ELECTORAL POLITICS IN

WILHELMINE GERMANY

STANLEY SUVAL

ELECTORAL POLITICS IN

WILHELMINE GERMANY

THE UNIVERSITY OF NORTH CAROLINA PRESS

CHAPEL HILL AND LONDON

© 1985 The University of North Carolina Press

All rights reserved

Manufactured in the United States of America

Library of Congress Cataloging in Publication Data

Suval, Stanley.

Electoral politics in Wilhelmine Germany.

Bibliography: p.

Includes index.

1. Elections—Germany—History. 2. Voting—Germany—
History. 3. Germany. Reichstag—Elections—History.
4. Germany—Politics and government—1888–1918. I. Title.

JN3838.S98 1985   324.943   84-17244

ISBN 0-8078-1631-0

TO ELIZABETH

CONTENTS

TABLES AND FIGURES

TABLES

FIGURES

ACKNOWLEDGMENTS

A study of this kind cannot be done without the support of many institutions and people. I would like to thank the staffs of the Geheimes Staatsarchiv in Berlin; the Bundesarchiv in Koblenz; the branches of the state archives of Rhineland-Westphalia in Münster and Detmold; of Hesse in Darmstadt, Wiesbaden, and Marburg; of Baden-Württemberg in Stuttgart and Ludwigsburg; as well as the city archives of Dortmund, Frankfurt, and Stuttgart. I would also like to thank the staffs of the Prussian State Library, Berlin, Duke University, University of North Carolina at Chapel Hill, the University Library in Marburg, the Hesse-Nassau State Library in Wiesbaden, the Library of Congress and, most particularly, that of the Württemberg State Library in Stuttgart and, at my own university, North Carolina State. Part of this study was supported by an off-campus assignment from North Carolina State University, which also provided the necessary computer funds. I am particularly indebted to those scholars who read all or part of the manuscript in various stages of preparation: James Sheehan of Stanford University, Lamar Cecil of Washington and Lee University, and my own colleagues, Robert Collins, Anthony LaVopa, and John Riddle. This last group has listened patiently to so many versions of Wilhelmine voting, offering constructive criticism and sustaining the author with what, given the state of the project in its early stages, might be considered excessive encouragement. I particularly appreciate the aid of my fellow German historian Professor LaVopa, in his careful and judicious critique of the manuscript and his high intellectual engagement with the project. Most of all I wish to thank my wife, Elizabeth, to whom this book is dedicated, for her encouragement and aid in completing the manuscript. It is very rare that another academic can be so honestly joyous over the successes and supportive in the failures of his or her spouse. And it is for this, even more than the energy and drive that she brought to the project, for which I am most grateful.

ELECTORAL POLITICS IN
WILHELMINE GERMANY

I

THE OUTLINE OF THE SYSTEM

1. The Wilhelmine Conundrum

Friday, 12 January 1912 was the day of the last national election in Wilhelmine Germany. Dead winter in Central Europe is hardly the time for public activity, particularly involving so many people. The last three elections but one had been held in midyear, once even on one of those unusual rainless days that can occur in a German summer. But the Bülow government became so enraged by the Reichstag in December 1906 that it dissolved the body and coincidentally punished the voters by calling an election in the worst winter in memory. Still, a higher proportion of eligibles turned out in the bad weather than ever had before. By 1912 the Reichstag elected in January 1907 had died a natural death at the end of its five-year term. Thus, barring another political crisis, Germans seemed doomed to continue fighting their campaigns at temperatures below zero. Fortunately the winter of 1912 was much milder than in 1907. The twelfth of January itself was a fine day. It was cold and windy, certainly; the high was 20° F in Berlin, 8 or 9 degrees colder in the south. However it was exceptionally clear, bringing particularly good skiing in the Alps and a modicum of decent sailing for shipping in the North and Baltic seas. But Germans were neither sailing nor skiing; they were voting in even greater numbers than in 1907.

From 10 a.m., various men appeared at the entrances of buildings, moving swiftly in, and then out minutes later. They were the voters; the buildings were the polling places—the offices of the Handicraft Union, Uhnstrasse 12, Stuttgart; the Restaurant Kopfmann, Märkische Strasse 1, Dortmund; the offices of the Holzhausen Estate in Kirchhain County, Hesse; the Town Hall in Biesigheim, Württemberg; and everywhere the local *Wirtschaft* or inn. It was one of the few acts in German society whose performance cut across class lines—everyone voted together. Almost all males twenty-five or over could vote. Most of the precincts were neither overwhelmingly working class nor middle class. From a great distance it would be impossible to tell the voters apart. Workman, doctor, farmer; they all wore black clothing. Against the snow they must have looked like those black birds of prey that still gather in trees in the old city parks of Central Europe. They were truly a faceless crowd, performing their tasks without humor, often without an exchange of greetings. For Germans, voting was less like a public festival and more like a visit to the post office.

Yet they were determined actors. By the time the polls had closed at 7 p.m., over 12 million German males had cast their ballots, 84.2 percent of those eligible. Most of these voters were not driven to the polls by a precinct captain or employer. The decision to vote was made freely and positively. Voters were undertaking an act that they considered important, although it is doubtful whether many understood the consequences of their actions. Even the intellectual supporters of universal manhood suffrage often felt engaged in an experiment that bedeviled its experimenters. They had extended the franchise, instituted direct and secret elections—and then came the surprises. Universal manhood suffrage with direct and secret election neither sustained nor brought down privilege, neither led to the redistribution of wealth nor ushered in the reign of virtue. The Benthamites were puzzled because voters seemed to cast ballots against their economic "self-interest"; conservatives like Disraeli and Bismarck were troubled because the voters were not as deferential as they had hoped; revolutionaries like Garibaldi found voters too timid, too willing to follow any authority. From the standpoint of the times, voting often appeared to consist of thousands of individual and unrelated decisions, reached in secret at odd places and in widely scattered moments, contrary to the traditional and more open ways in which individuals had heretofore expressed their relationship to authority.[1]

Two vignettes from the last Wilhelmine elections illustrate this complexity. Before the 1912 elections the *Frankfurter Zeitung* declared that the ever-increasing tempo of political life was making the average German more aware of the importance of elections. The paper declared, "We are not a state of citizens but we are on our way to becoming one. We used to be in a state where there was a small number of rulers and a great number of ruled. But now the rulers are a small minority among the great majority of the people."[2] In contrast to this picture of a self-aware and politicized electorate is the example of poor Hermann Runkowski, a "notorious imbecile" residing in Thorn County, West Prussia. Hermann was literally dragged to the polls in 1907 to cast his ballot against the Polish candidate. The Poles protested; Hermann had been too retarded to be drafted into the army; he had not even been allowed to attend the local school; and now he appeared as a qualified voter. All this fuss so disturbed Hermann that he broke into tears and attempted to flee the polling place. But his German friends would not allow it; they needed the vote. They subdued him, pushed him up to the ballot box, and forced him to place the ballot therein, a strictly legal operation since aiding the infirm to vote was within the law. Hermann fled the poll sobbing.[3]

German historians have tended to interpret their electoral history as if voters were marched to the polls in Prussianized battalions. After all, what else could explain those massive totals in a situation where voters could not help determine either the composition of national governments or national policies? This fits long-held assumptions that the nature of governments and the solution of issues were the principal reasons why voters went to the polls. Yet this is not the way any nineteenth-century electoral system worked. Even today a very high proportion of voters go to the polls for other reasons. As a recent summary of Anglo-American research states, "For the individual the chief functions of voting are emotional and allegiance maintaining. Only a limited fraction of the electorate are able or willing to act so that their votes consciously have for them the function of choosing governors or influencing governmental policy."[4]

The ballot then expresses other, perhaps more fundamental, social relationships.[5] Nineteenth-century voting, whether in democratic or authoritarian states, illustrates the same collective properties, performs very similar social functions, regardless of who wins or loses. In order to understand the importance of voting in creating a new political role for the individual, we should try to avoid keeping score. Explaining the complicated political and social phenomena associated with voting by winning and losing is like discussing nuclear physics from the standpoint of the atomic bomb. The things associated with scoring—ideas, specific issues, candidates' positions, all the stuff of intellectual politics—have minimal explanatory value when matched against the realities of nineteenth-century voting behavior. This is not to say that the motives of voters were simple or unidimensional. It is quite possible that many voters went to the polls to register their complaints against a government or to perpetuate their economic self-interest. But government support and economic self-interest do not appear, at least to this author, to have been the predominant motivations.

The Wilhelmine electorate thus cannot be described as making fleeting decisions based on immediate gratification. In fact, these voters' behavior was such as to frustrate any monistic explanation of their motives. This is particularly true when one tries to decide between the class-culture dichotomy. Class cleavages were strong and distinct in Wilhelmine society and were a determinant of voting behavior. But these class divisions functioned principally among German Protestants who lived west of the Elbe. Parties based on religious and national cleavages preserved what appeared to be more fundamental structural differences. Germans were unlikely to vote for Poles, whatever the class interest of the Polish candidate;

German working class Catholics were unlikely to join the Socialist party despite the possible economic advantages that might accrue from this act (see chapter 4).

While no single set of theories applies, all these unidimensional explanations are correct on one point. All describe persistent commitments that went beyond the ballot box. Two-thirds of all Wilhelmine voters can be identified as expressing loyalties to parties with a specific social referent. They were what I call affirming voters with identifiable and habitual voting patterns based upon their commitments to social groupings. This pattern emerges when social groupings and voting patterns are compared. The referent party vote can be associated with social and class characteristics. I discuss four such groupings in chapter 4—German Catholics, Protestant working class, rural East Elbian, Polish. Since these last two social groupings cannot be defined wholly by nationwide statistics, I have constructed two case studies (chapters 7 and 8) to substantiate the statistical data. Finally, there is a discussion of the Jewish social grouping, which has no referent party (chapter 4).

Other forms of data—government reports, newspaper articles, election materials, party publications—are used to describe the perceptions that accompanied these social and class divisions. This evidence tends to support the proposition that electoral cleavages were manifestations of the conflicts and struggles in everyday life and that social groupings were the perceived foci of these cleavages. The cohesiveness that sustained each social grouping was reinforced through physical and social isolation and ideological commitments, intertwined with cultural loyalties and economic interests to form a symbolic whole. This solidarity provided a formidable psychological barrier against defections from the social grouping and its referent party.

The German Catholics provide an ideal example of social grouping politics. The Center party can be defined by only one social referent, the percentage of the population that was Catholic. Catholic solidarities overwhelmed differences of region, size-of-place, occupation, or class. This unity was reinforced by an isolation that residentially and ideologically separated German Catholics from Protestants. It was sustained by the anti-Catholic sentiments in the dominant political culture and, through the 1890s, by the anti-Catholic policy of the Prussian government. The strength of this perceived isolation defied later efforts to bring Catholics into the mainstream of German political culture. For many in the Church leadership, this isolation was the surest means of guarding against defections from the faith and the Catholic community.

Just as the politics of belief supported German Catholic solidarities, so the politics of class created the new social grouping of imperial Germany, the Protestant working class whose referent party was the Social Democrats. Socialist voters and supporters tended to come from the less traditionally bound elements of the Protestant working class. They were younger and more urbanized than the German population as a whole, more ready to abandon old loyalties to bourgeois leadership in the workplace, on the street corner, and at the ballot box. This sense of class identification was buttressed by the perceived antagonism of most of the rest of Wilhelmine society. The ostracism of Socialists was so intense that they often referred to themselves as strangers in their own fatherland and felt the need to build their own organizations for leisure, culture, and self-help which the bourgeois world denied them. This isolation in turn fostered attempts within the social grouping to assert the vision of a more equitable economic and social system.

The non-German parties—Polish, Danish, French Lorrainer—followed the pattern described above, combining strong internal solidarity with defensiveness toward the dominant culture in quintessential in-group/out-group fashion. East Elbian rurals provide, however, a different pattern. At first glance, these conservative voters seemed scarcely to constitute the core of an isolated social grouping. Their leaders came from the large landowners who, except for a period in the early 1890s, most benefited from the proagrarian policies of the Wilhelmine regime. But this preferred status and the actions of a friendly government could not alter the process of social change whereby the balance of productive forces was increasingly shifting to the industrialized West. Rural East Elbians could be united by the threat of industrialization and urbanization. They formed an isolated periphery, separated not only by distance but in economy and lifestyle from the rest of Germany. This sense of separation was expressed symbolically in the articulation of the character of the German East. It was overlayed with an ideology that combined traditional Protestant virtues with aggressive agrarian stands, that emphasized the need to retain a hierarchical society buttressed by the army and the crown.

If affirming votes tied to social-grouping politics were the lifeblood of the electoral system, the failures would have to involve the inability to create blocs of habitual affirmers. The principal failure to establish affirming solidarities was in the Protestant *Bürgertum*, the main body of the non-Socialist Protestant community. The consequences of a loss of *Bürgertum* centrality disturbed many Wilhelmines, especially those in the progovernment parties, who could only sporadically unify this group through statements of bourgeois loyalty and fatherland rhetoric. The radical and populist methods that promised the most success at reshaping the *Bürgertum* were used in only scattered instances and would have to wait for their fruition in another era.

Yet *Bürgertum* voters could not escape the effects of affirming politics. Unable to create social grouping solidarities themselves, they were, in part, pushed into the electoral process by the successes of the affirming groups. *Bürgertum* voters could be relied upon to come out in contests where their dominant position was threatened by voters from deviant social groupings. Thus, at least in a negative way, the Protestant *Bürgertum* also was politicized by the entrance of great masses of affirming voters into the body politic (chapter 5).

Thus elections were battles that replicated fundamental social divisions. Voting was one of the many instances of social cleavages that were constantly articulated on the street corner, in the patterns of housing, in print, at festivals, and in the churches. Social groupings lent an orderliness and predictability to Wilhelmine electoral politics. Voting might be a seldom and easily forgotten act, but the loyalties that drove voters to the polls appeared to be almost permanently in place. Voters could be counted on to return year after year without orders, whether or not their candidate had a chance of winning. They recognized the right side (for them) and avoided the pitfalls of opposition entrapments. This kind of affirmation was at the root of electoral politics in the late nineteenth-century United States—it only changed later—as well as in Great Britain, France, and the Scandinavian countries. The Wilhelmine voter was genuinely engaged in a process that went beyond his parochial boundaries and was nationwide. One could make affirmations anywhere in the empire. It was Catholic against Protestant whether north or south of the Main; it was Pole against German whether in West Prussia or Westphalia; it was Socialist against non-Socialist almost everywhere (see chapters 6 through 9).

Such an electorate defies ordinary wisdom that citizenship means emancipation from previous traditional loyalties. The act of voting does not create a host of John Stuart Mills or Ben Franklins, or even Lenins or Kautskys, for that matter. Constant and repetitive balloting does create a new role for the voter; he begins to have a sense of political self along with his religious, economic, and family selves.

The result of all this activity was the Wilhelmine electoral system. Perhaps it is wrong to designate an electoral system as the sum of the structures that voting helped create. Certainly such structures were neither rationally nor systematically created. Yet something very much like an integrated system of voting and campaigning was built in the United States, in Great Britain, and Wilhelmine Germany, with each national system based on peculiar legal and constitutional circumstances, on distinctive social and religious divisions. In some instances it can be argued that these nineteenth- and early twentieth-century systems were more successful than the ones that followed them. This point has been made for the Unted States, and it appears even more valid for Germany. The Wilhelmine system worked better than the one in Weimar. What had worked before 1914 could not necessarily be applied to the postwar period. The Weimar system served to perpetuate the weakest links of politicization in Wilhelmine Germany. It even loosened the ties of the deputy with his district. More important, the balance and nature of social-grouping politics were changing after 1918. The German Catholics were losing supporters and the Socialists were losing their internal cohesiveness. The final success of Protestant *Bürgertum* reconstitution was not of such a variety as to increase politicization for more than a short duration. And ultimately the Weimar system added something new and very dangerous. Violence became a keynote of mass political mobilization and brought with it greater possibilities for system malformation and disintegration (chapter 11).

The paradox I pose therefore is quite different from the one usually discussed. It is not how badly Weimar worked but how well the Wilhelmine system functioned. The Wilhelmine electoral system demonstrated neither the impotence of the individual against the Prussianized state nor the reluctance of Germans to become involved in participatory politics. The authoritarian state could never dominate the electoral process, and this was not from want of trying.

2. The Response of the State

This view of participatory politics in Wilhelmine Germany is considerably different from the established interpretations. Elections are often seen as if they were inventions of cartoonist Rube Goldberg. They induce great meshing of gears, propelling transverse rods through space, leading to rapid and strong piston strokes; and then nothing is produced. Wilhelmine governments were appointed by and solely responsible to the crown; balloting did not necessarily lead to continuation or change in public policy. This resulted in clearly undemocratic solutions and led to the view that Wilhelmine electoral politics were permanently mired in authoritarian solutions.[6]

Even accepting these restrictions on outcome, the reaction of various Wilhelmine governments to the electoral system indicates that something different was occurring. These governments became increasingly involved in the electoral process. Their responses ranged across practically the whole gamut of possibilities—often authoritarian, sometimes liberal, on occasion even vaguely democratic. The governments eventually became entangled with affirming and habitual voters, an act that certainly legitimized the whole electoral process for many Germans.

Governments had no other choice: the Reichstag held the power of the purse, which became more important as successive administrations underwent a financial crisis. Only the Reichstag could set tariffs and a number of important taxes. Large indirect taxes on beer, wine, and tobacco raised sums in excess of the entire United States budget during the period. German historians have incorrectly maintained that the cost of financing the Reich was considerably less than that for the state governments. Gustav Stolper and others were misled because state budgets were padded by adding the entire expenditures of the railway systems. In Prussia and most other states, these systems made a profit. In fact, revenue from state-run enterprises paid for 65 percent of the Prussian expenditures in 1907 and only 5 percent of the Reich's. There were very few ways the Reich could make up this deficiency. Since subsidies to the state governments were about equal to the subventions received from them, the Reich received very little from the states, though such funds were supposed to be the foundation of its budget. The central government was forced to tax, and tax it did at a rate three times that of all the states combined. That this burden was unequal was a sign, not of the Reichstag's powerlessness, but of its inability to create a satisfactory pro-income-tax coalition—something that was not achieved in New Jersey until 1975.[7]

The Reichstag not only taxed and passed tariffs; it controlled expenditures. Certainly the legislature was manipulated by the government and was unable to control the military budgets fully. Still, the United States Congress has been in the same position during much of the cold war. Moreover, if the military budget was always safe, why did conservatives often believe that a coup d'état was the only alternative if the Reichstag turned it down?

Unfavorable Reichstag majorities might have had a decisive effect on military and naval budgets. They ensured a governmental response over a wide range of options. Of course, there was the pure authoritarian solution. Bismarck, who worked all the possibilities of the system, considered the strategem of doing away with these majorities by a coup d'etat, a *Staatsstreich*, particularly after the left-wing liberal gains in 1890. William II rejected such a policy then, only to reconsider the option when his pronavalist coalition seemed ready to fail somewhat later in the same decade. *Staatsstreich*, however, frightened as many as it attracted. Changing the electoral law by fiat meant abolishing the constitution. The various federal states could then reasonably argue that this ended their obligations to the empire and demand a renegotiation of the compact which set up the empire in 1871.[8]

Most governments also would attempt to deal with reality, that is, with elected representatives. This was not only uncongenial but a difficult task in the multiparty Reichstag. Bismarck's successor, Caprivi, governed through floating coalitions, needing left-wing liberal support for his trade policy and civil rights actions and using the conservative agrarians for his military bills. It was an unstable construction, particularly because the agrarians saw their whole economic future endangered by trade policies. Yet German chancellors after Caprivi still followed the same strategy. They had no alternative. The elections of 1893, 1898, and 1903 produced no clear progovernment majority. After 1898, governments did have some success in constructing a legislative package that united both big business and big agriculture behind the government while at the same time reaching an accommodation with German Catholics. This continued through the victorious election of 1907 (although Catholics were for a short time then in the opposition); however, the coalition fell apart on the problem of finding new finances for the Reich government (see table 1 : 1 and chapter 5).[9]

Governments also involved themselves directly in elections. In 1882 Bismarck planned to go to the nation by campaigning against an ineffective legislature. Bismarck could not scare up a permanent progovernment majority. He and others tried unsuccessfully to replicate the tactics of 1887, but there was no genuine success until 1907 when the Bülow bloc apparently permanently politicized those apathetic but marginally progovernment Protestant rurals. Yet even such successes only more deeply involved the government in political struggles. Elections could not remove chancellors, but they were viewed as indications of a public opinion that increasingly could not be ignored. Bülow's successor, Theobold von Bethmann Hollweg, survived the antigovernment landslide in 1912 but could not sustain such losses indefinitely. Even his son believed that his government would "have finally to become popular."[10]

This increasing involvement of government manifested itself in the choosing of candidates, the distribution of campaign funds, and propaganda materials. Yet the government also remained the chief protection for the freedom of the vote and the ability to campaign. In that curious Wilhelmine mix, voting was one of the most sheltered areas in the *Rechtsstaat*, where laws took precedence over the whims of man. Even at the height of the anti-Socialist policies between 1878 and 1890, Socialist candidates were allowed to campaign relatively freely. After 1890, government routinely protected freedom of speech during elections and efficiently supervised a permanent registration system and an honest count. Fraud and intimidation were almost always confined to local elites and were effectively policed by a Reichstag willing to invalidate the results of illegally won contests. The whole process worked in an efficient way, modeled on bureaucratic procedures. The undoubtedly unforeseen consequence of this process was to increase the prestige of the whole electoral process through its association with and imitation of the bureaucratic style (chapter 3).

The foregoing discussion only shows the intertwining of government and voting; it is not designed to undermine the proposition that Germany

TABLE 1:1. *German Parties and Their Development: 1887–1912*

Classification	Party Names	Areas of Strength	Highest % of Vote (and year achieved)	Trends of Strength	Stance on Government
Non-German parties	Poles, Danes, Lorrainers	Generally in border areas where nationalities resided	6.2 (1887)	Alsatians tend to decrease through time; Poles and Danes remain stable	Anti
Particularists	Welfs, Hessians	In areas recently annexed by Prussia	1.8 (1890)	Slow decline	Anti
Catholics	The Center	In German Catholic areas	20.1 (1887)	Relatively stable; suffers substantial losses in 1912	Pro (Anti for a short time after 1907)
Conservatives	Conservative, Free Conservatives (also known as Reich's party)	Particularly active in rural Protestant areas of the German east	25.0 (1887)	Strongest from 1887 to 1893; after that the percentage of vote remains stable although number of mandates varies	Pro (except when in opposition to low agrarian tariff)

	Parties	Area	% (year)	Trend	Position
Anti-Semites	German Reform, Christian Social, National Social, Economic Union	In only a few scattered rural areas	3.7 (1898)	These parties were formed out of the agrarian crisis of the 80s and 90s; decline after the crisis is resolved	Anti
Agrarians	*Bund der Landwirte*, Bavarian Peasants Union, various peasant parties	In only a few areas	2.7 (1898)	Same as for Anti-Semites	?
Right-wing liberal	National Liberal	Spread through Germany; differential voting base in each area	22.2 (1887)	Decline after 1887 to general stability	Pro
Left-wing liberal	Freisinnige, People's Progressives, Democrats	Same as for National Liberals	18.0 (1890)	After high in 1893, decline until 1907	Anti (Pro only for a short interlude in 1907 to 1908)
Socialist working class	Social Democrats	Strongest in urban, Protestant, manufacturing areas	34.8 (1912)	Rapid increase; only decline in 1907	Anti

was an authoritarian state. Voting was certainly a force that supported democratic impulses, but it did not democratize the authoritarian state nor cause governments to lose their authoritarian impulses. (For a fuller discussion, see chapters 10 and 11.) Yet the obverse is true as well. The persistence of the authoritarian state did not illegitimize the vote.

This last statement runs counter to the interpretations espoused by the dominant group of German historians dealing with the Wilhelmine period. Collectively called the "new orthodoxy," these historians have effectively demonstrated the authoritarian nature of the Wilhelmine state, the continuous reflex of Wilhelmine governments to authoritarian solutions, their resistance to reform, their attempts to depoliticize society and misdirect mass movement.[11] There is no question that "new orthodoxy" historians have redefined the nature of the arguments about policy making. Yet they tend to go further and deny that there was any possibility of attaining positive citizenship roles in the electoral system. Michael Stürmer believes that the Wilhelmine electoral system was shaped by Bismarck's successful Bonapartism, characterized by massive governmental interference molding an apathetic electorate, creating a "plebiscitary *Ersatz* Monarchy" which made the vote and other mass political actions meaningless.[12] In actuality, plebiscitary politics were relatively rare and not altogether permanent responses (see chapter 5), and these affirming voters loyal to social groupings were scarcely deferential to governments.

Hans-Ulrich Wehler, the dean of the "new orthodoxy," has arrived at a considerably more sophisticated view of German society and politics. He contends that these authoritarian attitudes had so deeply penetrated German social institutions as to make mass politics meaningless. Authoritarian attitudes not only permeated the state but were embedded in the family, economic life, and education as well as politics. This conception of an authoritarian monolith composed of dominant elites and apathetic or deferential followers has been effectively challenged by a number of American, British, and German historians. I generally agree with their criticism and have nothing to add to the argument.[13]

This conjuncture between high politics and mass politics is difficult to establish under the best conditions. It is an even harder task when considering the German experience since the German state and its bureaucracies have had considerably more prestige and power than similar Anglo-American institutions. Moreover this prestige and power have been translated into influence on the electoral system. However, this does not mean that Wilhelmine elections should be considered primarily as manifestations of manipulation by those on high or as a means for solidifying the dominant power structure (*Herrschaftssystem*) as implied in some recent studies.[14] This interpretation ascribes too much control to the state and its dominant elites and, in effect, leads to the unprovable assumption that failures in this governmental and elite structure would ultimately result in depoliticization.

The view that failures on the top would necessarily lead to failures on the bottom is reinforced by an idealization of the state and its potentialities. In the German context, the state is often viewed as a harmonizer of and mediator among varying interests. This conception conforms to the reality of German polities where the bureaucracies do mediate among local interests and national concerns. Thus a workable state is evidence of harmony, a weakened state is evidence of disharmony.[15] In these terms, electoral politics are prima facie evidence of disharmony since they are based upon unmediatable differences. Clear and articulated lines of social cleavage are required to bring people to the polls. Yet such enunciations of cleavage are often considered within the German experience as signs of fragmentation rather than the lifeblood of electoral politics and mass politicization. This is particularly relevant for the discussion of bourgeois politics, which is often considered narrowly focused on the particular interest rather than on the needs of the whole. However, such statements about fragmentation are also used to describe the whole electoral system, as Rainer Lepsius writes: "The parties were political action committees of highly structured and complex milieu. These parties confined their activities to their own milieu and allowed themselves to be entrapped by the complexity of its own specific interest politics. Parties were so unconcerned that all that did not pertain to these tasks slipped through their hands, . . . withered away, . . . or stagnated."[16]

This juxtaposition of a strong state against a weak and fragmented society is deeply rooted in the discussions of Wilhelmine politics. Almost seventy years ago, the American sociologist Thorstein Veblen argued that the supposed political backwardness of Germans was due not only to the strong state and its bureaucracies but to the inability of Germans to form a democratic consensus similar to that in other universal suffrage systems. Veblen argued that Germany evaded the natural order of social evolution. Industrialization in Germany had proceeded so rapidly that it outpaced the possibilities of creating what Veblen considered a modern consensus on society and politics. This situation supposedly provided an opportunity for traditional elites and ideologies to retain their dominance unchallenged by most Germans, who escaped the attitudinal changes that accompanied modernization elsewhere.

This explanation of German political backwardness was raised to prominence in the discussion about the causes of National Socialism. It has been extended in its economic implications by Alexander Gershenkron of Harvard and in its cultural-philosophical assumptions by Helmuth Plesser of Göttingen. Wehler has integrated this concept of political backwardness with conceptions of authoritarian polyarchy, each reinforcing his propo-

sition about political developments moving asynchronically with economic and social change.[17] The most impressive statement of this proposition is that by the dean of postwar German sociology Ralf Dahrendorf,
who identifies the root of German political failures in the inability of the
Wilhelmine system to eradicate traditional and authoritarian attitudes. It
is Dahrendorf who has coined the phrase which describes the result, the
creation of an "unmodern man in a modern world."[18] This is a perfect
statement of asynchronic development. And, if true, it undermines any
possibility of genuine politicization through the electoral system. Voting
in such a model becomes an isolated act within an authoritarian society.
The evidence of high turnout is, in Dahrendorf's words, only "a demonstration of the limits of statistical analysis."[19]

My reading of Wilhelmine electoral politics is almost precisely the opposite. Where Dahrendorf and Wehler see mass political activities robbed
of their ultimate meaning and springing from a faulted nation, I see
people operating according to their most profound beliefs. Such findings
are compatible with recent studies which argue that the process of both
political and social mobilization had proceeded less swiftly in all European countries than heretofore assumed, that asynchronic developments
between various spheres of society are quite common, and that the paradigm upon which the assumption of political backwardness rests may not
be useful. These findings are also compatible with some recent work by
Karl Rohe and his associates, who find strong patterns of politicization,
and the calls for further research by Werner Conze and Peter Steinbach.
They are supported by the scholarship of a number of British and American historians who have approached the problems of bourgeois politics
with differing methodologies, from differing ideological perspectives,
and with differing views on the nature of elite dominance. James Sheehan,
Richard Evans, David Blackbourn, Geoff Eley, all agree that the authoritarian state and its dominant elites were unable to depoliticize society
effectively. Thus a proven consequence of the Wilhelmine electoral system
was the raising of the level of politicization through elections and other
forms of political socialization. As Eley states, "it was the enlargement of
the public sphere—a vital 'reconstitution of the political nation' in Blackbourn's phrase—that *specified* the Wilhelmine conjuncture."[20]

3. The Human Responses

Since there is no particular reason to treat the responses of German voters
differently from those of their contemporaries in other nations, there is
no simple way of discounting the statistical descriptions used in this
study. Thus it was significant that Wilhelmines participated in the elec-

toral process at record-high levels. Almost 85 percent of those eligible voted in the last two Wilhelmine elections. When unavoidable absences are taken into account, the rate of nonvoting was less than 7 percent. The apathetic, the uninformed, or the principled abstainers were less than 1 percent. Although voting required only a minimal expenditure of time and effort, voters showed the strength of their inclinations by repeatedly returning to the ballot box at every reasonable opportunity allowed them. These repetitive acts were a sign of habitual voting in Reichstag contests as well as in state and local elections that were conducted under Reichstag rules, that is universal suffrage, secret ballot, and fair methods of counting. By the end of the Wilhelmine period, at least 70 percent of the eligibles in Baden and Württemberg voted in every state and national contest. These massive turnouts substantially reduced, if not eliminated, the different rates of voting due to class, status, occupation, urbanization, and region of residence. Moreover the higher turnout rates were matched by corresponding rises in the more intensive forms of participation that required a greater expenditure of time, money, and energy. There was a substantial increase in the membership of political and parapolitical organizations, in the distribution of printed campaign materials, in campaign activities of all kinds, including rallies and personal solicitations, in the numbers of party workers active on election day, and in the amounts of individual contributions to parties and candidates (chapters 2 and 6).

This statistical evidence is matched by conclusions drawn from more traditional research that shows increasing efforts to engage the whole society in the electoral process. There were attempts to gain the support of nonvoters, particularly the young and women. The politicization of voters in Reichstag elections was a principal reason for rising interest in municipal politics. The success of the national electoral process raised expectations that the Reichstag system of voting might be accepted in the unreformed states of the north, particularly Prussia and Saxony. Moreover, there appears to be a qualitative change in the levels of electoral rhetoric which I take as another sign of the increasing prestige of the system. All these statistical indicators move in the same direction toward an intensification of political life and increasing involvement in the electoral system.

This is true for qualitative measures as well. Wilhelmine Germans could readily draw on analogies that compared elections to military campaigns. There was some reason to expect that these terms would be understood by a wide range of potential voters where military service was the common experience. It seemed natural to compare voting to war. There was the obvious parallelism in terms such as victory and defeat, battle and fight. Campaign organizers were likened to officers, ordinary voters to common soldiers. The movement of voters was couched in terms of advance and retreat. The safe electoral districts were bastions or bomb-proof; defeated parties talked of counterattacking in the next election; moderates parried attacks from the Right and the Left.[21]

Yet more was involved than ease of communication and the need to channel voting. There were other analogies that might have proved equally useful, but none of these potential alternatives accentuated the seriousness of the act. Military symbols were used because they were not trivial, because they demanded the most intense loyalties and the hardest efforts. The Wilhelmine battle rhetoric was always placed in printed matter so as to catch the eye; it appeared in the peroration of an electoral leaflet or in boldface on the front pages of newspapers. And always it was the same, a call to arms.

The most convincing manifestations of battle rhetoric are the poems that appeared on handbills and in newspapers a few days before each election. The poetry was amateurish, scarcely ever replicated beyond the local electoral district, the work of convinced partisans rather than pro-fessional propagandists. Its scansion was particularly erratic, a fact not helped by the author's translations. The combination of local poet and the author's translations adds up to a crime against literature, but they communicate many of the images and enthusiasms that lay at the root of Wilhelmine voting patterns.

It was a prolific muse. In western Germany the National Liberal party often fought elections as representative of middle-class Protestant order. National Liberal election poetry tried to take advantage of the patriotic and anti-Socialist bent of its potential supporters. This was certainly the intent of the following poem from Gelnhausen, Hesse, in 1907; it was entitled "Before the Battle."

> Watch out, my people, be on your guard
> You German brothers all.
> The battle is now coming hard
> Keep awake lest no one fall
> As we battle for Germany's honor.
>
> Be strong, be brave, protect yourself
> As men did with spears in former times,
> Let right German thinking make you Germany's weapon.
> All arm yourself arrayed in battle lines
> And fight staunchly for Germany's honor's threatened.[22]

The 1903 Dortmund National Liberals expressed the same call to arms in a verse entitled "Germans Come Out: The Battle Begins."

> Proud waves the German flag
> Standing true as the Emperor's guard,

Striking fast against our enemies hard
So that behind our ancestors we never can lag.[23]

The Socialist poems in Dortmund speak of both recent oppression and recent victory at the polls. They are about equal parts anger and triumph. The following are two stanzas from two long electoral poems published just before the runoff election of 1907.

Now arm you voters for the last fight
Now show the people's power and might.
Now return to the ballot box man for man,
Now dressed in red and in rows thereon,
Now stand up for the freedom to fight.[24]

Now prepare for battle you voting masses.
Now prepare you proletarians to fight.
Jostling through the streets
As if a thousand catapults of fire,
Around which are piled the dead,
And roaring shall it to all announce
We're voting Red! We're voting Red![25]

The poetry of the Catholic Center is much more defensive-minded. German Catholics were a recently persecuted minority in a Protestant nation; German Catholicism was engaged in a fierce battle to hold on to the allegiance of Catholic workingmen. The following is a poem used in elections throughout Westphalia.

Onward you Catholics to the prize
In ever greater numbers mobilize.
From North and South, from East and West
True ones hold always to the Center fast.
The Center tower must always stand,
And flags shall wave high on its height,
Victorious and happy
For truth, freedom and right.[26]

The same kind of defensive images seems appropriate for left-wing liberals in Württemberg. The image of a beleaguered bastion fits the situation of all parties who have to maintain a skeletal apparatus between elections. The party was the *Volkspartei* (People's party); the poem was entitled "After the Battle."

Exhausted and fought-out, we forget
Battle's hot strife.
Still always invariably right

> In our old armor standing on the heights,
> In our own bastion on high
> Our good *Volkspartei*.[27]

Who read this poetry? Who quoted it? We do not know. But they were scarcely the precursors of an atomized totalitarian society or the antedeluvian mass that tramped deferentially to the polls. They demonstrated neither the impotence of the individual voter nor his reluctance to be involved in participatory politics. In reality, they may even help explain what can only be described as a rush to the polls.

2

THE RUSH TO THE POLLS

It is the conjunction of acts that defines the Wilhelmine electoral system. Each additional act is more expensive in time or money, requires more effort and commitment. It all seems so simple. More voting leads to (1) higher turnout and eventually to (2) habitual patterns of voting. This, in turn, causes (3) a rising level of commitment to the electoral system and the importance of the vote, which leads to (4) an expansion of partisan politics in local contests, and finally (5) the proliferation of campaign activities and organization. The result is to make participants politicized, that is, more aware of themselves as political beings, as performing important political roles, as functioning as part of a body politic with specific commitments that continued after the elections. It was a politicization recognizable in universal terms but distinctly and thoroughly Germanic in its ingredients.

1. Turnout

It was an extraordinary feat, but Wilhelmine Germany was on its way to making nonvoting unusual. In 1871, 52 percent of those eligible voted. In both 1907 and 1912, the last two imperial elections, the figure was about 85 percent. Such a high turnout left the confirmed nonvoters by choice to about 5 to 7 percent of the registrants. The remaining 8 to 10 percent fell away because of death, sickness, change in residence after registration, or unavoidable absence as the result of a job. At least this was the finding of two studies on nonvoting for Dresden in 1907 and Lübeck County in 1912.[1] The never-voted would naturally be an even smaller number, since there were undoubtedly some eligibles who voted only in one of these elections.

Moreover, Wilhelmine Germany did not have large reserve armies of disenfranchised male voters who were above the minimum age. There were very few exceptions in eligibility requirements. All males over twenty-four residing in the voting precinct at least twenty-eight days before the election were automatically registered unless they were paupers, in prison, deprived of their civil rights by a court of justice, or serving in one of the branches of the military. The number of enfranchised males in Württemberg in 1907 and 1912 was over 96 percent of those males over twenty-four listed in the census. The major proportion of the disenfranchised 4 percent was either foreigners residing in the state or those German citizens who were in military service. The paupers' exclusion applied to less than one-half of one percent of the adult male population of Stuttgart and was considerably less in the countryside. The numbers without civil rights were minuscule.[2]

This is in sharp contrast to pre–World War I Great Britain and the United States. In Britain suffrage was withheld from over one-third of the male population of voting age. In the United States voluntary registration considerably diminished the numbers of voters. The combination of new registration laws and disenfranchisement decreased the eligibles in the South to less than one-half of the male population of voting age.

2. Habitual Voting

Most of these new voters had to be habitual. The pool of nonvoters in Reichstag elections was decreasing dramatically, signaling that great masses of voters could no longer slip in and out of elections. This was also an indication that habitual and consistent patterns of voting were becoming the norm instead of the exception. There were other signals that these patterns of habitual voting continued in those state elections conducted under Reichstag rules, creating even more instances of repetitive decisions to turn out at the polls.

However, there are both methodological and theoretical problems in determining the precise nature of habitual voting. The voting data come in aggregate form so that it is impossible to trace any individual from election to election. Thus, we have to be satisfied with ascertaining statistical patterns instead of individual instances. And these statistical patterns must fit into some logical and empirically verifiable explanations that define habitual voting. This requires making some reasonable statements about voting behavior as well, thus fitting the statistical results into a wider framework.

The easiest way to identify linkage is to take the small group, the disappearing nonhabituals, and attempt to establish some reasonable pattern for their behavior. Nonhabituals should logically be most evident in elections where there is an upward surge of turnout compared with both previous and succeeding contests. These surges in turnout should be related in some way to exceptional characteristics for each election in question. This is the case for three such verifiable surges in Europe during the Wilhelmine period. They occurred in Germany in 1887, in France in

1877 and 1902, and in Great Britain in 1910 (see figures 2:1 and 2:2). These were all exceptional elections, characterized by calls to battle on the most fundamental principles of the political system: to save the re-public in France, to save Germany from war with France, to preserve de-mocracy in Britain against the power of the House of Lords. These are "easy issues," easy to understand, even by social isolates who tend to be apathetic.[3] But these nonhabituals were also notoriously fickle. The same apocalyptic calls might raise few voters in the next election. This is no-where more evident than in Britain where the highest prewar turnout was followed by very nearly the lowest in elections fought in the same year over the same ground.

Such arguments begin to carry us toward a definition, but they also produce difficulties, including the tautological problem. "Easy issue" elections are determined by their success in mobilizing these single-shot nonhabitual voters. In other words, the explanation is confused with the definition or vice versa. What is more, these surges can also be caused by institutional factors that have nothing to do with the issues. The jagged British curve evident in figure 2:1 is caused by the refusal of liberals to contest all seats in every election, forcing many convinced liberal voters to stay at home. These curves could be skewed by any number of other

FIGURE 2:1
Turnout in France and Great Britain
1884–1914 (in percent)[4]

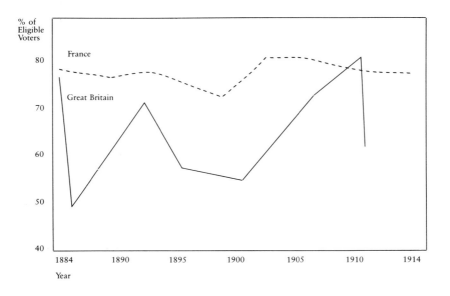

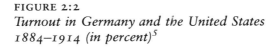

FIGURE 2:2

Turnout in Germany and the United States
1884–1914 (in percent)[5]

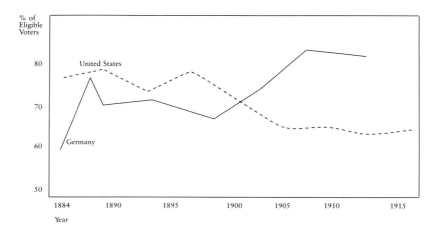

factors, particularly by the ability of each national set of politicians to fix the rules of the game.

The same kinds of problems occur in searching for habitual voters. The French turnout seems to be high from the 1880s onward. Does this mean that most French voters were already habituals? Perhaps, but it is difficult to be sure. Fortunately we have some theoretical and empirical evidence about curves that move in one direction. Herbert Tingsten, Stein Rokkan, and others have shown that the steady one-directional trends in turnout say something about voting patterns and commitments. Tingsten considers slow upward trends as a sign of the educational effect. Eligibles have to be taught to exercise their citizenship rights; like all learning, this information is acquired at differential rates, depending on the individual's status, group commitments, and geographic position. Therefore the slow but definitive rising of a turnout curve is a sign of increasing habituations as each election adds more and more voters educated to citizenship and committed to exercising their rights in each succeeding national election.

This upward curve characterizes the imperial German experience. It shows an increase of habitual voters and, if Seymour Martin Lipset and Walter Dean Burnham are correct, demonstrates permanent commitments to and integration into the political system.[6] In other words, it is a sign of a politicized electorate. A long-term downward trend should indicate a fleeing from the political, that is, depoliticization. This was characteristic of the United States at the turn of the century (see figure 2:2).

Many American scholars, however, have argued that the downward United States trend was due to institutional rather than attitudinal changes. They point to the imposition of the Australian ballot, voluntary registration and the decline of corruption. But, even with the British and American examples in mind, it is difficult to find any institutional changes that would explain increased voting. The ballot was made safe after 1903, but this did not create any noticeable upward deviation in the trend; there seems to be no reason to look for any downward revision either.

Upward and continuous trends can also be demonstrated by another measurement. Following is the first of many statistical explanations—some straightforward, others based on a minimal awareness of the discipline. Using numbers means making comparisons; making comparisons also inevitably requires a more formal structuring of results. Hopefully this process is not so filled with contortions that it would make the proverbial carnival rubber man wince.

In this instance, the statistic is called a discontinuity coefficient. It demonstrates that continuous trend in turnout which signified the educative function at work providing those habitual voters. A discontinuity coefficient of 1 shows the strongest possible difference in turnout for the four elections preceding and succeeding the midpoint. A positive sign indicates turnout is increasing through time; a negative sign shows decrease. The first two columns in table 2:1 show a continuous positive trend in turnout until the Weimar period; this is true when Weimar figures are revised to exclude voters between twenty-one and twenty-five and females, both groups enfranchised by the constitution of 1919. The last two columns of table 2:1 measure the differences in turnout from the general trend. Again, they show no statistically significant changes except for the Weimar period.

Dean Burnham has converted an old measure, dropoff, to account for repetitive voting patterns. The German data allow a measurement different and more precise than in the United States, by simply subtracting the turnout in state elections from that of the statewide totals for the national election immediately preceding it. A negative dropoff indicates that the state total is higher than the federal; a positive dropoff is the result of higher turnout in national elections. Burnham shows that habitual voters make up a greater proportion of the electorate in American state contests where the issues and candidates are less dramatic. Therefore a prolongation of low dropoff shows a high ratio of habitual voting among the electorate as a whole. The connection between habitual voting and commitment means that low dropoff can be taken as a sign of greater politicization.[7]

Translating this phenomenon into the German experience is fraught with problems. It is difficult to assume that national elections were more dramatic. Voters were often more interested in their historic states than in

TABLE 2:1. *Discontinuity Coefficients for Imperial Elections*[8]

Years	Midpoint Year	Coefficient on Raw Turnout	Adjusted for Inclusion of Females and Younger Voters in Weimar	Coefficient Based on Residuals	Adjusted Co-efficient Based on Residuals
1871–90	1880	.54		.30	
1874–93	1883	.74[a]		−.10	
1877–98	1886	.90[c]		.17	
1878–1903	1889	.84[b]		.14	
1881–1907	1893	.62		−.06	
1884–1912	1897	.68		.10	
1887–1919	1901	.92[c]	.91[a]	−.17	.40
1890–1920	1905	.95[c]	.95[c]	.34	.56
1893–1924[d]	1909	.87[a]	.94[c]	.24	.02
1898–1924[e]	1913	.17	.71[a]	−.52	−.30
1903–28	1916	−.63	−.37	−.50	−.83[b]

[a] Significant at $p = .05$ [d] First election of 1924
[b] Significant at $p = .01$ [e] Second election of 1924
[c] Significant at $p = .001$

the fate of the nation. Universal suffrage itself was a lonely experiment in constitution-making at the top that had left restrictive voting laws intact at the state level. Habitual responses were thus conditioned as much by electoral rules at the state level as by citizenship commitments. In the north, eligibles refused to move from meaningful national voting to meaningless state balloting. They particularly rejected Prussian and Saxon rules which overcounted the rich, disdained the secret ballot, and frustrated the will of the majority through indirect elections (chapter 6). The results for Prussia are demonstrated in figure 2:3. Turnout in nationwide elections increased among Prussian citizens; dropoff, however, still remained high.

Habitual voting in the south was much stronger. The dropoff curve declined at a rapid rate. Bavaria can be seen as representative of the south as Prussia was of the north. The Bavarian data show prolonged and decreasing dropoff from the national to state elections—coupled with increasing turnout, the prescription for an electorate of committed voters. More eligibles were entering the system and a higher proportion of them were habitual voters. There could be no better description of politicization.

To assure an accurate count, I have calculated the turnout in state elections as a percentage of the total eligibles in the state for the Reichstag

FIGURE 2:3
Turnout and Dropoff in Prussia and Bavaria[9]

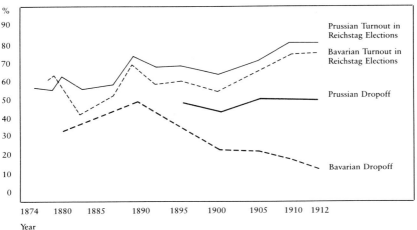

elections. This eliminates many problems caused by the fact that the numbers on the state eligible lists were smaller than on the statewide lists for national elections. In Bavaria and Hesse-Darmstadt, non-ratepayers were excluded. Baden and Württemberg did introduce universal suffrage during this period, but they still had a shorter list of eligibles. Germans with citizenship in other states could vote only in national elections. Given the patterns of migration and the complexity of the bureaucracy, potential eligibles in state elections often did not fill in the forms that changed their state citizenship. Without such a recalculation, dropoff in the south would be less than 5 percent in most elections.

Even then, more than 70 percent of the eligibles in national elections in Baden and Württemberg were repeaters. In Württemberg the eligibles outside of Stuttgart were given the opportunity to vote in at least three different elections within two months—normal state, national, and an additional proportional election (see chapter 4). The voters in Stuttgart were confined to two. Of those who could vote three times, as many as 75 percent may have availed themselves of the privilege. All this seems to indicate a massive number of habitual voters, confined neither to urban nor rural areas as the size-of-place data indicate. Even in the worst case, the Baden cities over 10,000, more than 67 percent of the eligibles for Reichstag elections voted in the state election of 1909 (see table 2:2).

Wilhelmine habitual voting has less to do with variations of perceived importance of state versus national issues than in the United States. There

TABLE 2:2. *Selected Turnouts and Dropoff by Population of Place of Residence (percentages)* [10]

| | Elections | | | | |
| | (1) Baden | | (2) Württemberg | | |
Population	1907 Reichstag First Election	1909 Dropoff to First State Election	1907 Reichstag First Election	1906 Dropoff to First State Election	1906 Dropoff to Proportional State Election
Less than 2,000	87.8	17.0	80.9	6.3	1.8
2,000–10,000	86.6	16.0	80.8	9.6	7.6
Over 10,000	88.9	23.6	81.4	10.2	n.a.

were always exceptions. Some voters tied to the extreme Right failed to move toward nationwide patterns of participation. Some parties still called themselves by their old pre-empire names in state elections, using only nationally recognizable designations in federal contests. There were special political deals that skewed the process. An example of this was the liberal-socialist coalition in Baden.

My own research in Württemberg and Hesse-Darmstadt; David Blackbourn's recent work on the Württemberg Center; Dan White's study on Hessian liberals; Dietrich Thränhardt's book on Bavarian voters—all substantiate the growing ties between state and national elections in the south.[11] Where repetitive and habitual voting is the rule, voters move from meaningful election to meaningful election, regardless of level of jurisdiction. These actions were never replicated north of the Main, where state politics remained unreformed (see chapter 6).

Just as the south led the nation in creating a nexus between state and national voting, so the Social Democrats led in the attempt to fight the same battle on all levels. It was a task to test the mettle of any organization. Social Democratic workers were driven from state to national elections, or vice versa, without time to catch their breath. This was the particular complaint of the Hessian Socialists as they moved from their November 1911 state (*Landtag*) contest into the national elections without a break. As the party report stated, "The political excitement of the *Landtag* elections did not lie behind us before the Reichstag election began. We had worked tirelessly for weeks during the *Landtag* elections. Instead of a well-earned rest, we had to begin a new election which placed new and greater responsibilities upon them [the party workers]."[12] A Württemberg official reported in the same vein about the activities of the Tuttlingen Socialists who fought five separate state and national elections within two months at the turn of 1906–7. "The Socialist party expended its strength to the utmost at the *Landtag* and Reichstag elections. It held meetings in all the important places and, when this was not possible, leaflets were handed out. At the election it brought out its supporters to the last man; even the sick and the crippled were dragged to the polls."[13] This paroxysm of activity exhausted the whole organization. The Socialists were unable to sustain their drive in the municipal election held early in 1908. The result was that they lost their majority in the city. Holding twenty-seven party meetings was not enough to stem the anti-Socialist tide.

3. Increasing Commitment

The elimination of nonvoters is both a sign and a cause of changing attitudes about the electoral system. Certainly this is the impression that one gains following individual elections during this period. I have systematically tried to understand local elections, using newspapers and government archives for a case study area that comprises all of Württemberg, both Prussian and independent Hesse, Westphalia, and West Prussia. Although the sample is weighted heavily in favor of the south and west, it does include examples from practically every type of German settlement—Catholic and Protestant, urban and rural, as well as both sides of the Elbe and Main. Most important, it is such a large area, comprising about 15 percent of the actual seats in the Reichstag, that it allows for the use of examples and even case studies of particular elections, which can be defined in their concrete local and regional context.

The following examples of voting permeating the popular consciousness are drawn from this search. Voting so captured the public attention that German advertisers would attempt to divert some of the enthusiasms of political campaigns in order to sell their products. An advertisement appearing in the *Frankfurter Zeitung* just a few days before the election of 1907 illustrates both the height of the national political culture based on voting and its ultimate vulgarization. The good bourgeois of Frankfurt were told, "With a majority of votes, the public prizes the Swiss chocolate Lucerna as having the finest quality and the best taste."[14] Forty years hence such an event would have been labelled "Americanization"; but what of that particular German manifestation taken from an electoral broadside for the same year in Hesse? The leaflet, entitled "To the Battle against Electoral Laziness," reproduced a picture of Bismarck voting. The former chancellor was dressed in the closest civilian approximation of a military uniform. Rigid in pose, he loomed before the table of the deferential election committee, the quintessential Junker. This was the feudal Bismarck in all his splendor. Yet the broadside maintained, "He never shirked his duty; he always voted. Follow his example; announce his deed from house to house." The leaflet closed with the peroration, "The Red troops of the revolutionary party threaten the fatherland. Fight back at them; the ballot is your weapon."[15]

These attitudes were evident in Eugen Würzburg's study of Dresden nonvoters in 1907. Würzburg interviewed about 80 percent of the non-voters in the entire city before his funds ran out. The results suggest that voting was becoming a universal act, which had acquired more meaning and more support than hitherto thought possible. Of almost fifteen hundred nonvoters questioned, only a handful suggested that they had been absent because of lack of interest or because of a disbelief in the efficacy of the political system. These particular responses varied little by occupational grouping (see table 2:3). There was divergence by occupation in other responses. For example, civil servants were much less likely to admit that they were forgetful than blue-collar workers, perhaps to avoid retaliation on the job.

The nature of the Dresden data is made even more clear when it is compared with the only other similar poll taken within twenty years, that for the Chicago mayoralty election of 1923. Cross-cultural and cross-temporal comparisons are bound to be suspect. The analysis is complicated by differences between national and local elections. The Chicago data can give only some possible starting points for coming to grips with the Dresden responses. Still, the comparisons are striking. Only 2.1 percent of the Dresden nonvoters polled claimed they were uninterested in the outcome of the election, compared with 17.2 percent of the Chicago male nonvoters. Only 1.3 percent of the Dresden sample (compared with 11.7 in Chicago) felt that their vote was meaningless, without political effect. This meant that just 20 eligibles out of 50,000 in Dresden were willing to state publicly that they had withdrawn from the political process. Eight times as many Chicago males refused to vote because they felt some alienation from the system. This comparison suggests that Reichstag elections created not only a new mode of political participation in Germany but also a new way of visualizing politics.

4. Transfer to Local Contests

The system fits together. High turnout causes a new way of viewing the vote, a view that was affected by and affected other areas of the electoral system. All of this culminated in an enormous spurt of activity in the last prewar decade. Stein Rokkan, the dean of European voting analysts, has argued that this activity indicated an entrance into a new stage of political mobilization. This stage was characterized by incorporating eligibles into more intense modes of politicization, signified by the entry of na-

TABLE 2:3. *Reasons for Nonvoting Males in Dresden 1907 (turnout 89.1%) and Chicago 1923 (turnout 62%), (by percentage)*[16]

Reasons Given	Dresden Occupations						Dresden Total (N=1,498)	Chicago Total (Males only) (N=1,681)
	Professionals (N=85)	Civil Servants (N=42)	Self-Employed in Industry and Commerce (N=218)	White-Collar Workers in Industry and Commerce (N=220)	Blue-Collar Workers (N=778)	Unemployed (N=155)		
Illness and death	21.4	34.1	25.2	14.5	20.7	76.1	27.0	9.3
Legal obstacles	31.0	16.5	14.2	16.4	28.9	9.0	22.3	11.2
Unavoidable absences due to employment	38.1	47.2	45.9	58.6	33.6	9.0	37.4	34.6
Forgetfulness or laziness	7.1	1.1	2.3	1.8	2.2	2.6	2.1	17.2
Disbelief in the efficacy of politics			1.8	0.9	1.5	1.4	1.3	11.7

tional parties into local elections and by greater participation in political organizations of all kinds.[17]

The nature of local politics, however, retarded the politicizing of German town councils. The bulk of city governments were elected under some form of restrictive suffrage that made it impossible for Socialists to receive anywhere near the number of seats to which they would have been entitled under equal representation. This kept the councils free, until very late, of the element that most disturbed entrenched interests. Even in 1911 there were only eight Social Democratic city councilors in the cities of Bochum, Gelsenkirchen, Dortmund, and Hörde. Berlin and Frankfurt did slightly better with over 20 percent of the city council members being Socialist as early as 1905. In the South German states the Social Democrats (SPD) were on the verge of some decisive electoral victories. By 1906 the SPD had nearly 40 percent of the seats in the Stuttgart and Heilbron councils. In the next year they almost elected a mayor for the capital city of Württemberg. By then every industrial town in Württemberg had an effective Social Democratic minority.

In any case, only one Socialist was needed to change totally the character of council meetings if not of city government itself. Until their entry, city governments had been the last refuge of an entrenched liberal oligarchy. This oligarchy could not help but be disturbed when the Socialist representative(s) kept an eye on the budget, criticized the management of affairs, and advocated a redistribution of city services in favor of the poor. Moreover, the Socialists emboldened other minority groups to demand their rights. In the Ruhr, in Dortmund in particular, Catholics began to complain about their traditional underrepresentation in the management of city affairs and the disproportionate numbers of Protestants in city jobs.[18]

5. More Intensive Levels of Participation

The last link in the system is the increasing intensity of involvement in mass political organizations. In Germany this did not happen right away. Before 1899 the Prussian Law on Associations forbade connecting local electoral organizations to a nationwide party except during Reichstag campaigns. It was a terrible nuisance and did discourage organizing.

Eventually the changes in social structure and campaign practices would overcome these obstacles. As James Sheehan states:

> In the late nineteenth and early twentieth centuries, party and pressure groups expanded in size and the range of their activities. . . . Of course these developments were unevenly distributed throughout the Reich; even in 1914 there were a few districts where the

level of political involvement was very low. But overall, participatory politics had begun to touch the lives of most Germans, to
whom organized political groups promised new sources of identity,
a way of defending special interests, and assistance in dealing with
the expanding bureaucratic apparatus.[19]

Organizing is imitative; once started, it cannot be stopped. The loyalties
of the committed were crystallized into the membership rolls of political
parties and parapolitical groups. The result was so phenomenal as to
challenge the prize for speed seemingly permanently retired by that other
wonder of the German world, the Prussian mobilization.

The industrial district of Dortmund-Hörde was not typical of all
Wilhelmine constituencies. There were less politicized areas or lightly
contested "Riviera" districts that only tangentially felt the quickening of
the organizational pace. Dortmund demonstrated the possibilities inherent in the Wilhelmine electoral system, the direction, we can almost say
the goal, toward which it was moving. Dortmund-Hörde was a high-
turnout area with a vote that reached 81.4 percent in 1903. Yet in 1900
there were fewer than 2,000 members of political parties in the entire district, almost all of them in the liberal associations. And then the dam
burst. By 1912 the figure had expanded to over 20,000. The Dortmund
parties were not composed of those groups that seem so prevalent in
America. They were not simply agglomerates of middle-class housewives,
students, businessmen, and professionals. Their numbers came from
every class and precinct in the city (see chapter 4).

What proportion of the voters were organized? It is impossible to give
a precise answer. Even the most readily accessible Socialist party data
have to be adjusted for age and sex. The party admitted anyone over
eighteen, although voting was limited to those over twenty-four; moreover, the party included large numbers of women after 1908. Still, it is
reasonable to estimate that by 1912 about 20 percent of the National
Liberal, 15 percent of the Socialist, and 5 percent each of the Polish and
Center voters in the district were party members. The figure was about
one in every ten voters for the entire district. Many of these members
were also election workers. In 1912 about one in every twenty-five voters
in Dortmund-Hörde left his job and spent the election day handing out
leaflets and ballots, taking eligibles to the polls, and watching the precinct counts.[20]

In addition to the political parties there was a vast reserve army of
nationwide associations based upon social, cultural, religious, and economic groupings. It would be wrong simply to equate this reserve army
with politicization. Religious, veterans', and fraternal organizations
sprang up for a host of reasons in the period after 1880. The nonpolitical
aspect of such associations did not preclude a political role. Veterans'

organizations were used to maintain the loyalty of all good Protestants to the crown; the Catholic *Volksverein* was eventually supported by the hierarchy as a device for avoiding defections from the Church and the Center party. Gymnastic and choral groups served such a purpose for the political Right. Special-interest groups such as the *Bund der Landwirte*, the proagrarians, were even more exclusively designed for political campaigning. The Socialist trade unions might vary in the intensity of their party loyalties, but there could be no question of the membership's sympathies.

The numbers are astonishing. In Dortmund-Hörde in 1912 there were approximately 20,000 members of political parties; at least 40,000 members of Socialist trade unions; 7,000 in the Catholic *Volksverein*; 13,000 in the veterans' organizations; 6,000 in the Patriotic Men's Society; 2,000 in the Naval League. There was little duplication among the membership except in the last three listed. Probably over half of Dortmund's voters were members of either political parties or the reserve army.[21]

And the Dortmund situation was not unique. This can be verified by a count of three variables throughout Germany—the membership of the Social Democratic party, the Catholic *Volksverein*, and the various veterans' organizations, since it can be assumed there was very little overlapping membership (chapter 4). The organizations accounted for over 30 percent of the voters in Westphalia and Württemberg, almost 30 percent in the Prussian Province of Hesse-Nassau (including both the *Regierungsbezirke* Cassel and Wiesbaden), and slightly more than 20 percent in West Prussia. The last figure would be about 10 percent more if the Polish organizations and *Bund der Landwirte* were added. These are remarkable statistics; they mean that almost a third of the German voters had at least some tenuous organizational connection which buttressed their political preferences.[22]

All of these organizations, parties and reserve army together, experienced an exceptional increase beginning in the late 1890s. Certainly there were technological and social reasons for these exploding membership rates; but some part of this change was probably due to more intensive politicization. The results displayed in figure 2:4 are phenomenal. The selected, but fairly typical, organizations double, triple, and then triple again. In contrast, turnout and membership rolls of those organizations still intact after 1919 declined simultaneously during the middle years of the Weimar Republic, a fact which supports both the hypothesis that these figures follow trends in turnout and that their membership was highly politicized. Only the trade unions moved on to a higher plateau after the war.

The influx of new members also transformed the political organizations they joined. In 1900 there had been no more than 5 precinct organi-

FIGURE 2:4
Number of Members in Selected Organizations[23]

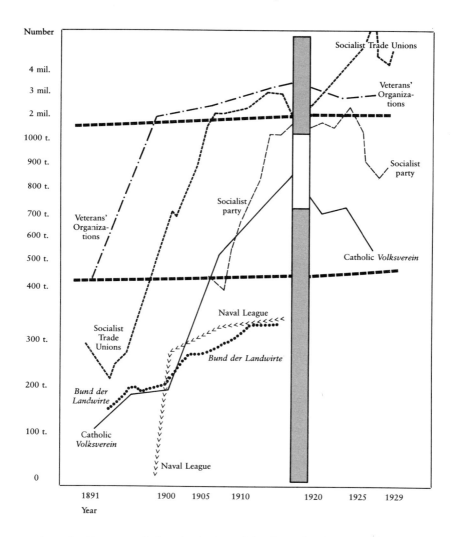

zations in Dortmund that had elected leaders, fixed times of meeting, and permanent meeting rooms. By 1912 the Socialists had 80 such precincts, the National Liberals 45. The Social Democrats held over 1,000 closed party meetings in 1912, the Center over 375. At the apex was a permanent party secretary to take charge of the electoral struggle. At least this was the alternative chosen by the National Liberals and Socialists. The Center and Socialists also had workers' secretaries who attempted to gain loyalists for their causes by aiding workers through the bureaucratic and legal jungles. All of this cost money. Thousands of marks were raised, mostly in the district, to finance permanent organizing efforts and political campaigns.

By the end of the Wilhelmine period education and propaganda efforts also proliferated. There was one official National Liberal newspaper in Dortmund city and eight more in the electoral district of Dortmund-Hörde. The Center and the Social Democrats each had one substantial daily in Dortmund city. At election time the press spewed forth instructions to the faithful and pleas to the unconvinced. Even more conspicuous were the thousands of handbills and leaflets posted on walls and littering the streets. The Socialists passed out over 2 million pieces of literature in the election year of 1912 in Dortmund-Hörde alone. Then there were public meetings. The Socialists held over 236 open meetings in 1912, most for election purposes.[24]

All these trends led in the same direction. Turnout increased; dropoff decreased; local councils became politicized; the number of voters engaged in more intensive campaign activity rose enormously. This is the Wilhelmine system.

As elections became closer, more and more efforts were directed at winning. The Socialists particularly appeared on the streets in great numbers to bring their less committed supporters to the polls. They called these campaign workers Schleppers, draggers. It has never been proven that dragging actually produced winners. It was most practiced in those areas already heavily Socialist, in working-class districts in central Berlin, in the mining and smelting areas of Dortmund-Hörde. Instead of dragging out marginal Socialists, loyalists may have principally demonstrated the intensity of their commitments.

It was affirmation, not electoral strategy, that brought voters to the polls and filled the political parties and the politicized arenas in the reserve army. They came out, if not to win, at least to be counted. The count was for many the most important task since it defined a social grouping's strength within the electoral district. Thus everything depended on the presentation of accurate voting results. It would be well, then, to turn to the count before going on to describe the various social groupings in detail.

3

THE CREDIBILITY OF THE SYSTEM

Elections, like games, are meaningless without a set of rules and referees to enforce them. The whole electoral process can be reduced to a sham by the lack of minimum fairness. The problem is somehow to find what this unmeasurable minimum is. Sometimes voters refuse to participate in a system with relatively little corruption, while other polities maintain credibility with massive intimidation and fraud. Talking about credibility is a tricky business at best. However, it seems possible to develop some method of judgment. One can posit that voters would support a system which meets all possible requirements of a fair count, a relative lack of fraud, and the ability to contain governments from undermining the process. Imperial Germany satisfies these tests; this chapter demonstrates how it did so.

1. The Count

German bureaucracies provided both the means and the model for operating one of the most complex electoral systems in the world. They did so with ease, punctuality, and accuracy. The principal beneficiary of all this efficiency was the prestige of the electoral system. As J. M. Mackenzie has stated, elections are anyway nothing more than great "confidence tricks,"[1] since the individual voter cannot possibly verify the count, but the Wilhelmine bureaucracy could and did.

Reichstag elections were administered by a combination of civil servants and members of local elite groups appointed by these civil servants. This was a typical German combination which ran everything from schools to cattle-breeding associations, differing from the French structure, which was totally in the hands of state employees, and from the British, which was run entirely by the local elite. Like so many other things in Germany, the holding of elections required large numbers of citizens who would and could emulate the actions of civil servants by following detailed instructions without deviation. For one day it turned factory owners and teachers into part of that large army of government clerks that ran the state. In the same way, the state bureaucracies were drawn into the process so as to assure a uniform functioning of the entire system. This was important because these bureaucracies had the responsibility for enforcing the rules; the federal government could only set the date of the contest.

The process started with the state government nominating an election commissioner for each Reichstag district within its jurisdiction. He was always a civil servant, in Prussia generally a county administrator (*Landrat*). The election commissioner would then supervise the construction of voting precincts and actual polling places. Much of this work was done by copying the old lists, but new precincts were also created. For example, shifting elections to the winter in 1907 caused a number of problems for eligibles who had rowed across lakes to polling booths in the summers of 1893–1903. In 1907 these eligibles would be forced to make a dangerous journey over the ice or take the long way around. In order to avoid wholesale losses by drowning, precincts were set up on the other side of the lakes.[2] In the cities precinct lines were constantly changed, since the law prescribed that a polling place could not serve a total population of more than 3,500 people, roughly 800 eligibles.

Once this was done, the armies of clerks began to work. Germany had automatic registration which allowed voting lists to be drawn up for each precinct. It was an enormous task. In 1912 14 million males over the age of twenty-four had to be listed in duplicate along with their occupations and addresses based on forms each resident had to complete for the police. The clerks had to exclude all who had lost their civil rights through court actions, those who had received poor relief during the preceding year, and anyone actively a member of the armed forces. The remaining names were placed in alphabetical order; in cities there also had to be an alphabetical listing of streets and then of voters by house number. In 1906–7 these tasks were completed in less than three weeks, including time off for Christmas and New Year holidays.

The principal copy of the election list had to be displayed in some official place twenty-eight days before the election. It lay there for eight days during which time anyone who believed himself excluded could file a written objection. If this protest was allowed, both copies of the list were amended, each amendation signed and dated by the proper official. The lists were permanently closed six days before the election; the election commissioner named the official chairman and vice-chairman of a committee for each precinct within eight days of the election. The chairman then nominated a secretary and at least three others to form the election committee.

On the appointed day, the election committee met and took an oath before the polls opened at 10 a.m. There were to be no fewer than three committee members present until the polls closed. The voter entered the polling place and, after 1903, took an opaque envelope bearing an official seal. The longest side of the envelope was no less than 12 cm and no more than 15 cm. Before April 1903 there had been no such protection. After that date the voter went to a table or a neighboring room where, hidden from the election committee, he placed the ballot in the envelope. The ballot itself was almost always brought into the polling place by the voter; he could have acquired it from a campaign worker just outside the door, or he might have been carrying it around for weeks. The ballot had to be of plain white, medium-weight writing paper whose longest side was between 9 cm and 12 cm. On it was written, but more often printed, the name and occupation of the candidate—Hans Schmidt, Cigar Trader; Hans Schmidt, Workers' Secretary; Hans Schmidt, Editor, etc. The voter then took his ballot, after 1903 his envelope, and went to the table where the secretary of the committee checked his name off the rolls. The ballot was placed in an urn. Voting urns in large cities were often of a special mode with optional handles that could be fitted to them after the voting ended so as to mix up the ballots automatically. In rural areas they could be just anything handy in the inn kitchen. The situation was eventually regulated in Prussia when the Ministry of Interior in 1911 urged all election committees to find an appropriate urn, preferably one with a slit in the cover so the ballot could be dropped in easily. The use of objects such as soup tureens was discouraged, because they threatened the secrecy of the ballot, detracted from the dignity of the process, and probably its cleanliness as well. Once the ballot was cast, the voter would leave the room. Loitering was discouraged; campaigning was forbidden.

At 7 p.m. the polls were closed and the count began. The instructions were again as explicit as possible. All the envelopes were counted and compared with the number of eligibles whom the secretary had recorded. Once this was done, one of the committee members opened up each envelope and handed its contents to the chairman, who then named the candidate. The chairman passed the ballot on to another committee member who verified the vote. The secretary added it to the count for the particular candidate and audibly gave the running total. The secretary was himself to be checked by another committee member. So it went, each vote adding to the total until all votes were counted. All questionable ballots were to be discussed on the spot. Ballots could be invalidated if they were not in an official envelope or if the envelopes were written on, if the ballots were not of white paper or were marked, if the writing was illegible or the person named not known to satisfy the requirements for candidacy. Any disagreement among the committee was to be settled by majority vote. The secretary then numbered each invalid ballot and placed the number in his official report besides the reason for invalidation. In addition, the secretary had to file that same night a description of the voting conditions, the number of ballots and envelopes used. The report was sent by mail, along with all invalid or disputed ballots, to the election commissioner. There was one more task that night; the results were also either hand-delivered, telegraphed, or phoned to the election commissioner. It was very rare when the commissioner did not know the outcome by early the next morning. The commissioner telegraphed his state government and the Reich Statistical Office immediately upon receipt of the totals. By the next day the pertinent officials at the state capitals knew the vote count by candidate and party for each electoral district. The process came to a conclusion four days after the election when the election commissioner called twelve private citizens together and went through the official precinct reports mailed on the night of the election. A count was then taken under oath and the results were reported officially throughout the district. Five days after the election, these results were on their way to the Reich Statistical Office. Ten days after the election the final forms were filled out. They listed each precinct in the district by population, number of eligibles, number of voters, number of invalid and valid ballots, number of votes for each candidate who received more than twenty-five ballots, and the name and party designation of the candidate as well. These forms would have provided an extraordinary data base for research on German elections if they had not burned up in an air raid in 1944.

A candidate receiving over 50 percent of the votes was declared elected. Otherwise the election commissioner had to set a date for a runoff between the two highest vote-getters. The dates would vary slightly, but most second elections were held between ten and fourteen days after the first. It was a considerable task; after 1890, 40 percent of Reichstag seats were settled by second elections. This meant that the whole procedure was repeated again with the same voting list and the same electoral committees. These rules also applied to by-elections when the Reichstag invalidated an election and when a candidate died or resigned.

It was an extraordinarily complex bureaucratized procedure, but it produced an honest count. Despite the fact that there were at least thirty petitions of electoral malfeasance after every election, there was just a handful of complaints that the actual count was incorrect, and none claiming that ballot boxes were stuffed. Accusations of falsified returns were generally confined to a few Polish-speaking areas in the east. Even in these areas, election officials were restrained from massive manipulation of balloting by the Reichstag's willingness to void elections. If the reader has any doubt of the Reichstag's willingness to do so, he should keep track of the number of invalidated elections in the case studies (chapters 7–9).

The effect of voting was much more skewed by the distribution of population. Although Reichstag districts were roughly even in 1871, by 1912 it generally took at least five times as many votes to elect a representative in the Ruhr than for an agrarian seat in the east. There had been essentially no redistricting from the foundation of the Reich in 1871 and, in most instances, from the creation of the North German Confederation in 1866. However much governments might support the continuation of an unreformed Reichstag, the failure to change was primarily a result of legislative inaction. Bourgeois parties feared such reform favored the Socialists. Reform was seriously discussed only just before the war, and then in terms of proportional representation rather than reconstitution of the districts (chapter 10).

2. Governments and Their Bureaucracies

The protection of the count by German bureaucracies should not be considered as setting an immutable course for their political neutrality. These bureaucracies were so strongly entrenched and so active in the society that it was more than possible that they had already malformed the political process at its roots, even before the count was instituted. Combined with the fact that the central governments were becoming much more adept at organizing coalitions and setting campaign issues, it is possible to imagine the creation of an authoritarian supremacy that would totally illegitimize Reichstag elections.

This vision did not materialize. Instead, the strange Wilhelmine amalgam prevailed. German state bureaucracies were more than willing to harass those deviant parties and organizations labeled enemies of the empire. In Prussia, especially, they made it difficult for these deviants to participate in state elections. Yet the same German state bureaucracies lacked the possibilities and often the will to control the outcome of Reichstag contests. They could not imitate the success of the prefects and other local officials who, during the French Second Empire, were able to construct large majorities through the use of force and patronage. The equivalent German bureaucracies were hemmed in by legal and moral precedents, by a vigilant Reichstag and the orders of their own governments, by cross-pressures between their loyalties to local elites and the commands of a hierarchical order. The higher civil servants tended to lapse into prosaic recapitulation of orders from above rather than to act as political catalysts for those below. They could not deliver the vote as the French prefects; they even failed to control totally their own lower ranks in Reichstag elections. It was the ultimate paradox that the powers of state bureaucracies were stifled by the fact of secrecy which they responsibly enforced in their role as protector of the count.

Ordinarily, the state bureaucracies were hardly beneficent but part of a repressive machinery that harrassed deviant political groups while protecting entrenched elites. Organizations supposed to contain "enemies of the state" would be closely watched by the authoritarian state; their meetings were attended by one or two police visibly taking notes. Even audible statements on the street might lead to police action, to arrest for disturbing the peace. Socialist and Polish organizers were jailed on the flimsiest of charges. Their freedom of opinion had very distinct limits. As late as 1900 almost three hundred Germans were convicted yearly of slandering a monarch or a monarch's family. The personages of the emperor and the various princes were simply not allowed to be an electoral issue. Although the numbers charged and convicted of this crime decreased substantially after 1900, Ernst Huber, the foremost German constitutional historian, argues that the very presence of this law mitigated against the creation of a liberal state. And this was not a lonely instance of oppression through law. In the 1870s and 1880s there had been special state laws directed against minority groups. First the Catholic clergy was effectively depoliticized at least in Prussia and Bavaria; then came the anti-Socialist laws in force between 1878 and 1890, which essentially abolished the rights of Socialists to organize, leaving them with only the right to stand as individuals for election to the Reichstag. It is true that not every federal state enacted anti-Catholic laws, that a few states did not even enforce the national anti-Socialist legislation. Yet there was no place in Germany where deviant politicians were totally exempt from harassment.

In some manner, voting was disengaged from these repressive acts. Perhaps because of its liberal antecedents or its place in the constitutions, voting was an extraordinarily sheltered act by contemporary standards. After 1890 there were no longer restrictive laws against any party or group campaigning for the vote. Freedom of the press in political campaigns was protected by the press law of 1874. Huber contends that the "extant and functional law governing political parties in the Bismarckean and Wilhelmine era was in reality just as protective as that of the late parliamentary democracy."[4] Nowhere could state bureaucracies find the legal and constitutional support necessary to malform national elections. State elections might be a different matter; thus bribes and threats in Reichstag contests usually brought not votes but trouble, not only from the press and elected representatives, but from the authoritarian state as well. The Reichstag was more than willing to invalidate elections that smacked of governmental interference. The threat was so strong that the Reich government advised all the state governments in both 1907 and 1912 to take pains that no electoral laws were violated and that civil servants were curbed from illegal acts. In neither year was there a complaint that a higher state official had tampered with the elections through force or bribery.[5]

Even before 1907 the instances of intimidation were widely scattered and very minor. For example, in 1893 the *Landrat* of Frankenberg

County, Prussian Province of Hesse-Cassel, moved through the villages offering bribes to the communities in return for large progovernment majorities. The bribes were very minor—a little public works project to provide a few jobs, a new cowpath, a foaling barn, some needed compost—scarcely enough to assure permanent prosperity of the inhabitants.[6] In Graudenz County, West Prussia, a young *Regierungsassessor* threatened to raise the taxes of some Jewish communities unless they returned substantial pluralities for the right candidate.[7] Both cases seem the actions of an overeager subordinate; neither was taken at the instruction of any government in Berlin.

The *Landrat* and *Regierungsassessor* were under close observation because they were higher provincial civil servants, responsible for the day-to-day administration of the various states. They were *Beamten*, a special class that entered the bureaucracy after academic training and moved up to the top posts. "Provincial" refers to the fact that they were generally in the service of the *Regierung*, about the equivalent of the French department, or the next lower level *Kreis* (county). For political purposes, the county administrator, *Landrat*, was the most important. Either through family connections, independent status, or the fact of the office, *Landräte*, especially in the east, were likely to find themselves at the center of local society serving both as arbitrators among local elites and as mediators between these elites and the state administration.

These higher civil servants were conceived to be both impartial and political. Logically, these are contradictory aims, yet the very fact that these roles were both legally and morally separated gives an important clue to understanding not only their position but also what society expected of them.

Governments, many elected politicians, and the bureaucrats themselves made a sharp distinction between illegal acts such as those engaged in by the *Landrat* of Frankenberg and ordinary politics. Higher civil servants were not exempted from the latter either by law or by tradition. Higher administrators in Prussia were just as susceptible to dismissal as any politically appointed official in the United States. They were even called "political officials." The situation in the South German states was more fluid, but there was no question that high officials in Baden, Bavaria, and Württemberg were expected to support their government's electoral position even if their political rights were legally protected.

In Prussia the state government went much further. Before 1900 it demanded that all political officials be members of the conservative parties. While Bethmann Hollweg and Bülow modified this policy somewhat, Bülow still warned political officials that membership even in the progovernment National Liberal party was not necessarily an adequate substitute for conservative loyalties.

Moreover, higher provincial civil servants were expected to perform a

number of political jobs thought to be within the law. In Prussia the
Landrat and his immediate superior, the *Regierungspräsident*, were or-
dered to use the offices in support of all legitimate progovernmental candidates from whatever party they might come. Both Bethmann and
Bülow instructed them how to field strong progovernment candidates
when none presented themselves, to make electoral lists readily available
to campaign workers from progovernment parties, and even help to distribute campaign literature. These were considered important tasks, to be
fulfilled promptly and to the letter. The government would surely react
against any failure to comply. Such was the case when the liberals complained that the *Landrat* of Gelnhausen, Hesse, was withholding election
lists. Since these liberals were government-approved in 1907, the Prussian
Ministry of Interior acted unusually swiftly with none of its traditional
regard for protecting civil service against citizens or keeping complaints
within channels. It immediately telegraphed the *Regierungspräsident* to
see that the lists were handed out.[3]

The governments had more problems in extending this political role to
employees in the lesser ranks who were clearly exempted from these laws.
Both government and its higher civil servants seemed to believe that
postmen, railway workers, and so on, received considerable prestige from
their government jobs, and ought to return the favor. This was especially
true in open state and municipal elections. The voter in Prussian state
elections had to proclaim his decision in an audible voice. The "wrong"
vote from a government employee would be followed by a number of calls
asking him to repeat his choice. Sometimes these negatives were recorded
and reported to the proper superiors; sometimes the votes of all government workers were inscribed.

Yet retribution was not as swift and sure as one might expect. The authoritarian state's demand for obedience was complicated by the power
of the *Rechtsstaat* and its proponents. Bülow was inclined to handle these
defectors with some care. A distinction was made between voting and
compaigning, a demonstrably higher level of involvement. Even then, not
all would be fired. Polish railway workers were transferred because they
attended Polish electoral meetings, although a teacher lost his job for attending Socialist gatherings.

Bethmann initially tried to crack down on all dissidents. In 1909 he
dismissed a number of federal and state employees for voting Polish in an
open municipal election. Bethmann found, however, there were even political limits in Prussia. Liberals and Socialists were so incensed about the
violation of civil rights that they pressed the government even into the
national parliament. Bethmann answered in a neat politics of the diago-
nal. He replied that voting Polish violated the civil service oath, even for
nonpolitical appointees. But then the government abandoned its policy of
wholesale firing.

It was difficult to extend this interference into national elections. Once at the polls, government employees could vote for any Reichstag candidate they chose. Governments could never determine whether the mass of their blue-collar workers defected to the Socialists. It was a real fear. The Prussian Ministry of the Interior was constantly reporting on secret organizing among the railwaymen. The head of the Royal Artillery Works in Schwarzenburg demanded that his employees vote against the Socialists. One boss after another predicted dire consequences for the wrong vote, but these threats never materialized as long as the ballot remained secret. What could be done? Bethmann and Bülow considered taking action against civil servants who did not vote, but this solution was based on the fantasy that all civil servants would vote correctly, and it was accordingly abandoned.[9]

Higher provincial servants were not so fortunate; they were expected to carry local elections even if it meant being candidates themselves. Running for political office might create problems, but they were generally not of a constitutional kind. It was perfectly legal to hold an administrative post and to be a representative, even in both state and national legislatures. Higher provincial officials generally chose the easier road, the one that led to a state legislature. These contests were most often based on restricted suffrage and on traditions that favored local dignitaries. The higher provincial civil servant benefited from the visible sign of trust, and the few months a year spent in the state capital could be very pleasing.

There were, however, potential conflicts between the local networks who elected the civil servants and the government in the state capital. Choosing to support these networks might be construed as violating the political oath to the crown, as with twenty-six Landräte in the Prussian House of Delegates who voted in 1899 against the government's canal bill and in favor of the agrarian-conservative opposition. The immediate result was that they lost their posts. Although the government's need for Conservative party support caused a number of these canal rebels to be reinstated, the line of development was clear. The Prussian government stepped up its efforts to discourage higher officials from becoming candidates for any office and, of course, these officials took the hint. The numbers decreased not only in the Prussian House of Delegates but in the Reichstag as well. By 1912 almost all of the local higher government officials who served in the Reichstag came from the small states of central Germany and from Bavaria.

Such conflicts not only discouraged higher civil servants from becoming candidates; it depoliticized them as well. Orders from Berlin were followed only mechanically. A Landrat might attend a strategy session or attempt to construct the appropriate coalition for the runoff. If he appeared on a platform, it was in the company of other local dignitaries. There were always exceptions, Landräte at the head of campaigns, visibly calling the electoral troops to rally around them. But most of these higher civil servants preferred their sheltered and useful lives within the hierarchy and appeared unable to find solace in electioneering.[10]

It is very hard to envision these high provincial civil servants as successful manipulators. Manipulation requires knowledge, which was precisely what high officials lacked. It is surprising how little they knew of the political process, considering how much information was available to them. They still viewed politics as an expression of local eminences and not as struggles among competing interests or affirming groupings. Certainly some of this kind of deferential politics was still practiced. The Conservatives in Hesse-Nassau used a very detailed report on these local eminences in 1912 as the basis of their pleas to *Regierungspräsident* Wilhelm Meister. They told Meister that he was the only possible choice if the seat were to be kept out of Socialist hands, "in reality the only collective candidate with any chance of success in our district."[11] Von Meister was ready to do his duty until the interior minister in Berlin warned him that his candidacy was opposed by large and vocal liberal parties. The poor *Regierungspräsident* never knew that he was part of a Conservative party ploy to take the district away from the liberals. There he was, the symbol of a bureaucracy overtaken and controlled by the electoral system rather than the opposite.

Thus bureaucracies were encapsulated by their own strengths and were unable to serve as the vanguard of plebiscitary politics. This was because electoral politics, universal suffrage style, was foreign to their role, which Eugene Anderson describes as perpetuating "the last phase of absolutism."[12] The paradox was the unwanted, unforeseen, and, until now, unnoticed effect of protecting the count and assuring the integrity of the vote. Thus these representatives of absolutism and believers in authoritarianism served, in this instance, as a means of increasing the prestige of the electoral system and fostering precisely the kinds of citizenship awareness which they generally despised.

3. Corruption

There were other means of influencing electoral corruption beyond the scope of either bureaucratic protection or interference. Bribery and intimidation always exist in some measure in every electoral system, but whether such acts are noticed or perceived as reprehensible varies with the political cultures from which the acts emerge. As one recent study suggests, perceptions of electoral fraud may be based more on prejudices than upon evidence. Moreover, there can be no assurances that correct perceptions of electoral fraud necessarily have an effect on the voter, causing apathy and depoliticization. The root of the problem is that one man's tampering is another man's legitimate profit. Payment for voting was favored by a large number of vote sellers; disenfranchised Southern whites in the United States actually approved of measures that lost them the vote as long as blacks were kept away from the polls.[13] If the motives of historical voters are considerably murky, the whole situation is compounded by inadequate data. There is no method of measuring precisely the extent of fraud and intimidation; the only way to find out about historical fraud is through written protests whose force and frequency did not necessarily relate to the extent of political corruption. For example, the method of invalidating elections in imperial Germany caused parties to make often the most frivolous protests in close elections while ignoring much more serious abuses in runaway contests whose outcomes they could not change.

But it is still possible to reach some minimal conclusion. Most Wilhelmine corruption arose from local circumstances: the breakdown of control by local elites who attempted to reassert their power illegally, often in conjunction with very minor officials but certainly without direction from the national and state capitals. As we have seen, the whole structure of German politics militated against the creation of local political machines to control the masses through bribery and individual favors. There was nothing in Germany like the widespread practices in Victorian Britain and in major nineteenth-century American cities. But the main protection against corruption was always the loyalties and convictions that drove eligibles to the polls. If these loyalties were high, then it would require enormous effort to push and pull the voters in other directions. In Wilhelmine Germany, government did not provide the push and there were not sufficient incentives to provide the pull. This view of minimal corruption reflects evidence derived from a number of sources. There were laws governing elections and legislative proposals to amend them. The petitions of fraud addressed to the Reichstag may not be quantifiable, but they are a sure way of determining the outer limits of corruption. There were also newspaper articles and government reports from the case-study area that comprised almost 15 percent of the Reichstag electoral districts.

The secret ballot was only a sign of important political changes. Along with mass enfranchisement, secret ballots ultimately circumscribed deferential voting patterns, that is, when eligibles follow local elites exclusively and are not politicized by economic interest or affirmative voting. In its purest form, local politics was simply decisions by a small oligarchy. A study by the Conservative party in Wiesbaden County showed a number of townships that could be won simply by capturing the local dignitary, often the village *Bürgermeister* (i.e. mayor), the Hessian equivalent of *Amtsvorsteher*. Sometimes there would be another figure, but it was always predictably one of political, moral, or economic influence. When the mayor of Scheirstein proved too lazy, the local Protestant pastor took up the political organizing. The hope was that this individual would bring the village along. There was great rejoicing when the local power in Michelbach, a mine owner named Pasevant, changed his political allegiance from liberal to conservative. Undoubtedly, this conversion was influenced by his two sons-in-law, both Protestant pastors.[14]

Deferential voting was a passive act. The foreman of a large landed estate might take his work gang directly from the fields into the polling place, which itself was likely to be the estate office. He would then observe the voting from an appropriate vantage point and take the gang back to the fields. The owner of the Geiswerden Iron Works in Siegen County, Westphalia, boasted that he led his workers to the polls like a shepherd leading his flock.[15] Once at the polls, the latent deferential voter was confronted with the local elite who formed the nucleus of the precinct election committee. Election committees were composed predominantly of businessmen, civil servants, and large landowners. Table 3:1 shows the composition of election committee chairmen and vice-chairmen for three typical areas—the city of Stuttgart, the working-class suburb of Borkenheim just outside Frankfurt, and the rural West Prussian county of Graudenz.

The relationship between the local elite and their followers alternately raised anger and amusement, as the following satire from the left-wing liberal *Dortmunder Tageblatt* illustrates:

> Peasant: Herr *Amtsvorsteher*, what do I have to do to vote?
> *Amtsvorsteher*: First go to the meeting. Hear the speech of the *Landrat* and continuously shout bravo. Then go to the Herr Count; let him press your hand and assure you that you will have a good harvest if you elect him. Then come back to me, and I will give you a ballot to place in the ballot box.
> Peasant: Jesus! I didn't know voting was that hard.[16]

Although the account was not true, it should have been. It illustrates all the liberal fears about the nature of rural majorities while at the same time showing how even the most deferential voters were expected to observe the forms of participation.

The structure of elections changed during this period. By the 1890s only stray and geographically isolated communities were immune from the new politics. Communities began to divide on social issues, on economic differences, on affirming practices. The aforementioned Conservative survey showed numerous townships where the local elite had relatively little power over the voters. Even in safe areas, the Conservatives knew that deferential politics were on the wane and advocated the building of political organizations and the mobilization of the potential voters as necessary steps in the new electoral world. Attempts to manipulate the

TABLE 3:1. *Occupational Distribution of Election Committee Chairmen and Vice-Chairmen (by percentage)* [17]

| | Administrative Unit | | |
| | Stuttgart 1893 (N=93) | Borkenheim 1898 (N=14) | Graudenz County 1912 (N=58) |
Occupation			
Free professionals	9.8	—	5.2
Civil servants	15.8	—	67.2
Owners of businesses and directors of corporations	35.3	42.9	3.4
Large landowners	—	—	17.3
Proprietors of small and medium-sized farms	—	7.1	5.2
Salespeople and shopowners	25.6	28.6	1.7
Master craftsmen	4.9	14.3	—
Craftsmen	4.9	—	—
Independent income or retired	3.7	7.1	—

electoral system followed the failure of these old elites to control their voters.

As long as the local elites held control, there was no need to use more expensive tools such as intimidation and fraud. This was all changed by the successes of deviant parties—the Social Democrats, the Poles, the Anti-Semites, sometimes even left-wing liberals. Deviant voters often found themselves confronting an impenetrable combination of local elites and officials. The local elites and their supporters would threaten to boycott any inns, hotels, and restaurants that rented their rooms to the deviant political parties for use as meeting halls; sometimes they would even break up meetings for which rooms were found. Such a prohibition never seriously affected the campaigns of the Anti-Semite Liebermann von Sonnenberg in Hesse in the 1890s. Liebermann simply moved his crowds out of doors in the mild June weather. The boycott was much more serious in the 1907 Reichstag campaigns of Württemberg Socialist Wilhelm Keil. Finding no room at the local inn in January was hardly a passing difficulty. Nor was Keil's situation unique. It was repeated through Württemberg, Hesse, and Westphalia. Socialist campaigners were in foreign territory once they stepped outside of the cities and their suburbs. Of course, there was no problem in cities like Frankfurt or Stuttgart, where Socialist parties controlled their own rooms and knew of many friendly inns whose clientele were exclusively working class, and often almost entirely Socialist.[18]

The local elite's harassment of deviant parties had a powerful ally in the person of that appointed or elected official who served as a combination of local administrator, town clerk, and village mayor—alternately named *Amts-, Kreis-,* or *Ortsvorsteher, Schultheiss* or *Bürgermeister.* These officials would harrass Socialist campaigners, wink at the destruction of deviant party placards, and even occasionally threaten violence. In a few Württemberg counties left-wing liberals would be threatened with a knock on the head, having their clothes stripped off, and being thrown out into the winter's cold. There is no evidence that this was ever done; however, in at least one instance such threats succeeded. During a state election, the election committee head declared to a potential voter, "Go over there to the oxen. You can vote over there; over here, never. Today we're fighting the election battle and you're safe. If it were only dark, you'd already be buried under the church."[19] The eligible did not cast his ballot.

In Reichstag elections, deviant voters ignored the threats and cast their ballots to affirm their fundamental loyalties to social grouping. The same secrecy protected the whole electoral system against bribery. Unlike Victorian Britain and the United States, nineteenth-century German workers could accept that occasional cigar and beer from the factory owners and still have voted Socialist. The real danger was, therefore, only to the secrecy of the ballot. This is where most of the attempts at corruption aimed, especially in the small towns and rural areas.

An agricultural worker might vote with his foreman looking over his shoulder; a member of an election committee might glance at the ballots. Light crosses or other marks could be put on ballots to discover the individual's preference. Even after the introduction of the envelope, there was always the reliable method of simply recording the order of voting and keeping the ballots in order of their being cast. Thus, at the end of the day, the committee had only to go through the ballots to find out how everyone in the precinct voted. This practice caused great uneasiness among the odd rebels in the villages. Few were as ingenious as Willy Brandt's grandfather, who assured the secrecy of his Socialist vote in a large eastern landed estate by "accidentally" spilling over the soup tureen that held the vote, thus making impossible a tally by order of who voted.[20]

In small towns the devices were likely to be more sophisticated. The best example of such an attempt was in the election of Friedrich Krupp to the Reichstag for Essen in 1893. The election went smoothly in the city itself, but the secrecy of the vote was challenged in the industrial suburbs. In the second precinct of Kettwig, Center election workers were restricted to the entrance of the building at which the poll was taken. The potential voter passed through a hallway and into a billiard room before he came to the actual polling place, the Great Hall of the Hotel Kaiserhof. In the billiard room, he had to walk by a table at which were seated three or

four directors and officials of the Schedt-schen Factory, the principal employer in the town. These directors asked his name and "what kind of
ballot are you holding there?"[21] Right at the entrance to the Great Hall,
just a few feet from the directors, was the Krupp election worker who
handed a Krupp ballot to every voter. From that point on, the potential
voter could be observed by one of two Krupp poll watchers so that it was
very difficult to slip a Centrist ballot in the envelope without being noticed, a trick which required a magician's sleight of hand. At the Hanker-
mann Inn, the same process was repeated, the only difference being that
five to nine factory executives were seated at the table in the billiard room.

Did this campaign harassment and election fraud undermine faith in
the electoral system itself? I think not. Full-scale harassment was too
hard to hide; the newspapers would have complained, and they seldom
did. Effective intimidation would have caused very low vote totals for opposition candidates throughout the rural areas and small towns. This was
not the case. Protestant areas almost always had a visible opposition
vote, this being defined as any time the leading party was held to less than
75 percent of the total. It is impossible to make any statement about predominantly Catholic areas, where opposition parties often simply did not
even field candidates. In the 1912 Reichstag election in Württemberg,
the victor gained over 75 percent of the vote in only 4 percent of the
Protestant townships. The proportion was even lower in the Hesse-
Darmstadt districts in 1907 and in the Prussian Hessian districts of
Marburg-Frankenburg-Kirchhain and Fritzlar-Ziegenhain-Homburg for
1912. At first glance there is contradictory evidence for the West Prussian
district of Graudenz-Strasburg-Briesen in 1907. The Polish party failed to
contest 40 percent of the townships in Graudenz County. However, many
of these townships were exclusively German. In Strasburg County and
the part of Briesen County in the district, less than 2 percent of the precincts were uncontested.[22]

The meeting of Pole and German east of the Elbe was a test at once of
the possibilities for corruption and the effectiveness of the corruptors. In
Schwetz County, West Prussia, in 1903 there was even a substantiated
complaint that a number of Polish votes had gone uncounted. In the
whole province Poles were struck off electoral lists, Germans were illegally added, Polish ballots were invalidated for the most trivial reasons,
and German ballots were almost always counted. This was a substantial
if not adequate attack on the vote. It is apparent that the Reichstag did
successfully police the most flagrant of abuses in the east, and that too
much manipulation would cause the election to be overturned. Thus the
German civil servants and election committees had to tread a fine line
between losing the election to the Poles or having it invalidated in the
Reichstag. Sometimes they succeeded. In at least one certifiable case,
the false invalidation of only two Polish votes cost a Reichstag seat.

But the problem was not only the count. Even more important, the Germans managed to establish an atmosphere of oppression at the polls. Polish poll watchers were sometimes forcibly removed from polling places; large landowners could threaten their employees with dismissal if their favorite lost the election. Rewards of cigars and brandy were offered, and, everywhere, there were fears for the secrecy of the vote.[23] In Marienwerder County in 1898 an incident occurred that sums up the whole campaign of oppression. A Polish civil servant by the name of Cieselski was handed a German ballot just outside the polling place. The election worker was another government employee, a certain Herr Teschner. Teschner then found that Cieselski had voted Polish; he followed the Pole home and demanded that the "secret" Polish ballot be withdrawn from the urn and replaced with the right one. It was a heated exchange, frightening Mrs. Cieselski with threats of her husband's dismissal, raising the whole neighborhood, even turning the pigs hysterical. Yet the Pole remained firm in his conviction, a symbolic gesture of how national commitments overcame the most blatant intimidation.[24]

The Poles themselves would not admit that intimidation and fraud changed their votes. The following speech of Father Milucki in Schwetz during the 1903 campaign was fairly typical. The good father pleaded with the faithful to be wary:

> I ask you then to be careful. If someone gives you an unfriendly greeting or looks askance at you, don't notice him and go off to one side. It is necessary that the things which happened five years ago are not repeated. [What things, we are not told.] The hatred against us is so great that we must be even more careful. For this reason no one of us should make trouble and all must go up to the ballot box. . . . Therefore I ask you not to go to the polls alone on 6 June but to drag along the lazy and the apathetic by their shirt collars.[25]

This is hardly disillusionment with the electoral system!

Statistical evidence indicates that Cieselski's response and Milucki's injunctions might only have been more dramatic statements of common practices. Table 3 : 2 represents data from the electoral district Graudenz-Strasburg-Briesen, West Prussia, which seems to show that Poles voted for their conationals. There was a high correspondence between the proportion of total vote for the Polish party and the proportion of the total population that was Polish. There are problems with these data, especially with the undercounting of Poles in the German census. Differential counting between city and countryside explains the fact that there was a higher percentage of Polish vote in Graudenz City than could be expected from extrapolating the census figures. However, estimates of this undercounting were never so large as to undermine the proposition that most Poles voted Polish. Nor could many Poles have been frightened away

TABLE 3:2. *Polish Nationality and Voting Patterns in Graudenz-Strasburg (by percentages)* [26]

Administrative Unit	% of Total Population Polish in 1910	% of Total Vote for Polish Party in 1907	% of Eligibles Who Voted in 1907	% of Total Vote for Polish Party in 1912	% of Eligibles Who Voted in 1912
Graudenz City	12.0	24.1	88.5	20.9	75.9
Graudenz County	39.1	39.9	92.0	38.4	89.7
Strasburg County	64.2	60.8	93.6	60.3	90.3

from voting entirely. The turnout rates were highest in the most Polish area of the district, Strasburg County, where nearly everyone voted. It would take an enormous restructuring of the data in table 3:2 to prove that the Polish vote was massively affected by the intimidation and fraud that went on in every election.

Poles, Socialists, German Catholics, monarchical Conservatives—none of these groups could be budged from their commitments, which drove voters to the polls and made the electoral battle important.

New techniques had to be developed if such voters were to be moved away from their fundamental loyalties. The affirming voter might be given misinformation that would turn him away from the polls, or he might be forced to reevaluate his choices among various social grouping loyalties. This is the case with a couple of dirty tricks tried against the Social Democrats in the Ruhr. In the first, the Socialist candidate was accused of immorality, a real sin in those Socialist circles that believed themselves even more moral than the bourgeoisie. In the second case, an attempt was made to turn Catholic Social Democratic voters back into the Catholic camp by playing upon an incident of church desecration.

In 1896 the conservative *Dortmunder General Anzeiger* published a trumped-up letter from a supposedly former supporter of Dr. Karl Lütgenau, the Socialist Reichstag deputy. The writer claimed that Lütgenau engaged in an improper chess game with the proprietress of a local inn.

Herr Doctor . . . retreated into the spare room with the proprietress and a bottle of Rüdesheim wine and began to play a game of chess for a kiss. That is in any case a strange occupation for a married representative of the people. The chess games must have been very short; there was kiss after kiss exchanged with such impetuosity that the Herr Doctor's glasses were in danger of falling off his nose and the chess pieces were clearly made to totter. This "chess game" between Dr. Lütgenau and the proprietress lasted so long

that many of the guests and even the cook became somewhat suspicious, especially since the door of the room remained always
firmly closed. They decided, however, to spy on this interesting
chess game through a tiny hole that had been bored through the
door. After they had seen enough in this way, they called the pro-
prietor. The curtain falls and hopefully also the blinds over the eyes
of the Dortmund workers.[27]

An effective trick occurred in the district Bochum-Gelsenkirchen-
Hattingen in 1912. The district had become Socialist during the great
disaster for the party in 1907. The Socialist candidate, Otto Hue, was the
head of the powerful miners' union and an extraordinarily popular man
in the Ruhr town. Hue needed Catholic votes to sustain him against the
National Liberal candidate and, while this was never a sure thing, he had
some confidence that enough Catholic workers would come over to the
Socialist camp to give him the election. A few days before the vote, some
grafitti appeared on a Catholic altar claiming, "Jesus speaks: elect Hue."[28]
Social Democrats accused their enemies of staging the event. The National Liberals distributed 175,000 leaflets accusing the Socialists of dese-
crating a church and warned that Hue's election would be a signal that
this would happen to other holy places. Hue lost the election, one of the
few incumbent Socialists defeated that year, perhaps because of Catholic
defection. But the strength of voters' convictions protected most contests
against intimidation and fraud. The electoral system satisfied the tests of
reliability so that affirmative voters would feel that their ballots counted
while, at the same time, relying on the commitments of these affirmers as
the best protection against attempts to make the vote meaningless.

4

THE AFFIRMERS

The affirming loyalties that served as the bulwark against corruption also constituted the bedrock upon which the electoral system was based. They provided the one essential for a functioning electoral system: meaningful and continuous difference that was ascertainable from election to election—cleavage. I believe that these differences propelled voters to the ballot box even when the circumstances were less dramatic than those of German versus Pole in the colonial east. Casting a Center ballot in 90 percent Catholic areas was certainly an easy act, supported by local elites and practically everyone the voter saw on his way to and at the polls. Yet I think that these German Catholic voters were motivated by just as strong ties. The fact of enormous individual diversity does not hide the similar nature of these commitments and their habitual exercise, whether by Pole, German Catholic, Socialist, Conservative landowner, and so on.

But the question of determining the voters' motivations is very difficult. Among many notions about these voters are attempts to explain Germany's failure to modernize or the state's inability to contain diverse economic interests. For Marxists, voters were controlled by class interests. Other explanatory systems demonstrated cultural functions and their political manifestations. Each of these notions protects a unidimensional theory that hopelessly attempts to assimilate the wide variety of cleavages which characterize Wilhelmine politics. With the tools at hand, it is impossible to connect any of these notions with individual motivation. Meaningful maps of the cleavages are needed. Any satisfactory resolution requires a number of constructs, including considering the state as an independent agent in explaining the nature of political commitments. Once these tasks are accomplished, it can significantly enlarge our view of how nineteenth-century electoral systems operate as well as help to amend the theories of voting behavior. This is as close as we can penetrate into the minds of the electorate; yet it does allow us to discard some notions heretofore mentioned and goes a long way to demonstrate the possibility that the author might be right.

It is important to remember that this is primarily a work of German history principally concerned with applying theoretical and methodological tools that explain the nature of the Wilhelmine system. Yet comparing the German experience both to theory and to the historical experience of other nations is a necessary function of the study since it aids in answering the most perplexing question in modern German historiography: Is Germany the same as other industrial nations? Even when the question of German uniqueness is set aside, it is important to untangle the nature of political cleavage in Wilhelmine Germany. At least two-thirds of all voters supported parties that were referents of economic, cultural, or regional cleavages, that is, the prerequisites of affirmative voting. If these affirming loyalties were the bedrock of the political system and if habitual political behavior was the result of strong commitments to the voters' own nests, then their ballots reveal much about the nature and strength of the political and social solidarities which sustained the vote, and they give some clue to the persistence and depth of such commitments over time.

1. Parties, Interest Groups, Classes, Political Subcultures, and Social Groupings

The nature of these cleavages and the limits of affirming groups must be demonstrated quantitatively. This requires not only a clear method of articulating these differences but also a precise means for connecting them with social and political realities and with theories of political behavior. Scholarship on both sides of the Atlantic presents an often unnecessarily confusing and contradictory analysis. Thus we are left with terms such as "class," "subculture," "milieu," "interest group," which purport to describe essentially the same phenomenon. Many of these terms' connotations make it difficult to link them with political and social reality. This is particularly true of the term "interest," which defines an electoral experience rooted in what individuals think are society's appropriate policy goals. Such a view of interest posits a process that is almost impossible to identify historically and often runs counter to statistical analyses which show voters making choices based on long-term commitments, some of which are not even necessarily congruent with their interest. This problem can be alleviated by defining interest loyalties in terms of group affinities.

An interest group itself is defined as a voluntary organization of individuals who attempt to move government policy in a specific or general direction. There are three qualifications: members join as a conscious act made without pressure; the group must possess some formal structure; the group must clearly demonstrate its connection with policy goals. Interest groups may have economic, cultural, or moral aims, but they cannot be operated predominantly for profit, elevation, or uplift. They are supposed to take aim at governments and affect policy through legislative or executive lobbying, through supporting candidates and parties in the electoral process, or any combination of the above. Most of the theoretical and historical research on interest groups has been confined to specific economic interests and goals. Without eliminating the wider approach, this study will follow the patterns already set.

Yet even when specifically defined, the relationship between interest group and voting is clouded by inappropriate assessment of both the power of interest groups and the nature of electoral systems. Electoral politics then become unnecessarily confused with the policy-making process in which interest groups often seem to structure political society. Using the American experience as a model, David Truman and Robert Dahl have suggested that the proliferation of interest groups provided an opportunity for organizing the political framework in a more democratic manner through conflict resolution, political socialization, and the reduction in the powers of arbitrary government. German scholars, on the other hand, have heretofore viewed the eruptions of interest-group politics as leading to eventual depoliticization by fragmenting the body politic. Even an economic determinist such as Hans Rosenberg could characterize Wilhelmine interest-group politics in the following way:

> In the foreground of party life now treads an unstoppable and prosaic following of interest by owners of large and small farms, big industrialists, bankers, large merchants, small artisans, day laborers, private white-collar workers and members of the free professions. Interests that until now were confined behind the scenes have become public knowledge, and open discussion of the goals of social classes and the material demands of various groups have substantially changed the outlook of individuals. In place of controversies over political freedom, the relationship of power, law and morality and the accomplishment or hindering of parliamentarization, the battles over economic security and social status, the intensification of the class struggle and the feeling of unhappiness which resulted from a fictive instead of real unification have become the focus of public conflict.[1]

This passage is doubly pertinent; it not only views interest groups as agents of depoliticization but also blames much of the problem on what Michael Stürmer has called the artificial nature of the Caesarist state. Thus the fictive state was characterized by fictive harmonizing of interest, bending primarily to the needs of the eastern agrarian elites who ran the bureaucracy and army, the group most committed to forestalling change in the political structure. The classic statement of this interpretation was made by Sigmund Neumann in 1932 when he warned that Weimar had inherited parties which had "lost their function in a crypto-absolutistic system . . . [and] were forced into politicizing private interest groups and not accepting the responsibility for the whole of the organism."[2]

The arguments are clean, precise, and unresolvable. There can be no wider divergence with the American view of interest groups as expressed by Truman and Dahl. Yet both of these views posit outcomes for an electoral system that no one can find. Electoral politics is rarely a force of national integration. This does not mean that electoral mobilization or the politicization that ensues from voting are unimportant, only that they cannot serve to articulate national goals; rather, they are based on asserting differences. Thus one ought to concentrate upon signs of interest-group cleavage, understanding that the cleavage itself drew people to the polls. The question then becomes not how interest groups controlled the electoral system, but how they mobilized voters.

Yet this clarification does not overcome the enormous problems associated with "interest." Even after interest groups are defined their role in the electoral system remains questionable. Thomas Nipperdey has pointed out that no such groups ever reached a goal of controlling policy in conjunction with the government. Moreover, very little attention has been paid to the fragility of these interest groups. The strongest of them, the *Bund der Landwirte* (BdL) founded in 1893, did play an imposing role in the electoral process (see section 4), but its strength and durability were a matter of conjecture. There is little evidence to prove that the BdL was more than a holding company for a wide variety of economic interests from small farmers in the west to the great landowners in the east, which led it to espouse political solutions from proto-Nazi to democratic and to include both peasant activists and passive agricultural laborers.

This same proposition was certainly true for another organization which influenced at least one election. The *Hansabund* attempted to replicate BdL tactics with urban liberal voters, a task conducted with some vigor and success in the 1912 elections. But its constituent groups were so disparate that the organization soon fell apart. The business associations that formed the heart of the *Hansabund* were generally more effective when they approached government bureaucracies directly. Thus they eschewed legislative lobbying and confined their electoral contributions to perfunctorily financing anti-Socialist candidates.

Even with all this increased political activity, it is practically impossible to find a pure economic interest group that contested in the political arena. The role of Socialist-oriented trade unions is ambiguous (see section 3). The BdL in western Germany was fast becoming an imperialist and anti-Semitic pressure group. This same meshing of cultural and political statements can be found in a whole series of interest groups like the Catholic *Volksverein* (see below). Shopclerks, white-collar workers, artisan and middle-class groups were only just beginning to define their political roles by 1912. These groups enveloped their economic interests with a whole series of political propositions and eventually would respond to appeals for a nationalist *Bürgertum* that stood above narrow articulation of interest.[3]

Such findings make it impossible to construct a theory of voting based upon class cleavages alone. Differences based on class would identify longstanding and inflexible antagonisms that could serve as the basis for this habitual and consistent voting described in chapter 2. But class cleavages did not overcome cultural solidarities among German Catholics, Poles, Danes, and certain regional groupings. In reality, class cleavages predominated only within the German Protestant community, showing the predominance of a cultural variable, in this case religion, over class lines.

Cultural approaches appear at first promising for demonstrating the nature of social distances upon which electoral cleavage was based. And, to understand this, there is a ready-made notion of political culture. As Paul Kleppner maintains:

> . . . *political culture* is the political aspect of group subculture . . . "an historical system of widespread behavioral, political values . . . classified into subsystems of identity, symbol, rule and belief." A group's political culture consists of its politically relevant purposive desires, cognitions and symbols. It refers to internalized expectations in terms of which political roles of the group's members are defined and through which regularized patterns of political behavior come into being.[4]

This approach views the individual not as a rational decision maker but as a member of an autonomous group that he may not have joined except through accidents of birth, place of residence, or baptism. Political propaganda moves beyond mere economic interest to include symbolic representation of existential need or fundamental cultural commitments made in daily life. Elections then can be seen as struggles among subcultural loyalists who come to the polls to affirm beliefs and vote regardless of the chances of winning or losing. It is a system amenable to definition by the use of aggregate statistics as Kleppner and other American scholars have shown.

Subcultural voting may run counter to much of the recent American experience where many decisions are made on the basis of interest. Middle Western farmers of the 1940s and 1950s are among the best examples of such voters, and they are not unique. Whether issue voting is supreme in the United States today is a matter of debate, but it was certainly of secondary importance in nineteenth-century voting systems. The Middle Western farmer in the 1890s was as equally troubled by economic difficulties as his twentieth-century counterpart, but he made his decision in the crucial 1896 contest on the basis of cultural values expressed through cultural loyalties. The fundamental political cleavages were based on religious groups roughly labeled as Pietists and Ritualists, on ethnicity and national origins that determined attitudes toward drink and prohibition.

The same argument can be made about British voting patterns. Although until very recently class has been the principal explanation for electoral cleavage in postwar Britain, the nineteenth century presented a different picture. Religion remained the chief reason for political cleavage in Great Britain through the 1920s. Non-conformers may have voted Liberal, but their basic loyalties were subcultural. These Baptists and Methodists would refuse to vote for any candidate who stood against disestablishment of the Church of England and teetotalism. By the turn of the century the Liberal party represented a hodgepodge of subcultures— not only Non-conformers but the Celtic fringe and Irish Catholic inmigrants. The same sets of cultural loyalists were present in French and Belgian elections; only here it was Catholic against secularist. André Siegfried, the founder of modern electoral research, characterized these groups as "two people living beside each other with two moral structures and two separate traditions."[5]

There is no question that some of these cultural cleavages have been overcome by the articulation of class lines and the increase of issue-oriented voting. Yet even today it is doubtful if issue-orientation applies beyond some American elections. A careful study of loyalty and the vote based on data from the 1960s shows that religious cleavage accounted for over 50 percent of decisions on voting in Austria, Belgium, France, Italy, the Netherlands, and Switzerland. Of the European capitalist states, only Denmark, Finland, Norway, Great Britain, and Sweden had a predominance of class voting, ranging from 37 percent for the British vote to 59 percent for the Finnish. In the United States, 16 percent of the vote is ascribed to religion, 20 percent to class, 11 percent to urban-rural differences. The corresponding figures for West Germany are 40 percent to religion, 27 percent to class, 17 percent to urban-rural differences, leaving very little to attribute either to candidates or to issues.[6]

Religion, ethnicity, nationality, and race—these variables determined the boundaries of nineteenth-century political subcultures. Germany possessed its fill of the first two with a strong Protestant-Catholic cleavage and the presence of discernible national minorities. In the German-speaking world, Dietrich Thränhardt has used these cultural cleavages to define two political subcultures in Weimar Bavaria; Adam Wandruska has done much the same with what he calls a *Lager*, a subcultural political camp, for the first Austrian Republic. Other scholars such as Rainer Lepsius have used the term "milieu" to describe something close to a political subculture. In fact, these historians and others, such as Guenther Roth, are prepared to expand the definition to include a Socialist subculture as well.[7]

This mixture of class and culture has some obvious benefits. It moves away from the culture-class dichotomy. Yet none of the cultural-subcultural approaches goes far enough. Such an approach requires a new term that would eliminate the necessity of fitting all parts into some sort of global explanation, that would carry at once fewer connotations and reduce the possibilities for defining groups in terms of polarities, that is, the dominant versus the dominated class, religion versus material goods, or class versus ethnicity. This new term would have to encompass more than the terms used above, and also provide good referents for statistical analysis. The concept of "social grouping" as defined by Richard Dawson and Kenneth Prewitt seems to fulfill both these tasks.

> The expression "social grouping" refers to the broad categories in the population. Societies are composed of a number of socially significant categories: social class, income level, occupation, race, religious affiliation, and national, regional and tribal origin. Persons belong to these groupings because they have certain physical attributes, or hold specified social beliefs, or belong to a particular social or occupational stratum. . . .
>
> Social groupings are not the same as secondary groups. They lack the formal structures and processes which characterize secondary groups. A social grouping such as the working class in Britain, Negroes in the United States, and the Christian population of Lebanon can, and should, be distinguished from a Labor Party club in England, the Congress on Racial Equality in the United States, and the Lebanese Church as a religious organization. . . .
>
> Social groupings have a tremendous influence on political orientations. Study after study of party preferences, policy choices or the level of political participation have shown that persons in different classes, occupations, and income categories, religions, geographic regions, and so on hold quite different political views. Social class variations are politically significant in Britain, Australia, Scandanavia, and most of Western Europe. Regional and ethnic factors are important in Canada, the United States, and Southern Europe. In the new nations of Africa, persistent tribal loyalties are often the source of political commitments.[8]

Social groupings in this study are defined when possible by party referents from one or more variables based on occupation, religion, and size and location of place. In addition, this statistical evidence is supported through more traditional investigations based on contemporary sources such as government reports, campaign documents, and contemporary newspapers. There are still a number of problems with such a definition.

Using "party" both as a definer and an end product of the system is strictly tautological. Moreover, the aggregate statistical techniques involve the ecological fallacy. If, for example, the bulk of Catholics voted Socialist in one election, the same statistical effect could be achieved in the next contest by an exchange of voters so that Protestants who voted anti-Socialist could be now voting Socialist, and Catholics could have almost uniformly changed their position by moving out of the Socialist camp. Also, these statistical techniques based on social correlates can cause bias if they are essentially segregated geographically, which is the case in Germany. In any event, these statistics refer at best to aggregations and cannot predict individual actions.

At least one-fourth of the Wilhelmine voters, chiefly liberals, were not even amenable to these statistical techniques. It is not so much that grouping analysis does not apply but that it cannot be shown to apply using the techniques available to me.

Yet everything is not hopeless. Sanity, common sense and knowledge are still the best guides. But there are standards of judgment derived from other disciplines. Angus Campbell et al. have devised a series of criteria for judging the effectiveness of social groupings. A grouping is judged effective if (1) there is a high identification of its members with each other, (2) there is a perception of the proximity of the grouping to politics, and (3) there are means for transmission of standards among the members of the grouping.[9] To these I would add the following, drawn from the cultural-subcultural approach: (4) these transmitted standards are based upon not only a clear identification of the grouping but some recognition of how it, as a distinct and isolated phenomenon, relates to other groupings and the state; (5) the sum of social transactions within the grouping increases loyalty among the members of the grouping, which is expressed by affirming and habitual voting; (6) the social grouping is clearly distinct and takes precedence over the political structures spawned in its wake, that is, interest groups, parties, informal clubs, and so on.

Measuring these criteria against the evidence, I have introduced three full-scale studies of social groupings—identified by the referents to Center party (German Catholics), the Social Democrats (working class), and the conservatives (East Elbian rurals). I have included a short discussion on the Jewish social grouping because of strong traditional evidence, although the statistical support that defines it is weak. Also included is a longer study of the Polish social grouping, which can be isolated statistically through the referent of Polish party but cannot be described with the same methods as those for the Germans. There are a number of other social groupings not discussed. There were too few Danes. Alsatians and Lorrainers had mixed loyalties to the predominantly German church and to their region; it is impossible to sort these out without considerably more information than I possess. It is doubtful if regional political parties were referents for a distinct social grouping, but their numbers were so small as to defy statistical manipulation or their vote totals did not necessarily indicate loyalties. An example is the Guelfs, where Catholic social-grouping loyalists were instructed to vote for the Hanoverian particularists.

When possible, I will try to describe all social groupings in the same manner, moving from statistical definitions and problems to campaign statements and other data that emphasize the isolation and enclosed nature of the grouping. I will attempt to demonstrate how each grouping is the source of secondary structures such as parties and interest groups, and how interest and cultural values were intertwined in the ways contemporaries defined their grouping.

These discussions based on social-grouping analysis are necessarily somewhat abstract; they do an injustice to the wide variety of conditions in which electoral contests were actually fought. Some of this variety will have to be sacrificed for the sake of analysis; some of it is not retrievable. However, it is important to appreciate how electoral conflict was related to local configurations of particular social groupings and continued from election to election with ever-increasing intensity, fought with noticeably greater passion. Therefore, I have introduced three case studies (chapters 7–9) to help construct the actual political map. Two come from West Prussian districts and examine contests between city and countryside, between German and Pole. The third is Dortmund in the Ruhr and is concerned with the multiple relationships among liberals, German Catholics, Poles, and Social Democrats.

I would like to know more, to tell what the priest in Zoppot really said to his congregation on election eve and if any voters really listened. I would like to know about the conversations that went on in the Polish electoral club in Langendreer or at the German *Stammtisch* at the local inn. But I think I know a number of things. I would not want to listen to the talk of intellectuals at the Cafe Central in Frankfurt. Intellectuals think of elections in terms of governments, political ideologies, universal aspirations; very little of this was translated into affirming votes. Yet these jarrings from the mass electorate could be just as important and even more frightening than the latest news of the Moroccan crisis and, perhaps, even more permanent too.

2. German Catholics

As we have seen, social and political segregation based on religion was one of the most salient facts of nineteenth-century political systems. The most imposing of these in Wilhelmine Germany was the one created by

German Catholics. Alternatively attracted and repelled by the political expressions of Protestantism, German Catholics saw the Center party not only as a statement of their security against enemies but as a structure stemming from their own strengths. The social-grouping loyalties as expressed in the Center were solidified by extreme attacks from the governing and liberal elites; but, in the end, the Center's most pervasive enemy was secularization and the change in social relationships that this entailed. The Catholic social grouping effectively preserved itself against both dangers by an articulation of culture supported by religious loyalties, by the use of the clergy and the Church as a point of reference, and by the lucky fact that most German Catholics were separated from the rest of Germany, creating an effective base for social-grouping politics in spatial, cultural, and sometimes ideological isolation.

The separation of religious groups was reinforced by geography and territorial history. The German Catholic vote generally followed the territorial lines that went back at least to the Peace of Westphalia in 1648. The two Christian branches were thus circumscribed within their own homogenous areas of settlement, a fact that persisted well into the twentieth century. In 1907, 270 of the 397 Reichstag districts were so constructed that at least 80 percent of their inhabitants were either Catholics or Protestants. The figure would rise to 312 if the 70 percent cutoff were used. Moreover, Protestants and Catholics often also inhabited different spaces in areas of mixed settlement. Helmut Croom has shown how even the massive in-migration into the Ruhr cities did not overcome the propensity of religious groupings to segregate spatially. These settlement patterns bred prejudice. Catholic and Protestant youths fought each other along the lines of demarcation; Protestants derisively referred to Catholic enclaves as "Colored Towns," *Negerdörfer*.[10] All of this served to confine interactions between members of the two religions to the most formal contacts. Most German voters would have their closest associations only with coreligionists whether at home, at work, or drinking at the local inn. Thus Wilhelmines were confined to a society of like-minded, at least as far as religion went.

Religion was a principal statistical determinant of voting behavior in Wilhelmine Germany, a fact forcefully represented by Catholic voters who were definitely German. Eliminating those districts in the 1912 election where Poles and Lorrainers (another principally Catholic party) got more than 10 percent of the vote, I estimate that over 90 percent of the Centrist voters for the remaining 343 districts were German Catholics.[11]

This is hardly a surprising conclusion, but it is an important one since it reinforces every statement of Catholic political exclusivity. The German world was sharply divided into Catholic or Protestant; 97.5 percent of the population declared themselves to be either one or the other. Almost all the remainder were Jews, Seventh-Day Adventists, Jehovah's Witnesses, and other small groups. Less than one-tenth of one percent of Germans were officially nonbelievers, even though such an affirmation automatically freed the individual from paying religious taxes.

Catholic voters were affirming their support for their church and the social grouping upon which it was based. For churchgoers, such a vote was sustained by countless traditions and a fair number of sermons. For nonchurch attenders, it was a statement of cultural solidarity. Whatever the case, the religious-cultural affirmations of German Catholics were so strong that they washed out the effect of urbanization and industrialization (see table 4 : 1; the explanations of the statistical terms can be found in the appendix). The regional concentration in the south and west, the economic predominance in agrarian areas, the demographic mix in small towns and villages still persisted. Yet the data presented in table 4 : 1, along with recent studies of Wolfgang Wölk, show that these are secondary characteristics.

It is only logical to expect that this religious solidarity would be demonstrated by data on German Catholic politicians. Again excluding Poles, Alsatians, and Lorrainers, 284 of the 318 known Catholic Wilhelmine Reichstag deputies were Centrists. Seven more were members of the predominantly Catholic Bavarian Peasants' League, which meant that only 8 percent of the German Catholic deputies could be truly called defectors. The obverse, Protestant defections to Catholicism, was even less evi-

TABLE 4:1. *Association of Catholic Party Vote with Selected Characteristics (N = 47 administrative units)* [12]

Characteristic	1907			1912		
	r	Significant Betas Only	Proportion of Variation Explained (Multiple R^2)	r	Significant Betas Only	Proportion of Variation Explained (Multiple R^2)
% Catholic	.865	.853	.748	.848	.757	.709
% of male work force in industry and mining	.081		.759	.056		.716
% of total population living in cities over 10,000	−.154		.763	−.144		.761

dent. Between 1887 and 1914 there was only one Protestant Centrist deputy.[13]

As long-term as the distinction, the majority religion for the whole nation was not politically decided upon until the *Kleindeutsch* victory of 1866 sealed the domination of Protestantism. One of the first effects of this victory was an attack on Catholics. The *Kulturkampf* of the 1870s was designed to force them into the status of a permanently weakened minority. Instead, the principal result of the oppression was to unify German Catholics into a nationwide political organization, the Center party, designed to protect the interests of the Church and its culture.

The end of the *Kulturkampf* might reduce the heat of oppression while at the same time allowing the Socialists to supersede Catholics as the undeniable "enemies of the empire." The adjustments on high also seemed to produce a reaction within the Catholic community. By the 1890s many German Catholics appeared to consider the *Kleindeutsch* Reich as the true expression of German patriotism. The following lyrics were taken from the songbook of the *Windthorst Bund*, a young Catholic group:

> On to life's highest height,
> Hold both the true watch,
> Fearing not the storms and cries,
> Noticing not the unlucky night,
> Our Emperor protects the homeland,
> Our Pope protects the altar.
> Hero Pope and hero Emperor,
> God keep you always there.[14]

Hohenzollern-hater and architect of Catholic resistance, Ludwig Windthorst would not have approved; but these sentiments represented an important strand of German Catholic thought and action.

Yet the inheritance of oppression still remained and acted as a brake upon the forces of assimilation. Catholics were no longer in the forefront of the oppressed, but they still carried the burden of both formal and informal discrimination in the allocation of power and influence. And the root of *Kulturkampf* rhetoric, the necessity for eliminating dual loyalties, continued to inform German opinion, especially in the attempt to secularize education, that is, to loosen the control of any religion including Catholicism. The Center was therefore still considered a bastion of Catholic defense, even called the "tower." Its propaganda emphasized its role in protecting the Church and the social grouping against the Protestant and secular majority. A Westphalian leader proclaimed, "We Catholic Prussians are a born minority. Whatever situation we find ourselves in, on all occasions, we have learned to be wary of our enemies and to protect our ideal interests. One goal must take precedence over all others . . . What protects the religious interest of all and every part of the Catholic population."[15] As the Catholic *Deutsches Volksblatt* (Stuttgart) argued, "So long as the liberal parties continue to construe politics with religion—and they will do so in the future—then the cats cannot let the mice play unhindered." Or, more specifically, "Down with the *Kulturkämpfer* and Catholic-haters."[16]

Thus it follows that the duty of every German Catholic was to vote and vote right, to follow the simple injunction: "A good Catholic man votes for the Center."[17] As the Wiesbaden Centrists stated in 1911, "True to the Church, true to the Center—that is our electoral slogan now more than ever."[18] Voting required putting up Centrist candidates, the absence of which was thought an admission of weakness. The Wiesbadeners refused even to consider a Protestant request that they not contest the 1912 race; to avoid the field was, in their words, "tantamount to suicide."[19] Such attitudes were not confined to German Catholic strongholds; even small communities were expected to field candidates. In 1903 German Catholics in Zoppot County, West Prussia, refused to withdraw their candidate although this action led to a Polish victory. A young teacher had negotiated a withdrawal agreement with the German Conservatives, but he was roundly attacked in the Centrist committee as being too naive and politically unripe. The six hundred or so Catholic eligibles in the district could not possibly bring the Center to victory, but the Zoppot committee was going to contest anyway, passing a resolution stating, "It is the duty of a Center man to vote for a Center candidate."[20] And it was the duty of the Zoppot committee to field such a candidate so that all the good German Catholics could perform the necessary political rituals.

The hierarchy and the party leadership worried about the pressure on such Catholics as those in Zoppot. As long as German Catholics lived within the densely settled Catholic areas, their loyalties would be constantly reinforced by those close at hand—relatives, friends, local opinion leaders. In areas of less dense settlement, Catholics were liable to hear a whole host of conflicting opinions. The result might be disaffiliation and defection from the Catholic social grouping. There were numerous signs of such a phenomenon, particularly the prevalence of church-leaving and intermarriage in areas of less dense settlement. German Catholic voters would react in the same way. Those in less segregated situations could be faced with a number of strong influences that created cross-pressures. Sometimes these cross-pressures could not be resolved, forcing the voter to abstain rather than to make a decision among them. Thus the first sign of disaffiliation from the Catholic grouping was lowered turnout in areas of less dense Catholic settlement.

Wolfgang Schulte (see table 4:2 and the appendix) has shown how this process worked in Württemberg. Catholics who lived in principally Catholic communities within Catholic counties tended to reinforce each

TABLE 4:2. *Correlation Coefficients of Center Party Vote with Turnout in Selected Townships in Württemberg*[21]

Year	Homogeneous Townships (N=20)	Mixed Townships (N=20)	Diaspora Townships (N=20)
1898	.990	.827	.552
1903	.974	.754	.542

other in their attendance at the polls; therefore the correlation between Center vote and turnout was very high in these areas. However, in the mixed settlements (Catholic townships in areas of no preponderant religious majority), and particularly in the Diaspora (Catholic townships in principally Protestant areas), there was a noticeable decline in the relationship between Center vote and turnout. The Diaspora voters, however, were a small minority of the German Catholic community. Most Catholics were protected within their geographic and cultural frontiers and remained stable habitual voters throughout the Wilhelmine regime. The Center party retained about 19 percent of the total vote for most of the Wilhelmine period. This was down from the highs of the *Kulturkampf,* but when combined with the fact that most German Catholics lived in predominantly German Catholic areas, it was enough to provide the Center with a large number of safe seats. The 1912 party sent 91 representatives to Berlin, precisely the same number as in 1874.

The continued safety of Centrist seats was only one more sign that disaffiliation with the Catholic cause was an uncommon response. Most Centrist voters were habituals and came out regardless of the issues. The erratic direction of German politics at the top makes it somewhat difficult to see this centrality of behavior. In 1874, for example, Catholic turnout was around 70 percent of the Catholic eligibles, about 10 points higher than that for Protestants, according to my estimates. Many of these were Centrist voters who came out in response to the apocalyptic vision of an oppressed minority and an injured Church. They were what we have called "easy issue" voters who disappeared once the *Kulturkampf* waned. The last year that produced a higher estimated Catholic turnout was 1887, and this election may have been skewed by an upsurge of Protestant voting in predominantly Catholic districts (see table 4:3 and the appendix for explanation of terms).

From 1890 to 1893 Catholic voting only slightly declined. This probably meant that the Center support was reduced to habitual voters, having lost those mobilized by the apocolyptic issue. Protestant turnout, on the other hand, increased, giving the impression of even more substantial

TABLE 4:3. *Catholicism and Turnout* (N=397 *electoral districts*)[22]

	% Catholic		Significant Betas for Conflict Variable	Estimated Protestant Turnout (%)	Estimated Catholic Turnout (%)
Year	r	Significant Betas Only			
1887	.105		−.137	76.6	79.0
1890	−.399		.569	75.5	64.0
1893	−.253		.223	74.1	68.5
1898	−.321		.301	70.9	61.6
1903	−.222		.164	77.4	72.3
1907	−.210	−.207	.114	86.1	82.3
1912	−.446	−.435	.149	87.2	80.4

habitual voting. However, this difference is problematic. Much of the variation between Protestant and Catholic turnout was due to the variable conflict, a measure I have used to indicate the closeness of elections. The higher the conflict, the closer the election, the more dramatic the contests, the more substantive the campaigning, the higher the turnout. When conflict is considered, until 1907 there are no significant beta relationships between the percentage of Catholics and turnout. In addition, the measured percentage of Catholics underrepresents adult males since the birthrates of German Catholics were higher. Considering both these observations, it is probable that Catholic and Protestant habitual voting was at about the same rate before 1907.

Thus there seems to have been little disaffiliation from the German Catholic social grouping until the last two Wilhelmine elections. While these differences were important, it must be remembered that they did not occur in times of low turnout. In both 1907 and 1912 the estimated Catholic turnout is above 80 percent. Thus while German Catholics were undoubtedly falling behind, their rate of participation was still higher than that of practically any other large social grouping in Europe and the United States (see below).

It was this social cohesion, not strong Church organization, that moved the German Catholic voter to the polls. The strength of affirming voting is that organizing is less necessary than feelings of solidarity. Such statements must seem strange when one considers the absolute centrality of the Church as an institution. If there was no salvation outside of the Church, then was there ever a time when the vote could be considered unorganized? The answer is a qualified yes. The Catholic political hierarchy was not necessarily coterminous with its religious hierarchy. The Catholic bishops controlled the central message of salvation; a considerably more secular leadership ran the political side of things. More-

over, the Center party leadership was becoming increasingly secular. In
1903 the clergy amounted to 15 percent of the Centrist Reichstag candidates and 20 percent of the deputies. By 1912 these figures were reduced
to 8 percent of the candidates and 11 percent of the deputies. There was
also a similar decline in the various provincial election committees and
the trustees, *Vertrauensmänner*, that ran the district organizations. In actuality, priests were often reduced to being followers and to loyally carrying forward the instructions of a predominantly secular leadership. In
electoral terms, they were messengers who were to get out the vote and
get it right.

But the Center was also the receptacle for the politics of belief and, as
such, religious figures were extraordinarily important. Their real and
symbolic position within the German Catholic communities sustained
social grouping solidarities and ultimately propelled those habitual voters
to the polls. As one Center leader stated, "Just once allow the clergy to
remain neutral and the Centrum will be shattered."[23]

The Center not only relied on the clergy to provide blessing for their
goals but also to dispense information to the voters. This was especially
true when Catholic voters were asked to turn to another party in runoffs
from which the Center was excluded. In rural Westphalia the Catholic
clergy was considerably more efficient and accurate in the transmission of
instructions than any of their Protestant counterparts.

Of course the responses of priests were not uniform. A few were apolitical and gave no instructions at all; others were ineffectual and could
not get the message right; some were opposed to the decision of the secular leadership. But the vast majority transmitted the message. And it was
at this level that it became impossible to separate politics from salvation.
The Wilhelmine political landscape was littered with stories about priests
who threatened excommunication for voting outside the Church, that is,
against the Center. There were numerous accusations about priests who
had abused their position as representatives of government and authority.

In 1907 a priest in Büren County used his period of religious instruction in the schools to urge the children to hunt out and burn any opposition ballots their fathers brought home. The same priest preached a sermon immediately before the election in which he deplored the necessity
of carrying politics into the church and then railed against the opposition. All of this occurred despite the fact that, while drinking with the
victorious Center election committee, he confessed that the opponent,
who was also a Catholic, "was really the right Reichstag candidate for
the district, but party discipline had to be maintained at any cost."[24]
There was a more authenticated case of a priest in Arnsberg County who
went from house to house, from school to school, urging the election of
the official Center candidate. The opponent was a good Catholic as well.
Immediately before the election, this priest, named Hatzfeld, preached a

sermon on "political obedience" in which he called the parish's attention to his superior education and training. Hatzfeld argued that the congregation had better listen not only to God but also to Hatzfeld, who was, at the very least, his political representative on earth.[25]

As long as religion remained the main focus of Centrist voters, the party and social grouping were not in danger. However, the modernization of transportation and communication, the penetration of the nationwide market, new sources of information about ideas and lifestyles were not easily dealt with by that combination of clergy and local notables who ran Catholic Germany at the local level. This secular threat was also enhanced by massive out-migration of Catholics into new areas, which increased the possibilities of interacting with Protestant, secular interests. If these secular economic interests prevailed, the Catholic social grouping would be fundamentally split on issues of class or economic interests and would disintegrate as a political force.

Unlike the Protestant inheritance, Catholic social theory provided a way out of this dilemma. German Catholic intellectuals and the hierarchy did not view the differences among various producer groups as necessarily divorced from belief but as parts of a cultural and economic whole. The great danger was conceived in terms of class conflict; the term "class" itself was viewed as an abomination since it presumed the division of society into autonomous groups. German Catholic social theorists attempted to substitute *Stände*, "estate," interests in place of class divisions.

Paradoxically the articulation of economic interest required a new type of political managers who were not necessarily in tune with this theory. Lawyers, schoolteachers, journalists like Karl Gröber in Württemberg, Robert Müller in Hesse, and Karl Bachem in the Rhineland obtained considerable influence over the choosing of Reichstag candidates and the direction of campaigns on the provincial and state level. They would have been the obvious beneficiaries of the Centrist attempts to achieve parity for German Catholics in government employment and political influence. Thus it was to their advantage to attempt to carry their varied clientele into the national mainstream. It was a task in which they were often frustrated since they proved more adept at accommodating local secular interests than at enforcing agreements with the elites that ran the bureaucracy and government.

The accommodation of local interests was in itself an important task and necessary for the continued strength of social grouping and party. Without new leadership, there was often rebellion. The small peasants in Lower Bavaria defected to the Bavarian Peasants' League in large numbers when their local notables failed to respond to the agrarian depression of the 1880s. A massive restructuring of electoral politics in Lower Bavaria was required to win back the majority of these peasant defectors. This was much harder than to legitimize interests and to reconcile any differences among them within the Catholic community. Center election committees in most of the rest of Germany carefully allocated Reichstag candidates among the various economic forces, especially the agrarian and artisan groups, and this seemed to forestall large-scale Bavarian-style defections.

Such actions merged national and local politics in quite unpredictable ways. As David Blackbourn states in his study of the Württemberg Center, "If there was a growing sense of national politics as politics at the local level, then in an important sense national politics became at the same time parish-pump politics writ large."[26] Blackbourn views the Württemberg Center as entrapped in the "economic backwardness" of its rural and small-town strongholds, thus becoming the principal vehicle for expressing grievances of artisans and small farmers, pursuing what he calls a *Mittelstandspolitik* that was especially insensitive to the process of modernization and the demands of the working class. Württemberg Catholic politicians had to use "demagogic" methods to hold on to their economic base. Rhetorically this was expressed in terms of stifling modernization; in practice it came to mean abdication before the most parochial interests of the electorate.

Blackbourn's study of Württemberg Catholics not only teaches us much about rural and small-town voting but also reinforces the proposition of mass politicization in the Wilhelmine period. Moreover it shows how the Center's Reichstag delegation responded to the economic demands of its clientele and how national programs were transformed to conform with local realities. The difference I have with him is that his parochials become my affirmers without any need for redefinition of function. The stronger they were bound into their local nests, the greater the preponderance of affirmative voting, the more predictable the electoral system, the more substantial the outcome.

What Blackbourn calls *Mittelstandspolitik* in Württemberg, Carl Zangerel defines as *Kulturpolitik* in Baden.[27] Zangerel's Catholics felt threatened by the Socialist-liberal alliances that controlled state politics in the first decade of the twentieth century. His Catholics were much more concerned about preserving their specific rights in the schools and the privileges of their church. Yet the social composition of Baden's Catholics was very similar to those in Württemberg, and the demands of artisans and small farmers throughout all Southern Germany were roughly similar. The fact is that Baden's Catholics had economic as well as cultural goals despite the fact that their leader, Theodor Wacker, was a priest and that Württemberg's Catholics had cultural-religious goals despite the interest of their leadership in social and economic questions. The Center strongholds in both states were in areas of preponderantly Catholic population, most often in the countryside or in small towns. Geographic isolation, cultural-religious bonds, religious questions at the state level, needs of economic security—all of these characterized German Catholic politics in the southwest. On the whole, they tended to reinforce Catholic isolation. Economic issues of *Mittelstandspolitik* often brought Catholic areas into conflict with a state government committed to industrializing; the same state government seemed bent on taking away important privileges from the schools. In the end, so many of these issues overlay one another that they could be intertwined in the generation of symbolic statements defining the Catholic social grouping, reinforced by the Church, in the family, at the workplace. When so iterated, such definitions relieved the cross-pressures that Catholics felt between their secular and religious selves and allowed for a more intensive organizational base than Catholics had heretofore.

The enveloping of economic interest by cultural-religious loyalties occurs again and again. Certainly this was the case with the radical peasant leader in Westphalia. Despite his noble lineage, Burghard von Schorlemer was a persuasive critic of old-style Centrist politics. He might even state an intention to withdraw from the party entirely if his demands were not met. But these were idle threats; Schorlemer was a convinced Catholic and a believer in *Ständepolitik*, especially in the intertwining of economic interest with religious belief. This was demonstrated in a petition of 150 farmers, which he drafted in 1893 to protest the high tariffs and demand an increase in agrarian representatives among the Center Reichstag candidates in Westphalia: "We stand and remain as Catholics, unmoved, tied firmly to the program of the Center party in religious-political and Christian-social questions and follow the flag that [our leaders] . . . have planted and nurtured. We want to exercise our Catholic belief as free German citizens and demand the revocation of all laws which hinder this aim. We wish also, as Westphalian farmers, to remain as our predecessors in possession of our inherited holdings and not to let anyone take them away from us without a bitter fight."[28] Similar agrarian objections continued in Westphalia for the next few years without causing massive defections or any breakup of the Center vote in the predominately agrarian areas of the province.

Much more difficult than controlling the *Mittelstand* in predominantly rural areas was the problem of reconciling the basic conflicts of the new industrial society. Many Catholic "social experts" believed that such a response meant remodeling *Stände* theory by recognizing the necessity of capitalist development for all German Catholics. Such was the task of the *Volksverein für das Katholische Deutschland* founded in 1890. From its headquarters in Mönchen-Gladbach in the heart of the Ruhr, the *Volksverein* sustained a strong propaganda machine, which produced over 500,000 pamphlets as well as numerous popular slide lectures. At the core of the *Volksverein* was an attempt to reconcile white- and blue-collar workers by undertaking specific studies on the possibilities of interclass unity and by explicating these theories in intensive ten-week training courses for both bourgeois and workers' leaders. The outcome was a great deal of practical help for Catholic workers, particularly through the so-called People's Bureaus, which were often staffed by professional workers' secretaries. These bureaus were designed to aid the less sophisticated in extracting social benefits from the government and often answered many more enquiries than their Socialist counterparts in cities like Dortmund and Bochum.

The greatest success of the *Volksverein* was in its sheer numbers; it had over 800,000 members by 1913. This led to expectations that it could perform a political role by "assuring a large reserve army for the Reichstag faction."[29] After all, there was one *Volksverein* member for every four Center voters by 1912. However, these were not equally dispersed by class. The *Volksverein* membership included 30.6 percent of Catholic males in Westphalia but only 7 percent in the smelting cities of Dortmund and Gelsenkirchen. This meant that there was a disproportionate membership in the rural areas and small towns around Münster and Paderborn. Its strength, therefore, was precisely among those rural and small town *Mittelstand* interests that David Blackbourn identifies in Württemberg and not among the working class. Yet even then this interclass reconciliation went too far for many in the *Mittelstand*. By 1911 special chapters had been founded in Westphalia for salespeople, farmers, and artisans, rejecting the principle that membership be open to all occupational groups.

The traditional Catholic hierarchy was less worried about the failure of the *Volksverein* to penetrate the working class effectively than the fact that it was attached to the whole trend of west German Catholicism toward advocating interconfessionalism and political interaction with Protestant Germany. The hierarchy, especially its Berlin direction, favored an approach that emphasized Catholic isolation as a means for guarding against disaffection and disaffiliation. This required the reiteration of cultural supremacy even among labor-oriented organizations. The bishops in southern and eastern Germany especially supported workers' associations, *Arbeitervereine*. These organizations were constructed in the 1890s based on the principles of the journeymen's associations, *Gesellenvereine*, created almost half a century earlier. In Württemberg and Silesia these *Arbeitervereine* were open to all Catholics and often led by a combination of priests, civil servants, and master craftsmen; many chapters were located in small towns where there were very few, if any, factory workers. Instead of new social theory, the *Arbeitervereine* practiced self-help measures by providing burial insurance, acting as agencies for the collection of health insurance funds, establishing adult education classes, and founding lending libraries. They were by law and by disposition "nonpolitical" and thus were considered to elevate Catholic commitment by "assuring the preservation of the religious-moral strength in the workers' estate, *Arbeiterstand*."[30]

Did these workers' associations serve the Center party any better than the *Volksverein*? One can answer with a tentative conclusion that those associations thrived only when they reinforced traditional cultural-religious commitments and patterns of isolation. This was not only demonstrated in the study of electoral geography but also in the case of certain Catholic organizations. An example would be the response of Catholic mine workers to the strike of 1905. The Christian unions had fought the 1905 strike along class lines in alliance with the nominally independent but Socialist-leaning *Alter Verband* "as a point of honor."[31] It was a costly point. The success of the 1905 strike and the assertion of the supremacy of class interests encouraged defections from the Christian unions and the Catholic social grouping. The Christian unions disappeared in a number of colonies around Dortmund and Bochum and were replaced by the *Alter Bund* and the Socialist party. The whole Christian labor movement in the eastern Ruhr was curtailed by the unambiguous representation of class and interconfessional interest. Catholic causes needed cultural-religious loyalties to survive, to sustain the social grouping and its Center.

As long as Catholic voters were attracted by their religious-cultural loyalties, they were secured for the Center and would produce evidences of a remarkable cohesion. They even voted together under instructions when a Centrist candidate was absent and, even more important, if they did not follow instructions, they were unlikely to vote for the opposition but would abstain from the polls entirely. This was the case in Württemberg, where the Center-Conservative coalition of 1912 was enthusiastically received. Habitual Catholic voters (see note 32 for definition) turned to Conservative candidates in districts where the Center party had declined to field a candidate. There is a correlation of .9 between Conservative vote in these instances and habitual Centrist voters. There are no other significant correlations with other parties. However, habitual Centrists who objected to either the *Mittelstand* or agrarian politics of the Conservatives, to their Protestantism or pro-Prussianism, could and would stay at home, as the correlation of −.5 with turnout increases and Catholic habitual voters shows.[32]

German Catholic loyalists were thus prepared to vote as instructed or to abstain. They would not easily defect to the opposition; the data for Catholic habituals in Württemberg shows no significant correlation with liberal or socialist voting patterns. This was an enormous power, particularly during the runoff elections where the Center was eliminated on the first ballot. In such instances, political Catholics faced an uncomfortable choice between two Protestant-based parties. Still the Center supporters were generally inclined to follow their party's instructions or to avoid the ballot box entirely when their personal choice conflicted with those of the party leadership (see chapter 9 for examples of this).

Yet this manifestation of Center strength and cohesiveness was also fraught with enormous peril. It removed the injunction that a Center man always voted Catholic and tended to sustain thoughts of defection, particularly among those Centrist voters asked to cast ballots against their secular interests. The choice particularly bedeviled a party leadership that sought to foster solidarities by diminishing class and occupational conflicts within the Catholic community. Formally allied with the SPD in 1907, the Hessian Center was particularly vulnerable in runoffs in Hanau and Wiesbaden. The party leader in Hesse, Robert Müller from Fulda, was forced to choose between two evils. If he turned to the Socialists, he would antagonize bourgeois Centrists. Supporting Protestant bourgeois candidates could overturn a whole series of electoral deals in western Germany and jeopardize the Centrist position nationwide. It was no wonder that he hesitated.

The situation in Hanau was particularly striking. On one side were Prince von Ysenberg and his dependents. Von Ysenberg was considered an unstable ally by the *Landrat* and the local progovernment elite. He had even allowed his own stonecutters to vote their conscience in 1903. In order to avoid a repetition, the local *Landrat* and a number of priests, even his own wife, all worked to keep him in line. The Prince actually became politically enthused; he even came down from his castle and attended a few political meetings. It all had the look of a feudal levy—a situation reproducible in the environs of the Ysenberg castle today, where his successor still annually receives a twenty-one-gun salute fired from sixteenth-century cannons. Ysenberg was led to each meeting by a number of renegade priests who believed in the national cause above the party. Their leader, a certain Deacon Deuffert, promised everyone that he would go through the district and "speak as a Catholic to Catholics about the election and awaken the opinion for Lucas [the National Liberal candidate]."[33] They were supported at least tacitly by all those Catholics who had become assimilated into the dominant Protestant community, who had engaged in formal political talks designed to create a bourgeois alliance, and who had much to lose if the Center came out for the SPD. Müller played his usual dubious role, placating all factions, but finally telling the Centrist voters in a series of mass meetings before the election that he gave them their electoral freedom. They should go out and vote, but they should not vote for Dr. Lucas. And they did vote for the SPD in enormous numbers. This political strength and the power of the Catholic grouping could not be shown if the electoral instructions were not followed precisely. In Hanau and Wiesbaden probably around three-quarters of the Center voters turned to the SPD in the runoff.

As long as the Centrists supported the government they could count on toleration from the dominant culture, but if they overstepped, a reversion to *Kulturkampf* terminology was not far away. In response to Müller's manipulations, the *Hanauer Anzeiger* maintained, "A monstrosity—one can scarcely understand how defamators and fanatics could celebrate these kinds of orgies. We will yet have the opportunity to return the score."[34] And they might have; after all, such is the logic of separation, and such is the nature of electoral conflict.

The politics of belief, a history of anti-Catholicism, a statement of uniqueness and possible oppression, a supportive clergy, the neutralization of secular cleavages, an intertwining of economic interest and cultural-religious commitments, a protective theology, an intelligent leadership dependent on a politicized mass—all of these factors reinforced the Catholic separation that solidified the base of the Center party. Still, there were signs of its disruption as well, particularly in the last few prewar years. These defections in runoff elections were transferred into lower votes in the first and most meaningful election. In 1912 the Center vote was down to 16.4 percent. Part of this was due to several long-term effects. The cities offered blandishments and a sense of cosmopolitanism, which turned Catholics toward secular interests and more cosmopolitan lifestyles that would form the base of competing loyalties and lead to disaffiliation from the social grouping. This can be clearly shown by dividing the number of Center voters by the number of Catholic males in a given population. The result yields an estimate of 54 percent of Catholic males voting Center in 1912 for Germany as a whole compared with 33 percent in cities of over 100,000.[35]

But long-term losses did not explain the exceptional slide of 1912. I think some of this decline can be accounted for by the behavior of Catholic leaders and the actions of Catholic organizations. These leaders and organizations had very little effect in maintaining Centrist habitual voting, which was assured by the dominance and stability of social grouping politics. However leaders, organizations, particular circumstances could move in the opposite direction, could accelerate the trends of disaffiliation.

In 1906 Julius Bachem, a Cologne publisher, seemed to encourage Catholic defections when he advocated that German Catholics end their isolation and leap "out of the tower" and join the national mainstream. Whether Bachem wanted to create an interconfessional party or simply prepare the way for the alliance with the conservatives is still a matter of debate. In any case, the strife that ensued probably disconcerted urban Rhenish Catholics. In 1912 there appears for the first time a regional variant in the West, a high negative correlation between the percentage of Catholics and the turnout. Long-term urban defections were combined with short-term disaffections caused by cross-pressures between secular and religious interest. The evidence is there. Cologne had the lowest turn-out of any German city with a population of over 500,000; Düsseldorf for those between 200,000 and 500,000; Aachen for the group between 100,000 and 200,000.[36]

These turnout declines in Rhenish cities were only a small part of the 1912 effect. The real crisis was measured in the rural vote. The Centrist share of the rural vote declined from 24 percent in 1907 to 20.5 percent in 1912 (see table 4:4). This sharp decrease was apparent in some of the strongest Catholic enclaves where voters were not usually subject to cross-pressures. What weakened the party and the social grouping in the rural areas and small towns? I think this was the result of the strength rather than the weakness of the Center party. This strength allowed party leaders to make multiple deals for Catholic votes in runoff elections, deals that often contradicted earlier electoral pronouncements. In 1903 the Cen-trists generally supported the government; in 1907 the working-class/ *Mittelstand* divisions in the party were heightened by an ostensible al-liance with the Social Democrats; in 1912 the Center turned to an alliance with the conservatives, a strange coalition of Prussian and Protestant blue with clerical black. While many Centrist deputies still won elections without runoffs and many Catholic voters had never been asked to vote against their secular or religious convictions, the knowledge of such ac-tions was sufficiently widespread to cause confusion, to increase secular loyalties which resulted in counter-pressures that ended in disaffiliation. These rural Catholics had been easily moved by the great levers of their commitments and the cohesion of the Catholic social grouping, but these levers could be used too many times. Thus 20 percent of the rural Cen-trists who had voted in 1907 probably stayed home or voted for other parties five years hence; their disaffection or disaffiliation started a skid that would continue through the Weimar Republic, that would be stopped by the formation of the Christian Democratic Union after World War II.

3. Socialists

Each social grouping was unique, formed by the combination of different characteristics. As the German Catholic social grouping was based pre-dominately on cultural-religious commitments, so the Socialist-oriented group was the result of secular economic conditions which created class divisions. Therefore what was a danger to one was a source of strength to the other.

But the similarities of social grouping politics were equally arresting. Both were politically defined in terms of oppression as a result of their divergence from the dominant political culture and progovernmental coalitions that sustained it. Both sprang from the loyalties and enmities of everyday life and were rooted in an isolation that formed their distinct nature. It is somewhat easier to deploy the arguments in the case of German Catholicism; the Catholic social grouping was attached to Church, tradition, and history, and could be statistically compared with votes for the Center party. The definition of the Socialist-oriented grouping is based on the strength of SPD voting, which makes it much more difficult to prove that a social grouping did exist independent from party and labor organizations and that there was a true class consciousness among German workers bred out of common experience. Yet I believe there were such experiences and that they can be measured by the Socialist vote in all its dimensions. Moreover, in contrast to the Catholics, the Socialists stood to profit by industralization and specialization of labor functions. The class and vote grew enormously from 9 percent of the vote in 1877, the last year before the extreme anti-Socialist measures, to 35 percent in 1912, from 493,000 voters to 4,250,000.[37]

Newness was the key to the composition of this social grouping—new places, new occupations, new men in terms of age and commitments. It is therefore surprising that Socialism would have a cultural-religious component at all. The strength of the Catholic social grouping essentially confined the SPD vote to Protestants. The high negative correlation with the percentage of Catholics in table 4 : 5 means that most Socialist voters were Protestant, since the proportion of Protestants and Catholics varies inversely.

The failure of German Protestantism to contain its working class was not lost on the Wilhelmines. The Catholic scholar Alois Klöcker analyzed the election of 1907 and was happy to find that over 90 percent of the SPD voters were Protestant. In part this reflects, of course, the fact that there were more Protestants in Germany, five for every three Catholics. Yet Klöcker appears to have been substantially correct when he stated that this ratio did not explain all. Using more modern methods, I estimate a figure of 83 percent Protestant for the SPD vote in 1912 and a ratio of Protestant to Catholic of six or seven to one for all other Wilhelmine elections after 1893.

Undoubtedly this was a sign of the strength of secular cleavages within German Protestantism. Yet something else was involved here as well. SPD voters were unlikely to be churchgoers, but they were unwilling to give up their designation as Protestant even when such an act would have freed them from paying church taxes. The German cultural majority was Protestant, and this designation was important even for secularists pushed down into the dominated class. Yet, once within the borders of Protestantism, the bulk of working-class Germans were moved by class interests and class loyalties, cultural ties being of secondary importance (see below).[38]

The close associations of Socialist vote with industrialization and ur-

TABLE 4:4. *Turnout and Party Strength by Population of Place of Residence in First Reichstag Elections from 1898 to 1912* [39]

Population	Year	Turnout (% of eligibles)	Party Vote (% of valid ballots cast)	
			Conservatives	Free Conservatives
Less than 2,000	1898	66.9	18.3	5.6
	1903	77.5	17.8	4.8
	1907	85.2	19.5	5.9
	1912	83.5	17.5	4.6
2,000–10,000	1898	66.9	8.1	4.3
	1903	74.5	6.8	3.7
	1907	84.3	7.4	3.9
	1912	84.8	5.7	2.6
10,001–100,000	1898	71.4	7.2	4.4
	1903	80.4	4.9	2.1
	1907	88.9	4.4	3.2
	1912	86.6	3.8	1.9
100,001–500,000	1898	75.5	1.9	0.6
	1903	72.8	1.8	3.0
	1907	83.1	2.6	1.2
	1912	84.1	2.0	1.6
Over 500,000	1898	66.5	4.9	0.2
	1903	82.9	7.9	0.0
	1907	80.0	3.6	2.4
	1912	84.9	2.5	1.1
Total:	1898	68.1	11.1	4.5
	1903	76.1	10.0	3.5
	1907	84.7	9.4	4.2
	1912	84.9	9.3	3.0

banization are less of a surprise. The interesting fact is that the proportion of the labor force in mining and manufacturing produces the least significant betas and the weakest correlation coefficients. Richard Blank, a contemporary Wilhelmine, argued that this was a sign that Social Democratic (SPD) voters were increasingly lower middle class and had created by 1900 "a great coalition party in which democratic elements of different classes strive for freedom, equality and social progress."[40]

| | | Party Vote | | | |
| | | (% of valid ballots cast) | | | |

Anti-Semites	National Liberals	Left-wing Liberals	Center	Poles	Socialist
3.4	11.8	9.0	23.4	5.1	14.2
5.8	15.3	11.8	24.1	5.8	17.1
—	13.2	7.8	24.1	6.0	14.1
4.7	12.8	8.8	20.5	5.8	19.4
3.2	13.6	5.1	19.5	1.9	32.8
2.8	13.0	9.2	22.9	2.8	35.0
—	14.6	11.0	22.9	3.5	30.6
2.7	15.0	12.1	19.8	3.2	35.8
2.4	16.2	13.0	14.0	1.3	38.3
1.3	18.4	10.7	17.7	1.9	41.0
—	18.1	12.6	15.5	3.2	38.3
1.8	15.6	15.5	13.0	2.7	42.3
3.5	10.6	19.8	8.2	0.1	47.7
1.8	15.4	16.2	11.0	1.4	51.2
—	14.1	15.5	11.5	1.5	45.5
0.8	13.5	17.3	11.3	1.8	50.1
9.0	9.0	12.1	6.9	0.1	56.2
3.7	9.0	10.3	3.2	0.2	60.9
—	13.1	14.8	6.6	1.5	56.7
1.3	10.2	13.6	6.0	1.8	62.7
3.7	12.5	11.1	18.8	3.1	27.2
2.6	13.8	10.3	19.7	3.7	31.7
—	14.5	10.9	19.4	4.0	28.9
3.9	13.6	12.3	16.4	3.6	34.8

Blank's arguments were essentially statistical, based on the proposition that there were not enough male wage earners in industry and trade over age twenty-four to fill the columns of the Socialist totals in the large cities. His assumptions led to as much error as insight although it would be wrong to disregard them completely. Berlin and Munich had large numbers of impoverished self-employed tailors and shoemakers who certainly could have joined unions in greater numbers and voted Socialist; in

TABLE 4:5. *Association of SPD Vote with Selected Characteristics* (N=47 *administrative units*)

	1907			1912		
Characteristic	r	Significant Betas Only	Proportion of Variation Explained (Multiple R^2)	r	Significant Betas Only	Proportion of Variation Explained (Multiple R^2)
% Catholic	−.624	−.515	.388	−.582	−.531	.339
% of male work force engaged in industry and mining	.526	.193	.647	.610	.213	.692
% of total population living in cities with populations over 10,000	.714	.472	.761	.723	.447	.773

any case, these cities began to develop Socialist settlements where service people—innkeepers, barbers and the like—were Socialist by either conviction or necessity.

Still, it would be wrong to view socialism as some kind of lower-middle-class eruption. The data available for the industrial cities show that Protestant cleavages were based essentially on class. Using designations drawn from the German census, I have classified by occupation over 30,000 listed eligible voters for Dortmund in 1903. Finally arriving at two categories, essentially blue-collar and white-collar workers, I found that voter response was remarkably uniform, relatively unaffected by industry or by occupational prestige categories within the white-collar group. The results in table 4:6 support the view of a Protestant working-class political isolation. This table shows a substantial class split among Protestants contrasted with a German Catholic response that bridged class differences. The Protestant National Liberals were almost all white-collar workers; the Protestant Social Democrats were mostly blue-collar. This is so although table 4:6 overestimates the white-collar response; it will be the same for any other measure used to show the propensity of Socialists to be blue-collar (Suval's definition), nontechnically trained wage earner (O'Donnell's definition), or simply working-class (Wuerth's).

TABLE 4:6. *Estimated Party Strength in Dortmund by Class (by percentage)* [41]

Class	Socialists	National Liberals	Center
White-collar Occupations	21	91	44
Blue-collar Occupations	79	9	55
Total	100	100	99

Workers voted Socialist; that is the message of the data in table 4:7, which presents the simple correlation coefficients between working-class (as defined) and SPD vote in three instances.

The third category listed in table 4:5, urbanization, includes only the effect of increasing urban population on the SPD vote after the effects of religion and work force have been removed. This procedure was followed because urbanization itself is a phenomenon that covers a host of social situations, and it is important to isolate just the effect of living in large cities from other considerations. Even when this is done, the beta coefficients for urbanization are very strong. Metropolitan areas like Munich, Hamburg, Berlin, Leipzig, and Dresden had a much higher proportion of the SPD vote than the religious and work-force variables would predict by themselves. There is room for some aspect of the Blank effect, a transfer of lower-middle-class SPD voters, but there were undoubtedly other reasons as well. I believe this indicates a strong working-class culture that enlarged the possible limits of the social grouping by including more workers from the foodstuffs, textiles, and clothing industries, which were generally without strong numerical representation.

Hellmut Hasselbach has argued that this discussion hides a counter-effect shown by the large number of SPD voters who lived in rural areas, defined as those places with less than 2,000 population. This vote varied from 14 percent in 1898 to 19 in 1912 (table 4:4). However, much of this vote was within rural areas close to large cities. Many of these eligibles did not live in rural settings at all but in small towns of over 1,000 population with large numbers of industrial or proto-industrial workers.

Still there was an irreducible minimun of rural Socialist votes that cannot all be explained away. In the Hesse-Darmstadt district of Giessen-Nidda-Büdingen the SPD obtained almost 35 percent of the rural vote. Much of this can be explained by the aforementioned reasons. Some of it was because the district was the home of SPD revisionists like Eduard David who believed in agrarian agitation; part of this was the result of the political situation in Hesse-Darmstadt, where the police had been less likely to harass Socialist campaigners than in Prussia or Saxony. Yet it is

TABLE 4:7. *Correlation Coefficients between Proportions of Blue-Collar Occupations and Socialist Vote*[42]

Source	City	Year	Number of Precincts	Correlation Coefficient *r*
Suval	Dortmund	1903	46	.871
O'Donnell	Dortmund	1912	70	.953
Wuerth	Göppingen	1907	7 (sample)	.81
Wuerth	Göppingen	1912	7 (sample)	.94

doubtful that all of these reasons can account for the SPD vote in the small villages and towns that bordered the Büdingen-Giessen railway line and created an ascertainable Socialist bastion. Nor can they account for the high rural vote in some of the more remote regions of East Prussia or figures reaching upwards of 40 percent in the Mecklenbergs.

Were these rural bastions possible outposts for a massive SPD advance into rural areas? I think not. As Tables 4 : 4 to 4 : 7 demonstrate, the greatest number of Socialist voters were in urban areas among working-class groups who had very little in common with peasants and agricultural workers. Energies expended in the recruitment of urban workers for party membership and voting were more than repaid, while the electoral returns for SPD agitation in rural areas were problematic as demonstrated by the disappointment after the 1893 elections. Moreover, rural voters in the 1890s would be increasingly seduced by agrarian parties and political organizations that even competed with socialism in propounding anticapitalist slogans, particularly against the stock market. All of this was a sign of the importance of class isolation, a fact recognized within the party, even if its leader, August Bebel, resisted. The SPD congresses that rejected agrarian programs were not only ideologically against preserving peasant holdings; they opted for supporting the widespread "cultural and emotional prejudices that made them [the majority of party delegates] see peasants as part of the backward-looking archaic forces that kept workers and their party isolated and scorned," an isolation which produced "the powerful emotional identification of the delegates with the good cause of the industrial workers."[43]

Protestant, urban, blue-collar, and then there was one more thing—young. The evidence for youth is much less substantial; it is based on a study of twelve electoral districts for the Prussian state election of 1908. The Prussian legislative elections were indirect, not secret, and had low turnout—in this case around 30 percent of the eligibles. Still, the results in table 4 : 8 are very striking: they show that the pattern of SPD voters is very different from that of the other parties. The four districts chosen for

TABLE 4:8. *Vote by Age Group in Selected Districts in Prussian State Election of 1908 (percent distribution)* [44]

Party	24–30	30–40	40–50	50–60	60–70	Over 70	Total
			Age Group				

Party	24–30	30–40	40–50	50–60	60–70	Over 70	Total
			Electoral District Magdeburg 4 (City Magdeburg)				
Conservative parties	—	0.1	0.1	0.1	0.3	0.4	0.1
Liberal parties	32.8	46.3	57.2	71.2	82.6	86.8	54.4
Socialists	65.4	52.5	40.6	27.9	16.5	11.7	43.6
Others	1.8	1.1	2.1	0.8	0.6	1.1	1.9
			Electoral District Minden 2 (Herford, Halle in Westf., City and County Bielefeld)				
Conservative parties	10.4	18.2	28.7	37.5	43.4	46.2	24.5
Anti-Semites	2.5	3.0	3.9	3.4	3.0	3.8	3.2
Liberal Parties	22.6	24.1	34.9	36.3	36.0	35.0	31.2
Socialists	54.1	37.3	20.7	12.7	6.1	4.0	29.9
Others	10.4	17.4	11.8	10.1	11.5	11.0	11.2
			Electoral District Potsdam 8 (City and County Kottbus, Spremberg, Calau)				
Conservative parties	14.8	20.8	29.0	39.1	45.6	36.4	26.1
Liberal parties	6.8	8.7	16.2	18.5	22.3	34.9	13.0
Socialists	72.4	62.7	45.9	35.1	19.8	13.7	52.2
Others	6.0	7.8	8.9	7.3	12.3	15.0	8.7
			Electoral District Frankfurt 7 (City and County Gruben, County Sorau)				
Conservative parties	22.3	32.3	42.4	44.9	46.0	42.1	37.2
Liberal parties	15.1	24.2	30.3	34.4	39.5	37.1	28.7
Socialists	47.0	33.1	18.3	11.1	4.2	4.2	23.9
Others	15.6	10.4	9.0	9.6	10.3	16.6	10.2

TABLE 4:9. *Working-Class Membership in the*
Social Democratic Party[45]

City and Year	Total Membership	% Working Class
Dortmund, 1912	1,258	95
Frankfurt a. M., 1905	2,620	94
Frankfurt a. M., 1908	4,940	94
Leipzig County, 1905	1,679	92
Marburg, 1905	114	95
Munich, 1905	6,704	77
Nuremberg, 1905	6,695	88+
Offenbach, 1905	1,630 (estimate)	92
Berlin, 1906	41,387	90

table 4 : 8 are typical of the twelve reported; the age-specific effect applied equally well to all districts and in urban and rural areas as well.

The party membership seems to have generally followed the outlines of the social grouping. It was predominantly working class (see table 4:9). The SPD did not appeal to those upper-middle-class defectors that made up a significant proportion of the French and Italian socialist parties. For example, there was not one local SPD member among the 1350 students at Marburg University in 1906. This was a situation impossible to replicate in a Rimini or a Navarre. Secondly, the party was also young. Table 4:10 shows not only a relatively young membership when compared to the nation as a whole, but also that the proportion of party joiners among the young was growing. This is an extraordinary fact when juxtaposed against the general rule in Western democracies, where the median age of party members is well above that of the adult population.

Taken together, these characteristics do not present a pattern for the integration of a social grouping; rather they describe the prerequisites for shaking off old obligations as a prelude to undertaking new loyalties. Despite the dangers of transferring aggregate statistics to individual cases, it seems altogether reasonable to construct an archetype of the Socialist-oriented as a young blue-collar worker, a Protestant in designation but not a churchgoer, residing in an urban setting. An excess of Protestants increased the possibilities of secular commitments instead of more traditional ties. Urbanization and youth are often associated with the disintegration of traditional values and breaking up of older patterns of socialization.

The newness of the party loyalties and their inability to penetrate into the Catholic and non-German national groupings have caused some re-

TABLE 4:10. *Age Distribution of Membership in the Social Democratic Party (in percent)*[46]

Age Cohort	Frankfurt am Main			Hamburg			Total Males in Reich Over 20 (N=17,913,774)
	SPD Membership 1/1/02 (N=1,138)	SPD Membership 12/1/06 (N=2,965)	Total Males in City Over 20 (N=101,391)	SPD Membership 1/1/03 (N=15,758)	SPD Membership 1/1/08 (N=34,428)	Total Males in City Over 20 (N=256,021)	
Under 20	1.4	1.8	—	1.9	3.1		
20–30	31.5	36.4	36.3	27.8	31.4	33.1	29.7
30–40	42.8	31.7	28.1	34.9	32.9	27.2	25.1
Over 40	24.2	20.9	34.6	35.3	32.6	39.6	45.2
Unknown		9.2					

cent undervaluation of the strength of the German working-class grouping. Yet it would be wrong to judge socialism by some abstract standard,
requiring the obliteration of Catholic and Polish commitments. The same
can be said about the relatively nonviolent behavior of the working class
in Wilhelmine Germany. Instead of emphasizing its difficulties, it might
be wise to look at the strengths of this social grouping. Unquestionably it
was the outcome of increasing solidarity among German Protestant blue-
collar workers at the workplace and in the neighborhoods. Miners, print-
ers, building workers and others increasingly voted Socialist.

The greater the SPD strength, the greater the reaction against the party.
The persistence of industrial conflict was, of course, not unique to Germany, but few Western European nations had introduced such oppressive
legislation as the anti-Socialist laws of 1878, which effectively forbade
trade-union activity, party organizing, or campaigning. The Socialists
were an illegal party with its leadership in exile, and their potential membership was both intimidated and subject to excessive control. The suspen-
sion of these laws in 1890 and the social welfare policies of the German
state alleviated some of the tensions between government and worker. But
the organized or unorganized worker was never totally free from controls
placed on his behavior through work rules or police action. Early in the
1890s union organizers were jailed for disturbing the peace, and Sunday
leaflet distributors might be arrested on the same charge. By 1900 laws
were less likely to be so explicitly enforced, but the opposition of the state
was always implicit, as when police officials attended Socialist meetings,
took copious notes, and filed reports. There was thus a kind of class administration that went along with a class justice, ending with a single political line which called Socialists *Reichsfiende*, official enemies of the empire. And finally there was always the threat of military intervention into
industrial conflict on the side of the bourgeoisie.[47]

The result was a labeling process by which Socialist-oriented workers
accepted the distinctions of separateness applied by the dominant political culture, a process of labeling that both generated and assured the isolation of their social grouping. This process has been discussed by J. O.
Nettl, Guenther Roth and, most recently, by Dieter Groh, who characterized the situation of the working class as sustained "on one side by continuous economic improvement and on the other side at the same time,
by the refusal of equal rights in the state and society and the continuation
of labor sweating and oppressive measures."[48]

Socialists thus were forced to turn inward to support from within their
social grouping. The images that sustained class loyalties called attention
to their plight as "homeless wanderers in the fatherland."[49] Home in this
setting becomes the locus of class loyalties rather than a physical place or
a traditional culture. The radical leader Kart Westmeyer exclaimed, "The
City Magistrate in Frankfurt has called Rosa Luxemburg a vagrant, a

homeless person. She does have a home, a home in millions of workers' hearts [stormy applause]."[50]

The party and its grouping were tied together by their isolation from the dominant and traditional political cultures. There were constant reminders of this fact in every election. Those loyal to other groupings, particularly to the bourgeois parties, would simply refuse to cross over the line and vote SPD in runoff elections. It was for this reason that the SPD had to win the overwhelming number of its seats in the first election or not win them at all. The SPD rate of success in runoffs was about one in three, almost half that of the Protestant bourgeois parties.[51]

These SPD failures in second elections were the result of its isolation. This is shown in table 4:11, which approximates the ability of parties to garner additional votes in runoffs. The percentage figure refers to the average differences between the proportion of the total vote won by a party in a runoff and that in the first election. The figure is obviously only calculated in those instances when a party made the runoff. The success of the liberals and anti-Semites is clearly apparent, especially when contrasted with the failure of the SPD to improve its runoff performance over time. Of course, such statistics must be viewed with caution. The percentage difference does not take into account those voters who stayed at

TABLE 4:11. *Average Percentage Difference between Runoff and First Election for Parties and Groups of Parties (number of electoral districts in parentheses)* [52]

Party	1887	1893	1903	1912
German Conservatives	9.5 (15)	11.2 (44)	14.9 (39)	11.9 (42)
Free Conservatives	6.6 (13)	11.7 (28)	13.3 (34)	14.3 (16)
Anti-Semites	—	19.7 (16)	20.9 (14)	17.8 (13)
National Liberals	8.3 (31)	13.2 (75)	18.3 (63)	18.8 (66)
Left-wing Liberals	13.4 (27)	19.5 (51)	21.8 (40)	18.2 (54)
Center	16.7 (11)	12.6 (27)	7.6 (32)	8.3 (29)
Poles	8.4 (4)	10.9 (8)	8.6 (7)	12.2 (10)
Social Democrats	8.7 (20)	8.2 (76)	8.2 (109)	8.7 (120)

home in the runoff; nor does it reflect differing political conditions and the placement of parties in various districts. It is supported by other evidence, particularly by Wolfgang Schulte's study of township-level responses in a number of runoffs in Württemberg, where the SPD was lowest on the hierarchical list of parties to whom voters turned in second elections.

All of this explains why even SPD party moderates met with resistance when they tried to deal with bourgeois parties. As one Frankfurt moderate bitterly complained, "They [the bourgeoisie] have no wish to have anything to do with Socialism or Social Democrats."[53] Certainly the sporadic electoral alliances with left-wing liberals could hardly be viewed as a sign to the contrary. The only important alliances were regionally based; they depended upon a mutual hatred of Catholics in Bavaria and Baden. Moreover, most of them were dissolved before the start of the war. All of them were severely burdened with the fact that liberal voters were often inclined not to follow any electoral alliance made between their leaders and the SPD. In the South German states, particularly in Württemberg in 1912, even the most democratic of the liberal parties could not convince its supporters to vote for the SPD candidates in the state legislative runoff. The result was that the SPD voters loyally went to the polls and increased the number of liberal victories while the bourgeois democrats abstained or voted for the opposition, causing a decrease in the SPD representation.[54]

This frustration was the cause of a dramatic Socialist intrusion into a left-wing liberal meeting in Herford County, Westphalia, in 1909. Led by the Bielefeld city councilor, Karl Hofmann, the Socialists accused the liberals of backing away from the fight against "our common enemy, the Junker, and, in this district, the clerical conservatives as well." The intruders were not placated by liberal reminders of their stands against the anti-Socialist laws of the 1870s and 1880s. Hofmann left the meeting complaining, "We have with some exceptions supported the Progressives and the Progressives have always left us in the lurch."[55] It was a prophetic statement that would come home to roost in Hofmann's own district just three years later. In the 1912 runoff for Bielefeld-Wiedenbrück, the Progressive district committee refused to follow the instructions of party central in Berlin. Instead of urging their supporters to vote Socialist, the district committee told them to vote their conscience, that is, bourgeois. Perhaps the committee had no choice; liberal voters were notorious for refusing even the slightest party discipline. They had to be treated very carefully. Faced with a choice between reaction and the SPD, a great many left-wing liberals deserted their national party and voted to defeat the Socialist incumbent, Karl Severing.[56]

These attitudes reinforced social-grouping isolation embedded in working-class attitudes and expressed in affirmative voting. Affirmative voting was expressed in habitual attendance at the polls and was based on working-class consciousness, not merely on belonging to the same party or union. Most Social Democratic habitual voters must have been unorganized and probably remained so. This priority of grouping, defined as voters, over the party was a historical fact. The SPD vote doubled between 1881 and 1890 while the party apparatus was underground and the organized Socialist electoral activity was forbidden by law. Even after the repeal of the anti-Socialist laws in 1890, the SPD was still shackled by the Prussian Law on Associations, which forbade permanent party organizations at the district level. Until 1900 every party had to form its election committees anew for each election. In some sense, this might have given the SPD an advantage since the Socialists created permanent nonelectoral organizations in every major working class area; however, the SPD membership figures remained relatively stable even after 1900. The party certainly did not grow faster than the grouping measured by the number of SPD voters. The Frankfurt am Main party membership total remained at about 5 percent of the SPD vote from 1893 to 1903. In Dortmund in 1903 the figure was less than .5 percent. A Frankfurt election broadside of 1903 complained bitterly about the fact.

> You can be a party comrade only if you understand the teachings of Social Democracy, accept the principles of the party, and put these principles into practice.
>
> Unfortunately these injunctions are not followed throughout the working class. Thousands of voters give their ballots to the Social Democrats; thousands of workers are organized in unions; hundreds belong to the working class choral societies, and only a handful are politically organized into the Social Democratic associations whose count bears no relationship to the other numbers.[57]

Nor is it possible to assert with the Frankfurt police president that Socialism's "best advertisement is to bring the outsider into the trade union."[58] There was evidence of numerical take-off. The proportion of organized workers increased enormously; the membership of unions who defined themselves as Socialist was never less than one-fifth of the SPD vote after 1890. Undoubtedly the unions socialized their members into a certain political leaning. Yet, too little is known about this connection to estimate its effectiveness. Moreover the struggles between the trade unions and the party are well documented. Many union leaders in the 1890s actively asserted that the free-union movement actually meant free of any party leaning. Robert Michels, the contemporary Wilhelmine sociologist, contended that this independence was carried to such absurdities as demanding that party leaders refrain from addressing union members as comrades.

It was not until after the Mannheim convention of 1905 that party and union unambiguously reinforced each other. After that they do often seem to be grafted to the same tree; both were overrepresented in skilled occupational groupings—woodworking, printing, and building trades—and underrepresented in those occupational groupings which employed a large number of unskilled workers and women—foodstuffs, textiles, clothing, and general trade. Yet the data base for these contentions is not altogether satisfactory; party records did not define the 20 percent of the membership defined as worker. Classifications such as metalworkers hid great differences of skill and pay. The miners especially did not join the party although their union membership rates were extraordinarily high. And there is no evidence of whether those occupational groups that dominated party and union were also overrepresented among the Socialist voters.[59]

No matter how strong or weak the combining of party and union were, both or either were scarcely the monolithic organizations that their opponents espied. Several recent studies emphasize that "the pre-organisation forms of individualist and spontaneous conflict continued beyond the control or direction of organisations."[60] Certainly the pre-1900 union and party were unable to undertake mass political organizing. In 1899 the average turnout for both union and party meetings in Dortmund-Hörde was 75. At the height of the agitation against the *Zuchthausvorlage*, the most virulent antiunion measure proposed in Wilhelmine Germany, the unions could gather about 1,200 in one mass meeting. In Frankfurt between 1897 and 1900 there was only one party meeting with an attendance larger than 450. Friedrich Naumann, with the small splinter National Socialist party, was able to rouse between 600 and 800 whenever he came to the city. In both 1898 and 1900 more people attended National Socialist than SPD meetings. This is a far cry from those mass meetings reported in chapter 2.

It was not until about 1903 in Frankfurt and Dortmund-Hörde that the party began to grow at an unprecedented rate and moved into a new phase of development. This growth rate was matched throughout Germany—the result of several converging factors. There was the increased propensity of Germans of all kinds to organize politically. The particular SPD expression of this growth was aided by the fact that the trade-union membership had begun to increase in the 1890s, that the unions themselves had become integrated into the party immediately before and after the Mannheim Congress in 1905, and that the party itself was reorganized in 1905 to place emphasis on the creation of new members. The results were phenomenal; the party doubled in size between 1900 and 1905, and doubled again by 1913 to almost one million members. This figure was surpassed in German history only immediately following World War I. In 1912 the party membership was about 23 percent of the SPD electorate, a very high proportion. Even when women and male youths are subtracted, this still represents about 15 percent of the electorate. It was a ratio beyond the experience of Great Britain or France. Coupled with the growth of union membership to almost 60 percent of the SPD vote in 1912, organized Socialism had moved from an embarrassment of poverty to a plethora of riches.[61]

Yet riches can be an embarrassment as well. It is probable that the party leadership never really knew what to do with all these new members. From the first there was enormous instability in party membership caused by the massive exchanges of population among the German cities. Preliminary research seems to indicate that around half of the population in the industrial cities had been there less than ten and, in some instances, less than three years. People came and left at incredible rates; in urban Germany the number of out-migrants from a particular city was four-fifths of the number of in-migrants. A large number of these out-migrants were Socialists. Forty percent of those who left the Frankfurt party in 1900 resigned because they moved out of the city. The occupational groups that tended to produce a higher ratio of SPD members were not immune from this tide. Skilled building workers were among the most highly organized and the most mobile of the occupational groups in Germany. Compared with the effect of this membership increase, the numbers of long-term party faithful, the core of any organization, was relatively small. To be faithful, one has to be around. Ralf Lützenkirchen has estimated that about 15 percent of the 1909 Dortmund city party had been members three years previously. The unions circumvented this massive exchange by centralizing their apparatuses; one could pay dues anywhere. But, although the party leadership established many nationwide controls, membership was an affair for local or regional associations.[62]

It would be wrong, however, to denigrate party membership. Joining the party at all was an important act for the individual. It required a good deal of effort and some money. Party members were expected to pay regular dues, generally at the rate of 30 pennies per month, at a special *Zahlabend* in the local inn. Thus even if these new members never attended a political meeting, they had moved meaningfully up the scale of political participation, and the fact that they might not be a well-organized army only testifies to the serious purpose of the membership. There was no checkoff system; there were no paid professionals to collect dues. The decision to join may have been influenced by peer-group pressures, but the continual payment of dues was an act of faith.

Recent scholarship has emphasized something different: that the party was more than a holding place for individual allegiances. Guenther Roth, Dieter Groh, and others have tended to view the SPD as the principal force in organizing a political subculture among the Socialist-oriented working class. This was supposed to lead to the creation of a separate society divorced from the dominant Wilhelmine political culture and to

create a negative integration characterized by a lack of contact with the
remainder of Germany. For Roth, Ernst Fraenkel, and others, the SPD organizational attempts are viewed as a workable form of social ghetto
politics.[63] Certainly these organizational efforts were numerous; certainly
they imitated the German bourgeois propensity to associate; certainly
joining these organizations would tend to reinforce loyalties toward the
SPD and help isolate the organized working class from the dominant and
traditional minority groupings. The problem is, who joined these burial
associations and buying cooperatives, these lending libraries and gymnastic societies, the choral and bicycling clubs, the soccer teams, the Sunday schools and dancing courses? Could it not have been a relatively
small number when compared to the entire party? The SPD hoped that
these subsidiary activities would appeal to the least politicized, would be
a first step in the education of a proletariat. Yet was this so? Except for
the lending libraries and choral societies, the SPD subsidiary organizations seem to have been organized later than the party and to be much
smaller than the party. At least this is the experience of the area around
Stuttgart, of Bochum, Dortmund, and Gelsenkirchen in the Ruhr. It
might very well have been that the convinced SPD members were encouraged to join the subsidiary organizations. Multiple membership among
the committed is generally less rare than single membership among the
marginally interested.

There is even some doubt that these subsidiary organizations were dis-
pensing actual proletarian culture. The lending libraries, the first of these
units to surface, were often centers for circulating romantic bourgeois
novels among proletarian women. The choral groups, which grew so
enormously in the last two decades of Wilhelmine Germany, were often
no more than vehicles for light entertainment. As they grew in size and
diversity of voices, they moved farther away from proletarian politics
and into Bach and Brahms. The whole issue of working-class culture is by
no means resolved. Lending libraries, choral groups, the gymnastic societies were transitional associations that not only heightened bourgeois
consciousness among workers but also were important in defining proletarian culture. At the moment, we simply do not know enough about
creating class culture and its connections with working-class consciousness and bourgeois society. Yet, even if we did, there seems to be no doubt
that the proletarian sense of separation did not grow out of culture as
with the German Catholics but came from perceptions of class drawn
from the workplace and the community as a whole. German workers
were originally self-defined culturally as dominated members of the Protestant society; it took a long while to see the possibility of a separable
cultural identity that went hand in hand with the separable class consciousness. To a great extent, these perceptions never came to fruition.[64]

Instead of falling into the party through bicycling, reading, or singing, the Socialist-inclined worker probably joined a union or affirmed his differences by voting. The vote expressed the isolation of these workers from the other social groupings and the dominant society; it connected everyday oppression with the process of identifying and responding to labeling of political and social deviance. But the vote also performed symbolic and practical functions for the Social Democratic party and its leadership. The vote and the successes associated with it became ends in themselves, forestalling revolutionary movement and containing radical elements of the party. It was the reason why the SPD central leadership did not always reward the most active participants in the party with the greatest influence. These active participants were less immune to radicalism, more likely to frighten away marginal voters and thus reduce the vote. This perceived threat of radicalism was a convenient excuse for the centralized party bureaucracy to sustain its domination over the most independently inclined local branches like that of Göppingen, Württemberg, where a well-led local party and trade union movement was easily undercut by the state and national party leadership.[65]

The Göppingen insurgents were radicals and, like almost all radicals, they fell into the trap of talking too much about suffrage. It is true that the party radicals who emphasized the extension of suffrage may have done so only because it was a useful slogan. "It is not the ballot stuffed in the box that we want," one of them stated, "It is the brain and heart."[66] But the masses of workers who took to the streets in support of universal manhood suffrage had no way of knowing this. And as for the rest of the party, the vote was sacred. The radicals may have been right when they accused the party majority of "electoral fetishism," particularly when often it was not even mandates but simply voters that were counted. The disapportionment of electoral seats made it impossible for the SPD to gain an equitable share of the mandates. So it was the count that presented the real measure of their strength. For this reason, the SPD contested almost all districts, including those in which it had no chance to win. Leaders like August Bebel and Wilhelm Liebknecht would allow their names to be put up in numerous districts, often just to rally a few hundred voters. They became called *Zahlkandidaten*, candidates for the count.[67]

It all started and ended with the vote and the need to support and strengthen habitual and affirming loyalties. To get the count, to win as many close elections as possible, Socialist campaign literature had to reach the widest possible audience within the grouping. The appeal was always understood to be circumscribed by class; the party expected few committed bourgeois or peasant voters, fewer if they were Catholic. Holding all the potential working class voters within the SPD camp was a formidable task in itself. The grouping was large and diverse, containing everything from convinced revolutionary radicals to those voters who saw social-grouping politics as essentially ameliorative. Party propaganda had then to keep the edge on the former without alarming the others. Generally, this goal was achieved by carefully balancing demands for short-term improvement with stories of oppression.

The SPD waged bread-and-butter campaigns after 1903, taking advantage of the unrest caused by the increase in food prices in the decade and a half before World War I. Many government officials believed that this was the reason for the party's triumph. Certainly it was an appealing issue. An SPD election leaflet in Frankfurt declared, "Look to your situation for once, and ask yourself why it is difficult to feed your wife and children when before you managed to live better with less income."[68] Moreover, the SPD might identify itself with all that was progressive without even mentioning class, particularly in the south. This was a technique of the Stuttgart Socialists, whose successes Württemberg officials attributed to the party's "moderate position and clever adaptation of their program to the times."[69] In Stuttgart it was often enough to identify the enemy as reactionary. In the state elections of 1906, a handbill for the incumbent SPD member Karl Kloss ended by simply characterizing the contest with his National Liberal opponent: "Kloss protects progress; Giessler means retrogression."[70]

This accusation of retrogression implied more than opposition to bourgeois programs; it was meant to warn about possible attacks. The SPD felt engaged in a struggle with a "Moloch of militarism and navalism."[71] SPD election literature often emphasized the threat. As a broadside from Hesse-Waldeck stated: "Voters! Your electoral law and freedom of movement are in danger. Down with the usurers of bread, the enemies of the people, the parasites upon the people. Elect men with stiff backbones, men who do not avert their eyes, remain silent, and slink away."[72]

The best electoral strategy would combine both sets of appeals, would subsume the rhetoric of evolution and of class warfare into an unambiguous struggle between good and evil. All of this should have been evident to the most casual reader of a handbill for the Dortmund Socialist Lütgenau against his National Liberal opponent. The document is reproduced in full.

> Electors of the Election District Dortmund-Hörde!
> Onward to the Runoff!
> Workers, Citizens!
>
> The decision has come. In a few days you will
> have to decide between Möller and me.
>
> Theod. Möller is an opponent of universal suf-
> frage. He longs to make the people politically
> powerless.

Dr. Lütgenau is for the exercise of this right
of the people and will fight decisively against
every curtailment of this right.

Theod. Möller is for the unlimited oppression
of the worker. He represents the one-sided
business viewpoint to the last ditch.

Dr. Lütgenau promises to work with all his
energy for the eight-hour day. Eight hours
sleep, eight hours work, eight hours to be
your own boss!

Theod. Möller supports every request of the
military and navy.

Dr. Lütgenau will put all his strength against
a militarism that lays burden after burden on
the people in order to find jobs for bankrupt
Junkers.

Theod. Möller will put a gag in the mouth of
the organized worker. Every independent worker
is for him an abomination. He cries for the
military and the police.

Dr. Lütgenau supports the right of free opinion
and the freedom to associate and create economic
coalitions.

Theod. Möller has declared himself to be in
favor of exceptional law dealing with politics
and religion.

Dr. Lütgenau is an opponent of all exceptional
laws.

Workers! Do not let the employers throw sand in
your eyes. Before the election, sugar bread; after
the election, the whip![73]

4. The Conservatives

Each social grouping was built upon a unique combination of indicators
and represents a unique problem of interpretation, but there are certain
commonalities. Whether defined by predominately cultural or class in-

dicators, the politically relevant social groupings had an effect of isolating their members and defining their differences from the rest of the community. This isolation was often enhanced by the reaction of the government and its elites. This was the case with Catholics, with Socialists, with Poles and Jews. The situation of the German conservatives was completely different. The conservative leaders came precisely from those elites who, according to Veblen, Dahrendorf, and Wehler, so deformed German political life. From where did this conservative sense of isolation spring? It came from the rest of Germany. By the end of the nineteenth century, conservative landowners were threatened with deposition not only from their land but from its accompanying political influence. Over 5,000 large eastern estates were sold at bankruptcy auctions between 1885 and 1900. As professional civil servants and military men, conservatives thrived in the new Germany. As large landowners, they were drowned in the economic and social change that accelerated with unification. No government could or would protect them against the new worldwide agrarian economy or the long-term depression of the 1870s through the 1890s. These economic changes were felt throughout the entire rural world, so that they did not serve to drive a wedge between large landowners and their followers. Instead they tended to solidify them both in the true politics of economic backwardness. Principally confined within the region east of the Elbe, conservative leaders and followers formed a spatial and economic periphery of the German state. All of this was intertwined with cultural statements to form a congery of symbols around the nature of the colonial east that conforms to Michael Hechter's definition of regional underdevelopment and political change. "It should be underlined that when objective cultural differences are superimposed upon economic inequalities, forming a cultural division of labor, and when adequate communications exist as a facilitating factor, the chances for successful political integration into the national society are minimized."[74]

Peripheral politics in eastern Germany carried with it the potential for enormous role conflicts among those conservatives who benefited from government patronage and worked in or for Berlin. Their regional and government loyalties could be opposed as in the struggle over the canal bill in the Prussian legislature (see chapter 3). Such role conflicts make for interesting character or family struggles; but they were hardly present in the Conservative case study in chapter 9 where the principal, Eluard Oldenburg-Janaschau, was some kind of East Prussian equivalent of John Wayne. Yet even at its greatest intensity, the struggle between center and periphery was blunted through the assertion of Prussian monarchical loyalties that were not focused on the monarch himself or government policy but on that region from which the enduring strength of Prussian monarchism came. It was a unique statement, but East Elbia, with its extreme

TABLE 4:12. *Association of Conservative Vote (Conservative and Reichspartei) with Selected Characteristics (N=47 administrative units)*

Characteristic	1907			1912		
	r	Significant Betas Only	Proportion of Variation Explained (Multiple R^2)	r	Significant Betas Only	Proportion of Variation Explained (Multiple R^2)
% Catholic	−.508	−.523	.258	−.567	−.615	.322
% of male work force engaged in industry and mining	−.509	−.623	.634	−.541	−.447	.632
% of total population living in cities with populations over 10,000	−.292		.636	−.337		.646

spatial and cultural isolation and its political programs of absolute neo-feudal loyalties, was a unique political manifestation.

Proving this is another matter. The statistical indicators for German conservatism require some explication. The results in table 4:12 show high negative correlations with the percentage of Catholic and of males engaged in industry and mining. Wolfgang Wölk's statistics also show a high positive correlation with the percentage of work force engaged in agriculture. We have already demonstrated that a high negative percentage of Catholics yields a high positive percentage of Protestants. Low associations between the percentage in cities of over 10,000 and conservative vote is more of a problem. The vote is obtained by adding the totals for the German Conservative party and the Imperial or *Reichspartei*, often called the free conservatives. In the following discussion, the word "conservative" (uncapitalized) refers to both parties, while "Conservative" (with a capital) refers only to the German Conservative party.[75]

Part of the discrepancy in the importance of urbanization was due to the strength of the work-force variable, which tends to neutralize the effect of urbanization or rurality with which it is correlated. If anything, the actual data show that the conservatives were becoming more rural.

The German Conservative party alone captured 18.3 percent of the 1898 rural vote as defined by residence in places of less than 2,000 population. By 1912 this figure had declined by less than 5 percent compared with a 50 percent decrease in Conservative vote in cities over 500,000 (see table 4:4). The actual numbers of rural Conservatives were also increasing. The rural Conservative vote rose from 12.3 to 14.6 percent as calculated in terms of percentage of eligibles. Only 68 percent of German Conservative voters came from rural areas in 1898 compared with 88 percent in 1912.

The weak statistical associations between rurality and conservative strength were also caused by discernible, small groups of urban conservatives. They were composed of civil servants who were urged to support conservative candidates above all others, Prussian elites who turned to the parties which displayed the most dependable monarchical instincts, and those mercantile and service people who were dependent on rural clienteles. In East Elbia these conservatives often supported the Imperial party rather than the older German Conservatives, since the Imperials were more likely to be univocal government supporters, willing to unite with other pro-state parties like the National Liberals, and less regionally based.

But these urban conservatives were a small and declining group, especially in the colonial east. Local cities appeared as centers of rival power and threats to the agrarians since they might drain away workers and therefore raise the price of labor on the rural estates. This remained only a theoretical possibility. There was little need to worry about a failing agrarian predominance. Although there was massive out-migration from East Elbia, the eastern provinces still gained three agricultural workers for every two added to the rolls in the rest of Germany.

Much of this regional anti-urbanism was cultural and was sustained by long conflicts between cities run by enlightenment-type liberals and rural landowners. Thus even better economic times that reduced the massive bankruptcies of large estates and external migration did not change this antiurbanism. The conservative leaders, and probably their followers as well, lived in an isolated periphery like the inhabitants of Brittany and Wales. Thus cultural and geographic isolation continued despite short-term gains. For in the long run, economic trends were against them. Neither tariff reform nor rising grain prices could alleviate the problem of inefficient production and high transportation costs. These long-term trends favored the industrializing regions, creating a situation of permanent crisis for East Elbia. Thus the farmers east of the Elbe were facing a different situation from the rest of German agriculture; their political conflict produced more than a basic town-country cleavage, which James Hunt believes to be the fundamental distinction for all of German political life. East Elbian politics was conditioned by the response of an agrar-

TABLE 4:13. *Party Strength East and West of the Elbe*

Party	1907 (1903 in parentheses)		1887 (1884 in parentheses)	
	% Vote East of the Elbe	% Vote West of the Elbe	% Vote East of the Elbe	% Vote West of the Elbe
Conservative party	24.4 (24.6)	3.8 (3.1)	36.7 (29.5)	7.6 (7.9)
Free Conservatives	5.8 (6.4)	2.5 (3.2)	14.7 (10.1)	8.0 (5.4)
National Liberals	3.2 (5.3)	18.4 (18.4)	5.7 (3.3)	26.2 (23.9)
Left-wing Liberals	13.4 (13.2)	7.4 (10.0)	17.2 (25.8)	13.8 (16.4)
% of total voters living in the area	29.4 (29.5)	70.6 (70.5)	26.1 (30.4)	73.9 (69.6)

ian group locked in a backward economic and culturally differentiated region. It was this region (as table 4:13 shows) from which the bulk of conservative voters came; it was this region where conservatism was still a predominant political force. Central to all was the belief that the region was the heart of Prussia, that is, of Germany, and that its strength was declining as the urbanizing and industrializing forces turned the ultimate balance to the industrialized west. The response was to hold on to what was, the intertwining of economic and cultural goods that characterized the east. (This is shown more clearly in chapter 7.)

As Frank Tipton's recent study explains:

> The regional focus of economic change contributed to agrarian intransigence. Previously, the eastern elite's defense of their principles had rested on a relatively secure economic foundation. As the foundations began to crumble, the new economic insecurity combined with the old traditions of principled opposition to give an increasing virulence to agrarian agitation. The centralizing thrust of urban and industrial development made rapid change imperative, but also made it progressively less likely that backward regions would be able to compete for resources and markets without outside help. In the absence of internally generated pressure from commerce and industry, the agrarian elite in the East opposed outside help whenever it threatened a change in economic structure. The result was to maintain and increase the region's dependence on a declining industry. At the same time agriculture was forced to become merely an industry "like many others" complete with organized political pressure groups, and this for many was the true essence of its decline. The Prussian tradition, the agrarian mystique,

an entire way of life were under attack, and from the point of view of the eastern elite seemed all the more seriously threatened by being so closely identified with those specific regions increasingly unlike the rest of the nation.[76]

Were these fears confined to the elites, or were elite statements the most visible expressions of an underlying general opinion that the culture of the colonial east was important and threatened? This is the central question for determining the viability of affirmative voting in the conservative camp. If these eastern rural voters were mere followers, then conservatism was not a social grouping. If these voters believed, then conservative rhetoric focused their economic interests layered within cultural traditions. They had become the stuff of affirming politics. But there was great doubt that this could happen in the rural east. The city liberals complained everywhere, especially in Danzig, that "conservative politics is also not citizenship politics [*Bürgerpolitik*]; it is not city politics."[77] This was a characteristic means of defining a world controlled by urban middle classes, including the use of the word *Bürger* to identify both citizen and city dweller. Yet, despite their ideological blinders, these liberals did have some reason to believe they were right; rural voters in the east were essentially deferential followers.

There can be no question that a few eastern voters were like those long-sought-after Prussian battalions obediently trooping to the polls. The large estate, the *Gut*, was at the heart of the agrarian society. A compact unit formed by the house and outbuildings, such a *Gut* appeared on the landscape as a center of control. The owner, the *Gutsbesitzer*, could demand deference if not obedience, particularly if his estate carried a noble title allowing him to be identified as a Junker, the possessor of a *Rittergut*. The overwhelming economic and social power of the landlord was reinforced by the social and geographic isolation of the *Gut* and the relatively low penetrability of deviant viewpoints and political campaigns. It was a recipe for deferential electoral politics, of following local leaders rather than affirming ties to a social grouping. It should be no surprise that at least half the German Conservative party deputies were noble landowners through the entire period. As one contemporary conservative explained, "The natural social differences found their robust political expression in the rich old-fashioned syntax of relationships based on obedience."[78]

However only about one-third of the cultivated land in the east was in large estates, and an even smaller percentage of the rural population lived under the direct control of local landowners. If deferential voting were to succeed, it would have to be grounded in more subtle relationships than naked obedience. It would have to be closer to the relationship that the historian Robert Frank described:

The Conservatives, however, stand in good relationship to all aspects of agriculture; they have the farsightedness which the villagers do not credit themselves with possessing, and they have the offices and relationships to achieve something for the electoral district. If many times they were overbearing, it is important not to forget that they were used to controlling gatherings by appeals to King and Country; they were almost always reserve officers accustomed to giving military commands at reservist gatherings. Thus they were usually spoken of as the Herr Major or the *Rittmeister*. Their political program was not rooted in an unknown future but was understandable and timeless: protection of the native soil and of the hereditary ruling house, and maintenance of the relationships of the estates in an order ordained by God.[79]

It was only one small step from such behavior to affirmative voting. These local landowners were indivisibly tied with county administrators and Protestant clergymen, many of whom came from landholding families themselves. Together they embarked on mobilizing. Their response to the agrarian crisis of the 1880s and 1890s combined an inculcation of deference with newer forms of participation, both enveloping a combination of new interest strategies and old symbols. Conservatives were not only for farmers, but they were the surest support of "prince and fatherland."[80] They viewed themselves as the principal barrier against a cold, rationalized, modernized Germany. The preservation of agrarian predominance in their region became in their minds and their electoral program the absolute sine qua non of this process, tantamount to the preservation of the monarchy and the retention of those attitudes which perpetuated neofeudal loyalties. In this way the most strident agrarian became encompassed in the general good whereby conservatives could maintain they stood for "the common good over special interests," "the fatherland over party."[81]

The necessities of affirming politics changed electoral campaigns. Instead of engaging in triumphal tours around the district, conservative candidates were making a large number of real campaign speeches. Hans Rosenberg has referred to this phenomenon as "pseudo-democratization," whereby the old elites learned to manipulate the mass electorate while at the same time fighting parliamentarization and the establishment of democratic polity. This is unquestionably true, as the case study in chapter 7 demonstrates. However, it is wrong to make too simple connections. As long as one considered the democratic model of voting as the only reasonable outcome, then undoubtedly the use of mass electoral manipulation for antidemocratic ends becomes a "travesty."[82] But affirming voters do not necessarily make the democratic connection. It is enough for them to express the needs of an isolated social grouping and to view their vote as some aid to the threatened social grouping, in this case attacking urbanism and its accompanying economic and political modernization.

The structure of social grouping politics was upheld by the BdL. Founded in 1893, the BdL created cooperatives and savings banks, provided inexpensive insurance and free legal aid, and discounted purchases of fertilizer and machinery. But it was principally designed as an interest group to influence policy by influencing electors and the legislative process. By 1912 the BdL had over 750 professional employees who carried out agitation for high tariffs on agricultural goods and other remedies for the agrarian crisis. Speakers were sent through the hinterland to gather support for its programs; in 1912 these paid propagandists gave over 10,000 public addresses.

The first target of the BdL and the principal reason for its existence was the so-called Caprivi treaties, which lowered cereal tariffs against Russia and Austria-Hungary. These tariffs disturbed an already hard-pressed agrarian elite in East Elbia. Under BdL prodding, the conservatives became a very successful pressure group, cooperating with big business to change government policy. By 1902 the agrarian tariffs had reached a new high and government was acting in a number of ways to alleviate the problems of eastern landowners, by sponsoring cooperatives, supporting the acquisition and retention of land by Germans instead of Poles, by easing credit and reducing transportation costs, and finally by giving eastern agrarians a subsidy for exporting grain.

Were these the result of BdL penetration and leadership? Certainly the BdL was influential in transforming the style of East Elbian politics from the expectation of deference to serious and consistent political campaigning. Yet much of this involved merely transferring old wine into new bottles; over 80 percent of the BdL leadership in the 1890s was composed of aristocratic landowners. Even there the BdL never predominated over the congeries of symbols and relationships that determined political actions in the German east. The BdL leadership could not even control the conservative parties. The majority of the conservative Reichstag deputies rejected the BdL attempt to hold them to its electoral platform, tariffs of 75 cents a kilo on grain. And they did so without fear of losing their seats. The BdL withdrew its support from many conservatives in 1903; the result was a dismal record in the campaign; only 4 of 54 BdL supported candidates won, as compared with 118 in 1898. Extreme interest group politics did not win the east. As a matter of fact, BdL efforts seem to have shown little effect overall. The greatest number of so-called BdL victories, 138, occurred in 1907 when the organizations remained relatively hidden inside a progovernment coalition. In 1912, after campaigning more avidly, the numbers were reduced to 78 and the rate of success to one elected for four supported. As the BdL-supported candidates won in the imperialist coalition of 1907, they lost as part of the general trend leftward in 1912. This hardly showed the influence expected of such a large and well-organized pressure group but is typical of social group voting patterns that operated in Wilhelmine Germany.

As the BdL failed to control those authoritarian East Elbian land-owners, it moved westward to establish bases in the remainder of Germany. By the end of the Wilhelmine period, the majority of BdL members were west of the Elbe. These areas of small and medium-sized farms dictated a new style of politics very different from the traditional Prussian-ized package. The BdL presented its own version of *Mittelstand* politics, which emphasized unity of agrarian and artisan interests. Occasionally also the *Bund* would modify its antidemocratic stands as in Bavaria and Württemberg. But, on the whole, the BdL in the west was more radical, more imperialist, more likely to emphasize anti-Socialism instead of anti-urbanism, almost sure to be anti-Semitic and extremely nationalistic. This new version of the BdL was propounded by a new leadership of pro-fessional propagandists and politicians who were less tied to the large east-ern landholding interests than their predecessors. These new leaders culti-vated ties with other political parties, particularly with right-wing liberal agrarians, and were more interested in forming national coalitions than conducting regional politics. Eventually this radical agrarianism would separate from its conservative base and join a broader national coalition. Although this trend was evident before 1914, the BdL-conservative al-liance was maintained throughout the Wilhelmine period, but it never undermined those conservative politics that were rooted in the cultural-economic peculiarities of the German east.[83]

The combination of interest group and subcultural needs was effective; they formed an ascertainable social grouping that had political conse-quences. It was also the newest of the social groupings to emerge in the political arena. The Prussian traditions and the hierarchical culture were, of course, of long duration, but their peculiar envelopment with agrarian issues came quite late. Thus it should be no surprise that there seems to have been some lag in creating citizenship norms; in fact, the un-politicized in conservative areas may never have been fully eliminated. The effect that the percentage of German Conservatives had on turnout was significantly negative for every election between 1890 and 1907 ex-cept for 1898, which was characterized by high absenteeism in any case. This effect is still significant when the conflict variable and the percentage of Protestants are accounted for. Excluding the effects of religion and conflict, the beta coefficients for the German Conservative vote on turn-out were for the elections of 1890, 1893, 1898, 1903, and 1907 $-.142$, $-.122$, $-.041$, $-.151$, and $-.128$ respectively. It is doubtful whether the effect could be caused by rurality or by intimidation. I believe the data describe an educational effect common to geographic and social periph-eries where knowledge and information about elections were likely to spread less rapidly because of differences from the majority political culture and the spatial isolation characterized by geographic peripheries. It was harder to pass the word in East Elbia,[84] particularly in areas where deferential politics was no longer working, and affirming politics with its various organizations was not fully in place. Yet even then the relationships are small, accounting for a maximum of 7 percent of turnout. The bulk of conservative supporters were undoubtedly affirming voters, tied to social-grouping loyalties that characterized the electoral system of Wilhelmine Germany. This will be clarified in chapter 7.

5. German Jews

The response of the German Jewish social grouping was an arresting and unpredictable variant of the backlash against modernization. Unlike the conservatives, this emotional attack against change came predominantly from outside the Jewish community, since Jews were one of the principal beneficiaries of economic and political modernization, which laid the groundwork for their own emancipation. Thus German Jews were willing to endure discrimination against their entrance into government jobs since they found numerous channels for upward mobility in the free professions, publishing, the retail trade, and so forth. The lack of the full range of possibilities placed German Jews in a number of well-paid occupations that were prevalent in large cities. Spatial and occupational concentration made them more visible than their numbers would indicate since they were never more than 1 percent of the population.

This increased visibility was taken by the Jewish community in the 1870s as a sign of their success and the fulfillment of their intention to become part of the mainstream of German society. For others, it symbolized the enormous changes brought about by industrialization that they felt were not to their benefit. Thus a strong antimodernism propelled numbers of small artisans and farmers to accept the leadership of certain rogue elements of the Protestant bourgeoisie who converted traditional and persistent cultural anti-Semitism into a political movement in the 1880s. This political anti-Semitism combined some urban lower middle classes who were threatened by the increasing size and complexity of business operations with a number of small farmers radicalized by the agrarian crisis. It cast strong shadows over the whole political society although the specifically anti-Semitic parties were not a threat by themselves. These political anti-Semites never captured more than sixteen seats nor got more than 3.5 percent of the total vote. They were a marginal political group, coming from disparate regions and social bases, combining different ideologies with strong and divisive personalities among their elected deputies. It is no wonder they they could never unite and form a political party cohesive enough to obtain recognition as a legal faction in the Reichstag (see chapter 5 for a fuller discussion). Their real power lay in the threat of transmitting populist-style politics to the constituencies dominated by the traditional parties. In order to forestall an anti-Semitic takeover, German Conservatives adopted a mild anti-Semitic plank in their platform of 1893 and National Liberals refused to defend minority religious rights, particularly in rural areas. In many instances, these tactics were influenced by an already persistent cultural anti-Semitism, particularly among conservatives who successfully blocked the entry of all but exceptional Jews into the officer corps, the bureaucracy and the court circles. This was reinforced by an increasing intellectual and social reaction to modernism among the German upper middle classes. Thus anti-Semitism could serve as a bond between the lower and upper middle classes, as a peculiar but understandable flexing of the anti-modernization muscle that turned the most visible beneficiaries of the process into a politically estranged social grouping.[85]

The anti-Semitic movement is fairly well charted; not so for the Jewish social grouping, where there are major problems with the data. Jewish eligibles were only 1.04 percent of the total possible voters. Even with their overrepresentation in urban centers, it is impossible to find any district that was predominantly Jewish; Jews were no more than 7 percent of the population in Frankfurt am Main, little more than 5 percent in Berlin, and less than 4 percent in most other cities. Precinct voting lines for Reichstag elections were constantly redrawn and never in such a way as to correlate religious data with voting. The best evidence comes from the distribution of officeholding, but this evidence is based on small numbers and is not necessarily indicative of voting patterns. For example, Social Democrats composed almost 30 percent of identifiable Jewish deputies elected to the Reichstag and state legislatures between 1893 and 1916. Yet it is doubtful that these represented a large number of Jewish voters. The working class was probably underrepresented among German Jews who were overwhelmingly bourgeois and paid taxes at rates six or seven times higher than that of the population as a whole.

The only reasonable response was to join with the left-wing liberals where Jews were already entrenched and whose principal vehicles, the Progressive Union and the Progressive People's party, had consistently favored emancipation and civil rights. Thus the number of Jewish pro-government legislative deputies (essentially National Liberals) declined from 70 percent in the period 1867–78 to 20 percent in 1893–1916. In contrast, the number of Jewish left-wing liberals increased to over half of all Jewish representatives in state and national legislatures. But these parties should not be considered Jewish referent groups as with the Center and German Catholics. Jews were only one part of the coalition that formed left-wing liberalism; various progressive parties relied heavily

upon Jewish intellectual and financial support, but their leaders such as
Eugen Richter and Theodor Barth were pragmatic politicians who were
not above making electoral deals with nominally anti-Semitic candidates.
The Jewish defense organizations, particularly the *Centralverein der
Deutscher Staatsbürger Jüdischen Glaubens*, were continually frustrated
in their attempts to seek binding commitments that these liberals take unambiguous and irrevocable stands against dealing with any anti-Semitic
parties.[86]

Despite the attempts of the *Centralverein* and other organizations to
chart a more independent course for their community, German Jews remained firmly entrenched in left-wing liberalism. There were good class
reasons for doing so. The only other party that openly supported Jewish
rights was the SPD, and bourgeois Jews were just as worried about the
threat of working-class politics as were their Christian neighbors. And as
Germans, they tended to reject any alliance with the deviant national
parties like Poles and Alsatians.

Why was there no Jewish party, no referent group to express social
grouping solidarities, either desired or forced upon German Jews? There
were some attempts in Posen to elect unambiguous Jewish representatives, particularly to municipal councils where as many as one-third of
the councilmen were Jews. But the Jewish community was unable to gain
a seat in Reichstag elections through arranging deals with the various
parties.

There are a number of reasons for the failure to create a Jewish referent
group for electoral politics. The German states still protected Jews. Prussian troops could be relied upon to quell anti-Semitic disturbances; they
did so three times in the Wilhelmine era. Governments generally resisted
political anti-Semitism as a dangerous radicalism. After an inauspicious
start in which it was powerless to control widespread vandalism, the Hessian government initiated legal actions against anti-Semitic leaders. In
Hesse, Prussia, and Bavaria, anti-Semitic leaders might find themselves in
jail for crimes from libel to perjury. Moreover the concentration of German Jews in larger cities meant that they had some control over those
bureaucrats who were charged with the protection of the Jewish community. The fact that many of the major liberal and independent newspapers
were in Jewish hands aided this feeling of safety. Even ordinary cultural
anti-Semitism was less evident in the major cities, which had become
both more liberal and more tolerant. By the end of the Wilhelmine period, 38 percent of the entire German Jewish community lived in Berlin,
which was the preeminent cosmopolitan environment and, therefore, the
one most friendly to Jews.

Jews also were unwilling to engage in any activities that they felt were
un-German. It was for this reason that Jewish communities in Posen supported the German Conservative Count Cuno von Westarp. He did make

it easier for Jews in his district to vote for him by issuing a statement that in effect changed his position from nominal anti-Semite to neutral. However the Junker never promised to vote for Jewish interests and cautioned the Jewish communities that elected him against believing in too much equality. German Jews voted German in the east to protect against the Polish menace just as some Jews even voted anti-Semitic in 1907 to save German imperialism and bourgeois society against the advertised Catholic-Socialist conspiracy.

At the core of such behavior was the desire of the bulk of German Jewry to disband the social grouping. There was a minority composed of the religious orthodox and the Zionists who desired to solidify Jewish loyalties against the outside world. However most German Jews viewed their ethnicity as only another historic accident, much the same as being a Hessian or Bavarian. This perception only struck roots in a limited section of the Christian majority, among a few intellectuals and ideological liberals. Most Christian Germans probably still considered the Jews in at least some mildly anti-Semitic fashion and were puzzled, if they thought at all, about Jewish demands to keep both their ethnic identity and status as German nationals.

In response to Christian perceptions, the German Jewish communities fought every assertion of their isolation from the mainstream and were committed to assimilation. The assimilationist strategy in both Germany and France was to make Jews invisible. Both German and French Jews had felt the dangers of strong anti-Semitic surges in the 1890s, in France culminating with the Dreyfus affair and in Germany with the election of political anti-Semites to the Reichstag. Both these communities responded overwhelmingly in the same manner. After all, they believed themselves essentially either Frenchmen or Germans and hoped that the onrushing tide of modernization would lead to the victory of toleration while burying populist anti-Semitism along with the old guards that sustained them. As Marjorie Lamberti explains:

> The Jews were not able to deal with the problem of double loyalties with the same ease as did the German Catholics who joined the Center Party. Knowing that anti-Semites denied their German nationality and feeling insecure about being accepted as Germans, they were reluctant to engage in any activity that might separate them from and could be used by anti-Semites to prop up their argument that the Jews were an alien body in Germany. . . .
>
> In politics Jews were psychologically inhibited by their anxiety that an assertion of particular Jewish interests might conflict with or call in question their loyalty to the German fatherland. . . . Even modest efforts to elect Jewish candidates provoked cries of "no ghetto candidates" and "no separate candidates." Jews should ac-

cept mandates only as German citizens and should avoid a separate position in politics.[87]

Jewish defense had not been extraordinarily effective against anti-Semitism. It never disappeared but was embedded in German political life. What changed was the ability of anti-Semites to be elected. In 1912 less than 1 percent of the voters cast their ballots for the anti-Semitic parties; only six anti-Semitic Reichstag deputies were elected and five of these immediately joined the Conservative party. In that same year two unbaptized Jews were elected as representatives of the left-wing liberals. Certainly political anti-Semitism seemed dead, and who would have known that it was even then reorganizing for another more successful assault.

6. The Poles

There were three principal national minorities in Wilhelmine Germany— the Lorraine French, the Danes in Schleswig, and the Poles. All three groupings were well defined, isolated, and isolating; all three were victims of intensive Germanization policies that tended to solidify the social and political loyalties of the nationals of which they were composed. However, the Danish grouping was very small, unamenable to both statistical and traditional definitions. The Lorrainers were often encompassed in assertions of rights made in conjunction with the Alsatians. It was only in 1902 when Alsatian bourgeois voters defected to the Center party that a Lorraine bloc was instituted. Moreover, these French speakers did not operate in the same legal environment. They were under federal control until 1911 and thus subject to different rules for the campaigning and voting as well as the treatment of deviant minorities.[88]

The Polish situation was, on the other hand, unambiguous. Although the tables used to define the other parties cannot be constructed for Poles, there is enough evidence to show, unsurprisingly, that 90 percent of the Polish vote was both Catholic and of Polish nationality.[89] And there is reason to believe these were the principal and perhaps only definers. If the strength of the work force and urbanization variables cannot be statistically accounted for, an inspection of Polish voters themselves shows that these social variables were not a test of voting behavior. The Polish party was equally strong in areas of the east where Poles composed 70 percent of the rural labor force and in settings in the Ruhr where they were 70 percent of the coalminers. They were the perfect example of a spatially and culturally isolated social grouping. Over 80 percent of the Polish population lived in areas almost entirely composed of Polish speakers. The majority came from regions that were attached to Prussia during the eighteenth-century partitions. Isolated areas of Polish settlement formed an arc around the Russian frontier encompassing southern East Prussia, West Prussia, and Posen with an extension up the line of the Vistula toward Danzig. It was these Poles who provided the bodies for the westward migration into the Ruhr coalfields commencing in the 1880s. But this migration should not be considered as a sign of assimilation. Ninety percent of the more than 3 million Poles in Germany still lived east of the Elbe. The Poles in the Rhenish Westphalian industrial area lived in settlements geographically isolated from the dominant German speakers, mostly in miners' colonies, that is, suburbs, or in a few sections of the towns.

Thus the Polish social grouping is a very good model to show the strength of national loyalties among affirming voters in both industrial and agrarian regions. There is one exception, Upper Silesia, where the historical experience retarded the growth of national identification; but, even there, the nationalist sentiments were moving toward fruition by the end of the Wilhelmine period (see below).

A linguistic and ethnic minority, the Poles were transformed into a national grouping by processes common to nineteenth-century Europe. An educated elite moved to reconstruct Polish history and culture in terms of its own uniqueness; this intelligentsia found ways of transmitting these appreciations to succeedingly less prestigious and less well educated elements of the linguistic group. In the end, popular manifestations like religious festivals were transformed into national gatherings. By the 1850s a unified national Polish culture faced the inexorable and efficient Prussian bureaucracy, unresponsive to nationalist demands but capable of mediating on other grounds between the national government and Polish elites if they both so desired.

The creation of the German national state intensified national conflict by bringing on a new justification for German political unity and a complementary set of threats against it. The *Kulturkampf* was the response to the perceived danger from international Catholicism; the so-called *Polenpolitik* was conceived by Bismarck as the answer to the siren call of international nationalism. Prussian Poland was the least important culturally of the three partitioned areas, and therefore susceptible to control by foreign Poles. Bereft of intellectual centers where the national movements were founded, Prussian Poles were dependent on ideas and leadership that came across the borders, especially from Russia. This was considered especially dangerous because these Poles were now on the national frontier of a unified German state and, as such, were considered more important at a time when their reliability in terms of crisis was being questioned.

Bismarck attempted both to neutralize and uproot the Poles. The Prussian government abolished almost all Polish instruction and thoroughly

Germanized the law courts and bureaucratic procedures. In 1885 it began the deportation of Russian and Austrian Poles who resided in the frontier region and the next year created the Royal Colonization Commission, which attempted to re-Germanize the frontier by buying up large Polish estates and parceling out the land to German farmers.

The Poles proved resistant to both these stratagems. They set up lending libraries and religious classes within churches to insure exposure to Polish culture. They organized a school strike in 1906 to protest the removal of the last vestiges of Polish religious instruction for the lowest elementary grades. This strike failed because German authoritarians threatened to fail all Polish students, but the method of boycott worked much better in the economic area, where many German businesses closed as the result of a buy-Polish campaign. By the turn of the century Poles had also found an effective means for undermining much of the Royal Commission's work. Polish peasant banks bought up Polish land to be resettled with Polish farmers.

The ability of the Poles to resist only spurred on the German and Prussian governments. Bernhard von Bülow, chancellor from 1900 to 1909, carried on the fight with a renewed intensity. Unable to gain enough Polish land, the Prussian legislature passed a bill that forbade Polish speakers to erect new buildings on recently bought property, essentially forestalling the Polish partition of large estates. And shortly before his fall, Bülow was planning to introduce an expropriation bill. Such a measure could be justified only in the crassest terms. The Conservative Elard Oldenburg-Janaschau answered the Poles in debate, "If you will not give us your hearts, gentlemen, we will take your land."[90] Radical nationalists went even farther. The *Ostmark Verein*, the Society for the Eastern Marches, served as a nucleus for German intellectuals and other middle-class elements who demanded the de-Polinization of the frontier. Other radical organizations took up this cause and formed with the more traditional Right an impenetrable obstacle to the lessening of tension. Thus Bülow's successor, Bethmann Hollweg, was never able to carry out his plans to defuse the Polish question. *Polenpolitik* had become too staple an issue for progovernment parties whose leaders and followers viewed the Poles as a foreign element that could not be mollified but only contained.

The result of all this agitation was to exacerbate the already tense relationship between German and Pole in the colonial east. Contacts that were based on equality between the social groupings were rare. Germans saw Poles in subordinate relationships; the Polish boycott of German shops tended to rub out those last links of civility based on cash nexus. Even contacts with coreligionists began to diminish. It was true that the German hierarchy and the Center leadership opposed discriminatory legislation and anti-Polish bureaucratic practice, but the Centrists in the east were also becoming increasingly nationalistic, that is, German. The last

ties were broken and observers in Posen believed that by the end of the
1890s these two national groups treated each other as foreigners.

The Poles in the eastern provinces had their own pure version of religion: A Pole was a Catholic; his Church led his nation. It was a connection that intensified through time as each new generation of believers defied the instructions of the German hierarchy to divorce their politics from their religion. Polish priests were particularly vulnerable since they were civil servants of the Prussian state and thus subject to governmental removal. Yet nothing stopped the priests from serving as the center of this intensified nationalist agitation. From the very beginning of the nationalist revival in the 1890s, they were also assisted by powerful new religious organizations, particularly the Polish-Catholic *Volksverein*, which was modeled on the German Catholic group of the same name. The *Volksverein* was especially effective because it had the sanction of Church authority and was difficult to destroy. How could the German hierarchy refuse to allow the Polish Catholics to create supplementary organizations to bolster their faith when it encouraged the general Catholic community to do so?

The result was an aggressive nationalist-religious ideology. As the *Volksverein* journal stated in 1903, "Our weapons are the Polish prayerbook, the pious song, the rosary, the Polish newspaper, the book from the lending library, the national anthem."[91] If this particular author had mentioned the vote, his bishop could have deprived him of his parish. However, writing outside of quasi-official Catholic journals, priests could be even more explicit. A certain father Milucki in Schekatowo, West Prussia, showed how Catholicism had become intertwined not only with nationalism but with the fate of Polish Reichstag candidates as well. "For that reason, none of us can stand aside; all must step up to the ballot box and vote for our Polish candidate, who is Pole by virtue of blood and conviction, and a true Catholic, who can represent us in Berlin as loyally as any soldier at his post."[92] At a meeting in neighboring Strasburg County in 1907, the Poles were admonished to vote "arm in arm for the defense of the law, for belief and fatherland."[93]

The push of discrimination and government pressure and the pull of national loyalties controlled the political responses even of the conservative large landowners who traditionally ran German Polandom. They did so at some sacrifice to their economic needs. If these Polish conservatives had been German, they would have considered raising the price of grain as a primary goal. Yet Polish landowners voted for the Caprivi treaties in the Reichstag because they supported the chancellor's attempts at reconciliation among the national groups. The Polish landowners wanted nothing more than acceptance by the Prussian government. "We are not waging a struggle with the *state*, but rather with the false direction of its policies. Our struggle with the government will cease when its policies towards us are based on the dictates of justice and political equality. If the government does this, it will see that it can rely on the Polish population."[94] But, of course, this was precisely what the government would not do; its actions continuously threatened the economic security and the cultural identity of conservative Poles. The Poles responded with a stubborn resistance that combined the need to maintain their estates, feelings of responsibility for the whole Polish community, and a genuine Romantic nationalism with far stronger roots than the late-blooming Romantic agrarianism invented by German landowners in the 1880s.

> We large landowners of the Grand Duchy of Poznań and West Prussia affirm that we have no intention of abandoning the lands of our birth. We will pursue in our hearts and our families and in our people our national and religious ideals with a fervor which persecution can only intensify and with a love stronger than even the hatred of our enemies. He who is expropriated will devote even more energy to the work of the national fatherland and of our people.
>
> Love is stronger than death. Love for our continually abused fatherland swells our breasts and our hearts sing a hymn of unshakable faith in our triumph over the spirit of destruction which seeks to eliminate the Polish nation, with its thousand years of service to Christian culture, so as to smooth the path for materialism and Protestantism.[95]

As with the Center party, this old-style leadership was challenged in the 1890s by a new and more aggressive political generation. In German Polandom they generally went under the name of National Democrats and broke with the old conservatives, who were neither democratic nor believers in the nation-state. The intellectual impetus for this movement often originated in Paris and came across the border from Russian Poland. It was an authentic nationalist movement following historical precedents (including the German), envisioning the need to reconstruct historical Poland, located in an urban bourgeoisie who were determined to educate and channel the opinions of working-class and rural voters. This national revival relied on a complex defense mechanism starting with a convinced clergy and a strong organizational base designed to support economic independence and cultural solidarities, and to make penetration of Germans into the Polish community extraordinarily difficult.

In Berent County, West Prussia, with considerably less than 15,000 Polish males, there were eight Polish banks and savings institutions founded between 1897 and 1912 with a total membership of 1,397 in the latter year, seven agricultural cooperatives between 1901 and 1910 with 377 members, seven religious clubs between 1891 and 1912 with 899 members, a salespersons' union (1909) with 20, a handworkers' and apprentices' association (1889) with 53, three choral groups (between 1902 and 1909) with 105, a gymnastic society (1912) with 51, and a Polish Electoral Committee (1903) with 350 members.[96]

Undoubtedly there was a great deal of plural membership. Still it is impossible to think that a great number of poor Poles would join cooperative banks and other associations that were more than 50 kilometers apart. Given this assumption, it is possible then to estimate that around 20 percent of the electorate as a whole and 40 percent of the Polish electorate was loosely organized in these unions. The Electoral Committee itself accounted for over 6 percent of the Polish voters.

The depth and breadth of this organizational effort suggests the possibilities of secular conflicts like those that characterized German Protestantism and which were slowly dissolving the German Catholic grouping. Yet the Poles remained socially and politically united during the Wilhelmine period. There were occasional outright conflicts, as those between the Polish Socialist and bourgeois candidates in Posen city in 1912, but, for the most part, Poles were able to apportion candidates among various factions in the manner of the Center. In Posen about a third of the candidates were from the conservative landowning faction and another third were National Democrats. The last third consisted of clergy and independents who played a moderating role between the factions. The conservatives maintained their strength outside of Posen; over half the Reichstag delegates elected in 1912 were possessors of ennobled land, *Rittergutsbesitzern*; yet the new national forces felt they had enough representation so as not to secede from the coalition. All candidates espoused the need for a united Polish faction in the Reichstag.

This affirming action was a sign for an army of affirming voters. Their fortunes might vary slightly, but on the whole the Polish delegation remained on solid footing, receiving between 3.5 and 4 percent of the vote. In 1912 the Polish party elected sixteen deputies, equal to their previous high in 1893. All of these deputies were elected from districts east of the Elbe, in Posen, West Prussia, and Upper Silesia. Everywhere, continuing electioneering reinforced national conflicts. The lines were clearly and consistently drawn, not only by the Poles but by the German opposition as well. As a broadside from the 1908 House of Delegates election in Putzig, West Prussia, stated: "The electoral slogan should finally become: Here Germans!——There Poles! That applies to all of us who think and feel German. We must unanimously do our duty in the electoral campaign."[97] Elections were not fought to win large numbers of unconvinced or to articulate issues in such a way as to win over interest groups. They were contests in which each side drew up troops of affirmers who were already both committed and counted. After all, almost everyone knew whether he was a German or a Pole; the important thing was to get one's friends to vote. On the Polish side, voters were instructed "not to go alone [to the polls] but take the lazy and apathetic with you even if you have to drag them by the seat of their pants,"[98] that "all the blind, and lame, the crippled and aged—have to appear."[99] And they did (see chapters 3 and 9).

There was regional variation in the rate of formation of this social-grouping consciousness and in the ability of Poles to elect deputies. In Posen, the center of Prussian Polandom, Polish electoral preponderance remained despite German attacks and out-migration. The number of Polish out-migrants was more than matched by the outflow of Jews who voted with the German minority. In West Prussia there was no comparable out-migration of German speakers; this eventually slightly altered the national composition of three districts in *Regierungsbezirk* Marienwerder. Yet the districts were so closely contested that shifts of less than 3 percent in the vote could lose the contests (see table 4:14 and chapter 8).

The losses in seats were made up by the late growth of Polish national consciousness in Upper Silesia, *Regierungsbezirk* Oppeln. Upper Silesia was acquired from Austria by Frederick the Great. The Silesian Poles lacked the tradition or the leadership that fostered national thinking in Posen, Pomerania, and West Prussia. Further, they were drawn into a cultural conflict between German-speaking Catholics and the Protestant Prussian administration that went on from the annexation of the province. Thus the *Kulturkampf* appeared in Silesia as a continuation of the struggle that involved all Catholics against the Prussian state.

The industrialization and modernization of the region after 1860 began to change this situation. Radical Polish nationalism came late, caused by a kind of false religious consciousness that overwhelmed nationalism. The Center did not feel constrained to nominate specific Polish-Centrist deputies until 1903. Even then the cities remained principally German in composition and vote. It was rural areas and working-class suburbs that gradually assimilated Polish nationalism. Agricultural districts would be transformed into Polish bastions, since the SPD began to make inroads in the mining centers in 1912. Despite such intrusions, the success was enormous; not only did the percentage of the vote increase, but also four Polish Reichstag deputies were elected from Upper Silesia by 1912.[100]

Upper Silesian Poles tended to migrate to places within their region, like Breslau or Berlin. They formed a smaller and smaller part of the Polish labor force in the Rhenish-Westphalian industrial area, which was dominated by in-migrants from Posen and West and East Prussia. In 1860 there were scarcely 300 Poles in the Ruhr; in 1890 there were 30,000; in 1910 there were 300,000. It was a swift and long move, not only in space but in occupation as well. The Poles that moved westward settled in mining "colonies," the suburbs around Bochum, Dortmund, Gelsenkirchen, and Essen. The rapid transition from agriculture to mining cut them off

TABLE 4:14. *Polish Vote in Selected Instances* [101]

Area	Estimated % Polish in 1910	Polish Vote in Election Years				
		1887	1898	1903	1907	1912
Province Posen	65	47.4	50.8	59.1	57.3	55.8
West Prussia	30	26.7	39.1	37.9	37.0	34.2
Upper Silesia	60			17.7	30.8	39.5
Westphalia	7			2.2	2.9	3.1

from their traditional agrarian leadership; the lack of good transportation among these "colonies" separated them from one another. But they brought their nationalism along with their other baggage. For the most part, they came after the national movement had spread through their provinces; they had learned how to found and use Polish organizations for cultural and political purposes. There were over 80,000 members in Polish organizations in the Ruhr by 1910. And finally, they carried along the memories of "Germanization" policies that were sustained by new information gained from the families and friends left behind.

As always, Polish consciousness was supported by German intransigence; the Ruhr Poles literally had come into a foreign land. They found little acceptance and a great deal of discrimination. The German hierarchy was very slow in providing Polish-speaking, let alone Polish-thinking, clergy. The Polish workers found themselves victims of special interpretations of work rules (all written in German) and the enmity of their fellow German workers. Even the trade-union movement was slow to respond to Polish needs, to make propaganda and give assistance in other languages, and to support Polish candidates for elections to workers' councils. The local police and other bureaucracies turned their elaborate anti-Socialist devices against the Poles as well. Policemen were in attendance at Polish meetings, some of which they would dissolve for whimsical reasons. The principal form of harassment against the Poles was the banning of foreign languages in public meetings as proscribed by the Law of Associations passed in 1908. The Poles in the Ruhr were not exempted from the law as those in the east were; not only did police dissolve all public meetings where Polish was spoken, but they used this provision as a basis for even more extreme actions, including refusing to allow the public display of banners with Polish slogans. This last interpretation was overturned in the courts, but it does demonstrate the reality of discrimination and the need for self-defense.

The Poles responded in their normal way by creating organizations in both economic and political arenas. There were the perennial religious and self-help groups but, in place of Polish land banks, there were the

Polish trade unions. From 1903, the Poles began contesting Reichstag elections and doing quite well. In Bochum-Gelsenkirchen-Hattingen the Polish party gained over 7 percent of the vote in the first election of 1912. By a very rough estimate, over three-quarters of the Poles in the district voted Polish. By then the process was well organized; there was one *Zahlkandidat*, candidate for the count, in the Ruhr; he was easily chosen. The process was ratified by local committees, and an intensive campaign ensued. It was a strictly affirming vote. The speed of the in-migration diminished the percentages of Poles who voted in the entire Ruhr, but the figures for Bochum, Dortmund, and Recklinghausen demonstrate that good organization and stable communities brought returns for the Polish party that were comparable with those in the east.

The problem was what to do in the runoff, particularly in close elections where the Polish vote could decide the contest. In 1907 the central electoral committee in Posen proposed different strategies. In Dortmund and Bochum Poles were to vote for the SPD; in Essen they were to abstain. In 1912 the Westphalian Poles took charge of their own eligibles, whom they encouraged to vote Centrist. This caused a conflict within the Polish community and among its organizations; the Polish union had become an ally of the *Alter Verband*, the Socialist-leaning miners' union. It was organized Pole against organized Pole, ending generally in the eligibles abstaining or voting their class interests.

Thus runoff elections did show the strength of secular pulls on the social grouping, but the first elections still maintained their national purity. Pole was to vote for Pole, not to win but to affirm commitments and protect the integrity of the social grouping. Moreover, this could all be done in Polish because the Law on Associations did not apply to elections. On one Sunday in 1912 as many as fifty raucus electoral meetings were held in the Ruhr, all filled with the new Polish sound. It was like a festival, a perfect recipe for affirmative voting. All the requirements were there: the spatial and cultural isolation of the social grouping and isolation intensified by actions of the government and dominant majority. As the Polish press wrote in 1912:

> Voting for a German candidate, be it Centrist or a representative of another party, puts the Polish people in a position of dependency on German parties, loosens its ties to Polish society. Through a hard struggle the Polish people have succeeded in protecting their independence against German parties, especially the Center. The fruit of this isolation was the powerful upturn in the national and civic enlightenment of the Polish people, the wonderment of a Polish community created from those thrown out of their homeland, the development of Polish associations and organizations.[102]

The victory then was isolation: Pole here! German there! These are statements of separation that are at once spatial, social, linguistic, economic, and religious, that range from where and what one eats to how one votes. But isolating the Poles is not enough; it is also necessary to define the nature of German as an electoral expression. This is in some part the task of the next chapter. Chapters 8 and 9 place these groups in the contextual relationships from which they sprang. The net result is only to increase the appreciation of the power of the nests and the ferocity of the contests among affirmative voters. These affirmations remained the basis of the Wilhelmine electoral system and sustained the vast majority of voters. But there were others as well. Chapter 5 goes on to explain the problems of nonaffirmative voting and the attempts to recreate the successes of the deviant social groupings among the dominant elites.

5

RECONSTRUCTING THE OLD MAJORITY:

THE PROTESTANT *MITTELSTAND* IN

WILHELMINE POLITICS

The process of electoral mobilization in imperial Germany undermined the former majorities of the preceding dominant political culture. For the most part but not exclusively liberal, these former majorities had relied upon old-fashioned politics run by local elites in predominantly Protestant areas. The new masses of organized affirming voters substantially reduced the size and reliability of these supporters and the industrialization and modernization of the nation greatly undercut the social bases upon which this majority was wrought. And, once the dominance was lost, the means for its reconstruction were not readily discernible. Based on local elites and their interests, the old majority was plagued by such a diversity of social groups as to make political alliances very fragile and of short duration. This fragmentation was only a mirror of fundamental conflict within the Protestant *Mittelstand*. Liberals, conservatives, even radical populists experimented with new political forms aimed at overcoming this fragmentation.

Their methods varied from mere patchwork enterprises to serious re-evaluations of interest-group politics, to the construction of overarching national symbologies or even a set of agreed-upon and convenient hatreds. Some of these methods did succeed in reproducing bodies of habitual voters, but these successes were never enough to reproduce the electoral and/or parliamentary majorities in place before the mobilization of those affirming social groupings.

1. The Liberals

The problems of reconstructing old majorities dominated liberal electoral politics in the Wilhelmine period. The amorphous social and ideological components of German liberals did not necessarily preclude efforts to both harden and extend the areas of their habitual support. Moreover liberals themselves sometimes transcended their differences through abiding by common rules, beliefs, and practices. However, the German liberals were never able to extend their narrow base permanently so as to reconstitute their old electoral strength. They were essentially the remainder, what was left after the disaffections and the massive introduction of new nonliberal voters that occurred after 1878 when Bismarck encouraged an extensive politicization of the rural masses in East Elbia. From the 1880s onward the liberals lost votes and seats to conservatives in the east and to Socialists in the industrialized areas of northern and western Germany. What remained were vestiges of the once-dominant majority. It littered the landscapes like glacial moraines without any perceptible pattern, sometimes in large cities or rural areas, both east and west of the Elbe. Consider the bulk of the Protestant political world as once being liberal, like a flat and uniform plain. Then came the conservative glacier from the east and Socialist from the north and west, cutting wide swaths through the landscape; the liberals were left on the hills, their local survival having depended on unique conditions such as the strength of the local elites and the nature of the local historical experience. Liberalism in industrial Saxony and the Ruhr was different from that in the Hanseatic states, Hamburg and Danzig. The agrarian liberal areas of Schleswig, Hesse, Hanover, and Württemberg pursued differing goals from both of the aforementioned groups.

This view of liberalism conforms fairly well to the ecological data. Because 1907 and 1912 presented different patterns, liberal first election votes were compared across four instead of two contests, showing a great deal of uniformity from 1898 to 1907. The liberal parties were strongest in Protestant, industrialized areas but declined with the strength of urbanization (see table 5:1). Since the work force and urbanization variables are highly intercorrelated, these high positive and negative beta weights represent a unique situation. It places liberals in a modernized and industrialized environment that lies midway between the traditional rural agrarian areas and the cosmopolitanism of the big cities. This is just such an arena from which American progressivism sprang or which describes voting habits in the mid-Victorian English industrial towns.[1] These characteristics yield a situation where local elites were still powerful and able to control the modernizing process and develop political factions that stood against traditional agrarian leadership and often big-business elites as well.

This interpretation of the data is not unique. James Sheehan, the best student of nineteenth-century German liberalism, states:

> The typical liberal voter, therefore, was a Protestant who belonged somewhere in the middle range of the class and status hierarchies. It was from these groups that the bulk of the two parties' 3.5 million votes came in the election of 1912. And it was districts

TABLE 5:1. *Association of Liberal Vote with Selected Characteristics*

Characteristic	1898 (N=46 administrative units)			1903 (N=46 administrative units)			1907 (N=47 administrative units)			1912 (N=47 administrative units)		
	r	Significant Betas Only	Proportion of Variation Explained (Multiple R^2)	r	Significant Betas Only	Proportion of Variation Explained (Multiple R^2)	r	Significant Betas Only	Proportion of Variation Explained (Multiple R^2)	r	Significant Betas Only	Proportion of Variation Explained (Multiple R^2)
% Catholic	-.542	-.612	.293	-.518	-.583	.268	-.548	-.617	.301	-.663	.721	.439
% of male work force engaged in industry and mining	.239	.493	.338	.326	.579	.358	.333	.518	.401	.058		.441
% of total population living in cities with populations over 10,000	.042	-.426	.432	.097	-.422	.450	.130	-.395	.480	.017		.487

where these groups were best represented that elected a majority of the liberals' eighty-seven delegates. In size and social composition, these districts tended to fall in between the small, agrarian *Wahlkreise* dominated by the Conservatives and the huge, urban and/or industrial districts controlled by the SPD. Characteristically, the liberals' districts were touched but not transformed by the social, economic, and cultural changes at work in German society. They were composed of small and medium-sized towns, not great cities or distended industrial suburbs; when liberals did win in large cities, it was most often in the relatively stable central districts where the urban middle strata still predominated. Similarly, their rural support came in places where agriculture was carried on by a large number of proprietors, not by a few big landowners.[2]

This is a fair estimation, although this form of ecological analysis is weakened by the propensity of liberals to win in runoffs, even in areas where their strength on the first ballot was very weak. This was true for the right-wing National Liberals as well as the various left-wing liberal parties (see table 4:11). By the end of the Wilhelmine period, the National Liberal runoff candidates increased their percentage of the vote by over 15 points from the first to the second election, and the left-wing liberals by almost 20 points. All these votes were needed. After 1887 neither the National Liberals nor the left-wingers won a majority of their seats in the first election. The ratio of seats won in the second to the first election for both liberal parties increased from 2:1 in 1890 to 7:1 in 1898. By 1912 only four out of the forty-six National Liberal Reichstag deputies and none of the forty-four left-wing liberal representatives were chosen in the first election. Less than half of those elected even led during the first round of voting.[3]

This combination of geographical dispersion and vague middling centrality fits other nineteenth-century liberal societies. Nineteenth-century British liberal supporters could not be described through clear bipolar definitions of class; twentieth-century Norwegian liberals showed the same geographic and social dispersion after they had lost their former positions of dominance.[4] The social and spatial referents of Wilhelmine liberalism are far from clear. Sometimes they represented clear Protestant middle-class interests against the working class; sometimes they represented a larger social group including many artisans and blue-collar workers. Sometimes they were united against the common enemy—the Socialists or Catholics; sometimes they divided along occupational lines themselves.

There were examples of simple bipolar class conflict within the Protestant communities, especially in the large industrial cities. As always, this bipolarity was conditioned by religion. In Dortmund in 1903, 44 percent of the Center party voters can be classified as white-collar workers, a close occupational approximation of middle-class. Thus many middle-class Catholics could be relied on to remain inside the ring of church and Center.

Consequently the National Liberal candidate was principally a representative of the Protestant middle class. And within Protestantism the figures are remarkable. I estimate that over 90 percent of the National Liberal votes came from the white-collar category. As shown in table 4:6, other studies based on similar definitions yield about the same results.

This high correlation remains the same even when middle class is defined in terms of proprietors, higher civil servants, business executives and technologically trained personnel. Such bipolar class distinctions are present in party membership data. National Liberal party members in both Dortmund and Frankfurt am Main as well as Frankfurt's left-wing liberals were overwhelmingly middle class (table 5:2). The left-wing liberals in Dortmund were a marginal party without a strong voting base. They thus demonstrated a larger blue-collar component similar to other marginal parties—the National Socialists and the Anti-Semites. Without doubt, the Stuttgart Socialist press was correct in characterizing the liberals as candidates of the "better people."[5]

However, bipolar definitions of class base are not very useful in those small-town and rural bastions of liberalism. Here liberals were divided along many lines, not the least concerning status and occupation. Each liberal party was an amalgam of such groups. The National Liberals had a strong agrarian wing in southwestern Germany to match their industrial bases in Saxony and the Ruhr; the left-wing liberals had strong bases in Berlin and Hamburg and in the small towns and wine-growing villages of Württemberg. Liberals also tended to divide even further in those areas where competition was safe. The National Liberals then would tend to come from higher status occupations and the left-wing liberals from the lower. In Württemberg and Oldenburg, left-wing liberals were the small farmers and the National Liberals dominated the areas of predominantly large farms. Left-wing liberals were more likely to be artisans, shopkeepers, and commercial clerks,[6] less likely to be civil servants or businessmen. As shown in the preceding chapter, left-wing liberal parties also relied on Jewish support.

Perhaps even this amorphous social structure could have been formed into a distinct social grouping if there were any popular support for this process. Liberals were likely to be divided on issues such as tariffs, levels and kinds of taxation, civil rights, military expenditures, and foreign and colonial policies. New liberal parties formed and disbanded on the basis of policy differences or leadership antagonisms. There were as many as four left-wing liberal parties in Wilhelmine Germany. The National Liberals were somewhat more stable, but they were also divided into bitterly

TABLE 5:2. *Social Composition of Political Parties in Frankfurt am Main and Dortmund*[7]

Social Group	Frankfurt am Main			Dortmund			
	Left-wing Liberals 1889–90 (N=417)	National Liberals 1893 (N=643)	National Socialists 1898 (N=130)	Left-wing Liberals 1907 (N=103)	National Liberals 1898 (N=146)	Anti-Semites 1898 (N=217)	Center 1891 (N=84)
Professionals	12.5	14.2	13.1	13.6	19.9	15.9	0
Civil servants	1.2	7.5	3.8	6.8	14.1	11.8	2.4
Teachers	7.9	14.0	6.9	4.8	14.4	1.1	1.2
Businessmen, directors, etc.	14.2	19.4	7.7	3.8	48.6	17.0	6.0
Shopowners and salespeople	50.8	30.5	12.3	44.6	8.2	38.2	10.7
Master craftsmen	5.3	1.4	15.4	0	1.6	0	10.7
Craftsmen and workers	3.1	6.5	40.0	26.2	0.6	12.2	56.0
Retired or unemployed	5.1	6.5	0.8	0	2.1	3.7	7.1
In four richest districts	8.9	10.3	1.5				
In four districts with the largest Jewish population	6.5	3.4	0.8				

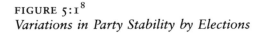

FIGURE 5:1[8]
Variations in Party Stability by Elections

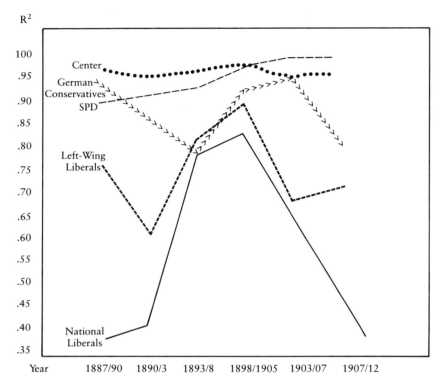

contesting factions. Liberal voters mirrored their parties; they were more likely to change party preference than affirming voters. Figure 5:1 is a graph of the total variation explained (R^2) in one party's vote by the same party's vote in the immediately preceding election. Thus a high R^2 through the period would indicate a body of habitual affirmers who came to the polls in election after election. The National Liberal curve indicates much more volatility. Some of this extreme in variation is caused by exchanges within the liberal community as progovernment supporters in one election defected from the National Liberal to the antigovernment left-wing liberals in the next contest, or vice versa. The left-wing liberal curve, however, does not move in total conjunction with the National Liberal; both liberal camps tended to be winners in 1907 and losers in 1912, indicating their weak hold on possible supporters, certainly striking when compared with those Center, Socialist, and even German Conservative curves, which describe the loyalties and solidarities formed by affirmative voting within isolated social groupings.

This lack of cohesiveness conditioned the liberal methods for influencing elections. Uncontrolled by the implicit limits of social-grouping politics, local liberal leaders were often able to make pragmatic decisions on candidate selection based on political needs. National Liberals in Wiesbaden County, Hesse, would choose a candidate from the party's left wing in order to place themselves in a favorable position in the runoff. In the neighboring Dillkreis and Oberwesterwald, National Liberals nominated a local *Landrat* in hopes of winning progovernment and conservative supporters.[9] Often separated spatially, in social composition, and in ideology from their nearest liberal neighbors, local elites were able to determine the direction of campaigns without reference to more national concerns. This brought about an ever-increasing range of responses conditioned by local politics, ideology, and economic interests. It placed these local elites at the center of district politics. Local election committees tended to remain independent of the central organizations even after changes in the law allowed for national party structures after 1900. The district liberals were able to continue on this course although much of their campaign expenses were paid by the national party. In fact, the national party leadership never got much beyond the role of beggars in dealing with these elites. The National Liberal chairman, Ernst Bassermann, had difficulties in assuring himself a place as a Reichstag candidate.

The articulation of interest also moved through the local elites. Big business organizations did not take over the National Liberal party in Dortmund as part of their nationwide practice. Long before the big business organizations became involved in national politics, the coal and steel interests in Dortmund had a controlling position in liberal politics at the state, municipal, and national elections. These local elites correctly recognized that electoral victories and political power were economically and socially beneficial in terms of prestige and in the resolution of economic conflicts.[10]

These local interests were much more easily subsumed under regional and state banners than within national interest groups. After 1884 the National Liberal party even encouraged the regional articulation of interest as the best means of saving what was a geographically and socially dispersed group of supporters. The social composition and particular state politics within the Grand Duchy of Hesse were especially appropriate for the creation of a conservative agrarian wing. The industrializing of the Ruhr and Saxony led to the domination of new industrial elites, who overwhelmed old-style and often left-wing liberals. Yet the very success of these regional coalitions undermined the view of a unified liberalism and, in the case of the National Liberals, put the party down what Dan White has called "the track of regional fragmentation."[11]

This fragmentation of interest and social composition was both a cause and a sign of a more fundamental problem dealing with liberal perceptions of their role in German society. Before 1850, liberals existed on both a firm social and ideological base, the quintessential citizens who represented the Protestant *Mittelstand* of educated and propertied. This group set standards and gave a sense of unity and purpose to the whole society; it should have the moral power to control governments as it was the natural core of political reform. The loss of this *Mittelstand* centrality in a pluralistic world was taken as a sign of liberal weakness and dissolution. The discussion of moral purpose often gave way to cultural pessimism laced with a strong sense of degeneration.

When combined with geographic, ideological, and social differentiation, varying policy statements and campaigning tactics, this loss of centrality presents a powerful picture of fragmentation and disunity. But this is only so when compared with the strength of affirming social groupings, with their definitive boundaries, their sense of separation and isolation, their ability to generate unity of purpose. The full meaning of liberal fragmentation is thus not altogether clear, particularly when placed within the historical traditions. German liberals retained their old electoral habits, which stemmed from a time when they could afford the luxury of diversity. They hark back to the era when liberals, in Lord David Balfour's terms, "could safely afford to bicker." [12]

There were statistical signs of definite limits beyond which liberals were not supposed to go. One of the most explicit rules in German electoral politics was that liberals always supported fellow liberals in a runoff. Failure to do so was tantamount to treason. When the Alzey-Bingen National Liberals in Hesse supported a Centrist in a runoff in 1909 rather than a left-wing liberal, the whole issue aroused enormous consternation in the party headquarters in both Darmstadt and Berlin. Such an action was treated as irreconcilable with liberal traditions. Arrestingly, even the closest allies of the Alzey-Bingen National Liberals admitted that the act itself was ignoble. The *Wormser Zeitung*, the organ of the agrarian wing of the Hessian National Liberals, stated that it could only have come about because the left-wing liberals had themselves violated informal rules by supporting Socialists over right-wing liberals. It was all done with the logic of some poor crusader who found himself fighting the French instead of the Moslems because he took the wrong turn on the road to Constantinople. "That is some situation: 5,000 National Liberal men vote resolutely for the Ultramontane after a gathering of National Liberal leaders even so resolutely gives the order. Evangelical men, evangelical pastors, high evangelical officers of the court; all decidedly support an evil that is the terrible fruit of the actions of the Hessian Progressives." [13]

Liberals not only supported each other in runoffs, but they were becoming distinctly less ready to fight among themselves in first elections. The data show clearly how the pattern of liberal candidature changed. Until the SPD spurt in the twentieth century, there was very little need for any liberal not to fight in the first election. But the increasing Socialist vote changed liberal election strategy. The correlation coefficients between the liberal parties became more and more negative, falling from .118 in 1887 to .049 in 1893, −.120 in 1898, −.288 in 1903, −.326 in 1907, and finally to −.454 in 1912. The trend was that the weaker group would withdraw from the contest, thus allowing all the liberal votes to cluster in one party for the first election.

There were other limits to liberal fragmentation. Left-wing liberals were unwilling to trust a priest-laden party. They endangered their chances of election in Danzig, Wiesbaden, and Stuttgart by remaining publicly anti-Catholic, by refusing to promise their support in revising even the most harmless sections of the state anti-Jesuit laws, by attacking clerical influence in the schools. They were supported by a strong strand of anti-clericalism in the National Liberal party, particularly among the Young Liberals group. Anticlericalism was matched by a permanent and emotional anti-Socialism. There were some dealings with the SPD; electoral coalitions were formed in Baden between the Socialists and both liberal parties. The left-wing Progressives joined in a runoff arrangement with the Social Democrats in 1912. Yet these were sporadic instances. As shown in chapter 4, left-wing liberal voters were often loath to follow their instructions and vote for a workers' candidate whom they believed to embody disorder and the end of private property. Coalitions such as the one in Baden were principally directed against political Catholicism. They were considered as temporary expedients and doomed because of differing views among the partners on the distribution of wealth. Thus the great coalition in Baden broke down after liberal reforms such as suffrage extension had been instituted and when the SPD first began to make serious demands for social reform upon their liberal partners. The slogan of a political union "from Bebel to Bassermann" was a concoction of Friedrich Naumann and was never considered as a serious part of any liberal platform. Even Theodor Barth, who emerged ultimately victorious as the left-wing liberal leader, only sporadically pursued his policy of alliance with the Socialists. Liberals preferred to stand against those deviant Catholic and Socialist camps. A liberal broadside from Bielefeld, Westphalia, called up images from the struggles against Napoleon as it urged its readers to fight in a "War of Liberation against the brutal Social Democracy, against the unbearably harsh and uncultured regime of the Center Party, against the Ultramontane."[14]

With Catholics and Socialists written off, liberalism depended on its ability to mobilize supporters in the Protestant *Mittelstand*, not only in slowing down the tide of defections to political socialism, but in extending the boundaries of habitual liberal voting. There were a number of alternatives for extending liberal strength, including a progovernment alliance with the conservatives. In the late 1890s such an alliance was formed to initiate a *Sammlungspolitik* of principally Protestant parties under the aegis of big business and large-scale agriculture. However, *Sammlungspolitik* had only limited application at the electoral level. Anthony O'Donnell has found a number of instances where National Liberals garnered electoral support from conservatives and a few places where an agrarian-industrial electoral alliance was possible. For the most part, conservatives and the industrial wing of the National Liberal party had little to offer each other because they were concentrated in different parts of the country. Thus the relationship of German Conservative and National Liberal voting changes very little through the period, indicating few alliances made in first elections, and it was strongly negative, indicating that their areas of strength were quite separated. The only beneficiaries from such an alliance were a few National Liberal agrarians in north-central Germany where there was some possibility of interchange of votes. For the most part, German conservative agrarians did not even stop attacking their nominal big-business ally and the National Liberal party, which represented it. Antiurbanism remained rampant in the east (see chapter 7).[15]

Sammlungspolitik effectively ended with the dissolution of the Bülow bloc in 1909. Created in 1907 and encompassing the widest possible economic and political diversity, the bloc split on the issue of taxation, with the conservatives joining the Center in forestalling major financial reform. This forced Bülow to abandon his attempts at instituting inheritance and property taxes and to return to regressive direct taxation. The conservatives not only destroyed the bloc's electoral coalition but precipitated a counterattack led by moderate liberals and focused in the *Hansabund*, founded in the year of the bloc's dissolution. The *Hansabund* was supposed to be a kind of urban BdL that would unite all possible interests against the BdL and agrarian domination. Organizations with strong ties to the *Hansabund* included both the representatives of heavy industry in the *Centralverband Deutscher Industrieller* (CVDI) and the finished-goods and high technology groups represented by the *Bund der Industriellen*. A mass base was provided by the addition of the proliferating organizations of the new *Mittelstand* of white-collar workers and from a large number of artisans, all hurt by the financial reform and its consequences.

In many ways the *Hansabund* was the fruition of Gustav Stresemann's hopes for creating an industry-led political grouping that would rely on the new *Mittelstand* of white-collar workers, small businessmen, and farmers for its mass support. Stresemann had attempted to transform the Saxon National Liberals into such a combination, and he appealed to the new middle class by advocating the extension of health insurance and other social benefits to white-collar workers.

The *Hansabund* not only promised a new base for liberal politics; it provided a new source of money for the liberal cause. Before 1909, campaign money came from a few donors in heavy industry who were increasingly using their power to threaten moderate National Liberals. The *Hansabund* provided a whole new means for gaining campaign contributions. It had around 2 million marks in its war chest for the election of 1912. With campaigns costing from 10,000 to 40,000 marks, such funds were a godsend. More than that, the *Hansabund* attempted to get *Mittelstand* workers out in the streets and even appeared to be responsible for the use of some new technology by which the dragger, the *Schlepper*, carried voters to the polls:

> When one won't vote, in an automobile
> Will gently be *Schlepper* led.
> With joy he then will ten times vote
> And on each journey dote.
> *Herr* Oske sniggers and thinks: so claps
> The *Hansabund* in gold enwrapped![16]

Usually these successes were short-lived and the promises of a unified liberal front were never realized. The experience of affirming voters shows the difficulties of constructing electoral coalitions based predominantly on economic interest. This was even more true when, as in the case of the *Hansabund*, these interests often had different goals. Thus the *Hansabund* leadership was primarily composed of representatives of the industries that were dependent on foreign trade and were opposed to high tariffs and other forms of protectionist legislation. Yet heavy industry, and the artisan and white-collar groups viewed government in a different light, if not as an outright protector then certainly as a regulator of unfair competition in all areas of life. These differences caused a split within the *Hansabund* almost immediately, bringing about the withdrawal of many elements of the CVDI in 1911.

Neither money nor effective propaganda was a satisfactory means for solidifying a great coalition of interests. The *Hansabund* leadership searched to find some stronger ties, hoping, for example, that artisans would realize that they were predominantly salespeople and would therefore see indirect taxation as a greater menace than free trade. But the main hope of unity continued to be based on attacking the privileged position of agriculture and the excessive power of the BdL. This even extended to the demand for electoral reform in Prussia, the only way to defeat the conservative agrarians who dominated the unreformed legislature. And finally the *Hansabund* appealed to those traditions of the old liberal *Mittelstand*, reformed but still recognizable in a pluralistic world of interest groups. The liberal *Mittelstand* could still proclaim its necessary centrality in German politics and society. The *Hansabund* adopted a kind of neophysiocratic ideology, redefined the *Mittelstand* as more than education and property, as more than reform and intelligence, as an alliance of those "active producers" against the working class and agrarians.

Assertions of centrality proved ineffective in the 1912 election, where the liberal parties sustained substantial losses. Coupled with an economic downturn, this was enough to turn the artisan groups to the right and to leave the *Hansabund* as a rump of convinced free traders and left-wing liberals, another example of liberal failure to find some satisfactory redefinition of the centrality. Dan White quotes Arthur Hobrecht, a contemporary party leader, who summarizes this weakness:

> . . . all other parties have their particular starting-points and focus to which they hold fast whether in the religious domain, in the representation of class or estate, or in the protection of material economic special interests. All of that is absent in the National Liberal Party. For us the protection of economic interests is an element of danger rather than of union. We have to seek our reputation in reconciling and harmonizing the opposed economic aspirations in our midst as far as it is in our power. We are likewise not the representatives of class or an estate; it is only an often-used rhetorical twist that we constitute the true representation of the educated middle strata—I have never been able to draw anything specific out of that phrase. The so-called middle classes are too indeterminate, varied and loose a substance to fit into one mold, and the German *Bürgertum* is too German to work particularly well in union or under obligation. All the more valuable for us is the cement of history, the cement that a long period of common effort in great tasks and of common struggles over great questions necessarily produced.[17]

Such sentiments might seem out of place among the interest-group contests of the twentieth-century world, but they bore a great deal of resemblance to the liberal inheritance of a classless society, of *Stände* unified under liberal leadership. It is true that this vision of the classless society was permeated by social imperialism playing upon threats from outside and inside the society, hiding real social conflict under the guise of nationalist rhetoric. But more was involved here than a vulgar statement of German imperialism to create a "false consciousness" among German workers and artisans. Fatherland rhetoric was the legitimate outgrowth of the longing for a classless society; it was enmeshed in German idealism and was an attempt to reunify the German ruling class with its Protestant *Mittelstand*.

It was certainly an effective electoral tool, always stated succinctly and clearly, particularly in struggles between National Liberals and the SPD. The following is a peroration from an electoral broadside used by the National Liberal candidate (Bartling) against the SPD (Lehmann) in Wiesbaden in 1912:

> Bartling or Lehmann?
> For or Against Emperor and Empire?
> For or Against Religion and Fatherland?
> For or Against Bourgeois Society?[18]

Emperor, fatherland, religion, bourgeois society—they were all united in a congery of symbols. National Liberal campaign rhetoric is filled with connections between national strength and moral order. This is the essential core of the runoff contests between National Liberals and Social Democrats. In 1893 Karl Siegle, a Stuttgart soda manufacturer, was engaged in just such a contest. Siegle campaigned as a nationalist and a supporter of fatherland for "protection of the Empire and the furthering of the common good." A vote for the Socialists was equated in the broadsides with a vote for impoverishment, cosmopolitanism, and against religious belief. Voting Socialist made one "also guilty" for the degeneration of the fatherland. Citizens were told to forget party loyalties. "No German of whatever party can live with his conscience by refusing the fatherland the necessary means for defense. The fatherland above all." "Unworthy is the nationalist who does not set everything upon its honor." And finally culminating in this advertisement: "A dangerous wrong is done to the fatherland by not voting. Tread into the polls, you voters, man for man, and give your vote. Do not let yourselves be swayed by unhappiness and personal interest, nor by personal inclination or antipathy, by slogans and counter-slogans, by seductions and demagoguery, but only alone look at the whole picture for the good of the people and the fatherland."[19]

2. The Protestant *Bürgertum*

The expression of fatherland rhetoric widened the possibilities of transforming the old liberal majority into a new constellation based on commitments to king and country and hatred for social democracy. There was some discernible but vague formation based on Protestantism, *Mittelstand*, and government, which was perceived as both loyal and moral. Yet this formation appeared only in indistinct outlines; it was always a group "in the making," very often more in the minds of its beholders than a reality. The task of the former dominant elites and the government was to discover somehow the nature of this structure, to solidify its outlines, and to use it as the base for a new political constellation. I have used the term *Bürgertum* to describe this group, since its very discussion in contemporary life defined the problem, at once meaning solid middle-class citizen, the moral unity of the Protestant society, and a class based on economic exploitation.[20]

The statistical delineation of such a group was bound to be very amorphous. Fatherland rhetoric was rooted in most of the Protestant-*Bürgertum* parties from liberal through conservative to anti-Semite. The principal associations of these parties are with Protestant indicators and not with other socioeconomic variables. Ideologically, they were too disparate a mass to be considered as a coherent force. Not all the parties so described accepted a relationship with each other. At one extreme the anti-Semites and agrarian conservatives attacked the free-trading left-wing liberals while, on the other side, some of these same liberals favored an alliance with Socialism. Neither group desired to include the other as an acceptable partner. Yet, even with these exceptions, there were some statistical footprints of a loose coalition, often expressed in runoff elections where these Protestant *Bürger* parties were the recipients of support from a larger than average number of voters whose candidates failed to make the runoff. The higher differences between runoff and first election percentages for these Protestant bourgeois parties have already been noted (see table 4 : 11). In the last three Wilhelmine Reichstag elections, the Protestant parties won two out of every three runoff contests they entered, including those among themselves. This compared very favorably with the Centrists and Social Democrats, who won only two elections out of every five.

Some of these parties undoubtedly served continuously or periodically as referents for Catholic and Jewish voters who identified with the dominant elites or the progovernment parties. Anyone was acceptable as a follower, but these parties retained a narrow Protestant definition for those qualified to represent the nation, particularly as Reichstag deputies. Catholics and Jews were acceptable as followers but hardly as deputies. Between 1887 and 1912 there were only eighteen Catholics representing the Protestant bourgeois parties, considerably less than 1 percent of the total. And of the eighteen, twelve were from that particular class of South German liberals, seven coming from Baden alone. The situation with Catholics was replicated within the Jewish community. There were only three listed Jewish deputies from all these parties in the period between 1887 and 1913.[21]

Fatherland rhetoric was the basis of new *Mittelstand* coalitions including sections of conservative and anti-Semitic agrarians, particularly those in western Germany. For the anti-Semites, an assertion of *Mittelstand* centrality was a means for averting attacks on their own deviance. The *Reichsherold*, a Hessian anti-Semitic organ, proclaimed as early as 1890, "We are an honorable *Mittelstand* and people's party of the working and earning classes in Germany."[22] However, the anti-Semites and the German Conservatives were by no means interested in including the traditional academic and propertied middle strata in their definition, since these were thought too liberal and antimonarchist to be unambiguously moral and profatherland. Thus German Conservatives and anti-Semites attacked the stock market and the power of great capital while asserting the rights of the small artisan and farmer to government protection through high tariffs and other forms of regulation. Even when the conservatives took up the rhetoric of *Sammlung*, union of big business and big agriculture, they did so from a peculiar agrarian viewpoint, asserting that business and the working class benefited from high tariffs. The key phrase uttered by the emperor in the *Sammlung* campaign literature was the assertion of the right for "national work," which became the anti-Socialist codeword in the 1898 election and beyond. A good example of such literature was a pamphlet that passed through rural Westphalia in 1903 under the title "Germany's Security and Prosperity." The pamphlet closed with a demand to support national parties "with honor for our emperor, our navy, and a strong Germany. The slogan for this election: Protection of the national work."[23] Or as a BdL broadside used in Hesse in 1898 stated:

> For a German *Mittelstand*!
> For Emperor and Empire!!!
> For a German peasantry [*Bauernstand*]!
> For Emperor and Fatherland!!![24]

As we have seen from the Stuttgart example, anti-Socialism was an integral part of fatherland rhetoric. It had some utility in liberal areas where the SPD garnered an increasingly larger percentage of votes. But the spread of anti-Socialist campaigns through the rural areas and small towns of Hesse, Württemberg, and Westphalia cannot alone be attributed to economic or class conflict or to the fear that urban disorder and cultural pluralism could spread into these areas. Anti-Socialism served as the symbolic referent for the internal enemy who resisted the national spirit. As one Westphalian broadside stated, the Socialists and left-wing liberals had "no love for or pride in soldiering." What could be done? In the present society, the broadside argued, force was impossible. The society therefore could only be preserved by supporting the *Mittelstand*, which was the true expression of the people against the fatherlandless SPD and the stockbrokers. The broadside's peroration was that old familiar refrain: "Up with the fatherland; up with national work; down the Social Democracy."[25]

As Charles Maier contends, this combination of vulgar anti-Marxism and vulgar imperialism was not unique either to or within Wilhelmine Germany. Maier, however, believes that anti-Socialism played a much more integral part in the consolidation of the German bourgeois than in other countries. He states:

German bourgeois consciousness thus developed into little more than rampant anti-Marxism. . . . "Bourgeois" became an attribute easily applied to political divisions as well as social ones, hence a characteristic eventually to be shared by agrarian or ennobled foes of sociologism as well as by middle-class opponents. The adjective "bourgeois" thus vaunted from reference to medieval citizenship rights to antisocialism. The older sense of "civic" was never really shed; but the intervening phase of reference to a generalized nation-state citizenship—such as the French Revolution had bestowed upon *citoyen*—never became prevalent. "Bürger" had been a title of pride in old Lübeck, but was little more than an antisocialist referent in the new Empire.[26]

But, as with the term *Mittelstand*, it would be well to view the inheritance of *Bürgertum*, which leads to somewhat different conclusions. Good citizenship carried a number of connotations in early nineteenth-century Germany that were substantially retained in later definitions. German Protestant *Bürgertum* was often perceived as a cultural verity instead of a set of class-based justifications. It is difficult to be very specific about the meaning of these cultural statements since there are no retrievable German data on religiosity or church attendance. Still there are good reasons for viewing German Protestantism as a cohesive group relative to the rest of the Protestant world. Historically, German Protestantism produced fewer different sects than other nations. By 1900 German Protestants were, for the most part, not even separated into Calvinists and Lutherans but were members of the numerous state churches, with their safe Erastian theology. This fact was of enormous importance even if these Protestants had become totally secular, since we know that in other societies sectarianism has had a lingering effect long after religious powers of the sects began to dwindle. And, lastly, German Protestants were not haunted by that major cleavage within the Anglo-American and Scandinavian Protestant communities—teetotalism. German Protestants drank like all good Germans. It was the patriotic thing to do, and in their drinking they also managed to create a greater semblance of unity within their Protestant bourgeois camp than in those other North Atlantic communities scarred by the Prohibition crusades. There were hopes that faith was alone strong enough to hold on to the Protestant working class. Although this proved a dream, the Evangelical Workers' Union in 1901 contended, "Who is evangelical [i.e., Protestant] is German because religion is the surest support for Emperor and Empire, for ruler and fatherland."[27]

The last element of this concoction was the moral position of the state, which stood above narrow interest and petty politics. Respect for the state was found in the strangest places—among Ruhr mineworkers, for instance—and was remarkably untarnished by the oppressive or un-popular actions of local bureaucrats and policemen. Thus workmen's compensation was considered an achievement of the state, surveillance of the trade-union movement was the work of local or provincial officials. The lowest rung of state officials in rural areas could, therefore, be excep-tionally unpopular because they refused to ban traveling salesmen from the neighborhood or demanded the inoculation of all children. Yet the same members of the Society against Forced Inoculation (*Impfzwang*) could also be strong Prussian or Württemberg monarchists and con-vinced German nationalists. There were other variants on the theme; the German Conservatives attacked the bureaucrats in Berlin or Stuttgart as unresponsive to the needs of agriculture, while genuinely proclaiming support of local officials as a sign of their loyalty to monarch and state. The state could not lose, escaping blame for the assaults of its bureau-cracy while accepting the real accomplishments of civil servants as medi-ators between local and national interests. This was buttressed by the genuine popularity of the reigning princes, especially in Bavaria, Hesse, and Württemberg, as well as the good will that William II himself engen-dered during the first years of his reign. As one electoral pamphlet circu-lated in Westphalia in 1903 stated, "Trust in the Emperor, your best friend, who has no comparison in the world as a loving and caring na-tional father." [28]

Michael Stürmer would correctly characterize such statements as ex-amples of plebiscitary politics, those waged on "easy issues," which were connected with unambiguous statements of loyalty. Yet even plebiscitary politics was becoming considerably more complicated as Germany moved into the twentieth century. Bismarck had considered his plebiscitary poli-tics in neofeudal terms, treating the vote as a statement of fealty, demand-ing that the voters follow the "desires" and "expectations" of the govern-ment. [29] It is doubtful that the voters responded in such a manner, even to his victorious calls of 1887. Certainly Bülow's attempt to repeat the feat thirty years later was undertaken in very different circumstances. The pro-state public had become the object of an intensive nationalist campaign through public festivals such as Sedan day, which celebrated the victory over Napoleon III, the erection of public monuments to the founders of the empire, the reconstitution of elementary-school curricula to empha-size patriotism and Hohenzollern destiny, the assertion of Germany's destiny in the daily press—all manifestations of a permeating nationalist ideology, which now overlaid and sometimes displaced the neofeudal conceptions of the electorate.

Bülow carried on an electoral campaign using strategies that seem very close to those of contemporary political advertising. The government carefully planned the targeting of materials with considerable sophistica-tion and expense. Bülow's voters were to be influenced rather than led by

the nose to the polls. But there the differences between the two chancellors ended; both envisioned the state as the centerpiece for national
campaigns. Bülow wrote to the various Reich jurisdictions before the
election: "Only a clear impression can be created in the case of mass elections. In my view, it would be best to place in the foreground of the coming election the principle of a responsible executive against the thirteen
legal parties and to use the issue of the honor of the German flag."[30]
Whether encouraged by the imperial government or springing from the
nature of the election itself, the campaign turf was littered with assertions
of the precedence of national loyalty above party. A leaflet in Bielefeld-
Wiedenbrück, signed principally by farmers and Protestant ministers,
proclaimed that attack on the power of the higher military commander
(the emperor) was unheard of in German history and argued that "he
who cares about the welfare of the fatherland and the power and honor of
the Reich will not have Germany dominated by parties and parliament."[31]

This so-called Hottentot election was a perfect tool for the conjunction
of fatherland rhetoric and Protestant *Bürger* politics. The Reichstag was
dissolved in December 1906 when the Center and SPD blocked the approval of funds for the coming colonial budget. It was a wonderful issue,
involving as it did the conceptions of a responsible state, alongside imperial drives and racial prejudices, isolating the two principal deviant parties and unifying all Protestant *Bürgertum* against them. Bülow claimed
that an election victory would demonstrate the stability of the empire,
protect against the possibility of revolution, and sustain the possibility of
a moral bourgeois life. His electoral policy was quite simple: to oppose
the deviants, the Poles, Guelphs, and Centrists.

Bülow fully mobilized nationalist organizations already in place such
as the Naval and Colonial Leagues. The most visible vehicle for this progovernment coalition was the *Reichsverband gegen die Sozialdemokratie*,
the Imperial Union against Social Democracy, founded in 1904. The Imperial Union was a careful construct of the loyal Protestant *Bürgertum*; it
even discouraged any possible Catholic joiners, still having 140,000
members divided into 287 local groups by the end of 1906. These members contributed toward a substantial war chest, which was used to finance the distribution of leaflets and to sustain local organizing activities.
Leaflet number 15 carried a picture of a black man ready to rape a German woman after having struck her son and killed her husband. The cap-
tion read: "This is the outcome if a Social Democrat is elected."[32] Such
racist sentiments found their way into other *Reichsverband* publications,
and anti-Socialist statements of all kinds prevailed in the campaign, especially in the popular "Handbook" for non-Social Democratic Voters,
which portrayed the Socialists as cosmopolitan antimoralists.

The *Reichsverband* was only the fermenting element in a massive anti-
Socialist coalition, which was expressed by all Protestant *Bürger* parties

and most newspapers, in government-sponsored publications and at election rallies. The 1907 election appears to have been the true test of the possibilities inherent in extending the *Mittelstand* vote. Certainly this was the strategy by both the government and the *Reichsverband*, which hoped to win back a few marginal voters who had gone SPD in 1903, and also to politicize permanently those peripheral voters who only came to the polls in special instances. And they did seem to have some success in both.

Fatherland rhetoric proved useful in plebiscitary elections as a means for capturing the moral high ground. In many ways, this was an easy task, since the SPD had always taken an anticolonial and antimilitarist position. Fatherland-rhetoric propagandists claimed this was a sign not only of weak national impulses but also of immorality and lack of communal responsibilities. Such statements put the SPD on the defensive. It was not enough for Socialist pamphlets to proclaim that the party members had higher morals than the rest of the working class, were better fathers, and cared more for the education of their children. Fatherland rhetoric had already made the connection between family life and national life. It was not enough for the Socialists to cry foul when Bülow labeled them "enemies of the empire." The Socialists might claim to represent the best of German nationalism, but the *Reichsverband* actually represented the nationalist coalition. The example of Karl Severing in Bielefeld shows how feeble were the SPD attempts to turn the nationalist message on its head by comparing the African rebels with oppressed Germans. Severing attempted to metamorphose a local hero who had turned back the Romans and become the subject of an enormous monument and national shrine in nearby Detmold.

> What does it have to do with the national honor of Germans which is supposed to be on the line in far Southwest Africa? It was the butchery and the eradication of the Hereros and the Hottentots, the original owners of the land, who through the cruelty and bestiality of the German farmer were tortured until they bled and were forced into rebellion, just as almost 1900 years ago Herman the Cherusker (Arminius) had been awakened against the Romans.[33]

This was hardly the winning ploy in Westphalia in 1907, even if Severing was personally elected with the help of the Catholic, not Protestant, *Bürgertum* voters.

The national coalition of 1907 produced a remarkable victory. The SPD may have gained a few voters and lost only about 2 percent of the total vote as compared with 1903, but the number of Socialist seats was halved. Narrow Socialist victories in 1903 were turned into narrow Socialist defeats in 1907 through the concentration of bloc parties in their instrument, the *Reichsverband*. The tactics of the bloc seemed to work everywhere, but they were particularly successful in rapidly industrializing districts that had turned SPD in 1903 or were in danger of doing so in 1907. One of the latter cases was Cassel-Melsungen, Hesse, where the SPD had lost the runoff in 1903 by fewer than 900 votes. Led by a retired lieutenant general, the *Reichsverband* worked early to gain a foothold in all camps of the Protestant *Bürgertum* parties. Their cause was taken up by the local establishment and the bourgeois press, including the influential *Casseler Allgemeine Zeitung*, which informed its readers two days before the election: "The whole civilized world will look at us next Friday. The fate of Germans abroad will be determined for years to come. Every individual is responsible for the outcome."[34]

The first election went quite smoothly; the National Liberal candidate carried the majority in Cassel city, the SPD won in the working-class suburbs of Cassel County, and the anti-Semite Wilhelm Lattmann gathered enough support in rural Melsungen to come in second, 5,000 votes behind the SPD. The National Liberals united behind Lattmann and were joined by conservatives, members of the Hessian Rights party, and a few left-wing liberals. The election was fought under the banner of the *Reichsverband* with scarcely a mention of particular parties. As proclaimed in a *Reichsverband* electoral gathering, "The fatherland is the party."[35] Turnout reached 89 percent in the runoff, high even for Germany, and Lattmann beat his SPD opponent by over 3,000 votes. Certainly much of the winning margin was due to the consolidation of the Protestant *Bürgertum* under *Reichsverband* leadership, yet in this district it could only postpone the inevitable. In 1912, with over 93 percent of the eligibles casting ballots, Cassel-Melsungen went Socialist by 800 votes out of 45,000.

This propaganda was only an example of what was hoped would be a permanent shift of voting habits among the entire Protestant *Bürgertum*, based on a distinctive combination of political, religious, and moral statements. Reconstituting the old majorities meant not recapturing the SPD vote but reversing the downward trends by attracting all possible followers of this coalition. There had come to be a general conviction among Protestant bourgeois leaders in western and central Germany that their share of the vote was declining because of their inability to mobilize all their potential followers. The assumption was that eligibles who belonged to the Socialist and Catholic social groupings were already highly politicized. Socialist voting required an active affirming commitment, and Catholic males were born and bred into a tight-knit social grouping that demanded the exercise of these commitments at the polls. Such loyalties were generally absent from the supporters of the dominant political coalition. The necessity was to construct commitments that would transform these supporters from apathetic and loosely organized followers into something like affirming voters.

This was the message of a campaign leaflet which the imperial government asked its administrators to help distribute in 1898. The writer of the leaflet asked only for a few simple calculations. He gave the fictitious example of a little village in which 350 out of 500 eligibles had voted in 1893. The result was that the Socialists with 175 votes had nearly gotten the majority. But if all 500 had voted, then the result would have been a severe setback for the SPD by a vote of 325 to 175.[36]

The same kind of deafening logic appeared in an anonymous leaflet used in Württemberg for the 1907 election:

> Three million eligible voters stayed away from the polls in the last election. That was favorable to the Center and the Social Democracy since both these parties denied national feelings on 13 December [by voting against colonial appropriations]. These eligible voters who stayed home belonged neither to the Center nor to the Social Democracy since these already understand how to bring every last man of their supporters to the ballot box.[37]

Or as the *Kreisblatt* in rural Frankenberg, Hesse, stated in 1898:

> The lax views have only up to now come to the good of the Social Democrats that thanks to their discipline can lead all their supporters on to the ballot box. In the election of 1893 the Social Democrats would have scarcely had a tenth of the 46 seats they got in the Reichstag were the elements that are true to the Empire correctly in their place.
>
> Thus man for man on the ballot box! That is our slogan on June 16 [election day]. "The most kingly act of free men" is what the Americans call the act of voting. That is what it is in fact. Giving the vote is not only a right; it is now, under present conditions, a serious duty.[38]

Once the problem was recognized, there were bound to be a whole series of solutions proposed with the wildest of hopes. In 1898 an ex-Prussian minister of justice advocated the direct method. Since pro-government voters tended to be lazy and failed to respond to traditional politics, the government should institute a fine of fifty marks to force them to come to the polls.[39] The *Darmstädter Zeitung* in 1912 suggested that the bourgeois parties would have to be kinder to each other, to "give up the hunt for complete victory," and that the voter himself would have to "understand that his vote is counted not only in its small party camp but also in the greater camp of the bourgeoisie."[40]

All the means for achieving this goal appeared to pale before the dubious allure of plebiscitary elections. The government would dissolve the Reichstag and form a coalition among the parties of the Protestant *Bürgertum*, conduct a campaign for national honor, God, King, and Father-

TABLE 5:3. *Association between Protestant Bourgeois Vote and Selected Characteristics* (N=397 *electoral districts*)

Year	% Protestant	Population Growth 1887–1912 (in %)	Conflict
		Significant Beta Coefficients	
1887	.804	−.123	
1890	.691	−.231	.130
1893	.628	−.235	.172
1898	.520	−.185	.135
1903	.281		.451
1907	.747	−.203	

land, and reap the reward. It apparently worked in both 1887 and 1907, increasing the turnout by 17 percent in the first year and 7 percent in the last, while winning victories at the polls.

These elections were actually different in context from those preceding and succeeding, but they did not lead to permanent changes in the composition of the electorate. The evidence is complex and contradictory, but there are signs that the 1887 and 1907 plebiscitary elections did engender temporary shifts in responses. Compared with other Wilhelmine elections, the strength of the parties of the Protestant *Bürgertum* was much more closely related to the Protestant portion of the population, supposing there was more identification with the Protestant *Bürgertum* in those years. They were the only two elections that did not bring forth significant relationships with conflict, meaning that Protestant *Mittelstand* voters went to the polls regardless of the closeness of the contest because they were more moved by the threat to national prestige and stability at home (see table 5:3).

While the 1887 and 1907 elections were different, neither was a "critical" or realigning contest that changed the direction of turnout and/or fundamentally altered party allegiances. The trend to the SPD was only temporarily halted in 1907. The influx of voters in 1887 was so unusual that it shows up in weak relationships between turnout in that election and all succeeding (see table 5:4). The 1907 turnout was highly correlated with both 1903 and 1912, the banner years of SPD growth, demonstrating no great variation in habitual voting.

In summary, these plebiscitary elections introduced small but not critically important changes in voting habits. The best way to describe the results of 1887 are as aberrant; the best way of viewing the election of 1907 is to consider it as a disturbance of long-term trends vis-à-vis the Socialists and an acceleration of political mobilization among certain

TABLE 5:4. *Correlation Matrix of Turnout for Wilhelmine Elections* (N=397)

Election Year	1890	1893	1898	1903	1907	1912
1887	.640	.581	.427	.474	.549	.395
1890	—	.704	.650	.613	.600	.620
1893		—	.790	.757	.680	.664
1898			—	.844	.663	.734
1903				—	.759	.750
1907					—	.746

groups of the Protestant *Bürgertum*. Taken together, these circumstances show a substantial if not enduring victory for the progovernment coalition. Table 5:5 compares certain elements of turnout from 1898 to 1912. Although the highest turnout figures were present in the small and medium-sized towns, I have chosen to present the extremes of rural and metropolitan areas as a means of demonstrating this fact (all data can be found in table 4:4). The evidence displayed in table 5:5 demonstrates again that there were no dramatic shifts in 1907. The correlation coefficients between turnout and SPD vote are remarkably stable, declining only slightly in 1907. What seems to have happened is that the large increase in turnout in 1903 in the most urbanized areas was matched by an extraordinary increase in 1907 in the rural areas, the holding place for those apathetic followers in the Protestant *Bürgertum*. In 1903 this turnout increase had been part of the SPD surge. The fatherland rhetoric and the strength of the progovernment coalition did halt the growth of the SPD, but only for one election. The surge forward was only delayed until 1912. But just as the progovernment victories of 1907 were interpreted as a sign of the Social Democrats' ultimate weakness, so the SPD victories of 1912 hid the fact that the increases in rural participation among Protestant *Bürgertum* remained substantially intact, only slightly decreasing from the 1907 highs. The statistical support for this scenario is even stronger when smaller units than Reichstag districts are used so as to articulate better the differences between the turnout patterns. The Württemberg data show a negative relationship between the indicators for industrialization and urbanization and turnout for 1907 only, after these associations had been positive for years. The 1912 responses did not return to the previous highs since 1907 permanently mobilized a number of voters from the least urbanized, industrialized, and Socialist areas (see table 5:6).

Plebiscitary politics fostered participation and entailed emotional

TABLE 5:5. *Selected Relations with Turnout for Wilhelmine Elections: 1898–1912*

Election Year	Turnout	Estimated Protestant Turnout	Turnout for Areas of Less than 2,000	Turnout for Areas of More than 500,000	Correlation Coefficient between Turnout and % SPD Vote
1898	68.1	70.9	66.9	66.5	.307
1903	76.1	77.4	77.5	82.9	.314
1907	84.7	86.1	85.2	80.0	.239
1912	84.9	87.2	83.5	84.9	.338

TABLE 5:6. *Correlation between Turnout in Reichstag Elections in Württemberg and Selected Social Characteristics*[41] *(Partial Correlation Coefficients [Controlled for percent Catholic] in Parentheses)*

Characteristic	1898	1903	1907	1912
Population growth 1870–1910	.353(.413)	.440(.457)	−.139(−.088)	.209(.277)
% of work force in commerce and industry	.429(.439)	.399(.388)	−.278(−.346)	.288(.349)
% living in cities above 2,000	.255(.257)	.236(.263)	−.374(−.346)	.179 (.186)
% of vote for SPD	.345	.347	−.366	.179
Turnout in previous election	.801	.819	.567	.198

drives toward unity of the Protestant *Bürgertum*, which could not be sustained. The number of voters permanently mobilized was still far short of a majority and it was impossible to channel them in every election in the most effective manner possible. *Sammlung* or bloc tactics could not be pursued for long periods of time within the Reichstag. Bismarck's coalition broke up by 1890; Bülow's scarcely lasted two years. By 1912 they were divided into many smaller coalitions, sometimes allied with those outside the bloc. The entire base of Protestant *Bürgertum* was itself too small to reconstruct the lost majority. Even at best, such a coalition could rely on the support of 40 percent of the voters into the Weimar period, but this was not a majority.

Protecting the base and searching for the lost majority, these were the reasons why political and governmental elites thought that the Protestant *Bürgertum* coalition needed stronger and more permanent supports like those that contained the nesting loyalties of affirming voters. Some of this was to be found in political associations which proliferated in this period, associations acting sometimes in concert and sometimes on their own. There were plenty of them: the BdL, the Colonial and Naval Leagues, the *Reichsverband*, the Evangelical *Arbeitervereine*, the Christian Book League, the Patriotic Men's Society, as well as countless choral groups and gymnastic societies. I have chosen to discuss the *Kriegervereine* as a model, because they were among the largest of these organizations and clearly represented an almost perfect mix of state loyalties and *Mittelstand* Protestant composition overlaid with fatherland rhetoric.

The German, particularly the Prussian, government was often enthusiastic about the possibility of transforming the soldiers' unions into the spearhead of an anti-Socialist drive. There were a great many veterans in Germany, and almost 2.5 million of them had joined a veterans' association by 1912. They represented a substantial body of men, united at least by the common experiences of soldiering and the *Stammtisch* at the local inn, where they held their regular meetings. These veterans' associations were often German versions of the American Legion, convivial gatherings at which all drank to the emperor and to Sedan. Members generally earned the right to join a burial association and, if lucky, eventually to have a military funeral—a matter of not only financial but moral relief for the family. In return for all this, one made some small accommodation to an ideology that was more vaguely Prussian, even in Württemberg, and Protestant even in Catholic areas. After all, Protestantism and Prussianism have long been tied together in the popular imagination. It was a way of establishing a Protestant *Bürgertum* tone to these organizations, of tying its membership toward the status quo and setting up boundaries against the Catholic and Socialist groupings.

The boundaries against these deviants were well patrolled. The *Kriegervereine* were supposedly nonsectarian, yet they constantly refused to accept Catholics as equals. The leadership especially rejected the idea of an interconfessional oath, even when this was to be used against the SPD. Catholics were supposed to play the role of good Germans, that is, vague Protestants, in their military unions. The national *Kriegervereine* leadership roundly refused the petition of a group of Munich Catholics to found a special Catholic veterans' organization. When Catholics in the Saar transformed a number of their associations into religious as well as veterans' groups, they were kicked out of the Prussian umbrella organization, and the emperor revoked their rights to fly a special flag.

This barrier against Catholicism can be seen clearly in the reactions of the eastern Westphalian leadership to two very different acts by two very different clergymen. The first was the horror of horrors. A Catholic priest was invited to an association meeting in Krwitz in 1912. There he delivered an address to five Protestant women on moral matters; the talk was kept discreetly out of the range of the men, who were typically carousing and singing patriotic songs. Such a simple act caused a regional scandal. The priest had to apologize. After all the veterans' groups were interconfessional; you could not mix religion and association business—unless you were a Protestant. In 1900 it was another matter when the Protestant pastor von Boldenschwingh attacked a number of veterans' groups for carousing at their celebrations. The response was direct and extreme. The *Kriegervereine* leadership in Westphalia was told to stop such acts; celebrating was restricted to only the Emperor's birthday and the founding day of each particular association. The organized veterans were also urged to find new membership in the more respectable portion of the community, schoolteachers and pastors being most prominently mentioned.[42]

Even in their least respectable phase, the *Kriegervereine* membership was *Mittelstand* as well as Protestant, coming from the crafts, independent farming, and the civil service. In the Rhineland there were a number of veterans' unions that were mainly working class, but they were a minority. In Danzig, Danzig-Höhe, and Zoppot (West Prussia), those associations that were predominantly composed of workers were in agricultural areas; therefore, it is almost certain that these workers were agricultural laborers and not an industrial proletariat. The typical Danzig area units were predominantly *Mittelstand* (see table 5 : 7).

Protestant, *Mittelstand*, pro-Prussian, immersed in fatherland rhetoric, if this was not the glue to bind the Protestant *Bürgertum*, what was? Still the results are mixed and equivocal. There was certainly some consciousness-raising on the anti-Socialist front. In numbers alone, the soldiers' unions appeared as a holding company for a national political majority. Even by 1912 in *Regierungsbezirk* Arnsberg, in the heart of the Ruhr, there were five members of a soldiers' union for every dues-paying Socialist. The organized veterans fought the SPD on two fronts. They attempted to slow the growth of Socialism by holding on to their own membership. Thus the soldiers' unions theoretically kicked out all SPD members with loss of burial rights. Moreover, they sought to sustain the moral force of patriotism among the voters in general and uphold the connection between local elites and their potential clienteles. A Socialist pamphlet in Württemberg warned workers about the consequences of joining such an organization. "Militarymen and pastors, *Landräte* and officials, employers and *Ortsvorstehere* decide on the business in these

TABLE 5:7. *Veterans' Union Membership in Danzig County, Danzig-Höhe, and Zoppot (percent distribution)*[43]

Occupational Class	Danzig Leadership 1913 (N=62)	Danzig 128 Reg. 1913 (N=102)	Danzig Uniformed 1913 (N=271)	Karwehrbruch 1912 (N=54)	Dornbeck and Gross Steinwart 1911 (N=65)	Total Listed 1911–1913 (N=1829)
Civil servants	35.7	63.6	19.7	3.7	—	15.5
Teachers	—	—	3.0	1.8	—	2.6
Other professionals	9.7	4.8	3.0	—	—	1.8
Independent farmers	8.3	—	—	50.0	20.0	15.2
(subcategory: those owners ennobled or possessing large estates)	(8.3)					(.05)
Businessmen	6.9	8.6	8.1	3.7	8.8	7.0
Salespeople	16.1	—	3.9	—	—	7.8
Craftsmen	19.1	15.2	47.6	7.4	16.3	29.9
White-collar workers	4.2	—	—	—	—	1.2
Blue-collar workers	—	7.8	7.7	22.3	53.4	15.7
Pensioned	—	—	4.4	11.1	1.5	1.8
Students	—	—	2.6	—	—	1.4
Total	100.0	100.0	100.0	100.0	100.0	99.9

unions and the worker must shout hurrah when he is commanded; he must vote on order and must on order fall on the backs of his comrades at work if they desire to improve their pitiful income."[44]

There is no reason to accept the SPD worries at face value or to think that the various local branches of the soldiers' unions were correct when they took credit for every SPD defeat. Responsible Prussian and Württemberg officials believed that the unions were unsuccessful in undermining SPD strength. In fact, there was some worry about the opposite, that the unions themselves were, in the words of a worried industrialist, "being penetrated by Social Democracy."[45]

Thus even the perfect mix of *Mittelstand*, Protestantism, and the state could not overcome strong social-grouping loyalties based on class. Fatherland rhetoric was almost always the weaker reed when confronted with affirming loyalties of all kinds. In reality, the Protestant *Bürgertum* were strongest in precisely the same areas where liberals thrived—the small towns, the half-modernized areas, the places with a more stable demographic history. Protestant *Bürgertum* organizing would not bring victory to the National Liberals in Bochum. The industrialist money poured into the Evangelical Workers' Union could hardly save the city. It was not so much that Protestant *Bürgertum* culture was being destroyed but that the class lines were hardening with the majority on the other side.[46]

Nor was Protestant *Bürgertum* saved in the electoral district that principally included Siegen County, in the same *Regierungsbezirk*, by the fact that it had a noted and effective deputy, the anti-Semite Adolf Stöcker. Siegerland, in the old Ruhr, had the very prescription for a successful defense of the Protestant *Bürgertum* culture. Although predominantly industrial, its inhabitants felt their prosperity endangered by the giant steel mills to the north and west. In the definition of Helmut Croon, they were old settlers who resented the new Ruhr. Thus Stöcker's victories were a viable expression of a political and social culture that held together. Its strength was mirrored in every statistic. Everything that was true in Bochum and in Dortmund was turned around in Siegen. In the former, Christian Trade Unions were outnumbered by the Socialist aligned labor movement in the ratio of $1:4$ and $1:5$. In Siegerland the ratio was $10:1$ in favor of the Christian Trade Unions. This unity of Protestant culture, Protestant churches, *Mittelstand* organizations and opposition to change certainly affected the vote. In Bochum-Gelsenkirchen the ratio of the percentage of the vote received by the Protestant *Bürgertum* parties to the percentage of Protestants in the district was $1:2$; in Siegen-Wittgenstein, the ratio was $1:1$.[47]

But there were not enough Siegen-Wittgensteins around. A number of Protestant *Bürgertum* leaders would become frustrated with the never-ending and never-successful battle to sustain only a minority position. For these leaders viewed the Protestant *Bürgertum* in terms very near to those of a threatened social grouping. Adolf Stöcker may have soft-pedaled his ideology in his Siegen-Wittgenstein campaign, but he saw the Germany around him in terms of the darkest pessimism. He thought that the Protestant *Mittelstand* was disintegrating under both capitalist and proletarian pressures reinforced by Jewish internationalism. Stöcker's views were only one example of a growing radical sentiment tied to demands for a radical reconstruction of the Protestant *Bürgertum*. Anti-Semites, radical nationalists, and convinced imperialists were all discussing means for transforming fatherland rhetoric into a reality, even if such action involved ungluing its social base and reconstructing the whole national policy along with the society that sustained it. These radical populist approaches are discussed in the next section.

3. Radical Populism

The traditional alliances of Protestant *Bürgertum*, those of religion, *Stände*, and connection to the state, were susceptible to challenge within their own camp for neither resolving the dislocations caused by modernization and industrialization nor fulfilling the needs for a more responsive politics on the local level or constructing a truly noncompromising nationalist policy everywhere. The response was to create more radical solutions, which disrupted the old connections between traditional elites and authorities on one hand and the mass of Protestant *Bürgertum* on the other. These solutions fundamentally altered the nature of political loyalties in a number of instances and, if only for a short time and with limited numbers, constituted movements based on an appreciation of society and politics something like that of an isolated and threatened social grouping.

There were three quite different brands of such radical populism within the Protestant communities of Wilhelmine Germany. The first wave of populism came, as in the United States, as a predominantly rural response to the agrarian depression of the 1880s and 1890s. As in America, this radical populism tended to be both antigovernment and anticapitalism. Such a confounding of authority with capitalism and modernization was not entirely new in Germany nor confined only to the Protestant segment of the population. Yet, in a number of Protestant areas, this populism overturned the nature of Protestant *Bürgertum* politics, causing the permanent rejection of these older elites by a portion of the voters. Old authority was replaced by a new movement that claimed to spring from the "small people" and proposed a better life based on the heady politics of nostalgia and using a campaign rhetoric that attacked most forms of traditional authority combined with at least a mild racism.

This kind of populism could never be more than an experiment. It required unique and dramatic personalities to drive a wedge between the traditional elites and their accustomed followers. Such charismatic leadership was difficult to crystallize into formal structures that would support durable electoral commitments. Thus the more traditional elites were often able to reclaim the districts lost to populism, especially when the economic situation improved in the early twentieth century. However, this new style of politics left its mark on the countryside. Traditional parties might be able to reclaim these districts by accommodating to the demands of a more mobilized and self-aware rural electorate and by adopting some of the styles and programs of the rural populists.

A second form of populism manifested itself in organizations that grew up to meet the needs of a wide range of social groups threatened by accelerated social change in the urban centers. These groups were often characterized as the new *Mittelstand* composed of retailers, commercial clerks, endangered artisans. They were politically mobilized by their fears of change and predictably followed leaders who advocated an aggressive antimodernism often but not always accompanied by anti-Semitism. Their organizations were envisioned as the mass component for a new *Sammlungspolitik* that combined the old and new *Mittelstand* against the Socialists.

The third group of populists consisted of radical intellectuals concerned with the failures of German governments to create viable popular support. They were rooted in the nationalist *Verbände* like the Naval League, the Pan-German League, and the Society for the Preservation of the Eastern Marches. They saw the need for a vital transformation of German politics based on radical ideology that would overturn the old elites and reconstitute not only the leadership but the whole basis of political culture.[48]

The rural populists were the first to reject old-style Protestant *Bürgertum* leadership. They were especially strong in regions of economic and political "backwardness" as defined by the preponderance of small and medium-sized farms, large out-migration, low income levels and low turnout rates in national elections. Anticapitalist, antiaristocratic, even anti-*Mittelstand*, these peasant movements dramatically asserted rural supremacy and were considered dangerous by both the traditional local leadership and the governments in Munich, Berlin, and Darmstadt. The joining of this rural radicalism with political anti-Semitism created an even more disturbing threat to the traditional political structures and was met as such, meaning that these populist movements were immediately given one of the bases upon which affirming voting strength rested. They were self-isolating from the rest of society and labeled as deviant by elites and governments alike.[49]

Populism also accelerated a change in the nature of candidates and electioneering. Political campaigning was already in a state of transformation, but the populist candidates became enduring examples of how to get elected in Wilhelmine Germany without friends or money, without social grouping or organizational support that was not built by an individual. They directly challenged the traditional Reichstag candidates who modeled themselves on the public style of bureaucrats, academics, and other kinds of gentry. These tended to be stiff, formalistic, unable or unwilling to use exaggerated rhetoric or to banter with their constituents. This style of politics was not only dominant in the bourgeois camp, but it was imitated by the Socialist as well. Rosa Luxemburg found her black-suited, high-collared German comrades were not only a disgrace to right doctrine but to the correct Socialist life-style as well.[50]

Within the bourgeois camp, Max Weber was also a critic of excessive formalism. Almost stifled by the formalistic traditions within his own family, Weber generated the concept of charisma to overcome this problem both in his personal life and in public life. Yet Weber and the educated elite he represented remained ambivalent about mass politics. He was personally more comfortable with the elections controlled by those whom he called *Honoratioren*, or local elites. Weber bemoaned the fact that these *Honoratioren* were being replaced by professional politicians, "'experts' in electoral battles."[51] He attributed this change to the increasing demands of electioneering. "The count of speaking engagements that candidates must now hold in every small crossroads in the district, his visits and reports to his constituency there . . . increase constantly."[52] Weber was not alone in his dislike of the give and take of mass politics nor in conceiving electoral battles as onerous. Such perceptions were turned into a powerful argument for proportional representation, a reform that would reduce contests to those between lists and not individuals. Friedrich von Payer, the Württemberg liberal leader, told the Reichstag in 1912:

> I would like to support proportional representation in this house through a practical point of view, that namely the modern electoral agitation that grows stronger with each Reichstag election would be redirected by the introduction of proportional representation. Now the candidate is demanded to exert extraordinary physical and spiritual resources (very right from the Right). In those districts that you already hold, let alone those that must by newly won—We have a number of those who are thusly called (laughter from the Right)—candidates question whether they can physically endure what is demanded from them (very right, Left and Right).[53]

Yet such statements say as much about the *Honoratioren* and their dislike of mass politics as they do about the reality of campaigning. Any agitation would be too much for those who had done very little in the past. The actual demands appear to have been much less than Payer stated. In some areas they were nonexistent; Dortmund-Hörde voters required very little campaigning by the actual candidates. There are only a few records of entire districts canvassed. Theodor Liesching, the young and vigorous Württemberg liberal, made eight speeches in eleven days during the height of a campaign. It was hardly an exhausting schedule. Extreme cases were not the fault of the system. Count Westarp found his superior in the civil service refused him any time off to campaign.[54] This meant that he had to motor at least a hundred miles every weekend during the campaign and attend between ten and twenty meetings on each trip. But campaigns lasted only three weeks and, Weber to the contrary, no one expected the candidate to "work" his district as if he were an American congressman, with periodic visits back home.

Electioneering was an entirely different matter for the anti-Semitic populists. They not only did not, they could not, rely on local elites or electoral bases. Political anti-Semitism was among the first manifestations of professional campaigning and, as such, drew on types of candidates different from the rest of Protestant *Bürgertum*. Anti-Semitic candidates could not model themselves on bureaucrats or local gentry; they required enormous energy to raise money and to "work" the district seriously, and had to have a personality that would draw in campaign workers and bring voters to the polls. Because everything depended on personality, anti-Semitic deputies came from unique backgrounds—sometimes as deviant as that of vegetarians, homosexuals, embezzlers, and sexual athletes.

The man who set the tone for populist anti-Semitism was Otto Böckel, who captured the electoral district Marburg-Frankenberg-Kirchhain, the fifth electoral district of the *Regierungsbezirk* Hesse-Cassel. It was a typical populist backwater district with weak participation before the introduction of Böckel's anti-Semitic campaigns. Hesse-Cassel itself was only annexed to Prussia in 1866, and Marburg city, which had doubled in size between 1866 and 1895, attested to that. The Prussian annexation provided the impetus that transformed the small hill town with its medieval churches, its sixteenth-century university, and its memories of Elizabeth of Hungary and Phillip of Hesse. But Marburg was not typical of a district that was still 75 percent rural. Most of the people lived in small villages of stuccoed and timbered houses (called *Fachwerk*), villages that are picturesque even today. Picturesque but poor described it. It was so poor that people left the area. Outside of Marburg, the population actually declined between the first Hesse-Cassel census in 1834 and the imperial census of 1895. Even with Marburg included, the district population growth was less than 0.4 percent. Rural, Protestant, backward—all of these adjectives summed up the social pattern of the district.[55]

It was no wonder then that the district was safely in the Conservative camp for most of the 1870s and 1880s. But the peasants were over-whelmed by a series of crises in the 1880s, and this changed its political complexion. Dear money, lower prices for their animals, hoof-and-mouth disease, and the new Prussian laws that forced farmers into a more capi-talistic agriculture—all of these pressed hard against a peasantry that had strong rebellious traditions even in the early nineteenth century. In Hesse, particularly in Marburg County, these discontents were soon to be mobi-lized by a young intellectual turned anti-Semite and populist. Otto Böckel was an extraordinary speaker. He promised simple solutions to the prob-lems of peasantry and handwork. Böckel told the peasants that their eco-nomic plight was the result of unscrupulous Jewish middlemen and moneylenders. These Jews were allied with the Berlin stockmarket and were supported by the confiscatory taxes of the Prussian state, which were used to finance the bureaucracy and the army, and, in the unkindest cut of all, to provide subsidies for the *Gutsbesitzer* in the east.

Böckel not only had skills at rhetoric but he also possessed a genius for organization. He founded the Central German Peasants' Union, which had over 400 chapters and 15,000 members by 1890. It was the van-guard of his revolution, holding meetings, spreading the message. The union set up seller cooperatives to attack the problem of the middlemen; it led boycotts of Jewish firms and markets. Böckel's populism was so suc-cessful that in many ways he was, as his opponents claimed, the un-crowned king of Hesse. But voluntarism has its limits. Fundamental reforms require government action. Thus in 1887 Böckel turned aside his earlier prejudices and became a candidate for the seat in Marburg-Frankenberg-Kirchhain. It was an event that would break apart the old system of Hessian politics. Five thousand new voters were mobilized by Böckel's entrance into the contest. The turnout rate increased from 49 percent in 1884 to 75 in 1887. And many of these new voters cast their ballots for the anti-Semite. Böckel won handily; he had become the crowned king of Marburg. His success was soon imitated throughout both Prussian Hesse and in the independent state of Hesse-Darmstadt.[56]

If Böckel represented the strength of populist politics, he also demon-strated its weaknesses. Anti-Semitism started to decline as the bite of the agrarian depression lessened through the 1890s. Without strong nation-wide organizations, all the agrarian populists were on the defensive, con-tinually at the mercy of their own devices. Böckel was especially vulner-able, since he had created a little empire in Hesse that became extremely difficult to finance. He began to take funds from earmarked contributions to keep his enterprises afloat, especially the new presses for his news-paper in Marburg, the *Reichsherold* (Herald of the Empire). Further-more, Böckel became involved in a series of sex scandals, and this lack of character seemed reinforced by the grub-street politicians whom he recruited from outside Hesse. The result was Böckel's expulsion from his own party in 1894 and his self-exile from Hesse, broken only for periodic Reichstag campaigning.

Böckel's problems encouraged a host of candidates to try for the now vulnerable seat in Marburg. In addition to all his other problems, Böckel was charged with both physical and ideological desertion. Even the Centrists, the Socialists, and the Hessian separatists thought they could gain something by running *Zahlkandidaten* in the district in 1898. The Conservatives found an appealing image in General Bartenwerfer, retired, and there was another anti-Semite opponent, Paul Bader. Hellmut von Gerlach moved his political activities from his native east and campaigned under the National Socialist label. There was no reason to believe that a new party would be an insuperable obstacle; after all, it was personality that counted in Marburg-Frankenberg-Kirchhain.

Conservative propaganda pictured the anti-Semites as disturbers and blamed Böckel for upsetting the district, arguing that he had unnecessarily turned the peasants against the large landowners. It proclaimed the Conservatives as the bastion of the state, order, stability, the family, and economic progress, and as the viable alternative solution to all those economic and social problems the anti-Semites had promised to resolve. The Conservatives addressed their literature to all "opponents of the anti-Semites."[57] Böckel's supporters viewed the Conservatives as the core of the anti-Böckel coalition. As one of their broadsides read, "Everything that is Conservative fights with his inheritance and with all means attempts to win back the district which Böckel took away from them in 1887."[58]

There was some truth to this contention. Böckel, after all, did stand against privilege as he saw it, against Jews, stockbrokers, bureaucrats; he opposed the naval bills outright and would vote only for an army budget that taxed the privileged equally with the poor. His literature called him a "radical democrat."[59] It was certainly a descriptive epithet, which he would accept. Yet incumbency had seen some softening. While he may have still labeled himself a democrat, he proclaimed himself by 1898 as loyal to the emperor, supporting Hessian rights and the need for political and economic protection of the *Mittelstand*. One Böckel broadside closed with the following peroration: "Hessian blood lives always. Forward for the emperor and empire, for freedom and the well-being of the people."[60]

For Bader and Gerlach, these statements were a sign of treason to Böckel's old radicalism and thus precipitated an even more dangerous attack by his fellow populists. As a Bader broadside stated, "Have you learned something from the old Böckel? Then you can only now vote for Bader."[61] Another pamphlet went on to list the differences between the old and new Böckel:

Old Böckel	New Böckel
The old Böckel was for secret and direct elections.	The new Böckel will be against this.
The old Böckel was an enemy of the Conservatives. He not only fought the Jews but the great landowners as well.	The new Böckel says nothing about this and is a dependent of the large landowners.
The old Böckel was against taxes on cognac and salt.	The new Böckel will be for these in the future.
The old Böckel was against the fleet.	The new Böckel will be for it.[62]

Or as a stanza from a poem in another Bader pamphlet put it:

> Before he had us all agree
> That *Schnapps* was good for little men;
> Now he answers stone and bone
> That *Schnapps* must more expensive be.
> Since the poor Junker to be without pain
> Must have his fill of caviar and champagne.[63]

The Böckel forces met such attacks by stating that Böckel had not changed, that voting for him meant a continuation of the anti-Semitic revolution in Hesse. As one Böckel leaflet asked:

> Shall Böckel's life work be destroyed?
> No, at no time! No again, and no for a third time!
> Up with the Hessian people's movement![64]

They did not convince everyone, however. Böckel won the seat against the Conservative in the runoff. The margin of victory was very narrow; it was less than 600 votes. Moreover, the whole campaign had seemed to confuse the electorate. The turnout rate in 1898 declined to 58 percent, 16 points below that of 1893. Many eligibles just stayed at home rather than make the decision about Böckel's true identity. Gerlach, especially, took heart from these results. Böckel had so personalized electoral campaigns that odd candidates with strange views might really succeed in the district. Gerlach went about making himself well known after 1898. He bought a newspaper in Marburg; he set up local organizations; most important, he continuously visited the villages. In a district where personality counted, this went a long way toward building his victory in 1903. But Gerlach could not succeed anymore than Böckel in following the example of numerous American congressmen who built absolutely safe constituencies on the basis of their own personality.[65]

Böckel's personalized populism left an imprint on Hessian politics that had nothing to do with economic need. His personalization of politics turned every election into an unwelcome contest with unpredictable results. Moreover the effect of personality might be geographically as well as temporally limited. Thus Gerlach won in Marburg city and Marburg County where his media blitz had an effect. He lost Frankenberg County, the rural stronghold, by a large margin to an assorted bunch of anti-Semites. This was enough to win the election in 1903 but less than sufficient to win the runoffs of 1907 and 1912.[66]

It was the weakness of anti-Semitic populism. The way out was shown by another anti-Semite, Liebermann von Sonnenberg, who had captured the neighboring district of Fritzlar-Homberg-Ziegenhain in 1890. At first a close ally of Böckel, Liebermann had gone his own way. By 1898 he was criticized as a traitor by the Böckel literature, which stated, "Liebermann is a conservative in his bones."[67] For once, Böckel was partially right; Liebermann had become an ally of conservative elites. He saw what lay ahead. Agrarian prices were rising; the lot of the pig farmers was improving. The Hessian anti-Semitic movement could survive good agrarian times after 1900 if it moved away from its earlier radical attacks on the state. Liebermann negotiated with the BdL for support, stood firmly for king and country. He waged a brand of anti-Semitic *Mittelstand* politics, promising to protect the Protestant *Bürgertum* culture against its enemies. Thus he was returned with over 70 percent of the vote in most elections. In fact, he lost only the urban areas of the district in 1907. This mattered very little in a district that was over 85 percent rural. Liebermann then was the recipe for continuing in office. He defended the barricades of the Protestant *Bürgertum*. Since his district had only a few Catholic and even less Socialist voters, this defense was enough to keep him in his seat. Only his death in 1911 lost the district. Böckel, the intellectual, the ideologue, the genuine political personality, went from bad to worse. Contesting Marburg in 1912, he got fewer than 2,500 votes, less than one-third of his majorities in the 1890s.

Böckel and his even more disreputable Prussian followers were scarcely the quintessential charismatic politicians that Weber had in mind. The man who most nearly filled this bill was Friedrich Naumann, who attempted to extend Protestant *Bürgertum* by allying it with working-class needs under an umbrella of social and democratic reforms with support for imperialism and eventually a total break with anti-Semitism. Despite Naumann's enormous popularity as a political orator and the immense crowds he drew, his kind of liberal renewal was losing rather than gaining popularity among the artisans, small businessmen, and salespeople whose fears about their economic future could not be satisfied with a vague reform platform. Even in Frankfurt, a democratic bastion and the scene of his greatest personal rhetorical triumphs, Naumann's influence was submerged by the union of a *Mittelstand* movement and political anti-Semites.[68]

These political changes in Frankfurt were a mirror of long-term trends throughout Germany. Symptomatic of these events was the transformation of the political loyalties of master artisans who had been almost uniformly radical democrats in 1850 and were split into radical populists and left-wing liberal factions by the turn of the century. Many of these master artisans believed themselves squeezed economically on one hand by large-scale enterprises in manufacturing, distribution, and sales, and on the other by increasing wage demands from their employees. Their answer was to create protective associations, particularly the *Allgemeine Deutscher Handwerkerbund*, which demanded salvation through government restrictions on competition, especially through increased taxation of department stores and the reintroduction of entrance requirements in certain occupations. These protective associations achieved some successes but not enough to quell the unsettled condition of the workplace. This in turn reinforced their belief in the general retrogression of society or their increasing distrust of liberal leaders who favored free trade and lack of restrictions on commerce and industry.

The last decades of the Wilhelmine era saw these antimodern artisans joined by other large groups, lower-ranking civil servants, white-collar workers, and retailers of all kinds. The flurry of economic organization among the lower middle classes was truly remarkable. Even the salespeople joined the rush. By 1913 the Association of Commercial clerks had 127,000 members; the German National Commercial Assistants Association had 148,000. Salesclerks and independent artisans were not necessarily complementary occupational groups with precisely the same interests, but they shared one thing: a fear that the increasing complexities of economic existence and the increasing size of economic units were to their disadvantage. They were thus united in policies that retarded economic modernization and that lapsed into nostalgic fantasies of a better organized and more secure past existence which became overlayed with anti-Semitic belief and action. The marriage of these diverse groups was consummated in the *Reichsdeutscher Mittelstandsverband*, which was founded in 1911. Definitely to the Right, definitely anti-Semitic, the new association embarked immediately upon a political goal, sending all prospective Reichstag candidates a questionnaire that inquired into their views on government regulation. It elicited a favorable response among almost all conservatives, anti-Semites, and Centrists, but it did little else. The union was too recently organized to have an effect on the 1912 election commensurate with the numbers in the protective associations that sustained it. The union's principal effect would come in the next decade.[69]

However, such organizations are not necessarily to be judged merely for the enthusiasms engendered in electoral politics. They were well on the road to a new kind of popular politics, especially when the economy worsened after the 1912 election. Their messages satisfied both the economic and cultural needs of a mass agglomeration. The antiliberal *Mittel-standspolitik* focused on the object of all artisan-retailer hatred, the Jewish-owned department stores—the perpetual conjoiners of economic and cultural fears.

A meeting of two hundred anti-Semitic members of the Protestant *Bürgertum* which took place in Dortmund in December 1912 illustrates this new-style politics. The speakers advocated a boycott of the department stores, 94 percent of which they claimed were in Jewish hands. Women were to be discouraged from going into the central city so as to avoid the temptation of shopping in big stores. A leaflet was distributed urging the populace to remember that Christmas was a Christian holiday and to buy accordingly. "Father! Mother! Begin your national duty as you search for your children's presents."[70]

The *Reichsverband* was only one of the groups that joined the last attempt at recreating Protestant *Bürgertum* politics. The *Kartell der Schäffenden Stände*, Cartel of the Productive Estates, pursued a *Sammlungspolitik* based on an agrarian/heavy-industry alliance. Like the *Hansabund*, the *Kartell* was organized in response to specific events. The election of 1912 had raised the fear of increased working-class militancy; the worsening economic situation at the end of 1912 and through 1913 substantially increased protectionist demands. Even the finished-goods industry abandoned its heretofore more tolerant stand toward working-class rights and its antitariff policies; the *Bund der Industriellen* was ready to join the alliance against Socialism and to seek protection for German industry endangered by a general downturn in the world markets. Thus big and medium-sized business were united with the BdL in demanding more protection. The *Kartell* not only consolidated the public viewpoints of the business community, but it sought to create a mass base by financing the *Mittelstand* organization and encouraging their participation as well as accepting the aid of bourgeois national populists from the Pan-German and Naval Leagues, the German Book League, the Eastern Marches Society, and so forth.

Geoff Eley correctly identifies this last group as crucial to the coalition, especially the Pan-German League, which had engineered the construction of the *Kartell*. But the middle-class intellectual workers who came to dominate the various radical *Verbände* had little desire to solve the needs of various interests. The *Kartell* was only an instrument in their campaign. Their main concern was to save a nation they believed to be in dissolution. The answer to cultural pessimism and the loss of bourgeois centrality was not the resolution of economic conflicts but the creation of a sense of mystical identity with the nation, an identity that often went hand in hand with a virulent anti-Semitism.

These radical nationalists sought to replace the older version of Protestant *Bürgertum* with a new populism, a fierce nationalist ideology that should be communicated to the white-collar workers of the new *Mittel-stand*. They were committed practitioners of a propaganda machine which published innumerable leaflets, sent out large numbers of lecturers, set up one slide show or evening of films after another. Their message was simple: advocating the necessity of nationalist expansion within and without Germany. And by 1913 they found a receptive climate for their views. Their programs seemed very proper when the government appeared to be failing in both its domestic and foreign policies. Eley describes the transition to populist politics:

> Thus the more pragmatic conservatives like Bülow laid down the rather modest objective of a united nationalist front which drew its common purpose from the principle of anti-Socialism, but took practical cognisance of the divergent sectional interests to which individual parties were committed—"the pairing of the conservative with the liberal spirit" on the "basis of national questions," as he once put it. The most radical spirits on the right, by contrast, wanted much more than this. They resented the tactical accommodation of sectional interests for what they saw as the lowest common denominator of nationalist commitment. The latter should be dominant and overridingly proclaimed in all its purity, rather than diluted by messy domestic agreements. The nationalist appeal should be wielded aggressively, slicing through the empty phrases of party politicians, fixing the public eye on "real issues" and not the selfish trivia of the "cattle-trading in the Reichstag" . . . radical nationalism also entailed a populist commitment—a systematic appeal to the people, not just as a formality of public agitation, but as a constructive ideological assault just on the old order, its parliamentary practices and forms of legitimacy.[71]

This brand of national populism appeared upon firmer ground. Unified and financed by economic interests, possessed with a strong set of cultural and nationalist symbologies, advocating a return to both nostalgic and classless politics, these national populists appeared able to create something like an affirming voting pattern among the Protestant *Bürgertum*. But such a movement would take time, more time than any temporary alliance of economic interests such as the *Kartell* would give it. There was no reason to suspect that agrarian and small and large business interests would remain united for the more than a few years that would be necessary to undermine the still formidable strength of traditional elites.

Still, the national populist propagandists were well on their way to turning at least part of an old majority into some new political form during and after the war. The Fatherland party founded in 1917 was such a radical nationalist populist attempt. There was, of course, some reconnection of these ideas with antidemocratic movements in the Weimar Republic, but they could never be properly reconstituted without a monarchical center; still, they were transformed and amalgamated into an inheritance that to a certain extent propelled the National Socialists and provided a tradition that they could rely upon to draw followers into their net.

6

THE COMMON RESPONSE

Cleavage, contradiction, conflict—all called forth negative images to the contemporary German mind, yet these same divisions produced the high turnout and other evidence of strong participation that seemed to indicate massive involvement of Germans in the system. A perception of threat from or dislike of others, a feeling of isolation or of the need to isolate, propelled eligibles to the polls regardless of divergence in socioeconomic status and spatial location, and caused the activation of the disenfranchised, of females and the young. This articulation of differences overcame unresponsiveness and parochial views of citizenship through varying combinations of *Mittelstand* morality, nationalist rhetoric, and strong affirming loyalties among deviant or self-labeled deviant social groupings. It alone produced similar strong and vibrant reactions that created a national electoral system characterized by very narrow differences in turnout and other levels of participation based on class, region, and religious and social groupings. In other words, it created the common response.

1. Narrowing Class Differences

The difficulties of using turnout for cross-national comparisons make simple conclusions impossible. Yet one thing seems certain in comparing socioeconomic distinctions in Wilhelmine voting behavior with the American experience. The wider the pool of nonvoters, the greater the effect socioeconomic status has on the decision to participate. Since large pools of nonvoters in Wilhelmine Germany were on the way to being eliminated, their existence constituted a transitional stage, the lag-end of a surge rather than the state of massive, permanent nonvoting that has characterized American voting behavior in the twentieth century.

This can be demonstrated in a number of ways. Although the medium-sized towns had higher turnout rates than either metropolitan or rural centers in every election after 1898, this lead in turnout decreased as other areas were able to mobilize voters. Over time the small towns lost their earlier advantages. Initially, unlike rural areas, they had a high enough level of communication to facilitate the distribution of political information. At the same time they had not experienced the atomization and disaffiliation from social groupings that made the transmission of information difficult in large cities. These differences in transmission, that is, political education, had already disappeared in many areas as the result of affirming voting or strong conflicts. In other areas, this transitional stage was maintained for a number of years (see table 4 : 4).[1] Some of this loss of differentiation was due to social forces, as argued below. But obviously, if everyone votes, all socioeconomic differences disappear.

Ziegenhain County, Hesse, was an area of transition. It was predominantly Protestant as well as rural and thus immune to politicization caused by affirming deviant social groupings. The district that encompassed the county was a typical bastion of Protestant *Bürgertum*, which initially responded with a short-lived enthusiasm for populist anti-Semitism, but by 1893 had relapsed into a relatively low turnout. Patterns in Ziegenhain seem to fit American and British theories on voting behavior, which explain differences in voting by socioeconomic status and the accompanying differential accumulation of political values. The premise is that the most favored go to the polls and the least favored stay at home. Participation is actually higher for those who are rewarded by society, who feel they have accrued actual economic and/or political benefits. The rewarded often take pride in the act of voting and are inclined to believe in the efficacy of their acts. These eligibles will invest what little it takes to gain the necessary information to vote in their interest. In contrast, the unrewarded see no reason to learn or to vote, reaping few benefits from the system and expecting that state of affairs to continue.[2]

The best measure of rewards is socioeconomic status, conventionally measured by income, education, and occupation. But the only indicator available historically is occupational status, an imprecise measure even in its contemporary setting. The task of demonstrating status differentiation is also complicated by the disparate nature and unavailability of useable data. Moreover, each preserved data set often requires a different mode of analysis, limiting comparability. Still, even with such problems, the Ziegenhain data seem to present a very clear profile of occupationally stratified categories as determinant of voting behavior. The results displayed in table 6 : 1 show that those with high status occupations such as professionals were twice as likely to vote as were the lowest status groups such as unskilled workers, mostly day laborers. Farmers and tradespeople (those engaged in commerce and trade) both had higher turnout rates than skilled workers, who would probably be considered as having lower social status. Further, a higher proportion of skilled workers went to the polls than unskilled workers. There are problems with drawing such fine

TABLE 6:1. *Voters in Ziegenhain Sample for Reichstag Election, 1893*[3]

Occupational Class	N	% of Eligibles Voting
Free professionals	97	97.2
Civil servants	51	86.2
Farm proprietors and occupiers	27	76.3
Engaged in trade and commerce	226	78.8
Skilled workers and craftsmen	730	62.9
Unskilled workers	380	49.2
Others	37	48.6
Total	1,730	

distinctions when it is difficult to transfer precisely occupational classifications into a status hierarchy. A number of farmers were not much better off than unskilled workmen; the tradespeople category includes both
shopkeepers and salesclerks, innkeepers and peddlers. Yet these occupational listings do have some connection with reality in the small towns
and villages that constitute the sample. They were drawn up by the township (*Gemeinde*) clerk, who knew all of the eligibles in question. In these
cases, occupational designations came closer to a conferred status. Day
laborers were less likely to be allowed to call themselves independent proprietors in such a situation; the township clerk would have changed the
record on anyone who did not pass muster as a legitimate peasant in his
eyes and presumably the eyes of the community as well. That this measurement is to some extent based upon a perception of status does not
reduce its validity. On the contrary, it underpins the premise that we are
dealing with real status differences here rather than twentieth-century
concoctions.

The socioeconomic status differentiation in Ziegenhain turnout rates
was most often the consequence of relatively low rates of politicization in
a "backward" area as measured in terms of conflict and the possibilities
for constructing affirmative social-grouping politics. Another factor that
delayed the surge to a high turnout district in the 1890s was the persistence of scars resulting from the annexation of the area into Prussia in
1866. This annexation caused differential benefits and thus differing responses among the various social groups in the province. It benefited the
free professionals and the "free enterprisers" while causing great anxiety
and some hardship among the artisan groups, particularly those joining
the labor force at that time. Rapid changes of status at the time of the
individual's entry into the political culture are likely to have a permanent

TABLE 6:2. *Voters in Selected Occupational Classes by Age Cohort,*
Ziegenhain Reichstag Election, 1893 (in percent of eligibles voting)[4]

Age Cohort	Unskilled Workers Residing in Places with Populations over 1,000 (N=169)	Skilled Workers (N=730)	Total (N=1,730)
25–30	43.6	62.8	60.9
31–40	50.9	66.3	66.9
41–50	41.2	56.2	65.7
51–60	51.9	69.3	68.4
Over 60	43.7	52.4	56.3

effect on his behavior, including his propensity to vote. This is demonstrated by the unexpected downturn in the turnout among all skilled
workers and unskilled town workers in the age cohort 41–50 (see table
6:2). This age cohort theoretically should be at the high point of the
curve, since younger and older eligibles tended to participate at lower
rates because of insufficient social integration on the one hand and problems with health and agility on the other.

Many of these aforementioned workers would have been apprentices
when Prussia annexed Hesse-Cassel, the state that formerly held sover-
eignty over Ziegenhain. One of the first acts of this new Prussian administration was to turn these apprentices out into the free market without
their old guild supports. These former apprentices had no political organization to welcome them except the weak and middle-class oriented
Hessian party; thus, they may have become apathetic rather than mobilized by their economic crisis, bereft of their belief in the beneficence of
government and the efficacy of political action. Those small artisans who
remained under the new rules never felt secure and were further disen-
chanted by the economic and social pressures of the 1880s and 1890s.
According to a recent study, they were inclined to view the pre-annexation
period as a golden age and never really became accommodated to the
new competitive post-1866 world.[5]

But the artisans and workers of Ziegenhain County would not present
these aberrant patterns forever. Eventually the rates of politicization as
measured by turnout would rise among those with lower socioeconomic
status, and those artisan and worker groups turned off by the system
would die off. The real wave of the future was in places like Dortmund
and Dresden, where turnout rates already approached or exceeded 90
percent. In contrast with Ziegenhain, Dortmund city in Westphalia was a

capitalist archetype, containing a high level of conflict, leading to high levels of turnout and other forms of participation (see chapter 9). By 1903 blue-collar eligibles were disposed to vote at levels comparable to the middle class. An ecological correlation between turnout and several social variables in the forty-six voting precincts in Dortmund city demonstrates no significant associations between occupational splits and turnout. The correlation coefficient between turnout and percentage working class was .074, between turnout and percentage middle class −.070.[6] It is true that an aggregate comparison is less precise than the actual count that was available in Ziegenhain; however, any trend as strong as in the former area would seem bound to show up in the statistical associations.

The same process of increasing homogeneity was present in Dresden in 1907, another high turnout area. Table 6:3 compares the proportion of Dresden nonvoters in various occupational groups with the actual proportion of these groups in the total male labor force. The results show some similarities with the Ziegenhain data; both areas had an overrepresentation of professionals and civil servants at the polls, although much of this was caused by heightened pressures on civil servants to vote in this plebiscitary election. But then the data diverge. Skilled and unskilled workers made up about the same proportion of the total labor force in each area; yet in Ziegenhain 76 percent of the nonvoters were workers while the corresponding figure for Dresden was around 55 percent. It is possible that very gross countervailing tendencies can be hidden within the Dresden data. For example, a similar study of Austrian voting shows large variations in turnout between owners of large and small businesses as well as among workers employed by these firms. Such differences would be hidden in table 6:3. The self-employed category is definitely ambiguous, since it includes both street peddlers and bankers. Still the general trend in Dresden is just as certain as that of Dortmund, and the melting of class differences is just as apparent.

TABLE 6:3. *Turnout by Occupational Class, First Reichstag Election, Dresden, 1907*[7]

Occupational Class	Proportion of Total Nonvoters Who Are in This Class	Proportion of Total Work Force in This Class
Professionals and civil servants	8.1	10.6
Self-employed in industry and trade	13.6	13.5
Workers	54.7	55.6
Unemployed and pensioners	9.0	8.8

2. The Disenfranchised

The process of electoral mobilization in a high-turnout system penetrates into areas that were heretofore immune from politics. Elections lose their exclusively "public" flavor and become even more entangled with the ways and institutions of everyday life. The common experiences become more common, more visible through the whole society, applying as in the Wilhelmine case even to nonvoters such as women and youths. As inevitable and powerful as were these processes of politicization, they were not necessarily greeted with enthusiasm by the electorate as a whole or by the political leadership in general. A full political socialization was not only a sign of family involvement that fortified the male at the ballot box; it could be something more, the attribution of equal citizenship roles to those of disenfranchized and socially inferior status. For this reason the process of politicizing the disenfranchised was undertaken often gingerly and with trepidation. Yet, in the end, there was no way out. Women were needed in the electoral battles, and the continuation of the natural apolitical trend among the young was considered as an invitation to their politicization by enemy forces; to forgo political agitation in the home was to open similar opportunities for your political opponents.

The clash of political needs and traditional values of citizenship was particularly striking in the politicization of women. I do not mean to imply that most Wilhelmine Germans favored universal suffrage for both males and females. The opposite was probably true. Bourgeois politicians of both sexes were generally lukewarm or opposed to the idea. What was important, then, was not the culmination of the suffrage movement but the eventual, albeit grudging, realization among all parties that even disenfranchised women had a political role. Close elections and the needs of affirmers both made it difficult to exclude any group from electoral politics. The result was most often a marvelous balancing act between the prejudices of male leaders and their supposed needs in electioneering. It was neither fish nor fowl, neither policy nor direction.

Only the Left unambiguously supported women's suffrage. And then the situation was clouded by the disagreements among left-wing liberals. Left-wing liberals were seriously divided; many tended to become suspicious about such suffrage extension while they were members of the Bülow bloc. It was not until female suffrage was enshrined in the Progressive party platform of 1910 that they appeared united on the issue. This is in sharp contrast to the Socialists, who had favored extension of the franchise from the 1880s. Apart from real moral commitments, the Left had hoped to benefit from the extension of suffrage. It was all in vain as the conservative women voters in Weimar would attest.

In fact the whole bourgeois women's suffrage movement had turned to the Right by the end of the Wilhelmine period. After 1908 the German

Union for Women's Suffrage, *Deutscher Verband für Frauenstimmrecht*, abandoned its earlier democratic and feminist positions and advocated property qualifications for voting. This was seconded by the conservative Alliance for Women's Suffrage. Only the left-wing German Women's Suffrage League, *Deutscher Frauenstimmrechtsbund*, favored extending the vote to all women, and this was the smallest of the three organizations. The fear of a deluge of Socialist women voters could be just as powerful a motive for bourgeois females as the worry about those SPD males trooping to the ballot boxes was for their male counterparts.

It was not the distant goal of enfranchisement but the immediate uses of women politically that really troubled the parties. Should they use women for agitation and propaganda or not? The SPD was, as always, the most anxious to utilize any displaced group; women could be useful even if they were disenfranchised. Louise Zietz in Dortmund, Klara Zetkin in Stuttgart, and Rosa Luxemburg everywhere were effective election propagandists, even if they could not vote or hold office. As early as 1903 there were large numbers of Social Democratic women campaigners in Westphalia. And after 1908, when women were first allowed to join political parties, they became an important factor in the party organizations. Before 1908 the separate Socialist Women's Educational Union had only a small membership, but by 1912 fully 20 percent of the Social Democrats in Dortmund-Hörde were women. This massive organizational effort obscured the conflict between women's rights and the cultural biases of most German Socialists. These biases tended to undermine both symbolic and practical attempts to change the position of women in the working-class world. The general contempt with which women industrial workers were held by their male counterparts did not aid the attempts to unionize women. Despite the fact that Socialist working women generally seemed to have more traditional views than their male coworkers, women workers were considered as inclined toward immorality, the only safe position for women being in the home. This was certainly the place of the wives of Socialist leaders who continued to uphold the image of the faithful helpmate and kept the traditional feminine skills and *Mittelstand* values.[8]

It was not a new world view that drew women into Wilhelmine politics; it was the need to mobilize all potential politicizing forces for elections and other purposes. This need caused often contradictory responses. The Center, the Conservatives, and most National Liberal leaders were opposed to politicizing women intensively in the SPD model. "What kind of women do we want?" asked one speaker at a Catholic workers' conference. "Do we want women like Klara Zetkin and Rosa Luxemburg? They are not to our taste nor to that of many Socialists either."[9] Yet the same speaker went on to illustrate the possibilities of engaging women in politics as an adjunct to their traditional roles. He argued that if all the good

Catholic wives would force their husbands to vote Center, the Center seats would increase by half. The same theme was repeated in the Protestant *Bürgertum* press. Conservatives winced at the possibilities of a politicized womanhood, yet they had every reason to believe that women were a necessary force for stemming the democratic and socialist tide. As one conservative women's magazine stated: "We live in a time of religious and political disintegration. The progressive democratizing of our people is slowly but surely killing the patriotic spirit, the religious and family loyalties; it is gradually burying all society. . . . It is therefore our holy duty to avoid the terrible downfall of our nation and, for this reason, we need our best helpers in the front line. We need OUR WIVES!"[10]

The response of the non-Socialist parties was the direct result of this conflict between immediate political needs and long-term prejudice. Most German parties organized women with a characteristic ambivalence. They moved, but they moved slowly and weakly. It was not until 1910, then, that the Center took the first tentative steps and admitted women into the *Windthorst Bund*. In the next few years the Center and the National Liberals would create a few separate women's branches. They proved failures. Bourgeois women were as reluctant to enter separate organizations as their Socialist counterparts. Women remained remote from the life of these parties and from politics in general. In particular I can find no instances of a woman every attending a Centrist political rally although some had crowds greater than one thousand. The apex of all these systematic attempts at simultaneous politicization and exclusion was the Union of Conservative Women, which was founded in 1913. Its charter provided that its membership would confine their interests to women's issues such as welfare, a very popular notion by then even in prosuffrage circles.

The same fears about too much politicization applied to young males. Of course, they were to be eventually politicized, but originally bourgeois politicians thought to retard this process until maturity or at least to the age of voting at twenty-five. But the process of politicization could not be contained, and this caused serious worries, particularly that adolescent males might desert the family fold in more ways than one. The Right was particularly frantic. Rightest journals would complain, "how easy it is, at the present time, to poison the souls of our children."[11] The Socialists as well sought to sustain the loyalties of children from Socialist families. All agreed that the key to the struggle was the impressionable age between the time the boy left school, generally at fourteen, until his entrance into the army at around twenty. Each side desired to gain control over "the physical and moral education"[12] of the youth as the key to channeling future political constellations.

The Socialists were at a serious disadvantage in these battles since the presence of youth in political parties was regulated by unfriendly governments. Until 1907 only Baden, Bremen, Hamburg, Hesse, and Württemberg allowed any young men to join political associations. Prussia was added to this category in 1907, but all such state laws were superseded by the 1908 federal statute on associations, which forbade the inclusion of anyone under eighteen in a political party. At first the law was enforced only at the discretion of the local police, but in 1911 the Prussian High Court declared all Socialist youth groups illegal, and other states followed suit if they had not already done so. The party was forced to reconstruct the youth movement into a bloodless sport and educational endeavor. Yet this act was not enough to bottle up the hounds. Thus even the relaxed officials in Württemberg would refuse to sanction many activities of reconstructed Socialist youth groups after 1908. And what the governments did not do to depoliticize the youth movement, the Socialist party leadership would accomplish itself. The moderate party leadership was anxious lest these groups be taken over by radicals and, therefore, did little to encourage their growth. It was no wonder that the SPD youth groups seemed so blatantly dull. As Otto Bauer stated, "The youth in the bourgeois youth movement have a feeling of greater freedom and independence, of being much less directed, than with us. They might be more controlled and more bound, but they don't consider it so." [13]

If there was any real politicization of youth it took place in the bourgeois youth groups. These bourgeois groups remained untouched by the police. The federal government itself would encourage the formation of the *Bund der Jungdeutschland* as a cover organization for all bourgeois-patriotic youth groups. While the Socialist youth groups were kept under constant surveillance, state officials had no trouble in certifying as unpoliticial any group that stated its purpose as the "upholding of the fatherland spirit." [14] Württemberg officials accepted unquestioningly the alleged unpolitical nature of journeymen's associations, church youth groups, and the like. Yet no one doubted that political purposes were among their major objectives. The Catholic organ in Stuttgart, the *Deutsches Volksblatt*, was only proclaiming the obvious when it contended that "the Red youth movement can be best fought through a strong-willed and self-conscious bourgeois youth movement that serves religious as well as educational needs." [15] It is impossible to estimate whether these aims were actually achieved, but there can be no question of motives.

Women, the young, then even the sacred portals of the German home would be threatened. In 1911 the Frankfurt police president called attention to the threat posed by SPD members going from house to house systematically gaining political intelligence and recording it all in little notebooks. In Württemberg in 1914, 274 out of the 304 SPD election committees engaged in some sort of house visitation program. The *Volksstimme*, the SPD organ for Frankfurt, declared, "We cannot rely totally on meetings for elections, but we imitate our opponents and visit the

voter in his place of residence."[16] The connection was thus complete, if
only tenuously established: from the affirming nests to politics and back
again, to family, the young, women, the foundations of the common
responses.

3. Overcoming Regionalism

The common response did not overcome regional differences in political
loyalties. German Conservatives were in essence a regionally based party;
the Center was dominant in those Catholic strongholds in the west and
south. The National Liberals and the SPD suffered from intraparty regional disputes. Recent work by Karl Rohe and Peter Steinbach, among
others, has demonstrated that various regions lagged behind the national
trend in creating viable class cleavages and meaningful interest politics.
However these regional variations in issues and cleavage formation did
not necessarily affect levels of participation, that is, the common response. To be sure, the rate of political mobilization varied from region to
region, from center to periphery, but the regional differences in turnout
and other forms of participation had considerably narrowed after 1890,
and in many instances, they had disappeared, at least according to the
evidence based on four regions: one east of the Elbe, one south of the
Main, one each for western and north-central Germany.

If Protestant districts tended to have greater political conflict, large
geographic areas that were almost entirely Protestant might possibly accelerate this effect. Thus beta coefficients for conflict and turnout were
higher in central Germany than those for the rest of the country. The
same intensified association is documented for the relationship between
the percentage that were Catholic and turnout in the predominantly
Catholic south. There the beta coefficients are generally more negative
than those for the rest of Germany. The major aberrations from the national trend, especially the Rhenish response of 1912, and the lowered
turnout in the German Conservative areas of the east have already been
discussed.

The usefulness of tables based on these regional differences is debat-
able. (1) The difficulties in dealing with statistical data nationwide are
multiplied severalfold when the data are broken up into geographic subgroups. These subgroups may be even more artificial than the nationwide
category. (2) The best means for categorizing these subgroups might not
provide the data base necessary for analysis. (3) The dominance of Prussia in both area and population skews regional effects, since Prussia composed over two-thirds of the empire and was spread through a number of
regions. The south presents a different problem, since this region contained three or four states whose countervailing effects could run counter

to regional or national trends. (4) The more times statistical data are manipulated, the greater the danger of error. This is especially true when the
strength of parties varies so much regionally. (5) The multiparty nature of
Wilhelmine politics makes it impossible to adopt techniques developed
for use in two-party systems.[17]

The most clearly ascribable regional variations were rooted in the inequalities of the federal system. The differing electoral laws caused very
different responses in turnout at the state level (see chapters 2 and 10).
There were also a few responses caused by asynchronous political developments. The movement of Württemberg Catholics into the political system
was such a case. Protected from the abuses of the *Kulturkampf* and feeling themselves a minority incapable of affecting state politics, Württemberg Catholics were not drawn out of their apathy by the new political
Catholicism of the 1870s and 1880s. Thus even as late as 1893, the association between the percentage that were Catholic and the turnout rate
for Reichstag elections in Württemberg was considerably more negative
than it was for the Reich as a whole. By the end of the 1890s, however,
the continuous, hard organizing efforts of Württemberg Catholic leaders
had begun to take effect. The result was a distinctly more positive trend
in the association of the percentage Catholic and turnout. The constitution of 1906 both abolished the privileged minority position of Catholics
in the lower house and the rights of clergy in elementary education. Either reform would have been enough to stimulate a storm of protest followed by the concomitant increased turnout in predominantly Catholic
areas. Church questions might be state issues, yet threats at the state level
propelled Württemberg Catholics into national elections as well as causing that remarkable association between turnout and the percentage
Catholic in 1907 (see table 6:4).[18]

In the end, even this phenomenon was overcome by the strength of
nationwide forces. The Württemberg association was only narrowly and
insignificantly positive in 1912; the beta relationshp had even turned
negative although it was just as insignificant. The powerful nationwide
phenomenon of politicization was too strong to succumb totally to peculiarities of state politics. Thus like regionalism and class, state loyalties
presented no insuperable obstacle to the creation of a unified response to
the stimuli that drove voters to the polls.[19]

In fact, Württemberg illustrates the ideal whereby state and national
trends reinforce each other, creating a politicized electorate at all levels.
At first the Württembergers' interest in state elections was almost as great
as in the national. Not all Württembergers were pleased with the national
unification. This trend of strong interest in state elections continued
throughout the period of constitutional reform, which also, by the way,
abolished the small-property-tax requirement heretofore tied to suffrage
at the state level.

TABLE 6:4. *Association between Turnout in Reichstag Elections and Percentage Catholic*

Year	Correlation Coefficient r	
	Württemberg	Nationwide
1893	−.447	−.253
1898	−.030	−.321
1903	.230	−.222
1907	.737	−.210
1912	.158	−.446

The result was to create strong habitual voters in both state and national elections. Even when Württemberg dropoff rates increased, they were still the lowest in the big states of the south (see table 6 : 5), fully half that of Baden and Bavaria and a third that of Hesse. High national turnout and low dropoff indicate that habituated vote discussed in chapter 2, making Württemberg the primary example of one alternative for state politics within the German national system.

4. The Nationalization of Campaign Styles

Some set of common inputs was required to produce the common response in campaigning among all types of candidates, in the relationship of elected deputies to their districts, in the ways in which local interests, styles, ways of doing business were encompassed within affirming loyalties and *Bürgertum* politics. Too much localism would tear the system up into never-ending and meaningless contests; too little localism would break the contacts of communication, the vital links by which ideas and emotional commitments are transmitted.

As nearly always, this problem was compounded by the special circumstances of electoral politics in the Wilhelmine era. Thus the German deputy neither became the representative of a nationwide elite controlling nationwide parties as was the case with the British M.P., nor did he emerge as the spokesman for a triumphant local coalition as American congressmen often did. Nor was he that ineffable compromise, the French deputy, who served as a reliable representative of local interests whether he supported the government or was in opposition. In German states, these functions were performed by bureaucracies, who not only carried through orders from the top but successfully mediated between local and national interests.

Both Catholic and Protestant politicians of the bourgeois party had to

TABLE 6:5. *Turnout Rates for Reichstag and State Elections in Württemberg*[20]

Year of Reichstag Election	Turnout for Reichstag Election	Turnout for State Election after Reichstag Election	Dropoff to State Election
1874	62.5	70.0	
1877	58.0		
1878	64.7		
1881	58.4		
1884	59.8	63.8	
1887	81.5	65.4	19.4
1890	73.6		
1893	73.2	74.9	3.1
1898	69.1	70.9	−2.5
1903	75.5	76.1	2.8
1907	81.0		
1912	86.4	77.7	11.9

handle this problem. They were often exposed to the situation that David Blackbourn describes with particular vividness for the Württemberg Center.

> This basic element of Centre politics was forged out of the leadership's uneasy relationship with the Catholic countryside and small towns where . . . the party had its chief support. In the early years between the 1880s and 1914 such areas were in a state of flux, caught between traditional parochialism and exposure to powerful outside forces. . . . These developments were signs of an important social leavening in Wilhelmine Germany; but their effects were partial and contradictory, particularly when it came to changing political consciousness. Social changes of this kind frequently meant only that traditional expressions of rural and parochial discontent were given a superficially new form. In 1848 the villages and small towns had argued about hawkers, the colour of the local militia uniforms and the neglect of the law-makers in Stuttgart. Fifty years later they argued about traveling salesmen, the local railway branch line and the neglect of the agricultural inspector in Ulm. At the turn of the century, no less than in 1848, political success was dependent on being able to effect a juncture between the narrow preoccupations of the local community and the broader mainstream of public life in which political leaders operated.[21]

Blackbourn argues that the answer of the Stuttgart Centrists was to construct a "demagogic" politics. In less pejorative terms, this seems to refer to a profession by both Catholic and Protestant politics that encompassed local issues with the reassertion of traditional *Honoratioren* tactics aimed at controlling localism. These German bourgeois politicians were also aided by relatively low expectations placed upon their effectiveness. Mediating local and national interests tended to be a function of state bureaucracies and, increasingly, state legislatures. Even the partial failure of these bureaucratic instruments would not necessarily lead to immediate political action aimed at rectifying the situation. The SPD found it especially hard to use local resentment against ordinances. Issues became lost in universal statements. Lower pork prices in Hesse ended up with a powerful anti-Semitic movement that attacked all the bastions of elite society; lower grain prices in eastern Germany precipitated a massive reorientation in German political life and intensified the struggle between urban and rural masses. The incipient tax revolt of 1912 was channeled, at least by the left-wing Socialists, into a statement against militarism and big business. Dan White has shown that getting elected in the Hessian tobacco-manufacturing districts in the 1880s depended upon opposing Bismarck's tobacco monopoly. But this was an unusual instance in which government ownership was involved.[22]

In any case, Reichstag elections were often immune from such issues as local improvements, the heart of the American congressional system. Local improvements were the principal concern of state governments. Reichstag deputies had no control over the building of canals and practically none over the placement of railway lines. Resentment over these issues, which was often intense, could only be indirectly transmitted to national elections. The failure of the Prussian government to dredge the Main beyond Frankfurt enraged enough citizens of Hanau that both Reichstag and Prussian state elections were more heated than they had been before or were afterward.[23]

Usually local governments could then be shoved into bureaucratic cubbyholes or become subordinated to universalized electoral stances. This universalization process occasionally occurred in state elections where such issues were supposed to be resolved. In the 1900 elections for the Württemberg state legislature in Welzheim, the People's party, left-wing liberals, fielded a young local lawyer as a candidate. They were intent on using the issue of local improvement to bring down the National Liberal incumbent, a certain Dr. Hieber. Hieber was attacked for failing to bring a railway to the town and thus jeopardizing the whole county's economy. He was castigated as a nonresident, unfavorably compared to his opponent who was the son of a local peasant. Hieber was pictured as a tool of the Junker interests who cared little for the dirt farmers of the district, and was finally attacked as not only a foreigner but a Gymnasium professor to boot. A People's party placard argued, "Many agricultural questions are settled in the state legislature. What can peasants expect if they are decided by professors?"[24]

Hieber's response was quite simple. In the time-honored manner of *Honoratioren* politics, his campaign subordinated local improvements to universal and vague national interest. He proclaimed himself a pillar of the Bismarck state and set himself up as a defender of Protestant *Bürgertum* against disturbers by implying that the young left-wing liberal lawyer was a tool of the Socialists and Catholics. In one stroke, he made state issues irrelevant in a state election. Instead of discussing the problems of Welzheim or even of Württemberg, Hieber's broadsides merely urged the voters "to elect the man who is independent in thought and speech."[25] In Welzheim, and throughout Germany, this was part of a code by which the Protestant *Bürgertum* identified themselves. And in Welzheim if not in other places this was the key to election and reelection.

This process was supported by the elite structures and the methods of candidate selection. There was no legal requirement of residency for Reichstag candidates; deputies did not have to be attached to their district at all. However, Wilhelmine Germany was too large and diverse regionally to develop a fully nationwide cadre of candidates in the British manner. Candidates tended to come from the most influential city in the region or from the state capitals in the smaller states. There was a matter of campaign costs, facility in the local dialect and a knowledge of local customs. But mostly this phenomenon was due to the fact that German elites were most often regionally based and that these cities represented their headquarters. In Württemberg Reichstag deputies came from the headquarters of the educated bourgeois and/or the centers of socialist organizations—Heilbronn, Ulm, Tübingen and the state capital, Stuttgart. This relationship appears even more clearly when it becomes possible to reconstruct the places of residency for all candidates. Between 1903 and 1912 over half of the serious candidates came from the capital alone. Seriousness is defined as 15 percent of the vote; it is a measure designed to exclude the candidates who were put up to increase their party's national count, *Zahlkandidaten*, and had no chance of winning. When this stipulation is removed, the ratio of Stuttgarters to the whole becomes even higher. A look at the other case-study areas verifies the findings for Württemberg. In western Germany, an occasional candidate might come from Munich or Dresden and quite a few from Berlin; however, over two-thirds of the serious candidates were from the provinces in which their particular district lay. About one-third came from the leading cities of the area—Bielefeld, Cologne, Darmstadt, Dortmund, Essen, Frankfurt.

There is still no reason to believe that this regional pattern of candidate selection was designed to overcome the stigma of nonresidency. Citizens of Cologne were treated as foreigners just a few miles either up or down the Rhine. Stuttgarters who represented the outlying Württemberg districts were often called the German equivalent of carpetbaggers. Friedrich Payer could be elected from the sixth Reichstag district for over thirty years and not be immune to this form of criticism. This was true although the heart of the district was only thirty miles from Stuttgart, a comfortable day's outing. A broadside for Payer's 1890 opponent attempted to exploit this issue by asking the voters to cast their ballots for "a candidate who lives among us, knows our needs, is more responsive to them, and is better able to represent our interests than a lawyer from the capital."[26]

The best method for a Protestant bourgeois representative to avert such an attack was to meet the charges about residency with the great "issue" of "honorable" politics, the statement of personal morality. This summoned up all those vague beliefs of *Mittelstand* centrality, as in Hieber's case, and was based on the character of a man who in Payer's case was laden with honors, not only as a Reichstag representative, but as a long-time state legislator from Reutlingen, also in the district, and as president of the Württemberg legislature itself after 1895. It was an impressive career for anyone, particularly for a lawyer without substantial influence. Much of Payer's success was due to an extraordinary platform presence, which made the Prussian minister in 1890 declare him "a dangerous opponent."[27] As one of Payer's colleagues wrote, "We have only to mention your name, and it seems as if the electoral district is bombarded."[28] Even Payer's opponents paid homage to his rhetorical skills.

Payer was the ultimate practitioner of *Honoratioren*, rhetoric cultivating the image of a self-made man; he emphasized his selfless service to the communities he represented and always impressed the voters with the enormous burdens that he faced. Morality and hard work were ostensibly traded for very little honor and status, no money or power. In 1890 Payer had a letter printed on a leaflet that he sent throughout the Reichstag district. It reads in part:

> I have truthfully been forced into this candidacy. I know from experience what sacrifices this means for my business and my health if I am to fill the post for another five years. I know in this case that greater demands will be made upon me than upon many others. I know from experience that I can count on such a strong agitation against me that my hair will stand on end. I have already been called a "demagogue without sense." . . . If the voters' trust should be given to me for a fifth time, I will perform the task to the best of my ability just as I have already done in the past. Should the voters agree with my worthy opponent that they are better served by another man, they will never find even the slightest hint of an inconsolable expression on my face.[29]

Even in those relatively rare instances where the issue of residency did have some effect on the election, it usually pertained to some hidden agenda, some set of irreconcilable differences within the party over the choice of candidates. The problem was not where the candidate lived so much as what he believed in and what interests he really represented. This was certainly the case in the agitation against Lieutenant General Albrecht Johannes von Roon, ret., a Silesian Junker who represented Minden-Lübbecke in eastern Westphalia from 1893 to 1903. Von Roon was the choice of the self-perpetuating conservative elite that had heretofore dominated the district. He was elected almost by acclamation in 1893. However, in 1898 his nomination was attacked by new forces that attempted to gain power within the conservative constituency. The *Bund der Landwirte* had been recently organized in the district; its leadership found Roon too aristocratic, too little interested in the problems of the medium-sized farms. Anti-Semites were more and more active in the district; they desired a politician that would mobilize the agrarian masses toward reform.

Roon and his supporters ignored these groups. The *Mindener Post*, the core of traditionalism, treated these attempts as tantamount to a declaration of war against the principle of Christian, that is Protestant, unity. "A strong sense of unity and the unbesmirched escutcheon of the party is more important than the possession of a parliamentary mandate."[30] The *Post* and Roon professed to believe the real reason for opposition was the candidate's nonresidence. Roon defended his position a few weeks before the election. He knew the district well, having already visited it once that year. Anyway, "What party demands that its candidate live in his district? Every party asks first: Is the candidate qualified? They ask first: Is he compatible with the district? The Reichstag is no *Kreistag* [county council]."[31]

Roon won the nomination and election against liberal and BdL opposition. The nonresidence question was scarcely raised. In fact, it would have been unwise. Many of his most petulant opponents were young pastors, new to the area themselves. These anti-Semitic ministers went from house to house urging their parishioners to vote for the BdL candidate. A certain pastor Winkler even burst into Conservative meetings and demanded that the crowd follow him out of the hall; he attacked as "green bumpkins" those who did not.[32] The BdL leadership was much more careful not to alienate the farmers of the district. They even scored points with old Conservatives by supporting Roon in his runoff battle against the liberals, arguing that it was too dangerous "to put the district in the hands of a man who has no understanding for agriculture and national productive work."[33]

In 1903 the BdL reaped its rewards. Even the *Mindener Post* was ready to ditch the Silesian Junker. Roon had become a redundancy in an area dominated by medium-sized farms. He was replaced by a good BdL man, someone who could be called a farmer instead of a great landowner. It is arresting that the last large landowner to represent the district in the Wilhelmine period did not even come from the Conservative party but was elected as a left-wing liberal in 1912. Neither the left-wing liberal nor, certainly, Roon or his replacement was essential to the politics of Minden-Lübbecke. The only essentials were the working out of various loyalties, interests, and ideologies. District politics were decided by the composition and mix of these elements, seldom by the personality or residency of the candidate.

The practice of affirming politics, the loyalties to Protestant *Bürgertum*, the articulation of interest at the local level—these brought voters to the polls and channeled their reactions. Leadership was often extraneous; too strong personalistic reactions were liable to fragment the system rather than make it workable. These interests, hatreds, fears, commitments, enthusiasms, symbolic statements, and so on could be articulated without strong candidacies. The stronger the loyalties and commitments, the weaker the need for some personal charisma. Even in those cases where charismatic leadership appeared, the forms of affirming politics were only temporarily skewed. Eugen Richter kept Hagen out of the SPD camp only until his death.

It is important to realize that even Payer did not move his constituents very far from where they had been in the first place. Tübingen and Reutlingen counties, which provided him with his victories, had been bastions of the Left in 1848. They may not have been the prototypical counties in terms of social composition for the People's party, but the historical traditions of left-wing liberalism ran so deep as to make Payer's views very acceptable among the voters. Payer did not then demonstrate the kind of personal magnetism of a Joseph Chamberlain who did lead a whole host of voters in a direction away from their earlier tradition. And even more striking, no matter how great his success, Payer was willing to give up the system that elected him and become a mere cipher on a list under proportional representation.[34]

Thus, if we want to understand the nature of local politics in Wilhelmine Germany, we must turn to those affirming entities for explanations. Their conflicts at the district level provide the best indicator of how electoral cleavages only mirrored the substantial differences of everyday life, how these cleavages were perpetuated and deepened by continuous conflict. Candidates were at most an aid in the struggle, never its end. Similar responses could be expected from that element of the Protestant *Bürgertum* that scrupulously followed the emotions engendered by fatherland rhetoric. And this was the ultimate answer. The greater the articulation of cleavage, the greater the electoral enthusiasms. The greater the electoral enthusiasms, the more widespread they become. The more widespread the enthusiasms become, the wider the area of common response. The greater the common response, the narrower the divergent responses among classes, regions, areas, and principalities. The less divergent responses, the greater the electoral energies at the local level. The greater the electoral energies at the local level, the greater the cleavages they represent. And we have arrived at a real system, circular in both its logic and reinforcements, as the next three chapters will demonstrate.

Excursus: Three Case Studies

There is always some question about the need for case studies in an analytic approach. Should not the nationwide analysis itself be of such depth as to obviate the need to go over the same ground on a microscopic level? Is this not especially true, given the common response? In politics, the answer is no. Following the analysis tends to remove the reader from the actual nature of the conflict at ground level; case studies bring the reader closer to the political realities of everyday life.

Thus case studies are necessary; the question is how many? Undoubtedly a study of every district would increase our knowledge and the explanatory power of the arguments. However, this is impossible as a research goal, let alone what it would do to the reader's span of attention. Originally I decided to have eight case studies, two from each of the historical regions in the case study areas—Württemberg, Hesse, Westphalia, and West Prussia. I eventually reduced this number to three. The other five case studies would have been informative, but they would have added little to the argument and a great deal to the length of the manuscript. Moreover, much of the information that would have been in the case studies was required to buttress the analysis in other sections of the work.

The three chosen are geographically skewed. All come from Prussia, and two come from the province of West Prussia. But there are good reasons for this choice. If there had to be only one case study, it would have to be Dortmund. Dortmund was the singular place where most of the affirmative social groupings competed alongside a strong Protestant *Burgertum*. The choice of the two West Prussian case studies has not so much to do with favoring that province as with the kinds of conflicts they explain. These are studies of the rural East Elbians and the Poles, the two major social groupings hardest to describe statistically and analytically at the national level, requiring local studies to buttress the analysis. Yet even reducing the number of case studies to three achieves the purpose I had intended, to make the reader aware that the analytical discussion has relevance in describing local events and to give the reader some notion of the excitement and adventure that accompanied grass-roots electoral politics in Wilhelmine Germany.

7

ELBING-MARIENBURG: 1903 – 1912

The first of three case studies focuses on the regional-rural base of the German Conservative party. Elbing-Marienburg in West Prussia is a wonderful example of the solidification of these agrarian-regional loyalties and the threats engendered by growing urbanization. The social grouping forming around German conservatism was placed in very serious straits by the growing power of urbanism in its own district. Conservatives in Elbing-Marienburg did not have to focus on some faraway urbanized region in central or western Germany; their own district provided a nearer and more obvious threat to their political domination. The conflicts between the conservative social grouping and the rest of the district enlivened the electoral struggles in the last decade of peace, increased the feelings of isolation and separation, hardening affirming loyalties and bringing forth strong emotions. The district was not only a thriving example of affirming politics, but it also represented a study in the strength and weakness of personalized politics. From 1902 to 1912 the German Conservatives presented a candidate who simultaneously maintained the barriers around the agrarian-monarchist position while calling forth a strong reaction against it. The responses to this candidate so concentrated on urban-rural differences that they even temporarily overwhelmed embedded religious antagonisms, founding an alliance of both Catholic and Protestant *Bürgertum* directed against a German Conservative who was feared as some kind of proto- or neopopulist.

In the end, it all came back to that curious vision of the German east: when nothing was left to be said, when nothing had even been said, East Elbian politicians would outdo each other in claiming to preserve "our German east." They often purveyed an ersatz romanticism built upon the myth of a heroic German civilizing mission. The victories of German knights in the thirteenth century and Prussian armies in the sixteenth were merged into one mythic whole. Thus the annexation of West Prussia from Poland in the eighteenth century sounded in their rhetoric more like a combination of the drama of salvation and a land reclamation project than the act of conquest that it was. Elard von Oldenburg-Januschau, Elbing-Marienburg's Reichstag delegate from 1902 to 1912, was particu-

larly adept at conveying this message. As he told an assemblage gathered
to honor the Prussian crown prince in 1912: "The border between East
Prussia and Russia is a small brook, as wide as this table. The ground and
soil are the same. Over there is disorder and poverty, here is order and
prosperity. That is the work of Frederick William I. Standing on the
border of West Prussia with Russia, one is struck by a similar impression:
he knows that this is the work of Frederick the Great."[1]

Unfortunately for myth, West Prussians were more concerned about
their relative status vis-à-vis other Germans than their superiority over
the Russians. And this could cause problems. West Prussia was a province that impoverished the rich as well as the poor. The large estates that
dominated the economy were sinkholes of indebtedness. Their owners
were in a constant struggle against bankruptcy. The bulk of the rural
population were agricultural laborers who worked on the large estates.
The ratio of farm laborers to farm owners was over three to one, a figure
in 1882 about a third higher than for western and southern Germany.
There was a trend in the opposite direction; the number of independent
proprietors was increasing faster in West Prussia than anywhere else in
the Reich, partially due to an attempt to settle German peasants in the
areas of Polish domination. Still it was a poor and dependent life. Even in
prosperous villages, less than one-quarter of the male heads of house-
holds were craftsmen or self-employed farmers who could not assure
their own lot for their younger sons. These would swell the ranks of an
already overcrowded labor pool and thus keep West Prussian wages
among the lowest in the Reich. Only workers in neighboring Posen and
East Prussia were paid less. The best solution to this massive pauperiza-
tion was to get out. Commencing in the depression of the 1880s, a wave
of young West Prussians fled their villages to Berlin, Hamburg, or the
industrial regions of Saxony and Westphalia. Between 1880 and 1910
over 10 percent of the total West Prussian population had migrated westward. In 1910 over 75,000 persons born in West Prussia lived in the
Rhenish-Westphalian industrial area, and another 115,000 in Berlin.

As migrants changed the complexion of the Ruhr, and to a certain extent Berlin, they left untransformed an apparently immutable political
and social structure in West Prussia. The large estate, the *Gut*, remained
the principal unit of agrarian society well into the twentieth century.
Forty percent of the West Prussian land was cultivated by farms of over
100 hectares; a third of all land was in holdings of over 200 hectares.
Thus about a thousand large estates dominated the rural economy up to
1945. The impression these estates made on the landscape pointed out
their function as centers of control. The compact units formed by the
house and outbuildings were often the only dramatic relief against the
dull, flat landscape and the small villages that seemed to disappear into
the unrelieved gray skies.

Inhabitants of the *Gut* were economic subjects of the owner, or *Gutsbesitzer*. He might no longer have judicial rights over the peasant, but custom often still allowed him to exercise informal police and judicial power. It was this custom that made the *Gutsbesitzer* so powerful. He could rely not only on unquestioned economic control of the peasants but on his traditional right to demand deference and obedience. There might be distinctions among them. Slightly less than 40 percent of the West Prussian estates carried noble titles with them, allowing their owners to be identified as Junkers and possessors of a *Rittergut*. A *Rittergutsbesitzer* held somewhat higher status than an owner of a regular *Gut*, but the nonnoble gentry were by no means excluded from rural society. The Junkers set the example that was followed by all the estate owners; thus, there was no noticeable differentiation between noble and nonnoble lifestyles. Both groups had roughly the same political and social attitudes and maintained their estates according to similar rules. All the large landowners participated in the attempts to salvage the East Elbian economy through intensive lobbying and political action. They were a united, homogenous group who were running the province and intended to continue in their privileged position.[2]

The East Elbian gentry were extremely suspicious of the cities in their midst. Danzig, the provincial capital, was an old Hanseatic town, a cosmopolitan city with closer ties to Hamburg than to the neighboring *Gut*. It was no wonder that the gentry viewed Danzig and cities like it as intrusions into their area of control, potential centers of disruption and as loci of antagonistic political powers. Moreover, the West Prussian cities were often growing more prosperous, expanding their area, creating new riches. Such prosperity quite naturally stirred jealousy in the rural areas, which faced continual crises of lower prices and increasing poverty throughout the 1880s and 1890s.

The distrust between city and countryside was at the root of the political conflicts in the district Elbing-Marienburg. Elbing was a Hanseatic city founded in the thirteenth century. Its handsome buildings fronting on Vistula quays made it appear that a part of Belgium or Holland had been transferred intact to East Elbia. By the middle of the nineteenth century the old mercantile core had expanded into a prosperous medium-sized Prussian administrative and manufacturing center. In 1895 the population passed the 50,000 mark, about a third of the total for the district. It had a teacher training academy, theaters, a large shipbuilding and machinery industry. In 1907 over 60 percent of the work force was engaged in manufacturing. Elbing city was much more closely tied to Danzig than to the rest of the electoral district. Its voting pattern bears out this assertion. Elbing city moved from a stronghold of left-wing liberalism in the 1870s to that of Socialism in the early twentieth century. It was not a place where the inhabitants of a *Rittergut* could feel comfortable.[3]

Marienburg city, a county seat of 10,000, was less frightening to the countryside than the more cosmopolitan Elbing. The administrative and marketing town was constructed on a more comprehensible scale. The patterns of deference in the small city more closely resembled those of the countryside. The leader of local society was the *Landrat* (county administrator), who was often of Junker origin and always of Junker sympathies. Still, Marienburg city had never been an adjunct of the rural area surrounding it. It never served the function of similar county seats in Iowa or Kansas that acted as centers for the agricultural society. On the contrary, Marienburg city had a history of domination over its hinterland. It had served as the administrative center for the German Order of Knights, who ruled West Prussia from the fourteenth to the sixteenth century. The seat of their government until 1439 was Marienburg castle, an extraordinarily imposing relic intact until 1945, whose enormous rectangular towers seemed to signal a strength that could at any time cause a renewed domination over the land.

The actual situation was more prosaic. In the period before World War I, Marienburg city was less controlled by the countryside than separated from it. Like the other small cities in West Prussia, it had a clearly defined boundary that did not trail off into the suburbs, villas of the rich, or noncontiguous working-class settlements. Marienburg's limits were bound by the Nogat River on the north and west and the more recently built apartments in the working-class districts of the east and south. These crisp, well-defined lines in space were social and political boundaries as well. Marienburg city was filled with a bourgeoisie and craftsmen who chafed under the political and social dominance of the agrarians. They might not be as radical as their fellow workers in Elbing city, but they were just as reluctant to accept Conservative rule. The Conservative party never got more than 17 percent of the vote in Marienburg city in the last four imperial elections.[4]

Beyond the borders of Marienburg city and the suburbs of Elbing, the situation was entirely different. Tenants, small farmers, and agricultural laborers all appeared united under the direction of gentry landowners. This was true for both Elbing and Marienburg counties, although they had undergone very different kinds of development. Most of Marienburg county was composed of medium-sized peasant holdings growing grain on the flat lands south of the Baltic. Almost 20 percent of the land in Marienburg and over one-quarter of Elbing county was in large holdings. When the forested estates are included, over one-third of Elbing's area was in *Gutsbezirke*, even after the end of the Wilhelmine period. Thus the district had its share of those romanticized country houses and a gentry that took pride in its leadership role. If not quintessentially East Elbia, it was close.

In both of these counties, farmer and farm laborers all felt the brunt of the agrarian crises in the 1880s and 1890s, which lowered the prices of everything from estates and grain to wage labor. The overwhelming majority of rural voters in both counties were willing to follow the hybrid of old conservative ideas and new interest-group politics associated with the BdL. And, as was traditional in times of trouble in the east, the small and large landowners alike had turned to the Junkers for leadership. Sometimes this was the result of intimidation by this Junker elite; but, on the whole, the greater part was freely given as a result of both the natural and new order of things in East Elbian politics.

Thus Elbing and Marienburg counties delivered substantial majorities to the German Conservative party, overwhelming the liberals and Socialists in the cities. German Conservatives lost the seat only once between 1871 and 1907, that time in a fluke defeat by a National Liberal. Between 1887 and 1898, the Conservative party candidate was able to achieve a majority in the first election and did not even have to fight in the runoff. Elbing-Marienburg was a safe seat for a succession of Junker deputies who often carried distinguished names into the Reichstag. Between 1893 and 1902 the representative was the closest thing to a political boss in West Prussia. When Puttkamer-Plauth resigned in 1902, it caused no surprise that the Conservative party committee turned to another *Rittergutsbesitzer*, Elard von Oldenburg-Januschau, a promising combination of patriarchial leader and proto-populist.

Oldenburg was almost a textbook case of how to achieve influence among local East Elbian elites. He combined actual presence with economic success, became a leader and spokesman for local agrarian interests, received notice and honors from the Prussian monarchy and finally worked up through a series of offices. It all began with a characteristic case of a young man resigning a commission in order to satisfy pressing family needs. But, unlike so many in his position, Oldenburg proved to be a good manager. Migrating to West Prussia to care for a small property in the 1880s, he made money in farming, paid off his mortgages and used his profits to buy new estates. Starting with the run-down family estates of Januschau, he created an agrarian empire consisting of six *Güter* and over 80,000 acres. He did this all while many other gentry sank deeper into debt. This same activity and intelligence turned him quickly into a leader among the West Prussian gentry. Oldenburg became a *Landwirtschaftsrat* in charge of issuing agricultural loans and then also a member of the chief agricultural advisory bodies to both the state and national governments. Most important, he never let his own success cause him to lose sympathy with the proliferating anxious and impoverished gentry. He was an early leader of the BdL, becoming provincial leader in 1895.[5] Oldenburg also had a social position that tied him directly to the monarchy. And he had made an advantageous marriage, which brought him into contact with the circles around William II, where he eventually received the title of court chamberlain and formed a close friendship with the emperor's eldest son. His serviceable legislative experience included election to the Prussian House of Delegates in 1898 and again in 1901.

Known locally, certified by the emperor, possessing a remarkable record, this Junker appeared the natural candidate to succeed von Puttkamer. He also promised to be an excellent campaigner. Oldenburg's political style was ideally suited to East Elbia, if perhaps nowhere else. He was a political natural, having a strange combination of characteristics peculiarly associated with old-style Junker leaders—part aristocratic paternalist, part exploiter, part gunfighter. If he could not command respect for reasons of deference, he would take it out of fear. His wit was a sharp weapon; his temper was uncontrollable. In debate, he frightened his friends as well as his enemies. He attacked everyone who disagreed with him—young or old, king's minister or Socialist. When speech failed, he tried fists. This is his own account of an incident during the Reichstag election of 1912:

> I campaigned in a small town in the Niederung. As I came into the room, the innkeeper stated that it would be necessary for me to speak from behind a table. The crowd seemed to be against me. I believed that I knew my West Prussians better than that and placed myself calmly in front of the table so that everybody could see me.
>
> Right at the beginning, I saw that it would come to blows. After only a few minutes a gigantic fellow rose out of the audience and, with encouragement from the crowd, pressed closer and closer to me. I waited a bit to lull him into security and then seized him by the throat and threw him out of the hall. After some grumbling, the rest of the crowd shut up as I told them: "Now I'll talk and you hold your tongues. After that you can speak and I'll be silent."[6]

He did not record any subsequent challenge. This all sounds more like a story out of West Texas than West Prussia.

The incident is indicative of the difference between an Oldenburg-type Junker and the aristocrats trained in the western European mold, men like Bethmann and Phillip von Eulenberg. Oldenburg could trade punches with an inferior. His paternalistic control did not mean that he would set insuperable physical or rhetorical distance between himself and those he called "his people." Oldenburg could adapt to peasant manners, relish country jokes, eat plain food, speak naturally in the East Elbian dialect. These were not merely affectations. At the root of his politics, at the core of his beliefs, was a conviction that lord and peasant in the east formed a community of interests whose ties took precedence over all other loyalties, including those due to the government. His father instructed him, "When you yourself are a landowner, mark this. You might be forced by necessity to lie to the provincial president but never do so to your people."[7]

Oldenburg's intention to preserve this hierarchical community represented his entire political platform. Both landowner and laborer benefited from high farm prices, but the "noneconomic side of living together" was even more important.

> I came to a simple but profound understanding of this deepening relationship with my own people through the example of my old nurse. . . . She was sick and near the end so I visited her frequently and read to her from the Bible or the hymnal. At my last visit, a few hours before her death, she said to me, "The good God has laid as much work and as many burdens upon you as few have to endure. Forget not the good God in your work!" What great truth lay in the words of this simple person. It has become the exhortation for my whole life.[8]

His politics were just as simple. He envisioned the BdL as far more than an economic pressure group; it was to be the organization dedicated to preserving his West Prussian way of life. This commitment to the BdL was extraordinarily intense, made with a characteristically swift resolve, and steadfastly pursued as long as the institution existed. "I put the greater part of my efforts into the battles of the *Bund der Landwirte* so that my life was inextricably bound up with the life of the *Bund*."[9]

Oldenburg could accept the BdL argument that agrarian influence would diminish without strong representation in the German Reichstag, that is, without obtaining control of the German Conservative party. It was not that he ever had any love for traditional Conservative leadership, which he attacked as too deferential to authority and not enough attuned to its East Elbian base. He was especially critical of the party's propensity to unite with liberals on any issue, even those that benefited agrarians. For him, politics stank of compromise; he could hardly tolerate sitting in the Reichstag. He was generally disgusted by debate and usually listened only to himself. Oldenburg claimed to be more interested in how many pigs comprised a litter in Januschau than in the most fiery and intellectual speech.

Hans-Jürgen Puhle, who has written the best study of the BdL, argues that Oldenburg was a transitional figure among the older Conservative and new BdL agitators. Unlike the publicists and impoverished landowners who comprised the bulk of the BdL leadership, Oldenburg could move easily in court circles and had an aristocratic distaste of politics, even as he succeeded in it. Oldenburg did not support a number of BdL positions, advocating primogeniture and lacking expansionist beliefs. Finally, his hatred of politics made him suspicious to this new group of leaders whose principal activity was not economic but political. There is some truth to this assertion. Oldenburg was older than the new generation of BdL leaders who had come to the fore in the first decade of the twentieth century. He never participated in those fashionable *Mittelstand* anti-Socialist, antiparliamentary movements. In the end, Oldenburg was what he had been in the beginning, a man who lived within the confines of the hierarchical society—monarchist, antidemocratic, agrarian.[10]

The synthesis of these beliefs became obvious every time the Junker rose to speak. On 6 November 1899, Oldenburg told a BdL gathering in Elbing that agriculture was the principal source of national greatness. He feared that too rapid industrialization would undermine the predominance of agriculture in Germany, that the new industrial cities were breeding grounds of a treasonous Socialist movement which could at any time infect the East Elbian laborer as well. His version of the BdL not only protected the economic interests of German agriculture but also preserved the monarchy by fighting the urban forces. The audience of *Gutsbesitzer* were never to forget that their economic survival had merged with the preservation of the dynasty. The peroration concluded: "Whether in grace or out of grace, we are inseparably bound to our King, and we will serve him to our last breath. Thus see to it, my men; let us hear the old victory cry: Long live His Majesty, Emperor and King! (Lively and sustained applause.)"[11]

Armed with Prussian patriotism, possessing good organization and encouraging profit, it was no wonder that Oldenburg won the seat in the first election. However, a problem soon developed. While Oldenburg had run far ahead of the second candidate, his majority over all the opposition had been only four votes. This slender majority was challenged because there had been only two poll watchers in one precinct instead of the prescribed three. Although the absence had occurred for only a short period of time and involved just a few voters, the Reichstag's Elections Committee recommended that the precinct's votes be declared invalid. Once this was done, Oldenburg would have received only a plurality, not a majority, in the first election; thus the Conservative victory itself was in jeopardy. In March 1903 the Reichstag declared Oldenburg's election invalid. No one doubted that the Conservatives would be the ultimate victors when the seat was contested again. After all, even the corrected totals gave Oldenburg over 49 percent of the vote in the first election. This plurality could easily be turned into a comfortable majority during a runoff. However another special election could not be held in the time before the term of the Reichstag expired. In May, Oldenburg announced his candidacy for a regular five-year term in the forthcoming June elections. It appeared that this time he would be unambiguously seated as the deputy from Elbing-Marienburg.[12]

Unfortunately for Oldenburg, the political climate had changed in the thirteen months between elections. In 1903 the urban centers of West Prussia were counterattacking the agrarians. The agrarians seemed more and more vulnerable as Germany urbanized; a new candidate might be beatable. The left-wing liberal *Danziger Neueste Nachrichten* set the tone for the entire province. It attacked the agrarians for being undemocratic and opposing the principle of direct elections to the Prussian House of Delegates. The paper warned that another defeat in West Prussia would weaken the liberals for the full five-year term of the new Reichstag. It urged its readers to support liberal candidates everywhere. The liberal press in Elbing-Marienburg seized upon this wave of anti-agrarianism to advocate Oldenburg's ouster. The *Elbinger Zeitung* and the *Altpreussischer Zeitung* (Elbing), the *Marienburger Zeitung* and the *Nogat Zeitung* (Marienburg), all supported Oldenburg's liberal opponent, a certain Mr. Schmidt.[13]

Schmidt campaigned principally against the agrarians. He had to make an occasional bow to old-line liberal themes by identifying himself as a candidate of freedom and democracy, but his main issues concerned the fundamental split between urban and rural interests in Elbing-Marienburg. For example, Schmidt favored long-term trade treaties that might lower agricultural tariffs in exchange for promoting trade and commerce. It was an issue designed to bring him support in the port and shipbuilding city of Elbing although it would raise cries of consternation in the rural areas of the district. In other cases, Schmidt reaffirmed the interests of the cities just as surely as Oldenburg attacked them. The liberal candidate criticized the Conservatives because "they fear the political influence of the great cities will increase at the expense of the agrarian regions."[14] He argued that these fears caused the Conservatives to construct a policy that met their anxieties, that would defend their special interests whatever the outcome. Schmidt contended that urban liberals were the wave of the future, that they were determined to gain prosperity for all Germans, not just a few *Gutsbesitzer*.

Schmidt started his campaign with certain advantages. Heretofore the National Liberals and the left-wing liberals had each put up separate candidates in the district. Now, in conformity with national trends, they ran Schmidt under the unified National Liberal banner. Their candidate was a pleasing speaker; he could draw upon a group of enthusiastic supporters. His problem was that he could not turn these advantages into votes. The liberals of Elbing-Marienburg had permanent disabilities. Their programs were too urban and bourgeois-oriented; their ideology forced them to attack the power of organized religion in an area less secular than the rest of Germany. If they staged a weak campaign, they would find no satisfactory candidate for the next election. If they made a strong effort, the *Rittergutsbesitzer* would be furious with them for splitting the property holders' vote. Schmidt's campaign managed to bring about both of these consequences. Despite the renewed liberal agitation, his share of the vote in 1903 was no more than that of both liberal parties in 1902.

An even more serious urban challenge to Oldenburg emerged from within the ranks of the Conservative party. Town conservatism had always been a fragile phenomenon of the German east, tied to old Prussian mercantile traditions. It was under severe attack as the conservative-based social grouping became more ideologically rural. Oldenburg's victory might signify the end for urban conservatism. The bulk of the West Prussian Conservative party organizations were already in the hands of the gentry and tied to the BdL. The *Elbinger Zeitung* may not have exaggerated when it contended that the *Bund der Landwirte* had already conquered the field.

Even in terminal battle, the urban Conservatives could make trouble. Oldenburg's candidacy received considerably more scrutiny in the urban Conservative committees than it had a year previously. The Conservative committee from the small town of Neuenkirchen asked the Junker whether he strove for an exclusively agrarian party or believed that all Germans might find a place in the Conservative organization. It was a question designed to elicit a favorable response, and even Oldenburg was not so stupid as to respond incorrectly. The Junker assured the Neuenkirchen committee that he supported an open party. In a small town economically dependent on a conservative countryside filled with its clients, this answer had to suffice, but the Elbing and Marienburg committees were not as easily pacified.

These urban Conservatives fielded a second candidate under the Conservative party label. Herr Heidenhein claimed to represent both urban and agrarian interests; yet the main focus of his campaign was an attack upon the BdL. Heidenhein admitted that the BdL served a useful purpose when agricultural prices were low and the worth of farms had sharply declined. He contended, however, that the worst of the agricultural depression was long past. Only the superfluous anxiety remained from these bad times, an anxiety upon which Oldenburg played. If Oldenburg were allowed to campaign in the same manner as before, he would ruin not only Germany as a whole but also the fabric of life in West Prussia itself. "The setting in motion of the farmers against the other estates, *Stände*, is an act that endangers the peaceful coexistence of city and countryside in our East." [15]

Oldenburg's problems were multiplied twice again by affirming deviants. The Socialists were determined enemies. They were the second strongest party in the district and had some faint hopes of winning the seat for themselves. The Centrists were resolved to maintain a separate identity from the other parties based on the Catholic-Protestant separation, which was uninfluenced by the town-land division in the German east. In 1903 Catholics in Elbing-Marienburg were still suspicious of a

Conservative party that had strong ties to the Prussian state church. It was this Conservative majority in the Prussian House of Delegates that had not yet revised the law forbidding Jesuits to enter Prussia. Oldenburg was a member not only of the Reichstag but also of the House of Delegates and could, thus, be held accountable for any delays in overturning the anti-Catholic laws. Conservative, National Liberal, Centrist, Socialist—it was a long list of opponents and threatened by its very size to overturn the agrarian dominance of the district.

The opposition was tied together by one hope, the defeat of Oldenburg. Yet all this agitation did not even bring forth a record turnout, let alone substantial shifts in party loyalties. The Centrist and liberal proportion of the vote remained very close to previous levels. The Social Democratic share rose to over 31 percent, but this was only the continuation of a long-term trend. The total Conservative vote decreased by only four points; the difference was that it was divided up between two candidates. Oldenburg received only 29.6 percent of the vote; Heidenhein had 15.3. Almost all the urban Conservatives defected to Heidenhein. Oldenburg received only 142 votes in Elbing city, less than 2 percent of the total. Heidenhein received 1,200 votes, about the same number as the liberal Schmidt. The anti-urban positions of Oldenburg and his Junker friends had finally come home to roost (see table 7:1).

There is a Prussian version of God that looks out for good Conservatives and other fools. Oldenburg was assured of winning the seat, not through his own exertions, but because his opponent in the runoff would be a Social Democrat. There were some problems. The Center press seemed aloof from the contest. Some Catholic workers in Elbing and Marienburg cities probably voted Social Democrat although it is impossible to verify this assertion without precinct returns. The left-wing liberals apparently defected. The left-wing liberal *Altpreussischer Zeitung* despaired of the choice between the black reactionaries and the reds but still declared that the Socialists would better serve the interests of the majority than would the BdL.

Oldenburg could count on Heidenhein and Schmidt to instruct their supporters to vote Conservative. They were not fully obeyed. Urban voters still were reluctant to cast their ballot for the Junker; the Socialists, thus, captured Elbing city by a majority of four to one. The rural areas again provided the margin of the Conservative victory. Elbing county went for Oldenburg by a margin of better than three to one; Marienburg county by an only slightly lower ratio. Oldenburg was able to win the district with 11,215 against 9,344 votes for the Socialist, a difference of 6 percent.

This was too close a call for the Conservative-BdL coalition. The aristocrats in charge hoped to modify their organizational structure and their propaganda in order to reestablish those massive first-ballot victories that had heretofore characterized the district. In the fall of 1903 the Marienburg County committee took the first halting steps by promising to share the selection and election machinery with nonagrarian conservatives. Yet these promises were never fulfilled and, even if they had been, there was no way for Oldenburg to make significant gains in the cities.

More important and more lasting were the real organizational changes made to meet the new levels of politicization. The Conservative committee for Elbing-Marienburg actually collected a war chest of 3,000 marks. While this sum was relatively small, it represented a whole new way of doing political business. Cash was necessary only when noble landowners could no longer fully mobilize their clientele. This organizational change was paralleled by a change in electoral propaganda. Oldenburg's campaign managers accepted the logic of Protestant *Bürgertum* politics. They sought to transform their intrepid and obdurate agrarian into a candidate of the *Mittelstand*, hoping at least to rally the artisans in the small towns to their cause. It was a particularly good tactic in the plebiscitary elections of 1907 when a petition was circulated maintaining that Oldenburg fought for the interests of the common man of both city and countryside. Surprisingly, 2,361 voters were willing to affix their names to the document. With a tenth of the eligible voters in agreement, the BdL-Conservative coalition had apparently won their argument by the sheer weight of numbers, if not of truths.[16]

The Conservatives would never be considered urban; their folksy Junker candidate with his fake country accent would hardly pass as a statesman of liberal urban politics; in the cities, he was often considered a stand-in for Satan. The liberal hatred of Oldenburg was so strong that it undermined the possibility of constructing even temporary alliances between urban liberals and BdL Conservatives. In 1907 the Elbing-Marienburg liberals rejected the instructions of their national parties to make a compact with the Conservatives in order to fight the Socialists and the Center. The liberals argued that the principal obstacle to unity was Oldenburg himself. When the Reichstag was dissolved in December 1906, the *Nogat Zeitung* pleaded with the Conservatives to nominate a candidate the people could trust, that is, not Oldenburg. Heidenhein publicly urged Oldenburg to withdraw from the race on patriotic grounds lest the Socialists win the district with the support of the Center. The liberal organization had almost agreed not to contest Elbing-Marienburg in exchange for a similar Conservative concession elsewhere. However Oldenburg's nomination quashed the deal. The liberal constituency simply would not allow their district to fall into the Junker's hands without a fight.

With all these disadvantages, Oldenburg still emerged a victor in 1907;

TABLE 7:1. *Elections in Elbing-Marienburg, 1903, 1907, and 1912: Turnout and Vote (in percent)* [17]

Area	Turnout	von Oldenburg (Conservative)	Heidenhein (Conservative)	Schmidt (National Liberal)
		First Election 1903		
Elbing City	69.7	2.0	17.0	15.7
Elbing County	70.4	43.0	23.0	3.4
Marienburg County	62.8	46.6	8.5	5.2
Total	67.1	30.5	15.2	8.2

Area	Turnout	von Oldenburg (Conservative)	Fischer (National Liberal)
		First Election 1907	
Elbing City	83.6	22.5	19.9
Elbing County	83.6	68.8	3.7
Marienburg County	80.1	51.6	14.2
Total	82.5	45.9	13.4

Area	Turnout	von Oldenburg (Conservative)	Schröder (Free Conservative)
		First Election 1912	
Total	81.9	39.5	30.3

First Election 1903		Second Election 1903		
Zagermann (Center)	Crispien (SPD)	Turnout	von Oldenburg	Crispien
10.0	55.2	68.9	18.2	81.7
12.0	18.4	69.0	74.7	24.6
20.7	19.3	61.0	71.3	27.7
15.4	30.7	65.2	54.6	45.4

First Election 1907		Second Election 1907		
Richer (Center)	Crispien (SPD)	Turnout	von Oldenburg	Crispien
9.9	47.6	76.5	45.5	54.5
14.6	12.9	78.0	86.3	13.6
19.8	14.3	71.7	84.7	15.3
14.9	25.7	75.6	71.2	28.8

First Election 1912	Second Election 1912		
Crispien (SPD)	Turnout	von Oldenburg	Schröder
30.1	83.7	43.7	56.3

it was, after all, a reactionary year, and he certainly qualified on that point. He regained that part of the Conservative constituency he had lost in 1903; he got 45.6 percent of the vote in the first election of 1907.

And 1907 was precisely the wrong year for a rebellion inside the Protestant *Bürgertum* camp. Any anti-Socialist, promonarchist incumbent could count on the wave of national enthusiasm engendered in this plebiscitary election. The influx of voters that characterized 1907 did not overwhelm the German Conservatives. Oldenburg maintained an urban percentage of the vote equal to that of both conservative candidates in 1903. The Junker got 17.2 percent in Marienburg in the first election and 22.2 percent in Elbing, even more than the liberal candidate. And these achievements were more than matched in the runoff against the SPD candidate where even the left-wing liberals supported him. Sometimes these endorsements were the barest of compliments. Heidenhein stated, "We may have many reasons to fight Oldenburg, but he is honorable and pro-fatherland. There can be no doubt that these stands separate him from his opponent; thus, man for man, we must vote for Oldenburg."[18] And in contrast with 1903, such instructions were followed. Oldenburg got almost three-quarters of the vote. He managed to get 45 percent in Elbing city and to win Elbing and Marienburg counties by margins of over five to one.

Oldenburg's 1907 triumph was just an interlude in his struggles with the cities. His reputation guaranteed that urban-rural conflict would continue to dominate politics in Elbing-Marienburg. In fact, Oldenburg was rapidly becoming hated throughout Germany. He never kept his mouth shut when an attack would do. In a 1910 debate on the emperor's power of command, Oldenburg offered a simple solution: "The King of Prussia must be able at any moment to say to a lieutenant, 'Take ten men and shoot the Reichstag.'"[19] The Junker had achieved the impossible, embarrassing the German government by antidemocratic statements. Both the Conservative party leadership and the German government began to put some distance between themselves and this mad Junker. The West Prussian leader had to be treated gingerly since he had a following in the Reichstag; thus, he was politely informed that he was a credit to the Reich but bad publicity forced the emperor to refuse him further honors. It is impossible to say whether these hints were understood in Marienburg, yet there is no reason to believe that the world of the West Prussian *Gutsbesitzer* was so narrow as to be totally divorced from the gossip of the capital.

Oldenburg's accumulated liabilities engendered oppositional responses. In 1910 the *Hansabund* appeared in both Elbing and Marienburg cities, proclaiming itself as the urban answer to the BdL and complaining that the BdL was too influential in an urbanizing Germany where two-thirds of the taxes were paid from the profits of industry and commerce. These arguments appeared to take hold in the district; the *Marienburger Zeitung* stated in 1911 that the *Hansabund* had a larger membership than the BdL. The liberal-oriented *Bauernbund*, the *Hansabund* twin, also appeared in the district in 1910, seeking to convince proprietors of small farms to throw off the leadership of the large landowners. If the outcry that ensued is any indication, the *Bauernbund* was at least partially successful. The *Danziger Allgemeine Zeitung*, a BdL-Conservative organ, proclaimed: "For a long time the liberals have unsuccessfully attempted to delude the farmers. Finally they have found the means of inciting a small landowner against the large landowner and to sow mistrust and discord. Unfortunately, many had let themselves be incited because they have forgotten or have never understood how it was before, how the great landowners did our work for us despite the outcries of the liberals."[20]

Oldenburg was thus to face a difficult campaign in 1912. The liberal war chest was larger than before; the liberal newspaper opposition was more intense; and liberals were electioneering in rural areas where they had never been seen before. Some left-wing liberals actually held a successful meeting in Rosenberg, the small country town just a few miles from Januschau. When Oldenburg came to find out what was happening, he was greeted by a city lawyer who did not even recognize him. The Junker was furious; he pushed his way into the meeting and requested permission to speak.

> I wished to ask the gathering whether the inhabitants of a small country town are better off following the Progressives [left-wing liberals], the representatives of the world of banking, or by remaining steadfast by the old banners of agriculture. I closed thusly: "I can honor your fete no longer because my wife has cooked Brautklops today, and they are already getting cold." My Rosenbergers understood this speech. During the next week, my joke made the rounds of the entire province.[21]

For the first time, Oldenburg was actively challenged as he went about the district. He retaliated with his fists and his mouth; both results tended to backfire. When pressed too hard by one crowd, the Junker retorted, "The voice of the people is the voice of pigs."[22] This "joke" undoubtedly did make the rounds of the province as well. Oldenburg knew he had made a mistake; he later complained of being falsely accused of originating a phrase that was coined by General Wrangel as he put down the revolution in Berlin in 1848. It was scarcely an explanation that would pacify anyone.

All these disadvantages might not have defeated Oldenburg if the liberals had not pulled a clever trick in choosing candidates. The Center and liberals did not field one of their own but supported a conservative who

TABLE 7:2. *Voting in Elbing-Marienburg, 1907 and 1912, by Population of Place of Residence (by percentage of votes cast)* [23]

Population	1907				
	Turnout	German Conservative	National Liberal	Center	SPD
Less than 2,000	83.4	70.5	4.8	15.2	9.4
2,000–10,000	79.6	30.5	13.1	30.3	25.9
More than 10,000	81.8	21.8	23.3	10.8	43.9

Population	1912			
	Turnout	German Conser- vative	Free Conser- vative	SPD
Less than 2,000	82.5	65.8	20.6	13.5
2,000–10,000	79.4	29.6	33.5	36.8
More than 10,000	81.9	14.0	39.9	46.1

united the bourgeois opposition. City Forester Schröder was a safe candidate; his occupation put him neither in the agrarian nor in the industrial camp; he was right in supporting patriotism and attacking Socialism. Schröder campaigned under the banner of the free conservative party, whose moderate policies frightened neither urban businessmen nor rural *Gutsbesitzer*. But he was clearly an urban candidate. When viewed from the standpoint of the district as a whole or from a trichotomy based upon size of place, the election statistics seem to prove the success of this tactic. Schröder's totals appear to coincide with the combined Centrist and National Liberal vote in 1907 (see table 7:2). He had become the candidate of a unified urban bourgeoisie, gaining 53 percent of the vote in Marienburg city and, with 37.5 percent, giving the Socialist a very close race in Elbing.

Oldenburg was still king in the countryside. He lost only 5 percent of the vote from the 1907 totals in the rural areas of less than 2,000 population. The Conservative proportion of the vote in Marienburg city was larger than it had been in 1907. The Junker's only substantial losses were in Elbing city where his vote was halved from the 1907 figures. Still

Oldenburg got almost 40 percent of the vote and emerged again as the leading candidate going into the second election.

The election was actually decided by the fight for the second place in the runoff. Schröder won this battle with the Social Democrats by a plurality of only 66 votes out of more than 17,000 cast for both candidates. Many of these were urban Catholics who, because of their fears of Oldenburg, refused to honor the blue-black coalition of 1912. Luck had finally deserted Oldenburg. Instead of counting on the urban bourgeoisie to help him defeat the Socialist, the Junker now faced a situation where the Socialists supported his opponent. His rural bastions held firm, but they were decreasing in numbers. In 1903, the last close election, the district had been 48 percent rural; in 1912 it was only 42 percent. Oldenburg got 43 percent of the votes cast in the runoff, an election that set a record for levels of participation.

The Junker who was so maddeningly combative took his defeat with surprising grace. He had never liked the Reichstag anyway. The BdL and the Conservatives sought to honor him for his work; Oldenburg spoke to an agrarian gathering called together for this purpose: "I have the feeling that this is no farewell but a harvest celebration, not the kind when one envies the other but one in which we all participate, he that receives the crown as well as he who gives it. My men, you bring me the harvest crown today because my life is entwined with yours. We belong to each other in a way that no one can deny."[24] Oldenburg's sense of community, his loyalty to the land and its people, are all expressed here. But it is well to remember that there was another side to Oldenburg's character that was not capturable by the bucolic muse. The urban image of Oldenburg was just as sharp, most pungently expressed by a statement in the *Königsberger Volkszeitung*, claiming that "the Junker lusts for blood."[25] The truth depended upon the place of the beholder, whether he was in a *Gutsbezirk* or on the quays of Elbing. And the differences in these answers truly captured the nature of political conflict in the German east.

If there was any doubt about Oldenburg's moral integrity or his strength of character, it should be dissolved by the reminder that the aged ex–court chamberlain, well into his eighties, was the only one with the courage to inform the sick and guarded Hindenburg about the Nazi atrocities in June 1934, at a time and place long distanced from his native monarchist East Elbia, but not from his sense of moral purpose.[26]

8

GRAUDENZ-STRASBURG IN WEST
PRUSSIA-BRIESEN: 1912

As wrenching as were the disputes between the countryside and city in
the German east or among other social groupings, there was still one area
of conflict that unleashed greater heat at a lower flashpoint: the time-
honored and time-worn battle between German and Pole. The electoral
conflicts were only an extension of these national rivalries, which produced deep divisions in the east over the distribution of land, educational
policy, civil rights, and finally emerged in a number of political statements
from boycott movements to election campaigns. Thus electoral politics
was only one part of a continuing set of responses rooted in daily life.
This makes the Polish-German division an ideal example of affirming
politics, for examining not only their intensity and strength but also how
the contextual relationships at the local and provincial levels continually
reinforced and extended the duration of these conflicts.

The struggle in West Prussia was particularly pertinent since one out of
every five inhabitants of the province was a Pole; 6 percent more came
from allied Slavic groups like the Kassubians. These national groupings
formed loyalties that overrode almost all other allegiances based on class,
occupation, and religion. On one hand they solidified the Protestant *Bürgertum* in ways impossible for all of Germany, overcoming interest-group
tensions and other divisions, thus forming something like a coherent
social grouping. On the other hand, the Polish reality consisted of an ex-
emplary affirming social grouping composed of shopkeepers, ennobled
landowners, urban and rural laborers, where nationalist loyalties took
precedence over all other considerations.

These distinctions were very real; the lines of battle were very finely
drawn and instantly recognizable—that is, to West Prussians. The inhabitants of the province knew who were Poles, even if they spoke German and had a perfectly good German name. The distinction was only
somewhat blurred by the Poles' slow rate of assimilation into the dominant German culture as demonstrated by the low but constant rate of
intermarriage. Moreover this blurring was countered by the willingness

of certain urban Poles to stand up and be counted as shown by the decline in the numbers of registered German Catholics and dual speakers after 1890. Part of this decline may have been due to the propensities of census-takers, but much seems to have been the result of renewed Polish consciousness among those heretofore labeled as German Catholics or as dual speakers.[1]

Thus we have the classic confrontation where the politics were determined by the basic demographic strength of each social grouping and by the ability of each social grouping to bring out all its voters, not by issues or candidates. The demographic dispositions in the early Wilhelmine period favored the Polish minority. If the Poles had been distributed evenly through West Prussia, there would have been comfortable German majorities in each electoral district. Instead there were only 115 Poles—men, women, and children—among the 55,000 inhabitants of Elbing city in 1912, while there were counties where the Polish majority was four to one. The Poles were in a majority of thirteen of the twenty-nine administrative units of West Prussia. These patterns of homogenous settlement reinforced the bonds of national grouping and made penetration of disconcerting information very difficult. In the case of the Poles, it increased an already enormously strong propensity to stay inside the social, cultural, and political borders of Polandom. The result was electoral success; in 1890 the Poles won six out of the thirteen West Prussian seats, the high-water mark of their electoral power in the province.

"Pole here!—German there!" were the watchwords of the Wilhelmine east. They established indelible lines of political conflict around those already hardened boundaries of social and economic cleavage. These conflicts were reinforced by the government's *Polenpolitik*, which focused on re-Germanizing the province. The Poles responded by asserting their exclusivity and by forming a ring of institutional supports to defend the barriers of their social grouping: the Polish priest in the Catholic church, the gymnastic and choral societies, the savings banks and agricultural cooperatives, the political clubs and election committees. Pole here!—German there! did really describe the nature of the organizational as well as the demographic bases (see chapter 4, section 6).

But after 1890 the demographic tides changed. The German areas began to grow faster than the Polish. By 1898 the Poles retained only three of the six seats previously held. The changes over the province were very slight; the Polish losses were due to a swing of only 3.15 percent of the voters. Much of this swing was caused by the out-migration of Poles from the province to the Ruhr or Berlin without a commensurate loss of German voters as was the case in Posen. The ratio of Poles to the total rural population declined as much as 3 percent between 1900 and 1910 alone. As the proportion of Poles decreased in their rural strongholds, the German majorities in the cities were further enhanced. Rural West Prussian

Germans were more likely to stay in the province and wind up as workers in the ports or factories of the coastal or river-front cities.[2]

These slight demographic swings were supported by an intensification of the organizing effort within the German community as a whole. From the 1880s the government had embarked on resettlement plans to increase the proportion of the German population. While these plans did very little to bring in Germans, they encouraged an enormous propaganda effort which solidified national loyalties. This effort was supported and to a certain extent exploited by the radical nationalist propagandists established in the Eastern Marches Society and other anti-Polish organizations. There were 8,937 members of the Eastern Marches Society in West Prussia in 1908 with sixty-two local branches. The membership came from those categories of educated *Mittelstand* Germans committed to new-style radical populism. One out of four of the total was a civil servant, one out of ten a teacher, one out of five a free professional.[3]

The real front line of battle against the Poles swept up not only the government and radical pressure groups but those representing the traditional *Bürgertum* and the agrarian aristocrats as well. Thus the government placed pressure on its civil servants. The *Rittergutsbesitzer* showed a renewed interest in controlling his clients (see chapters 2 and 4). The BdL became increasingly involved with anti-Polish agitation. In most close districts, all German interests united under a single candidate, a kind of anti-Polish *Sammlung* representing all the local elite groups. This was quite different in content and form from the Oldenburg petition of 1907 which attempted to diminish attacks on the candidate as a representative of narrow elite interests and for that reason included a large proportion of workers and independent farmers (see table 8:1). The petition signed for the anti-Polish candidate Sieg in Graudenz–Strasburg–Briesen was designed to show a united elite of which Sieg was an ideal representative as a National Liberal landowner with strong nationalist leanings whose estate's name, *Siegsruhe*, seemed also to recall the best traditions of conservative landholding. The Sieg petition therefore was a manifestation of a Protestant *Bürgertum* elite that drew heavily from civil servants, free professionals, and large landowners. It represented both the groups that spewed forth the populist anti-Polish agitation and the staid center of rural and urban Germandom. Protestant *Bürgertum* centrality did work when the enemy was large enough, when the enemy appeared to challenge the entire national and local enterprise. The Sieg petition closed with the following call to battle:

> The enemy is a Pole! The electoral slogan reads short and clear:
> Here German! There Polish!
> Laziness or neutrality are treasons to the German cause. Every Ger-

TABLE 8:1. *Occupations of Signers of Two Electoral Petitions in West Prussia in 1907 (percent distribution)*[4]

Occupational Class	Oldenburg Petition In Elbing-Marienburg (N=2,631)	Sieg Petition in Graudenz-Strasburg (N=254)
Civil servants	11.7	21.7
(of these, railway workers)	(6.7)	
Teachers	1.7	13.8
Free professionals	.5	9.1
Businessmen	8.4	9.8
Salespersons	1.7	6.7
White-collar workers	1.6	1.2
Craftsmen	21.5	13.8
Workers	19.0	3.5
Large landowners	.5	14.2
Other independent farmers	30.6	3.1
Retired	2.8	3.1
Total	100.0	100.0

man voter must know that every German vote is needed. No one should be absent from the polls on January 25.

Who does not fulfill his electoral duty as a German man helps the Poles to victory, weakens Germany in the East, encourages all enemies of the German Empire at home and abroad.[5]

This German elite confronted a massive Polish resistance. In Graudenz-Strasburg-Briesen these two forces faced each other in continuous battle along a whole series of fronts, economic, social, ideological, and eventually political. And, as in most cases, these struggles were reinforced by homogenous patterns of settlement. The Poles lived in the countryside. In 1880 the bulk of the district was both rural and Polish. About two-thirds of the population in Briesen, Strasburg, and Graudenz counties were engaged in agriculture; over 60 percent of the population of Strasburg and Briesen counties were Poles as well. Even though only 40 percent of Graudenz County was Polish, there was a clear majority of Poles in the countryside which found its expression in the rural vote. The Polish party also dominated in the small market towns, especially Strasburg city with a population of 8,000 (see table 8:2).

It was a quintessential Slavic countryside, bleak and poor. Unlike those around Danzig and Elbing, the flat lands were broken up by numerous rivers and lakes. There were more woods and fewer people than on the Baltic coast. Farmers tended to produce the coarser grains like rye, because modest rainfall befitted their inland condition. All of this resulted in considerable poverty. The average income taxes paid in Strasburg were two-thirds those of Elbing County and only one-half those of Marienburg County. The poverty was reinforced by the national character of the process of exploitation. This was particularly true in Graudenz County, where the Germans owned two-thirds of the large estates while the Poles provided 60 percent of the agricultural laborers.[6]

But whether the Polish rural laborer worked for a German or Polish landowner, he was organized and would vote Polish. As with the rest of eastern Polandom, this was accomplished without any social revolution. The Polish leadership in Graudenz-Strasburg-Briesen rested on traditional lines; all of the Reichstag candidates were ennobled. When the Central Office in Posen objected to the district's candidate in 1912, the ennobled lawyer and landowner in question was replaced with another specimen of the same breed. The free professionals and businessmen accepted their "natural" leaders and willingly served on the central electoral committee for the district which represented a wider cross-section of society. And if Strasburg in 1912 can be taken as an example, the base of local organization extended even deeper into the community as a whole, including proprietors of small farms, priests, even a mason as well as the predictable large landowner or two.[7] The propensity of all classes in the Polish community to accept the lead of Polish notables was attacked by German Conservatives and especially by Social Democrats. The SPD argued that nationality conflict only benefited the employers since it split the workingmen into competing camps. "We must remember," stated one Socialist broadside in 1912, "that, when the Kingdom of Poland still existed, the Polish nobleman sucked the last drop of blood from the Polish people. Was he then the brother of the Polish peasant and the Polish artisan?"[8] All of this was, of course, quite irrelevant to the nature of the political cleavage in the district.

Poles voted for Poles regardless of class or conviction. This was particularly true in the rural areas which formed the heart of the Polish vote in Graudenz-Strasburg-Briesen. There strong national pride and resilient institutional supports, the links formed by those economically and culturally exploited, resulted in an extraordinarily high and persistently strong Polish vote (see table 8 : 2).

The percentage ratio of Polish vote to Poles in the entire population was very high in the two predominantly rural counties, even higher in the cities where the figures were wildly skewed by the large amount of declared dual speakers who were really Polish thinking and Polish voting (see table 8 : 3). The figures for Briesen County are not available since only a part of it was included in the district. However the other data

TABLE 8:2. *Voting in Graudenz-Strasburg-Briesen, 1898–1912, by Population of Place of Residence (in percentage of votes cast)*

Population	Turnout	National Liberal	Center	Poles	SPD
		1898			
Less than 2,000	90.3	46.2	0.1	53.4	0.3
2,000–10,000	82.0	42.5	0.5	56.0	0.8
Graudenz	83.4	72.9	0.4	20.9	5.8
		1903			
Less than 2,000	94.5	44.5	0.3	53.6	1.6
2,000–10,000	75.4	42.0	0.5	56.1	1.4
Graudenz	75.4	57.3	1.1	19.1	22.4
		1907			
Less than 2,000	94.2	48.3	0.1	50.3	1.1
2,000–10,000	91.4	42.8	4.7	50.6	5.7
Graudenz	88.5	58.3	0.5	24.0	17.2
		1912			
Less than 2,000	91.6	47.4	0.1	50.2	1.5
2,000–10,000	87.3	44.5	0.8	46.7	5.6
Graudenz	75.5	53.2	1.6	20.9	16.0

clearly demonstrate national solidarities matched by high turnout particularly in rural areas, and by consistently high levels of voting throughout all administrative units, indicating little absenteeism due to intimidation (see chapter 3).

Despite these advantages, the Polish presence in the district began to decline. The Polish party had won three out of five elections between 1881 and 1893. But the margins were never secure. In 1890 the Polish victory was by less than 300 out of 20,000 votes, 87 percent of the eli-

TABLE 8:3. *Strength of Polish Voting in 1907 and 1912 Elections*[9]

Administrative Unit	Ratio of % Polish Party Vote to % of Poles in Total Population		Actual % of Total Vote for Polish Party in 1912
	1907	1912	
Graudenz City	2.01	1.74	20.9
Graudenz County	0.98	0.98	38.4
Strasburg County	0.94	0.94	60.3

gibles participating (see table 8:4). Thus it took only very small shifts in the voting population to make the district German. The elections still continued to be very close until 1907. In 1903 Sieg won the district by only 400 votes out of 27,000 ballots cast in the runoff, with a turnout of over 90 percent of the eligible voters. Gradually the pattern of out-migration reduced the Polish lead in the countryside, decreasing their margin from more than 6 percent to less than 1 percent in areas of less than 2,000 population in the first election.[10]

The second prong of the German advance was small but perceptible urbanization of the district, particularly the growth of Graudenz city. The proportion of the district that lived in Graudenz city increased from 16 percent to 23 percent of the total district population in the last two decades of Wilhelmine Germany. And Graudenz was distinctly German.

Poles did not come to Graudenz in great numbers; it was not a city overwhelmed by undercounted dual speakers. German peasants came to Graudenz and stayed; they joined the rowing union; their children be-came part of the amateur theater group. They strolled down Marien-werder Street past the Schwarzer Adler and in the city forest and, most of all, they opened up small shops and carried on light trade. The city thrived on this. There was not enough industry to yield an enormous SPD vote, but there was trade and commerce. Goods moved from the east through Graudenz and up the Vistula to Marienburg or across its famous bridge to the west. This tended to connect the Germans in Graudenz with those in Elbing, Danzig, and East Prussia and to reinforce their already strong national attitudes by isolating them from the sur-rounding countryside.

This isolation was reinforced by a striking physical separation between the city and countryside. The lines were drawn cleanly between the neigh-boring *Güter* and the city. Moreover the city had its striking features. On the castle hill was the surviving watchtower of the medieval bastion where the German Order had ruled the neighboring Slavic countryside. And dominating the entire landscape was the eighteenth-century fortress on the cliffs of the Vistula, named after its commander, and still in use in 1914.

TABLE 8:4. *Polish and German Voting in Graudenz-Strasburg-Briesen: 1890–1912 (percentage of votes cast)*

| Year | First Election | | | | | | Second Election | | |
	Turnout	National Liberal	Other Protestant Bürgertum Parties	Center	Pole	SPD	Turnout	German	Pole
1890	83.6	35.0	17.0[a]	0.2	47.0	0.8	86.2	49.2	50.8
1893	80.0	18.7	30.1[b]	—	49.0	2.0	83.0	49.0	51.7
1898	88.7	50.1		0.2	48.4	1.2	—	—	—
1903	88.7	46.5		0.5	47.6	5.2	90.6	50.7	49.3
1907	92.7	49.8		0.2	44.9	5.1	93.8	52.3	47.7
1912[c]	87.1	48.2		0.5	43.5	5.2	89.2	54.1	45.0

[a] Left-wing liberal.
[b] German Conservative.
[c] In 1912, 2.6 % of the ballots were unmarked.

Over 30 percent of the male labor force in Graudenz was in the army. This might not have any direct effect on elections because soldiers serving under the colors were disenfranchised, but it must have contributed to the flavor of political life and the political views of the town's inhabitants.[11]

After all, the fortress had withstood a siege in 1807 by the French and had held out until the entire Prussian army had surrendered. Such facts created a kind of central mythology for the city, which was constantly used during elections. Each new election created another call to defend the bastion against foreign enemies. As an electoral broadside put out by the soldiers' unions in 1907 stated, "Shall Graudenz that in 1807 withstood the Corsican be lost in 1907 to the Poles who even then sought to make the fortress fall through their mutinies and desertions."[12]

There were defections from the overwhelmingly Protestant *Bürgertum*, of course. The SPD made heavy inroads in the city, reducing the National Liberal vote by about a fourth. Graudenz city itself was a curious anomaly, a place of between 10,000 and 100,000 that produced a lower turnout than the rural area surrounding it. And the nature of this effect was unpredictable—1903 and 1912 yielded very low turnout; 1898 and 1907 produced a much higher figure. If we posit that the 1907 response was a one-time plebiscitary effect which did not fully integrate all city voters into the electoral system, this could mean that a "normal" turnout rate in the city was as much as 15 percent lower than that for the countryside. This lower turnout counterbalanced some of the demographic effect caused by the relatively rapid growth of Graudenz vis-à-vis the Polish rural areas. Thus, instead of adding 5 percent of the total vote to the German cause in the 1890s and the first decade of the twentieth century as its population growth would predict, Graudenz city added less than 2 percent of the total vote to the German side. This was a swing of 4 percent, since another 2 percent would be subtracted from the Polish. But, with the gradual increase of German vote in the rural areas and smaller towns, it was enough to make the district safely German by 1912.

The increasing inevitability of Polish losses did nothing to lower turnout and other forms of participation. The German-Polish struggle remained always the central electoral question, win, lose, or draw. This can be demonstrated by the fact that turnout rates in runoffs were uniformly higher than for first elections in a Polish-German contest. Usually, some party loyalists would drop out after the first election, but this was not the case when the major affirming contest was in the runoff. In 1907 the runoff voters in Graudenz-Strasburg-Briesen included almost 94 percent of the eligibles, an extraordinarily high number; Sieg won the election with 52.3 percent, a margin of over 5 percent of the vote, the equivalent of a landslide in this district.

Yet the strength of their affirming loyalties brought the Poles out again in 1912. They made lame excuses that it was otherwise, claiming that they

could emerge victorious with only minor adjustments. The candidate himself, a certain Domrinski, argued that the losses sustained to the SPD had
cost the election, but the SPD was not even in the runoff. Then there was an
even more fantastic belief that large numbers of Poles had not voted in
1907. Father Doering preferred this thesis in a meeting of the district electoral committee, claiming that 1,500 lazy Poles had lost the contest. But
only 1,700 of the total eligible voters were no-shows; raising the level of
turnout to the good Deacon's expectations would have meant voting the
dead and dogs, as long as they were male and over twenty-four.[13]

The Poles campaigned harder and more consistently in 1912 than in any
previous election. In Strasburg, in the heart of West Prussian Polandom,
one meeting after another was held in January of 1912 with attendance
sometimes running over 200. Yet at the end of the first election in 1912, the
Polish candidate trailed Sieg by 1,324 votes, only 30 fewer than in 1907.
Even then, the national hatreds and national commitments made affirming social-grouping politics work. Everyone was to be counted, both German and Pole. The Germans in Graudenz were moved certainly by much
the same calls that appeared in the neighboring *Schwetzer Kreisblatt und
Zeitung.*

> Do we want to be represented by a delegate of a small uninfluential
> party that belongs to the enemies of the Empire and the Emperor?
>   No, we don't want that.
> Do we want a delegate that believes in the sharpening of national
> differences?
>   No, we don't want that.

The antiphonal responses continued until the peroration:

> German Brothers
> Let no man of you be absent from the ballot box on
> January 25.
> You brothers of the Polish tongue!
> Free yourself from the control of the demagogues
> that damage us all and poison our life.[14]

Or there was the speech of Deacon Klatt to the Poles in the small town of
Lautenberg in Strasburg County: "The purpose of the runoff elections
has already been discussed. It has already been stated that all—blind and
lame, cripples and retired—have to appear. In the last election 42 Poles
were missing."[15]

It was not for want of trying that the Poles lost in 1912. Sieg gained
54.1 percent of the vote in the 1912 runoff, almost two points better than
he had done in 1907. Certainly the Poles tried hard enough; and with
almost 90 percent turnout in the runoff it is difficult to find any substantial Polish group that was untouched. The truth was that the demo-

graphic and political tides were against the Poles and Graudenz-Strasburg
was increasingly becoming safely German. But what did winning or losing mean? The struggles between German and Pole on the periphery
could hardly be taken as indicating national trends or approval of government policy; they were small-stakes contests and caused hardly a ripple
on the national scene. But it was never winning or losing that vindicated
the system nor elicited common nationwide responses, nor created affirming voting patterns. These Poles and Germans were the quintessential
affirming voters, moved by their loyalties and commitments, attempting
to meet perceived and often real threats and dangers, necessarily articulating the boundaries of their political social groupings, reinforcing
through politics the fundamental cleavages present in everyday life. Politics was the one totally legal, if not totally legitimized, expression for
these differences. Electoral politics crystallized and heightened cleavages
that went back generations and promised to continue indefinitely. Losing
in 1907 did not mean the end for articulating Polishness; one could do
the same in 1912 and presumably, if there had been no war, in 1917.

9

DORTMUND-HÖRDE: 1898–1912

Dortmund in Westphalia represents a textbook case of the growth of affirming social-grouping politics. A stronghold of the Protestant *Mittelstand* at midcentury, the city and the district that surrounded it were transformed by massive in-migration and social change into a battleground between the Protestant *Bürgertum* and deviant affirming groupings. Dortmund-Hörde elections were waged with increasing intensity and ferocity. There was seldom any thought of compromise or making political alliances in a district where the nature of the contests dictated a runoff. Instead of using the French tactic of coddling possible runoff supporters by refusing to attack them in first elections, Dortmund's electoral rhetoric was characterized by constant, repetitive, and threatening attacks on all others. This especially undercut the advantages that the National Liberal candidates might have as centers of an anti-Socialist *Sammlung*. But the refusal to understand and act upon the aspirations of others was not confined to the middle-class leadership of the German Protestant *Bürgertum*; it was the way the Center and the SPD treated the Poles. It characterized the nature and persistence of affirming social-grouping politics and, as with so many things, was both its fundamental strength and its most substantial weakness.

Wilhelmine Dortmund was a city of the industrial revolution. A Hanseatic town and important trade center in the late middle ages, it had declined in status to a small Prussian administrative and marketing town in the early nineteenth century. The population had risen to an appreciable level by 1850 with 10,000 inhabitants, but there was nothing in Dortmund's history to prepare the city for the vast influx of people in the next half-century. By 1900 its population had reached 142,000. The trend continued into the twentieth century; there were 214,000 residents in Dortmund by 1910. The electoral district comprising the city and Dortmund and Hörde counties grew at almost the same phenomenal rate. With over 500,000 inhabitants in 1912, it had become the fourth largest electoral district in Germany. This meant that substantial towns and cities grew out of crossroad villages and small market towns in just decades. By 1900, eight cities had populations greater than Dortmund's had been in 1850. They bore names that conjure up images of steel and coal—Castrop, Hörde city, Schwerte. The cities spawned "colonies," most often in the shape of truncated quarter-moons spreading out over the landscape wherever there was a mine. It was a quintessential industrial setting. By 1907, the date of the last imperial occupational census, over 80 percent of the male work force was engaged in industry and mining. Over 60 percent of the inhabitants lived in cities with populations exceeding 10,000; less than 8 percent lived in places with under 2,000 people. And a good number of these rural inhabitants were nonfarmers residing in small mining colonies.

This influx even refashioned the topography of the district. The rolling hills and the church steeples were replaced as principal points of reference by the thirty or more Bessemer converters and the high shafts of the mine elevators. The converters threw up a constant gray smoke that dirtied not only the bricks of the factory buildings but the fashionable shopfronts in downtown Dortmund as well. Luckily, the smoke would periodically be dispersed by those prevailing and predominant North Sea winds, which chill to the bone even in mid-July. Only these winds and the ever-present Prussian *Sanitätionsrat* stood between the average Dortmunder and those airborne diseases such as typhus which reached almost epidemic levels in similar towns in southern Europe.

Each in its own way, the *Sanitätionsrat* and the converter were symbols of the flood of activity and purposefulness that characterized life in the district. The inhabitants were mostly new settlers or the children of new settlers. The population bore those demographic characteristics associated with a high proportion of recent in-migrants. It was younger than the Reich average with a higher ratio of males to females. The new settlers came mostly from Westphalia and the neighboring provinces of Hanover and Hesse. At the turn of the century there was a massive in-migration of Poles and Massurians, who comprised about 7 percent of the population by the time of World War I. The Poles remained separated by nationality and language from the Germans; they did not thrust themselves into the life of the district. But they were the exception. Elsewhere new men overwhelmed the old settlers; they formed not only the bulk of the organized proletariat but the middle class as well. They replaced the old settlers in the positions of leadership in social and cultural activities and in local government and politics. Middle class, craftsmen, steelworkers—all seemed to have at least one thing in common: they appeared not to recognize the old, the traditional, particularly in German civic life. The educated bourgeoisie, the *Bildungsbürgertum* as it was called, played scarcely any role in Dortmund or other cities after 1900. Dortmund had no opera house, hardly any theater. It was a plain, workday city, the center of a plain, workday district.[1]

Yet this massive in-migration did not lead to a total disordering of local political life. This is particularly striking when we consider that this in-migration was accompanied by a massive out-migration. The district's population was clearly on the move, changing as much as 10 percent of its residents in any one year. Yet all these new voters simply lined up along social, religious, and national lines, very often based upon commitments they had held before they moved into the district, and would hold after they had moved out. There were in Dortmund three recognizable social groupings: German Catholic, Socialist working class, and Polish. These social groupings organized Dortmunders, old and new, in separate clusters, like the steel filings that cling to the poles of the various magnets in high school physics experiments. Elections were one of the means by which Dortmunders affirmed their loyalties; the results show a high and persistent turnout, reaching over 88 percent in the first election of 1907.

By 1900 these in-migrants and natives had coalesced into patterns of settlement, which formed the distinctive electoral geography of the district. The National Liberals were strongest in the cities of Dortmund and Hörde, which had the largest concentrations of males in white-collar occupations—clerks and commission agents, proprietors of small stores, civil servants of all descriptions. The largest number of Center voters were in the mining colonies and the working-class cities of Dortmund County. The Poles were particularly numerous in Dortmund County, comprising 13 percent of its population and almost a quarter of the inhabitants of such cities as Castrop. The Socialists dominated in overwhelmingly Protestant Hörde County and in the mining colonies and suburbs around Dortmund itself.

This in-migration not only changed the electoral geography; it fundamentally altered the mix or proportions among these social groupings and thus determined the direction of electoral politics within the district. The waves of migrants overturned the traditional system of Dortmund politics whereby elections were principally contested within the Protestant *Bürgertum*. After 1890 the SPD emerged to challenge the domination of the Protestant *Bürgertum* in a series of runoffs with National Liberals. Finally, in 1912 the force of these new migrants totally prevailed; the liberals were eliminated from the runoff and the contest was between the two new boys on the block—the Center and the SPD.

Spatially rooted with secure institutional and ideological supports, these social groupings set the tone for elections in Dortmund-Hörde. Campaigning consisted principally of asserting the differences among affirming voters. Specific issues, unrelated to cleavages among the groupings, were seldom discussed; candidates were almost inconsequential to the process. Only the National Liberals consistently fielded a local; the SPD and Centrist candidates were almost always nonresidents who seldom even visited Dortmund. Theodor Bömelburg, a Hamburg trade-union official, represented Dortmund-Hörde from 1903 to 1912 but was rarely in the district between campaigns and spent only a few weeks there before each election. There was very little opportunity to challenge Bömelburg on the basis of his service to the Reichstag since the delegation voted as a unit. In fact, the only serious attacks against him came as a result of his activities in the annual party meetings, where his outspoken revisionism required explanation in a "radical" district.[2]

Bömelburg's case was not unique. In 1912, the most intense of the prewar campaigns, there were over three hundred political meetings in Dortmund-Hörde. At least eighty of these were held in the three weeks before the election. No more than ten of these meetings were addressed by various candidates.[3] This was not replicated everywhere throughout the Reich, yet it shows how far things could go in an intensely politicized district. In Dortmund the candidates had become almost irrelevant. What mattered was to hold those eligibles already committed to one's own grouping, to undermine the loyalties that other voters held to their groupings and, in the end, to become the second choice of a majority of those voters whose real choices were excluded from campaigning in the runoff.

All of this gave a specifically Wilhelmine tone to the campaign. Dortmund elections were not defined by any sort of consensus or decided on the personality of an individual. One did not talk to an opponent; one talked *through* him. The attacker and the person thus attacked were robbed of a common linkage, except when they had a mutual contempt or fear of a third social grouping. This is why Dortmund electoral rhetoric was so maddeningly unperceptive; why Socialists, at least in public, could understand no other loyalty but class; why German Catholics pretended to believe in none but religion; why Poles considered only nationalism.

The classic example of such rhetoric and of social-grouping politics from which it sprang was in the treatment of the Poles. The very fact that there was a Polish social grouping caught the older elements unaware. There were practically no Polish speakers in Dortmund before the Wilhelmine period. By 1910 almost one in every ten inhabitants of the district was Polish speaking. Coming from East and West Prussia, from Silesia and Posen, these new migrants became adherents of the Polish party. The process was accelerated by the anti-Polish actions of the German government in those eastern provinces from which they had migrated, by the unwillingness or inability of the Ruhr bishops to provide adequate numbers of Polish priests, and by the discrimination Germans practiced at work and in the settlements (see chapter 4, section 6).

This grouping consciousness was expressed in a flurry of organizational activity. The Poles had produced what the government called a state within a state. In the Dortmund of 1911 there were Polish fraternal and national societies, religious associations, organizations of Polish journeymen, artisans, and manual workers, gymnastic and choral groups, lending libraries and banks. And, most important, there were two large electoral committees with a membership of over 250. In 1903 the Poles had fielded their first candidate and took 3.5 percent of the vote. In 1907 the figure rose to 5.5 percent, in 1912 to over 6 percent. How much of the Polish population voted Polish? The in-migration was too rapid and the count too tenuous to give more than a very tentative estimate. Still, assuming that very few Polish party voters were German, it seems that over two-thirds of the Poles voted for the Polish party in 1903 and 1907 and only a slightly smaller proportion in 1912. This was a clear case of social-grouping politics. Since the Poles could not hope to reach the runoff, most of their ballots were just to affirm their separateness. The Polish candidate did not live in the district; he did not even have to campaign. Polish votes were designed to show the other social groupings that the Poles had arrived and were to be reckoned with.

The primary losers from the creation of this new voting bloc were the Social Democrats and Catholics. Since the Poles were principally working class and uniformly Catholic, both of these parties had hopes of capturing much of their vote. Yet neither Socialist nor Centrist politicians had any idea how to accomplish this end. This failure was particularly crucial for the Centrists. In both 1903 and 1907 Polish Catholic voters could have easily placed the Center in the runoff with the SPD. The Poles voted for their own and placed a German Protestant industrialist in the second contest. The Poles felt this was deserved; the German Catholic response was too little and too late. It was only after the Poles began to show political clout that the Ruhr Centrist leaders talked about some amelioration of Polish grievances. And then they addressed only problems already over a decade old. In 1908 Lambert Lensing, the Dortmund Centrist leader, warned that the Poles in Rhineland-Westphalia might "get up to 50,000 votes for their own candidates and, thus, put the Center in a difficult situation without achieving any purpose. On the other hand, it is not to be denied that an ever-increasing number of migrating Poles, suffering from a lack of pastoral care, might become enraged and embittered by the conditions in their motherland and, under the heated influence of radical leaders, become more and more a prey for the Social Democrats."[4]

The crucial phrase in the argument is "without any purpose." They clearly demonstrate the traditional insensitivity of the German Catholic minority for Catholics of other nationalities. The Centrist leadership considered only religious loyalties. Lensing commented, "One goal must always take precedence over all others. All Catholics of whatever party must recognize only that which protects the religious interest of any and every part of the Catholic population."[5]

The Dortmund Socialists viewed the Polish vote as similarly superfluous; but they saw it through the rosy tints of class consciousness. The

SPD leadership was concerned about competition from the Polish workers' organizations and unions in the mines. Such organizations vitiated
the need for unity which was at the core of the union message. Moreover,
the vast majority of these Poles were blue-collar in-migrants; and yet they
refused to vote their class interests in both first and runoff elections. In
1898 and 1907 Poles withheld their votes in a runoff rather than vote for
a Socialist. The *Arbeiter Zeitung* claimed as early as 1898 that the Polish
political organizations were seriously undermining SPD strength in the
district. It calculated that 95 percent of the Polish vote was working class
and that, if the Poles had voted in the runoff, they would have overwhelmingly turned to the SPD. The paper concludes: "The task of the
class conscious workers is to win the Polish proletarians to the workers'
cause, these same Poles who are cut off from the working-class thinking
through the oppression of national chauvinism and the power of the
Catholic church."[6] All the bases were touched and an enormous propaganda effort ensued, but the injunction proved impossible to follow. Both
the Centrist and the SPD Polish policies in Dortmund were unmitigated
failures. Affirming politics was good at isolating and separating, not at
bringing together diverse groups under single banners.

The refusal to recognize the legitimacy of some affirmers was a longstanding tradition in Dortmund. The Centrists and Poles had been consistently attacked as divisive elements by the German Protestant *Bürgertum*. The Protestant *Bürgertum* was so accustomed to pronouncing its
own centrality that it at first refused to recognize even the existence of
dissident social groupings. As late as 1887 the elections in Dortmund-
Hörde were conducted as if they were familial struggles within the old
Mittelstand majority. The chief contests were between the various liberal
contingents. In 1881 and 1884 the left-wing liberals won the district;
after 1887 they were succeeded by the National Liberals, who were more
attuned to the newer industrializing elites. It was not until 1890 that this
Protestant *Mittelstand* domination was seriously challenged. The Center
presented a candidate for the first time in years, and the SPD increased its
vote fourfold in the first election (see table 9:1). Together these deviant
parties gained over 50 percent of the vote.

The liberals responded in a number of predictable ways. Gone was the
luxury of deciding between different brands of the same product. Liberal
voters seemed to recognize this and concentrated around the National
Liberal camp. Left-wing liberalism never got more than 4 percent of the
vote in the first election after 1890. Yet this consolidation was not enough.
The liberal parties were no longer broad coalitions that cut across class
lines; thus, the Dortmund liberal leadership could not count on large
numbers of deferential blue-collar workers trooping to the polls in their
support. In fact, they could hardly count on any blue-collar workers at
all. In 1903 in Dortmund city, the National Liberal vote was estimated to

TABLE 9:1. *Major Party Votes in Dortmund Elections: 1887 to 1912 (by percent)*[7]

Year	Turnout	National Liberal	Left-wing Liberal	Center	Socialist	Poles
1887	85.2	57.3	36.9		5.7	
1890						
1st	75.4	30.3	10.7	26.1	26.7	
2nd	72.5	53.9			46.1	
1893						
1st by-election	73.4	33.3	4.0	27.5	35.5	
1st regular election	78.4	34.8	0.1	28.2	36.7	
2nd	72.1	50.1			49.9	
1895						
1st	—	35.8		29.5	34.7	
2nd	—	46.6			53.4	
1898						
1st	78.1	31.0	3.9	30.3	34.7	
2nd	77.9	51.9			48.1	
1903						
1st	81.4	27.2	1.4	25.1	42.8	3.5
2nd	82.5	49.8			50.2	
1907						
1st	87.6	27.9	0.5	24.1	42.0	5.5
2nd	75.9	40.6			59.4	
1912						
1st	86.8	23.2	0.7	23.6	44.8	6.3
2nd	80.4			44.6	55.4	

be 90 percent white-collar (table 4:6). This made liberalism into a permanent minority in a city that was blue collar by about two to one. Not all of these white-collar workers were in the Protestant bourgeois camp; a fair number must have voted Center—a party whose supporters seemed unrelated to occupation. Thus, although the Protestant *Bürgertum* had made enormous strides in unifying everyone who came under the rubric of *Mittelstand* inside the city and probably within the district, this fact did not halt their slide into the status of a permanent minority in Reichstag elections. And if the National Liberals lost the district, their dominance might be threatened in the city council, in the regional assemblies, and perhaps even at the factory gate.

The result was a mild panic and the attempt to reassert their electoral power by intimidation through their control of the local police and bureaucracy. Unaccustomed to dealing with, and unable to control, the opposition, some of the liberal leaders considered flattening it. This was a typical reaction of a hitherto dominant elite to deluges of deviant voters (see chapter 3).

In 1890 the small mining towns of Hörde County were flooded with regular police, gendarmerie, and other officials who served as visible signs of the forces of law and order. These police not only served as symbols of intimidation, they practiced it. Known SPD sympathizers were discouraged from entering the polls. The most visible corruption was in Hörde city, where the mayor called out the *Landwehr* and filled the streets with a bourgeoisie in uniform. SPD and Centrist voters there were harassed by the police in combination with the supervisory employees of the Hörde Mining and Milling Association. Furthermore, the National Liberal ballot was so marked as to be distinguishable by polling officials. Officials of the Mining Association and police sergeants loitered around the polls to make sure that this ballot was cast. Around noon the Center party leaders thought of reprinting their ballots to conform to the National Liberal specifications. This worked only for a short time; the National Liberals appeared with a new ballot at 3 p.m. Such techniques used in the first and runoff elections achieved a final victory by 3,000 votes for the National Liberal candidate, Theodor Möller, over the SPD.[8]

The Reichstag naturally invalidated the election. Möller had to stand again in a by-election that was held in June 1893. But then the beleaguered National Liberals were hit with another blow. The Reichstag was dissolved between the time of the first election and the runoff. This necessitated a new first election and a subsequent runoff in which Möller again won—by only 64 votes out of 43,000 cast. That was not yet the end. There was more fraud and intimidation. This time it was localized in the Catholic areas of Dortmund County. In May 1895 the Reichstag Committee on Election Validation was again ready to bring in another unfavorable report. Möller by then had a surfeit of elections and invalidations; he resigned from the Reichstag.

On 23 May 1895 the Reichstag met to consider a whole series of reports on the validity of their membership. The Centrist leader Julius Bachem joined the SPD in advocating that Möller's resignation not be accepted. Bachem and the SPD speaker Paul Singer wanted to invalidate the election and kick Möller out of a Reichstag from which he had already resigned. After all, something had to be done to stop the mess in Dortmund. Bachem and Singer were unsuccessful. The opposition pointed out that such a precedent might lead to the invalidation of a seat held by a dead member. A majority of the membership seemed frightened by the task of delivering a message at least figuratively into the depths of hell.

Some message was heard in Dortmund; the enormous fraud stopped, with a predictable result.[9] The by-election of 1895 brought the election of Dr. Franz Lütgenau, the first successful SPD candidate in the Ruhr, and his margin of victory was over 3,000 votes.

Unable to undermine the electoral system, the Dortmund liberals would have to cope with their enemies. They would have to win the runoff with the help of voters outside their limited sphere. The requirement of a majority vote in a runoff is the peculiarity of primaries in the southern United States and Wilhelmine Germany. Victory in both systems was determined by favorable placement and by making deals with candidates who were excluded from the runoff. In Dortmund the liberals were not as favorably placed as they were in other areas where they had a larger vote in the first election or where they could garner conservative voters against the Socialists or Socialist votes against the conservatives. Therefore the National Liberals would have to make deals, which they were reluctant to do. Making deals was anathema to a former majority; it meant considering Catholics as equals. Since it was the Center which was eliminated after the first election in Dortmund from 1890 onward, German Catholic voters would be needed to beat the SPD.

Thus the National Liberals in 1898 only brushed up their images and refurbished their campaign rhetoric rather than dealing with the Catholics. They had a new candidate, the personable industrialist Alexander Hilbck. Hilbck seemed so attractive that the *Arbeiter Zeitung* warned its readers against inadequate political enlightenment and urged them to consider "the party and not the person . . . especially when a candidate of the upper classes has a winning personality, is an ingratiating speaker and is an honorable man in private life."[10] The editors did not have to worry. Affirming and not personal politics dominated the Dortmund electorate, and affirmers would still be labeled as deviant by the Protestant *Bürgertum*.

However reasonable it might be to charm Catholic voters, the liberal press never seemed able to avoid that last anti-Catholic jab. On 26 May 1898 the *Dortmunder Zeitung*, the National Liberal organ, began its election campaign with an article attacking Centrist election tactics. Entitled "Political Support by Sucklings," the article heaped scorn on the statements of a single priest that even Catholic children should be mobilized for the campaign. A few days later the whole district was alive with rumors that the National Liberal candidate still supported the ideas of the *Kulturkampf*. These rumors were fed when it turned out that Hilbck had refused to relinquish his membership in the Evangelical Union, a virulently anti-Catholic organization. Meanwhile the *Dortmunder Zeitung* published a strong piece just three days before the first election, which challenged the Catholic Church as a political institution.[11]

On the day after the first election, however, the same paper could demand that the Catholics support the National Liberals, since the latter party had not attacked the Church or Center party during the campaign. Like so many representatives of *Kartell* politics in 1898, the *Dortmunder Zeitung* editors emphasized the alliance of *Bürgertum* parties against the disturbers of the empire and the opponents of the military budget (generally agreed to be one and the same). It was the perfect example of that combination of fatherland rhetoric and statement of *Mittelstand* centrality which characterized Protestant *Bürgertum* politics. The "good industrialist" and good Protestant Hilbck transcended all particular interests. In their minds, he was "a candidate whom everyone can support regardless of his estate or profession, Protestants as well as Catholics, industrialists as well as agriculturalists, salesmen as well as artisans, civil servants and workers . . ."[12] The message was even translated into poetry. The following poem appeared in the *Dortmunder Zeitung* just a few days before the second election:

> It has to do with good and bad
> For the whole people whether rich, whether poor,
> Whether it is tied to the herd,
> Whether it is produced in knowledge's realm.
> Let there be only one thought at hand
> Bursting forth in a fire bright:
> In every storm I shall not take flight.
> My heart belongs to the Fatherland.
>
> Fresh on to battle you men of the pen,
> You men in homely worker's clothes!
> To the Empire and Emperor loyal all
> In battle now and for all time we stand.
> Let us not through speech be deceived;
> They can never you mislead
> The phrase: It is the Fatherland.[13]

For the Centrists, then, there were no promises, only a renewed assertion of Protestant *Mittelstand* centrality and, of course, the continuation of Protestant, industrialist control in Dortmund. But the Center had its own ideological irons in the fire, and these kept them from an alliance with the SPD. After all, the SPD was not only anti-Catholic; it was anti-God as well. Moreover, the Socialist allure leading to the defection of Catholic workers was much more keenly worrisome than the attractions of the National Liberals for middle-class Catholics.

Therefore the Westphalian Centrist leadership decided to abandon their policies of 1890 and 1893 where the party had remained neutral. The Center urged its supporters to vote for all liberals over the SPD.

These instructions were translated into dogma at church services on the Sunday intervening between the first election and the runoff. If the priest was not inclined to instruct his parishioners, they could still find their marching orders in the form of leaflets reinforced by as much informal social control as the Catholic social grouping could muster. The result was that National Liberals reclaimed the district by 3,000 votes.

The Centrists did expect some rewards for their aid in returning the district to the National Liberal camp. More than any other party, the Center was used to trading votes for recognition and support of Catholic causes. In Dortmund this raised hopes that the liberals would share their entrenched power in the cities and in society. As late as 1900 *Tremonia*, the Catholic organ, was still praising Hilbck. For the National Liberals, however, the alliance had only to do with runoff voters. The liberal domination of civic and provincial government remained intact. After all, they had never promised to share. On the contrary, by 1902 the National Liberal speakers and the *Dortmunder Zeitung* were regularly talking about the ultramontane menace. National Liberal committees were organized around the specifically Protestant symbols of monarchy and religion. There was a plethora of patriotic family evenings in which the chief entertainment was provided by the anti-Catholic Evangelical Singing Association.[14]

The National Liberals were, after all, the representatives of the German Protestant *Bürgertum*, and this meant they had to support the cultural as well as class and national aspects of this group. Anti-Catholicism was one of the strongest cultural goods of such a *Bürgertum*; even the flimsiest and more fleeting support of Catholic causes would call forth attacks upon the utility of allying with the "ultramontanes." Members of the Evangelical League argued that any alliance with the Center might oblige the National Liberals to support the Centrist in a runoff against the Social Democrats. The specter of Protestant voters electing a Catholic deputy was more than they could bear. And the Evangelical League was not alone. At the turn of the century young Protestant clergy in eastern Westphalia were organizing their own edition of the anti-Semitic political movements. In Dortmund the anti-Semites worked among the shopkeepers and salesmen. Instead of creating their own party, however, they preferred to exercise some influence upon the National Liberals, and part of their influence was manifested in an increasing pressure to maintain a separation between the Protestant and Catholic communities.

Despite these problems, the election of 1903 was almost a replay of 1898. The National Liberals attacked everyone in the first election and got the support of the Center in the runoff. The runoff poem this time shows how the National Liberals even more fiercely defined their position by an exclusive fatherland rhetoric. The Bömelburg or Bömel Castle refers to Theodor Bömelburg, the nonresident SPD candidate. It is also one of the very rare pieces that mentions any candidate, referring to the opponent Hilbck as well:

> In the District Dortmund-Hörde
> The days have come for each to aid the other.
> To stomp the Reds into the ground at this decisive hour,
> Each German is bidden by duty and honor.
> Hurray! you upright German men,
> Today brings the happy longed-for time
> When we can show the insolent Reds uncouth
> What we understand by the unvarnished truth.
> When unbelievably dissolute figures
> Called comrades constantly conquer
> That remote little fortress Bömelburg,
> Then German voters must decide
> That down must go those Red boys.
> Rise up happy and unafraid
> Vote, Germans today all and stick with Alexander Hilbck.[15]

The Centrist leadership endorsement this time was hardly overwhelming. The party's literature for the second election admitted that German Catholics had strong disagreements with National Liberals over church policy and that there was more than a residue of anti-Catholicism among the Dortmund National Liberals themselves. In the election a number of National Liberal speakers had attacked the Catholics. The decision for Catholic voters was then between two evils. Yet the choice appeared to be clear. The SPD had made enormous gains in the first election. It would be a mistake to increase these gains by supporting Socialists in a runoff, because "the Social Democracy has become since the election of 16 June [the first election] the greater danger to the throne and altar." The instructions were as follows: "We leave our electors the decision on whether they wish to participate in the election between the National Liberals and the Social Democrats. We expect, however, at the very least that our party supporters will under no circumstances give their vote to a Social Democrat."[16]

The National Liberal leadership, the Social Democrats, assumed that even such a weakly worded Center endorsement could still carry the bulk of their supporters. The reality of the Centrist response was much more complicated on other occasions but not in 1903. The Dortmund city Center party was almost evenly divided between white- and blue-collar workers, but the Center response was to vote National Liberal although this might be against class interest. As table 9:2 shows, an estimated 90 percent of the Center voters turned to the National Liberals in 1903, while National Liberals and Socialists rarely changed their allegiances.

TABLE 9:2. *Estimated Movement of Vote from First to Runoff Election in Dortmund City: 1903 (by percent)* [17]

Voted in First Election	Voted in Second Election		
	Socialist	National Liberal	Did Not Vote
Socialist	111	−10	−3
Center	8	92	7
Liberal parties	3	97	−6

The influx of new voters in the runoff and the regression bias leads toward some inflated percentages and negative numbers, yet there is no question about the responses. And the pattern shown in Dortmund city seems to apply to the district as a whole. The National Liberals gained 17,000 additional votes in the runoff compared with only 6,000 for the SPD. Dortmund city went for the National Liberals, but the rest of the district opted narrowly Socialist, giving Bömelburg the victory by a few more than 300 votes.

The lessons of 1903 were ambiguous. The National Liberals had antagonized Catholics in the first election, yet they had gotten their votes in the second. Would the Center party leaders continue their subordinate position? The 1907 election provided the Center with an ideal opportunity to try to improve its position in the district, to become recognized, bona fide kingmakers instead of a political tool of liberalism. On 13 December 1906 Bülow had dissolved the Reichstag and initiated his campaign against the SPD and Center. The Center and SPD became the targets of the entire Protestant *Bürgertum*. Thus there was every good reason to believe that the Center might support the Socialists in the runoff.

Given such a possibility, it is difficult to understand why much of the SPD campaign was directed at the Center. On New Year's Day 1907 the *Arbeiter Zeitung* carried a copy of a leaflet that was being distributed across the district. It argued that the Ruhr Center was a vehicle of Catholic industrialists and was directed against the working man. The leaflet questioned:

Who has voted for all those new cannons?
    Principally our Center.
Who has generally supported all the plans of the military?
    Principally our Center.
Who has approved the great naval law which requires the raising of indirect taxes to support it?
    Principally our Center.[18]

On 3 January the paper declared, "The Center belongs to the enemies of the rule of the people; it belongs to the reaction;" on 5 January it published a "register of Center misdeeds."[19] On 18 January it carried an article entitled "How the Center swindles the workers on the Electoral Law Question"[20] and went on to say that the Center party opposed the extension of universal manhood suffrage to Prussia. On 19 January it lumped all Christians together. "The church whether it be Catholic or Evangelical is ruled by the spirit of Mammon." A later edition of the same paper defended a disturbance caused by workers at a Centrist electoral meeting. Replying to attacks from *Tremonia*, the Centrist organ, the *Arbeiter Zeitung* claimed that the workers were incited by a priest who proclaimed, "If you worked, your children would not starve. You are yourself to blame [for their hunger]."[21] There were, in addition, thirteen electoral meetings in which the "lies of the Center" were exposed, as well as two anti-Centrist leaflets distributed with a circulation of 25,000 each. A compilation of the SPD attacks on the Centrists ran the gamut. The Centrists claimed to have been called "those who seek to make the people more ignorant, men who overweigh bread on fraudulent scales [an allusion to the grain tariffs]; . . . Centrist scoundels and house boys of the Jesuits."[22]

The SPD attacks were an excuse for the Center to use its key position and attempt to deal with both sides. Everywhere in 1907 (chapter 4) local Centrist parties were forced into making painful decisions between supporting the SPD and parties of the Protestant *Bürgertum* in the runoff. The Dortmund Centrists were free to attempt the role of kingmakers by selling their votes to the highest bidder. They first offered themselves to the National Liberals in exchange for a share of the power at the local level. Only after negotiations had broken down with the National Liberals would they turn to the SPD. Evidently some deal was made. No one talked of an explicit or implicit understanding, but there was at least one visible sign. The SPD reversed its earlier position and instructed its Dortmund County electors to aid in the selection of a Centrist deputy to the Prussian legislature in 1908 (see table 9:3).

The SPD responded to Centrist endorsement with that typical Dortmund political etiquette, never mentioning Centrist voters in their runoff campaign. All the propaganda was addressed to the party faithful, to holding the self-enclosed social grouping intact. On 31 January the *Arbeiter Zeitung* commented on the numerous losses that the SPD had already incurred at the national level. "The election of 25 January has shown that there are not any bomb-proof districts anymore. And our district is not bomb-proof. It can only be held when we exert ourselves to the fullest."[23] There was no mention of other aid. The SPD electoral poetry was addressed only to their own kind.

TABLE 9:3. *Results in Dortmund-Hörde by Administrative Unit: 1903 and 1907*[24]

| Administrative Unit | First Election | | | | | | Second Election | | | |
	Turnout % Valid Ballots	National Liberals	Left-wing Liberals	Center	Socialists	Poles	Turnout % Valid Ballots	Turnout in 2nd as % of 1st	National Liberals	Socialists
Dortmund City										
1903	85.6	30.7	2.0	30.4	35.3	1.5	86.7	101.2	56.2	43.8
1907	91.5	31.4	0.8	27.0	37.5	3.4	76.9	84.0	46.3	53.6
Dortmund County										
1903	75.9	24.0	0.6	24.5	44.0	6.8	75.9	100.3	47.6	52.4
1907	—	23.2	0.2	25.1	41.5	9.9	—	85.2	36.1	63.8
Hörde County										
1903	81.9	26.9	1.7	19.2	50.4	1.6	83.9	102.7	45.2	54.8
1907	—	29.2	0.6	18.8	48.7	2.5	—	92.8	40.0	60.0

Now arm you voters for the last fight,
Now show the people's power and might,
Now return to the ballot box man for man,
Now dressed in red and in rows thereon,
Now stand up for freedom and fight!

The bosses hate all that by freedom is told
The people who know what the future will hold.
In spiritual darkness shut up for all time,
In slaughterhouse, factory and mine.
And They say it is the order of "God."

Thus, forward to the battle of votes, do not cower
You masses, you masses! Use your power
To the ballot box, to the ballot box in red and in rows you lurk.
The victory must be for the people who work.
Red must the banner fly.[25]

Paradoxically, the appeals to Catholics came from the other camp. Going down for the third time, the National Liberals began to realize the error of their ways. The *Dortmunder Zeitung* pleaded, "It is political robbery that is undertaken here, robbery that can never bear good fruit. Those voters who cast their ballots for the Center on January 25 must give up a quiet quarter hour to the process of political conversion in which it will be made clear to them what it means to put the Dortmund district in the hands of the Socialists."[26] Yet, to no one's surprise, all these injunctions were in a losing cause. The SPD got almost 60 percent of the votes in the runoff and won the election by over 15,000 votes.

Now that the Centrists finally had some kind of deal, it was with the wrong group, one that could promise very little and which was subject to much more abuse in the Centrist press than was the Protestant *Bürgertum*. Blind loyalty was often needed to vote SPD in the runoff; thus the strength of the Centrist response would be conditioned by the strength of the social groupings. The German Catholics in the impenetrable rural areas would vote their instructions regardless of the nature of the candidate or the party he represented. In four overwhelmingly Catholic townships in nearby rural Wiedenbrück County, the SPD totals increased from 143 in the first election to 3,341 in the runoff. This increase was almost equivalent to the 3,200 Center votes in the first contest.[27]

Thus the Dortmund response in 1907 was very different from Wiedenbrück and from that in the city itself in 1898 and 1903 where the great bulk of Centrists had followed their instructions to the letter. Some of the Center voters in Dortmund had strong *Mittelstand* loyalties, which put them into daily conflict with the Socialist-oriented working class; others must have been conditioned by the urban propaganda machine, which had long cultivated the image of the SPD as the party of godlessness and disorder. Instead of creating cross-pressures that could lead to disaffiliation among such Catholics, the Center leadership always allowed for abstention as a legitimate response to their instructions. And some German Catholics probably did abstain. There were 8,000 fewer votes in the runoff than in the first election. The bulk of these were probably Poles who were instructed to remain at home, but a few thousand were probably German Catholics.

German Catholics in Dortmund had another alternative which allowed them to affirm their loyalties to their social grouping in public while casting invalid ballots. These voters felt the unavoidable duty to go to the polls to demonstrate Catholic power, but then they did not vote. The number of invalid ballots jumped from 326 in the first election and 742 in the 1903 runoff to an unprecedented 5,686 in 1907.[28] Most of these invalid ballots were probably caused by striking out a candidate's name and inserting another. It seems probable that many Center eligibles came to the polls, took the Socialist ballot that a Center campaign worker handed to them at the entrance to the polling place, and struck through that ballot once in the privacy of the voting area. Many of these strike-outs must have been Center since the Polish numbers were not large enough to account for all the invalid ballots and, in any case, the Poles boycotted the runoff.

The choice may have been monumental for the Centrist supporters, but it was almost inconsequential to the SPD. Staying at home or casting an invalid ballot was almost as good as voting SPD. The SPD runoff totals were 9,000 larger than the first election, a figure only 2,000 greater than in 1903, when the Centrist vote had gone in the other direction. The National Liberals, however, increased their vote by 8,000—10,000 less than in the previous election. Thus these absentees turned the National Liberal majorities in Dortmund city into SPD victories in 1907 while increasing the Socialist margins of victory in the two counties (see table 9:3).

The Dortmund Socialists had every reason to be proud. They never thought of being thankful to the Centrists. The *Arbeiter Zeitung* proclaimed the message of the runoff on the day after the election. "The land of the red earth [Westphalia], the land of the red flag." The Dortmund Socialists were elated. They saw the election as enhancing the grouping solidarity and establishing lines of boundaries against the outsiders. The *Arbeiter Zeitung* had gained 3,000 new subscribers during the election campaign and the Socialist party 1,000 new members in Dortmund alone. "But we must not rest on our honors won. Our slogan must be: 'now but farther.'"[29]

It had been not organizations but the basic demographic and economic trends that had provided the Socialists with a majority of the electorate. Still the activity of the SPD was remarkable. And if the Socialists could make the moral of the election that organizing succeeded, how could the losers avoid feeling that they had failed because of lack of energy and organization? As the Westphalian Centrist leader stated in 1908, "God helps only those who do something, not those who are lazy and lie in their caves like the bears."[30] For this reason, the Centrists began to prepare for the next election in 1908, four years in advance of the projected date.

The year 1912 saw the end of any liberal shred of power. The demographic shift in the district increased the Center first ballot vote vis-à-vis the Protestant bourgeoisie. The Centrists believed it was all due to their good work, to their emphasis on the need of Catholics to vote Catholic. Once into the runoff, however, they adopted the *Bürgertum* rhetoric of the National Liberals. A Centrist advertisement stated, "Here it does not have to do with the confessional question. We must, whether Catholic or Evangelical, stand together against the red flag."[31]

Unlike the National Liberals, however, the Centrists were well placed for the runoff. The Centrists had large numbers of workers who might have become SPD recruits at any time. The National Liberals were almost entirely middle class. It was simply inconceivable that these liberals would turn toward the Socialists. Left-wing liberals in Dortmund did at least theoretically support the SPD, but they were only few in number. Thus the Centrists then gained almost 20,000 votes from the Protestant *Bürgertum* since the first election. The SPD increased its numbers by only 7,000. This would not change the outcome because the Protestant working-class grouping was growing even faster than the Catholic one. The SPD almost won it all in the first election and ended with a comfortable margin of 55 percent of the vote. Dortmund-Hörde was the first Ruhr district to go Socialist, and it would be the first to become "bombproof" against attacks from any bourgeois group. Yet no matter how the SPD margins grew, the proponents of other social groupings would continue to present candidates and campaign hard. For in Dortmund elections were not only about winning or losing; they were votes that affirmed profound loyalties and unleashed profound hatreds. In this the Dortmund voters were not unique.

10

REFORMING AND RESTRUCTURING THE ELECTORAL SYSTEM

The three case studies complete the description of the electoral system as it was, but for many Germans, particularly on the Left, it was just as important to consider what the electoral system might become. The demands for reform and restructuring centered on (1) finding means for constructing a system whereby elected deputies more closely mirrored the actual vote; (2) extending the system of universal suffrage, the Australian ballot, direct and secret elections to the various states and municipalities north of the Main; (3) producing a situation where the locus of power shifted from the executive to parliament. The sum of all these reforms would have meant restructuring the authoritarian state, a premise that German governments and the elites which supported them found unconscionable.

But whether formal constitutional reform was possible or not, the electoral system still afforded the promise of a substantial reconstitution of the ways of doing politics. The precise nature and direction of this reshaping is very difficult to determine. What can be demonstrated is that the constitution itself and the problems of its development did not restrain but, in a very real sense, enhanced the process of politicization and extended the prestige of voting.

1. Reapportionment and Alternative Methods of Selection

The authoritarian system did, in one way, channel the views of electoral reform. Since compromise was usually more difficult to achieve than in democratic societies, reformers would pay less attention to those possibilities involving slight modification. Thus instead of emphasizing reapportionment as was the eventual American solution to similar problems, the German Left turned toward basic structural changes in the methods of electing Reichstag representatives. And they had almost achieved their task by the end of the empire, while American state legislatures would go unreformed for five more decades. Whether successful or not, all these attempts at reform certainly added to the prestige of universal suffrage in general and Wilhelmine elections in particular. Nor did their incompleteness seem to call the system into question.

At first glance, it seemed that the German Left should have been satisfied with what they had. The system of electing individual deputies in districts by a majority vote seems a good democratic procedure. The elections at the district level concretize those great nationwide contests among affirming social groupings or between the German Protestant *Bürgertum* and its various deviant enemies. If nationwide returns were sometimes ambiguous and difficult to interpret, the district was always clearly won or perhaps just not lost. For it was as important to deny victory to certain parties as support the attempts of others. Time and time again, campaign literature used the phrase "keep their hands off the district,"[1] as if some deviant party were equivalent of a burglar in the night who had to be thrust out of the house.

The distinctiveness of the district was encouraged by laws on political associations. Before 1900 there could be no campaign organizations except at the district level. This was also interpreted as a legal bar against candidate selection at the national level. Once established, autonomy in candidate selection became a Wilhelmine tradition even if, as with the Center, Poles, and SPD, the local committee often just ratified decisions made at the capital or in the provincial committee.[2]

The districts themselves provided remarkably uniform vehicles for both conducting and analyzing the results of campaigns. They had been constructed with an eye for common history and tradition; their boundaries never crossed state, and seldom crossed provincial, lines. Instead of mirroring the diversities of German society, districts often provided comfortable settings for homogeneous social and political experience. The very fact that these boundaries never changed served to make them appear less as artificial creations and more as irreplaceable, authentic parts of the political system. After all, electoral districts were not less artificial than the counties of which they were composed, and county names had long been used to delineate a particular rooted tradition. It is striking then that by 1912 electoral propaganda referred to the district not only by its official designation, *Wahlkreis*, but sometimes simply as *unser Kreis*, "our county."[3]

Despite these advantages, the district electoral system was under attack, especially because of the failure to induce reapportionment. The original districts had been allocated to the states by population under the proviso that each state would have at least one representative. This not only benefited the very small states, but the whole process favored the safe, that is, rural, areas. However, apportionment was not wildly out of line at the beginning, generally fairer than that in most nineteenth-century American states, and much superior to any contemporary British system. In 1871 over half the districts had populations of eligible voters that fell within 10 percent of the average and three-quarters were within 20 percent of the average. The problem was that the system never was changed. The whole system had become skewed by 1912, when less than 20 percent of the districts had populations of eligibles within 10 percent of the average; less than half were within 20 percent of the mean. Thus 8,000 voters constituted a majority of all eligibles in the East Prussian agrarian district of Heiligenbeil-Preussische Eylau. The same figure for the Ruhr district of Bochum-Gelsenkirchen-Hattingen was over 60,000. These divergences were generally the result of urbanization. The district Berlin Center was an exception to the rule; it declined in population as commercial and government buildings displaced residences in the central city. In 1912 less than 7,000 eligibles constituted a majority of all possible voters in the district, while the same figure was almost 110,000 in Berlin District 6, which comprised the rings of working-class tenements in the north and northwest of the city.[4]

As would be expected, the failure to reapportion did not affect all parties equally. It hurt those with the largest urban bases, particularly Socialists and liberals of all varieties. There is no precise way of estimating losses accrued through this malapportionment. Winning and losing were equally controlled by the mix of party supporters in individual districts, by the placement of these parties for the runoff elections and by the content of individual elections. The displacement caused by all of these variables, however, can be measured by constructing a simple equation, which yields a figure with the measure of malapportionment as one of its major components.

$$\begin{array}{c} \text{Net Advantage} \\ \text{for Party A in} \\ \text{Election A} \\ \text{(in percent)} \end{array} = \left(\dfrac{\begin{array}{c}\text{Average number of voters} \\ \text{needed to elect a deputy} \\ \text{in Election A}\end{array}}{\begin{array}{c}\text{Average number of voters} \\ \text{needed to elect a deputy} \\ \text{for Party A in Election A}\end{array}} \times 100 \right) -100$$

The results are shown in table 10:1. A positive percentage shows the party had a net advantage in a particular election; a negative advantage shows that party had less seats than would have been allotted under strict proportional representation. Since these figures do not have the same base, they are only a very close approximation of the differences between parties. Still, it did take over 110 percent more voters to elect an SPD candidate than a conservative in 1887 and over 50 percent more to elect both left-wing liberals and SPD candidates in 1893.

TABLE 10:1. *Net Advantage Accruing to Parties under Various Electoral Systems*[5]

Year	German Conservatives	National Liberals	Left-wing Liberals	Center	Socialists
1887	+33	+11	−37	+22	−83
1890	+46	−36	+ 2	+42	−56
1893	+11	−15	−42	+ 5	−41
1898	+24	−10	− 1	+33	−49
1903	+36	− 7	− 6	+28	−35
1907	+60	− 6	+ 8	+36	−63
1912	+ 8	−17	−14	+ 3	−20

The exigencies of practical politics dictated the positions that various parties had on electoral reform. And here the SPD and liberals diverged. Any alternative solution would aid the SPD—(1) simple reapportionment, (2) the introduction of a plurality system of election whereby the candidate with the most votes in the district won regardless of whether he achieved a majority, or (3) the introduction of a system of proportional representation.

There was very little support for the first alternative. The German politicians divided into supporting the status quo or retrogression on one hand or demanding one of the two structural reforms on the other. The conservatives and Center were opposed since the introduction of either proportional representation or the plurality system would have resulted in substantial losses. Many right-wing liberals joined them, fearing that the introduction of either electoral system would mean substantial gains for the SPD (see table 10:2).

However, the last two alternatives would have differential advantages. The Socialists would probably benefit from either reform; the liberals only from one. If Germany went to the plurality system, the way the British Parliament and American Congress are elected, then the left-wing liberals would especially suffer, since they were much more thinly spread through the nation and thus were less likely to be leaders in many contests. Of course, the projections in table 10:2 do not tell the full story. The liberals would benefit while the Socialists would lose from Protestant *Bürgertum* coalitions that would replace runoff coalitions in districts where the SPD had a chance to win. However, such a single election coalition seemed less frightening to the Social Democrats and less enticing for the left-wing liberals than the accustomed runoff agreements of the Wilhelmine system. Thus the left-wing liberals rejected the plurality system in favor of proportional representation. It was not untried, having

TABLE 10:2. *Relative Advantage Accruing to Parties under Various Electoral Systems*[6]

Party	1907			1912		
	Actual Seats	Under Proportional Representation	Under Plurality System	Actual Seats	Under Proportional Representation	Under Plurality System
German Conservatives	67	41	74	43	37	57
Free Conservatives	24	16	24	14	12	13
National Liberals	54	58	47	45	54	25
Left-wing Liberals	49	43	38	42	48	14
Center	105	77	101	91	65	98
Socialists	43	115	73	110	138	144

been introduced into Belgium in the 1890s and given limited use in Württemberg state elections after 1906. It was also used for elections to the industrial courts, mining councils, and local health agencies. Increasingly, proportional representation was seen in these instances as a means of electing *Bürgertum* deputies in areas that under other systems would produce almost exclusively Socialist victories.

Thus moderate and left-wing liberals joined the SPD in supporting proportional representation. The system would benefit both and could be equally ideologically justified in both camps. As one liberal proponent stated, "The system of proportional representation . . . allows in this manner for the endless variety of modern social, economic, religious-moral, cultural situations which underlie the psychological motivation of the individual person."[7] The Socialist Karl Gradnauer wanted to make the Reichstag "a correct mirror of the political decisions of our people."[8]

There was some opposition in both camps. Within the SPD Eduard Bernstein asked for reconsideration of proportional representation, believing that it would weaken the process by which large parties were being created. Bernstein feared that proportional representation would splinter the electorate and make the necessary compromises between parties more difficult.

But Bernstein was certainly not the majority in his party. Radical Socialists liked proportional representation precisely because it encouraged each individual to vote his conscience, because it was a bulwark "against

the spirit of compromise that leads to corruption."[9] Even in more congenial quarters, Bernstein's solution was rejected. Most democratically inclined Socialists believed that proportional representation would hasten
the political reform of Germany. Gradnauer stated:

> You need only to introduce a representative and a good representa-
> tion of the German people in this house in order to make the reac-
> tion into a hopeless minority! You can in this deed turn around the
> balance of power in the German Empire and, if the liberals really
> practice liberal politics, then our party will not lack support. (Aha!
> from the Right—Very correct from the Social Democrats)—Cer-
> tainly, gentlemen, your Ahas support my proposition completely
> since with proportional representation your power dies out. You
> know as well as we that we will fight for the power you have until
> we win because your power rests on injustice. (Very correct from
> the Social Democrats).[10]

The liberals may not have joined in this particular discussion; it may even
have raised their fears of introducing proportional representation. But
the fact remains that most liberals voted for the Socialist resolution on
proportional representation in this debate in 1913, and the resolution
lost by only one vote. From then on it was obvious that proportional representation would be the new electoral system of the German Reich. Even
before the empire fell, a modified system was introduced. And after its
fall, it was almost a foregone conclusion that the new republic would
adopt this form of suffrage.

2. The Extension of Suffrage to the States

The movement to extend universal manhood suffrage, the Australian ballot, direct and secret elections to the states, was at once the most visible
sign both of the success and the failure of the attempts to reform German
political life. In the south, Baden and Württemberg essentially adopted
the Reichstag system of elections in the first decade of the twentieth century, while both Bavaria and Hesse substantially extended their electorate and provided for greater security during elections (see chapters 2 and
6). North of the Main, however, reform was blocked by a persistent coalition of governments with conservative, German Catholic, and right-wing
liberal politicians who saw the extension of suffrage as further diminishing their influence at both the state and local level. In northern Germany
restrictive legislation remained essentially intact, retarding the growth of
politicization by making state elections less important and diminishing
the possibilities of meaningful habitual voting in state elections.

The result was a situation similar to that of the American South from

1890 to 1964, where "undesirables" were kept from the polls by constructing legal obstacles. The Prussians and Saxons might not use grandfather clauses and poll taxes, but they found methods just as complex and overarching and, what is more important, just as effective. There was one crucial difference: the Wilhelmine voters north of the Main had a constant reminder of their disenfranchisement. Restrictive clauses in the American South applied in all elections; in Germany they only pertained to those of the states. This disparity between state and national rules encouraged the movement demanding adjustment of the Prussian, the Saxon, the Hamburg electoral systems. The decade before the war was filled with organizing and demonstrating for the extension of national suffrage to the state level.

The most complex instrument of electoral repression was the Prussian three-class system of voting, which was neither direct, nor equal, nor secret. Established by the Constitution of 1850, the three-class system counted marks, not people, as equal. This is how it worked after several amendations, the last in 1893. The male ratepayers over age 24 in each township or city ward were hierarchically ranked immediately before each election on the basis of the amount of taxes each paid. The appropriate state official would then go down the list until he counted a third of the total tax revenues for the unit; this group constituted the first class of voters. The official then repeated the act for those still on the list so as to demarcate the line between the second and third classes. The remainder on the list and all eligible nontaxpayers were lumped into Class III. In 1888, 3.6 percent of the voters were in Class I and 85.6 percent in Class III. The rate of discrimination changed little during the Wilhelmine period; in 1913 the corresponding figures were 4.5 and 79.8. Under the provisions of the Constitution of 1850, each class chose an equal number of electors so that the average vote in Class I had over twenty times the voice of the average vote in Class III.

It was a system ideally designed to dampen enthusiasm at the polls. As table 10:3 shows, the turnout for Class II was higher in every election than that for Class III, and the rate for Class I was always higher than for Class II. This statement applies to the particular as well as the general. The provinces replicated the national figures; indeed, in 1908 every administrative unit in Westphalia and West Prussia conformed to this rule. Third-class eligibles were simply intent on staying at home rather than have their vote discounted; cheapening the vote depoliticizes. It is difficult to determine more. These differences in turnout between electoral classes were hardly proof of divergences among social groupings. In the first place, taxes paid are not necessarily good indicators of social status. Even more important, the classes themselves did not define distinct groups of taxpayers. Voters of very similar wealth could be grouped into very disparate classes or vice versa. If over two-thirds of Class I eligibles

TABLE 10:3. *Turnout Rates for State Elections in Prussia by Electoral Class* [11]

Class	1893	1898	1903	1908	1913
I	48.1	46.2	49.2	53.5	51.4
II	32.1	30.7	34.3	42.9	41.9
III	15.2	15.7	21.2	30.2	29.9
Combined classes	18.4	18.4	23.6	32.8	32.7
Turnout for immediately preceding Reichstag election	73.6	69.1	75.5	81.0	86.4
Dropoff			53.5	50.2	53.4

in 1913 paid over 100 marks in taxes, at least one-third of those in Class III did the same. Much more strangely, some first-class eligibles in the working-class precincts of Berlin paid less than 100 marks in taxes, while there were third-class voters in the suburbs who paid over 30,000.

As if ambiguous results, partial disenfranchisement, and indirect elections were not enough to depress turnout, Prussian elections were also conducted in public with the concomitant opportunity for intimidation. Reformers argued that this fact alone turned a great many away from the polls. Potential opponents of the regime would think twice about voting against a government which was usually supported by a local elite that could easily retaliate against them.

However, I believe something more was involved than threats of intimidation. Nonvoting in Prussian elections reflected a systemwide effect; it was a statement of alienation from, and dissatisfaction with, the political processes in Prussia. And this is why the Prussian situation contrasted with the British, where open voting simultaneously brought out high turnout and large majorities for the local elite. Abstention was the rule in Prussia even among Class I eligibles whose turnout was seldom higher than 50 percent. The entrance of Socialist voters into the fray after 1908 could not move large elements of the *Bürgertum* to the polls even when their votes were overcounted. Turnout rates for Class I eligibles approached the Reichstag levels only in certain areas in the east where Polish-German conflicts predominated. The system has to be credible and the fight has to be at least relatively fair for voting to work. In Prussia this was simply not so. [12]

Such were the hard facts of reaction. They represent the irreducible core of the antidemocratic edifice and the structural limits of the political culture of voting. In the minds of the monarchical elite, reforming Prussia meant abolishing it. William II may have had greater German loyalties than his grandfather, but the younger sovereign understood that his monarchy depended on the support of unreformed legislative majorities. This was the primary difference between Prussia and the South German states. William of Hohenzollern despised his namesake, William II of Württemberg, for the innovation of equal balloting. The Prussian William knew how to solve the Württemberg constitutional crisis—with the sabers of his cavalry. It was no wonder that South German democrats thought themselves lucky. Konrad Haussmann once came dangerously close to lese majesty in one of the heated *Landtag* debates in Stuttgart on constitutional reform. Haussmann recognized that his speech would have landed him in deep trouble in the colossus to the north. Slumping in his seat, he was heard to mutter that South German litany, "Thank God we're not in Prussia."[13]

Yet the monarchy was not the only obstacle to reform. The kings and grand dukes of northern Germany formed only one of the buttresses of reaction. They needed the support of other political forces to preserve the status quo. In the 1890s a cohesive political constellation was formed against the "tyranny of the count." The monarchical elite had always thought that the vote was Bismarck's mistake; they would be joined by right-wing liberals who believed themselves the most capable and least recognized group in Germany. As one Hessian pamphlet read, "The educated minority is the backbone of political and cultural life."[14] The decreasing liberal strength in the Reichstag was seen as a sign that their special brand of elite politics would be doomed if the Reichstag election system was introduced at the state level. A contemporary law professor, Leo von Savigny (not to be confused with Friedrich Karl) expressed the views of this elite when he contended that all voting should have been confined to the educated and propertied minority. It was not right for this minority to have its ballots counted equally with "the young who, with the inexperience and naivete of youth, are not hindered by the weight of experience," or "the craftsman whose work never changes day in and day out, whose experience does not go beyond his county line, and who is too tired to be able to grasp the great political questions of a world he neither knows nor understands," or "the day laborer who in his hard, dumb work has long forgotten his school lessons about the great men and the history of the fatherland," or finally "the propertyless who have nothing to lose if the state itself collapses."[15]

Obviously there was more at stake in these issues than good government. Suffrage questions are fundamentally questions of power. Conservatives, right-wing liberals, and Catholics all had an interest in preserving restrictive suffrage. The Catholic Center party had made the most important challenge to the three-class system during the early years of the empire, but by 1900 the Center leadership worried that reform would seriously jeopardize its leverage in Prussian politics. If the Reichstag suffrage had been introduced in Prussia in 1908, the Center would have lost 25 seats, fully a quarter of its representation. The conservative case is even easier to document. Universal suffrage and proportional representation would have meant the loss of two-thirds of the conservative seats, 140 out of the 212 in 1908.

The National Liberals, the embodiment of Prussian right-wing liberalism, would have lost less than 10 percent, a total of 6 seats; however, this party would suffer just as severely from the fallout of these reforms as would the Center and conservatives. Once universal, direct, and equal suffrage was introduced at the state level, there was no way to avoid extending equality to the cities, which were the National Liberal refuge from mass politics. Conservatives and Centrists were more insulated against local suffrage reform by their rural majorities and a bureaucracy that exercised more power in unincorporated areas than it did in the cities. Cities, on the other hand, had wide powers of self-governance and taxation; universal suffrage in the city would not only have destroyed this refuge but directly attacked the economic power and social privileges of the *Bürgertum*. The fear was that a Berlin, a Frankfurt, a Breslau might produce a Socialist mayor and a revolutionary program. The Socialists in Dortmund, Frankfurt, and Cassel first worked to alleviate the worst anxieties of the liberal nightmare by claiming that they only advocated a balanced representation instead of an exclusively middle-class council. But this was merely a temporary strategy on the road to power. In the end the Social Democrats meant to rule the major cities of Germany. In Frankfurt and Dortmund, Socialists waged political campaigns on the premise that working-class criticisms of the local councils could never be satisfied in coalition with *Bürgertum* interests. The main obstacle to this rule was always understood to be beyond city control and to reside in the restricted franchise supported by a reactionary state government. Red city councils, like red state legislatures, required electoral reform. When the bourgeois-Socialist coalition failed in Frankfurt in 1902, it was the final blow to any hopes of cooperation. The Socialist *Volksstimme* then proclaimed: "Above all, all comrades must strive to revise the electoral law. The Democrats are in retreat; we are in the advance. There will never be any more talk of compromise in city council elections."[16]

It was no wonder that the Socialists preempted the suffrage movement at the beginning of the twentieth century. Left-wing liberals could legitimately complain that they had carried the banner in former years when the Social Democrats had been disinterested. But it was the Socialists who took to the streets, co-opting the issue and making disparaging comments on the enthusiasms of left-wing liberals. The event that triggered the response was the Russian Revolution of 1905. If the czar, the most autocratic ruler in Europe, could agree to universal manhood suffrage, it stood to reason that the kings of Prussia and Saxony could be convinced.

Anyway this was the rationale of the striking workers in Dresden and Hamburg in the last months of 1905. On 21 January 1906 the whole Socialist working class took to the streets to announce their support for the Russian Revolution and to demand universal manhood suffrage.

Class divisions would seriously undermine the effect of these actions. The bulk of the bourgeois press thought the demonstrations were signs of social unrest and saw these lines of peacefully marching workers as the vanguard of revolutionary battalions. There was some justification for these fears. The Socialist radicals cared nothing for universal suffrage; Rosa Luxemburg thought that marching was much too tame and had wanted to turn the universal suffrage movement into a general strike. She hoped that this would lead to police repression, producing intensified class antagonism and propelling the proletariat closer to revolutionary actions. There were violent disorders. Richard Evans has recently shown how a suffrage demonstration in Hamburg just four days previously had erupted into violence based on deep-seated class antagonism, leading to looting and the inevitable police repression.[17]

The intent of the majority of the Socialist leadership and its followers was quite different, however. They appeared to believe in the efficacy of introducing the national political culture into the states. The addition of 100 Socialist deputies to the Prussian House of Delegates would have turned that chamber into a miniature Reichstag and fundamentally altered the power relationships in the Reich. The left-wing liberal *Berliner Tageblatt* alluded to this when it praised "Red Sunday" as serving to both "strengthen the prestige of the Reichstag and act as a death blow to the three-class electoral law."[18] It was a vain hope; the restrictive franchises in the states were still in place at the end of the empire.

This failure to build a nexus between state and local politics in northern Germany may have fostered depoliticization in some areas, but it also had the effect of increasing politicization in others. In the first place, the failure of the attempts to bring the Reichstag electoral system to the states had the paradoxical effect of increasing the prestige of the Reichstag elections as the only viable mass political outlet. In the second, the continued demands for suffrage extension began to infiltrate the hitherto antidemocratic establishment as well as providing a convenient vehicle for Socialists and others to politicize the masses.

The national vote was increasingly viewed after 1906 as the chief barrier against a projected return to absolutism. As a left-wing liberal broadside in Ziegenhain stated, "The Reichstag electoral law is a holy right that the German people achieved in bloody combat. Hold it holy! Do not misuse it. Do not play games with it, and don't avert your eyes from it! It is in danger!"[19] At the Mannheim Social Democratic Party Congress in September 1906, the Socialist chief, August Bebel, argued that the leadership failed to authorize a general strike because it would have called forth a counterattack against the Reichstag franchise. Bebel assured the Congress that any threat to the Reichstag suffrage would be met with just such a work stoppage. Part of this statement was undoubtedly a stratagem to protect his flank by rationalizing the leadership's inaction in January. Yet it was also partly a realistic estimate of achievable goals. The Socialists needed the Reichstag vote to impress their growing strength on the rest of the population and to feed their own self-confidence.[20] The political culture of high turnout voting was an absolute essential for the party's development; it made good its defeats in other areas. *Bürgertum* critics might argue that the Socialist failure to achieve reform in the states was a sign of their "impotence," but the Socialists had a ready answer. They would simply transfer the contest out of the arena of state politics altogether and place it onto a more favorable terrain. This is just how Franz Mehring responded to the charge of Socialist "impotence" in 1906.

> The decisive answer to this question will be given in the next Reichstag election. We can already see the clear signs of the outcome. The subscriptions to the party press, we must say, are increasing at a feverish rate in those areas where the "victors" on January 21 have most violently "won" and still yet "win"—in Königsberg, Hamburg, Breslau and Leipzig. But I have heard nothing since "Red Sunday" of the patriotic press penetrating into the workers' world even to the depth of a single straw.[21]

It was a tradeoff that the SPD could not continuously make without distorting its program. But there were others who would seize on this possibility of maintaining state politics on the dormant level. From the 1890s onward, Prussian and imperial governments were willing to exchange intensified political activity in the Reich for a depoliticized state electorate—that is, as long as this did not mean an antigovernment Reichstag. This kind of thinking came clearly to the fore in a meeting of the Prussian Cabinet held in 1898 to decide on the dates of the Reichstag and Prussian House of Delegates elections in that year. Reich and Prussian premier Hohenlohe preferred the earlier date for the state elections lest the "excited labors of uprooting before the Reichstag elections would have an effect on the state vote."[22] In the end, other difficulties arose and the Reichstag elections had to be held first, before the hay harvest dispersed the farm laborers from their homes in late June and weakened the agrarian majorities in the east.

Hohenlohe's successor, Bernhard von Bülow, also believed that state elections had to be protected from the politicization inherent in Reichstag elections. The force of the demands for state suffrage reform was so strong and the rumors of *Staatsstreich* against the Reichstag suffrage so prevalent that Bülow had to break precedent and discuss the Prussian suffrage reform before the Reichstag in March 1908. Yet precedent was all that was broken. Bülow was at his cleverest, his most facetious and obscurantist. His argument was simple: why should the Reichstag suffrage be extended to Prussia since the Prussian government never demanded that the Reich take up the three-class system? He went on in the same manner:

> Thus, gentlemen, the direct, common, secret electoral right is not a dogma because it is what the Socialists want to impose on us (laughter).
>
> They make a dogma into a fetish, into an idol. I am no servant of fetishes, no worshiper of idols or dogmas; I believe that they have no place in politics at all. If you wish me to tell you the hard truth, it is that no electoral system absolutely serves all lands and all purposes equally well.
>
> The day before yesterday, Deputy Naumann graded the various federal states on their constitutions and their electoral laws. The South German states got 1a, Prussia 3b (laughter), Mecklenburg 5b (renewed laughter). Do you gentlemen really think that the welfare and freedom of a country overwhelmingly depend on the form of its constitution or even of its electoral law? Deputy Bebel once proclaimed the model to be England or France. England does not even possess the common vote (hear! hear!). Do you really believe that Mecklenburg, so attacked by Naumann, is ruled worse than Haiti (great laughter)? We have just now received an interesting dispatch; Haiti has equal and direct franchise (stormy laughter).
>
> In order to clear up a misunderstanding, I give you assurances that the federated state governments plan no change in the standing electoral law. But what is good for, or at least bearable in, the empire does not need to be transferred to every individual state. The national thought is expressed through the Reichstag electoral law; the federal nature of the state is confirmed in the *Bundesrat*. Just for that reason alone, it is not permissible for Prussia to be considered as an equal with the Reich.[23]

Such constitutional theory was more an articulation of the past than a statement of future possibilities. The pressures for reform continued to grow throughout the Wilhelmine period; the governments in the north would respond first by accepting some changes, merely window dressings on the system. In the end, these proposals made the talk of real reforms more respectable and thus undermined the intellectual supports of the system that they were envisioned as supporting.

There were several such window-dressing reforms proposed in the years immediately preceding the war. The Saxon government after 1909 abandoned the three-class system, which it had only introduced thirteen years previously, and opted for a direct, secret but plural franchise, which awarded up to three additional ballots on the basis of age, education, income and property. Plural voting had long been considered the best means for saving the power of the propertied and educated elite, which was the core of liberalism. It was instituted in Hamburg and in the Hessian reform of 1909, which gave a second vote to all those eligibles over fifty. In defense of the Hamburgers, Saxons, and Hessians, this was not a unique reform in Europe. The British Whigs forestalled its abolition in the 1870s, and it had only been recently introduced into Belgium in the 1890s. But the direction of the reform in Germany was much clearer—to create an unbreakable alliance of all propertied interests against the national political culture.

In 1910 the Prussian government attempted to introduce a similar reform. The franchise was to become equal and secret as in Saxony. In Prussia, however, the three-class system would be maintained. The propertied and educated in the cities were to be additionally rewarded. Anyone who paid above 5,000 marks would be in Class I regardless of the composition of his district. All university-trained males would be promoted by one class if they were not already in Class I. New districts would be created in the industrial areas which would, under the three-class system, give greater power to the industrial plutocrats in Westphalia. Surprisingly, even such a tenuous reform was bound to fail. The Catholics and the Conservatives were united in rejecting the secret ballot and direct voting.[24]

The majority of Prussian right-wing liberals joined the Left in refusing to consider any reform that satisfied the Center-Conservative coalition. Only the left wing of the party rejected this position. Prodded by Ernst Bassermann and Gustav Stresemann, the National Liberal party abandoned its earlier hard-line position against the extension of the suffrage. In 1911 the National Liberals joined with the Left in the Reichstag vote that extended to Alsace-Lorraine the universal manhood suffrage with direct and secret ballot. This vote did not usher in the era of wholesale conversion. Most National Liberals remained only marginally convinced of the necessity of democratizing Germany. There was a substantial body of conservative and right-wing liberal intellectuals who feared that the agitation for reform would disrupt the whole society, even if they could present no more than a pitiful alternative.

Demonstrations in the streets were renewed in 1908 and 1910. And by 1910, in Frankfurt at least, they had lost their exclusively working-class character. Hans Delbrück, for example, declared it was important that "some reform comes to fruition. This would naturally not satisfy the Social Democrats; they can never be satisfied. However, such a reform would awaken a feeling of confidence in the broad masses that follow them without fully belonging to them. It would also do the same for the wide circles of the *Bürgertum* who are convinced that the present class system must be abolished, an opinion that something serious and honorable must be undertaken."[25]

3. The Possibilities of Reform

The movement for what Delbrück called "serious and honorable" suffrage reform was only one of the many items on the political agenda in the last years before the war. As the agenda was growing, the number of solutions kept declining, or at least this is the general consensus of historical opinion. A number of historians have gone so far as to delineate a permanent crisis in late Wilhelmine domestic politics where the forces both inside and outside of parliament were so excruciatingly balanced that any reform was impossible. The result was political stalemate, disillusionment, and a flight into foreign adventures. The "new orthodoxy" historians view any solutions based on consensus for reform as impossible and believe that essentially only authoritarian antiparliamentary alternatives would work. The suffrage model for such a new national political system might have been the unreformed state legislation rather than the Reichstag electoral system.

In contrast, there is a growing body of scholars who envisioned the reform movement as ultimately victorious, pointing out that it was achieved during the end-of-the-war crisis and in the Weimar Republic (see chapter 11). Neither possibility was certain. Both of these alternatives were possible outcomes within the Wilhelmine framework. That is all that I believe can be said. Guenther Roth pointed out a number of years ago that the "hopeful" or "skeptical" versions of Wilhelmine constitutional development were often the product of a number of extraneous factors, including the author's spatial and ideological position.[26] What is true now was true then. There was for some Wilhelmine Germans enough hope to validate their efforts despite the prevalence of a reactionary government and great impediments to reform. And, as with so many things about Wilhelmine voting, these hopes for change served to solidify commitments already strongly in place and to increase the appreciation of many Wilhelmines of the importance of exercising their citizenship rights at the polls and extending their citizenship roles into even wider arenas in the political world.

II

CONCLUSION AND EPILOGUE

This work is founded on the assumption that German history is comparable. Thus any study of Wilhelmine elections can make some contribution to theoretical and comparative historical dialogues as well as to understanding German history and politics. The most fundamental error made in Wilhelmine electoral history has been to emphasize the uniqueness of the German experience so strongly as to establish a false view of the cleft between its national development and that of other industrialized states. This "German error" is opposite from that which often characterizes French historical writing. The French are inclined to believe that every study of every locality is somehow immersed in universal significance. But then French intellectuals have rarely had to uphold the historical distinctiveness of their nation against neighbors who threatened its intellectual dissolution. Nor have they had to explain a phenomenon as morally evil as National Socialism.

Assertions of uniqueness or universality can equally encapsulate particular actions that are similar and comparable. Such assertions can also be used to resist explanations built upon methods used in other nations, particularly in the refusal to accept conclusions based on Anglo-American studies. This drive to encapsulate the national experience has also been far more common in nineteenth-century studies than in those involving National Socialist voting patterns. Even the present disputes about Wilhelmine comparability tend to focus on methods of domination, policy making, and intellectual development. Voting plays a relatively minor role in these discussions.[1]

Discussions of voting based on traditional elite practices ultimately obscure and undervalue the process of politicization and overvalue the antipoliticization rhetoric that was common among Wilhelmine intellectuals, many of whom clung tenaciously to the concept of the "unpolitical" German. While this concept does play an important role in the intellectual appreciation of politics and thus had some bearing on attitude formation, its use as a description of mass German phenomena is dubious. In Wilhelmine society the consciously "unpolitical" tended to come from the intellectual elites. This is in sharp contrast with the United States in the same period, where the "unpolitical" were most visible at the bottom of the socioeconomic scale, often illiterate, certainly not literary, and probably part of the growing pool of habitual nonvoters. This is precisely opposite to the effect of the Wilhelmine electoral system, where the non-voter was disappearing. However, the German distinction received considerably more credence among contemporaries while American concerns about abstainers tended to remain relatively isolated and weak until much later in the twentieth century. Thus American nonvoters could pass rapidly out of public consciousness for a long time and were often considered as aberrants in a highly democratized society while the German "un-politicals" endured with such eloquent spokesmen as Thomas Mann. The preservation of "unpoliticals" thus clearly has to do with who can write and who will read. Armed with its readers, the "unpolitical" myth not only remained alive but was actually reinforced by the idea prevalent among German intellectuals that cleavage was a sign of dislocation rather than a manifestation of intensified citizenship. Thus electoral campaigns, which in American mythologies are almost always vibrant demonstrations of democratic belief, are transformed in the German case into examples of division, fractionalization, unnecessary and debilitating controversy.[2]

Such differences in style and perception, as important as they are, do not undermine the possibilities of comparing structural similarities. Thus I can stand safely on the side of comparability while accepting real differences in both style and structure in the German electoral system and without justifying the authoritarian state by giving it too much or too little emphasis. Viewing the German electoral system in a comparative light allows us to understand the integration of the system as a whole, its place in specifically German developments, its nature and structure. When reduced to its essentials, the Wilhelmine electoral system can be described by a number of straightforward propositions.

1. The Wilhelmine electorate exhibits all the signs of a fully politicized body demonstrated by high turnout statistics, evidences of consistent and habitual voting, penetration of conflictual politics into the state and municipalities, rapid increase in political and parapolitical organizations, and finally, attempts to politicize the disenfranchised and to extend the system of universal suffrage to the state governments north of the Main.

2. Wilhelmine electioneering and voting were essentially protected by law and by governmental actions. The policing mechanisms controlled by the Reichstag effectively retarded intimidation and corruption, and the bureaucracy supervised procedures for registration and vote counting that were fair and equitable. All of this added to the prestige of the electoral system as demonstrated by the positive relationship between this system and the state that protected it.

3. The Wilhelmine system consisted of essentially nationalized citizen-

ship responses regardless of political differences based on region, class, and status. The high turnout was only one sign of an increasingly politicized electorate who viewed themselves as citizens and believed their votes to be both meaningful and necessary, even if they did not necessarily lead to changes in governments.

4. The importance and the prestige of the electoral system is demonstrated by the seriousness attached to elections, not only by the Left but by antidemocratic, progovernment elites and antidemocratic politicians of all stripes.

5. The basis for the strength of the electoral system lay in the affirming loyalties of social-grouping voters. These voters were not only the reason for the stability, strength, and persistent importance of electoral politics, but they also created a model that the old-style majorities used in their attempts to reconstitute themselves into a viable political coalition.

6. The durability and intensity of their sentiments led affirming voters to the polls regardless of the formal structure of politics. There was very little outright manipulation of the voter by party or parapolitical organizations. Organizing was designed to bring the already committed to the polls and influence those marginal members of the social grouping to perform in the manner of hard-core loyalists. Attempts at misinforming of voters in other social groupings were rare and, then, unsuccessful.

7. Politicization through affirming social groupings does not necessarily lead to democratization. Yet it did produce demands for reform of the system in order to extend, strengthen, and regularize the process and increase the prestige of the electoral system and of voting in general.

Nothing in the foregoing descriptions contradicts the notion of comparability between the Wilhelmine electoral system and other contemporary universal suffrage states. Accepting comparability allows us to identify those aspects of the German experience that were truly unique as well as reinforcing or altering general statements about long-run historical developments based on suffrage. In the end, the effort hopefully will also slightly expand the operational view of voting in any society. Precisely identifying what is unique and what is the same is not an altogether easy task, but I hope that the following propositions will not surprise the reader. I have attempted to keep my mind focused on the logic of this approach throughout the study and will now repeat a few statements that summarize the possible accomplishments and deficiences of such an approach.

1. The Wilhelmine experience generally reinforces the applicability of American and British culturally based methodologies. Using this approach allows us to conceive of elections based on persistent and continuous division—many of them cultural in origin—described partially through statistical methods derived from American historical research.

2. The German study adds a new dimension to this approach by de-

monstrating how class divisions exist within cultural bounds and by including the state-directed loyalties within a frame of reference. The Wilhelmine state is completely comprehended neither by theories based on governmental change nor upon third-world polities where the state is the most active mechanism of modernization. The state in Wilhelmine Germany was both an upholder of tradition and an instrument of economic and social modernization. The first attribute served as a referent for the attempts at creating a new majority political culture based on fatherland rhetoric and *Bürgertum* centrality. The second attribute formed as much opposition as support, sometimes undermining and sometimes strangely reinforcing those traditional loyalties. These relationships were undoubtedly not as unique as traditional German scholarship believes. Such persistent attitudes may have been more noticeable in Germany, but they existed elsewhere as well and represented an important variable to be used in discussing historical change.

3. Anglo-American research focuses on describing political cleavages and changes through time. This is less a concern for Wilhelmine Germany, where long-term trends of cleavage seemed well entrenched and where changes in voting behavior did not necessarily lead to changes in government personnel. Therefore, any Wilhelmine study is bound to emphasize politicization, which is one of the most important characteristics of that age, and thus to concentrate on turnout and other forms of participation. This approach can connect turnout data with that of cleavage and demonstrate how the interrelationship between the two variables can show trends of affiliation or disaffiliation within social groupings.

4. Finally, cross-national perspectives reinforce and widen our appreciation of the institutions of mass political culture in general and allow us to form and test certain theories about politicization in different and unfortunately unreplicable situations. The German experience adds new dimensions which at once both confirm and question the standard theories of politicization, particularly those offered by Stein Rokkan. We need much clearer definitions of class and cultural differentiation, of the feedback among individual and collective acts whereby voting at once influenced and was conditioned by the individual and collective acts of the participants. These achievements require both more knowledge and better theory which means, for universal suffrage systems, more national and local studies. It is that old academic complaint: the more we know, the more we need to know. But I believe that this does describe the situation and hope that my work can make some contribution to this task because understanding universal suffrage systems is an absolute requirement for understanding our own age and its peculiarities.

There is another form of issue emanating from comparison on which this study has not concentrated, that is, the relationship of the specific national polity through time. However, the findings of this study do have implications for the interpretation of long-term trends in German politics, particularly for some generally accepted notions about the place of the Weimar electoral system.

There can be no question that the Wilhelmine and Weimar electoral systems were interrelated in the most specific ways. The majority of political officeholders and a large (but, of course, decreasing) percentage of voters in the Weimar period were politicized in the Wilhelmine era. The prevailing interpretation among postwar historians has been that this relationship was for the worst, that the Wilhelmine inheritance undermined the possibilities of democratizing Weimar. They attribute much of this supposed failure to what Theodor Eschenburg, the dean of postwar German political science, identified as a lack of proper preparation in the period before 1914. The result was an "improvised democracy" without any historical roots, thus "not only lacking the political motor from below but also the intellectual preparation from above."[3] This notion of a rootless democracy is continually emphasized in postwar scholarship, particularly in the interpretations of the rise of Hitler. Karl Dietrich Bracher, who has produced the most authoritative postwar account on the failures of Weimar, concludes, "The fact that the first attempt to introduce democracy into Germany was a failure was due less to the compromise character of the constitution than to the lack of prior political preparation of the population and of the political parties."[4]

Such an interpretation runs counter to findings of this study. Wilhelmine Germany produced precisely those politicized electors who constituted in other polities "the motor from below." The Wilhelmine political system might not have been able to reconstitute itself democratically before 1914, but Wilhelmine politicians did not lack the experience of accommodation and conflict resolution that characterized other polities. Following the lead of Werner Frauendienst, a number of postwar historians have contended that the Reichstag often effectively used the leverage that accrued with its competence in budgetary and revenue affairs. Manfred Rauh and Dieter Grosser have emphasized the intensive workload undertaken by the Reichstag and the willingness of second-level governmental officials to cooperate with deputies, the increasing use of interpellations to challenge specific government policies in the Reichstag. Recently, the American historian David Schoenbaum has demonstrated that the Wilhelmine regime was surprisingly successful in resolving political conflicts. Peter Doman has shown that the lack of revolutionary intention among Socialists was more than a sign of irresolvable ideological difficulties. He believes that the majority of the SPD leadership and party intellectuals had become so parliamentarized that they had abandoned their republicanism for all practical purposes and were beginning to visualize themselves as participants within a parliamentary regime. The persistent commitments of the Weimar working-class masses to a democratic and parliamentary regime do not have to be taken as a sign of excessive political apathy. These commitments can be as easily viewed as a statement of a hope for a future based upon an assessment of possibilities learned in the past. Although there was not a parliamentary government at the national level before 1919, there is a growing body of evidence to suggest that it existed in fact in the southern states at an earlier date and that this fact altered the balance of power in the Wilhelmine upper house, the Bundesrat, in favor of accommodation with the parliamentary system.[5]

Thus the Weimar electoral system was without a legitimate depoliticizing or authoritarian inheritance. In fact, I believe the opposite was true: that the weakness was acquired, not inherited, that the Weimar system was unable to assimilate the viable politicization and expressions of citizenship roles that Wilhelmine voters had acquired. Part of this difficulty lies with forces external to the electoral system—war, defeat, economic chaos, new forms of control and politicization. However, part also lies within the structure of the electoral system itself. The concept of these structural changes also goes against the grain of received opinion. Students of Weimar politics and electoral history have tended to view the party allegiances of Weimar as resting upon foundations inherited from the empire. There is good evidence for such a contention, at least in the outward manifestations of Weimar political life. The continuation between pre- and post-1918 voting patterns can even be identified in groups whose referent party disappeared in 1918. Thus the movement of the various National Liberal factions into new parties and their merger with other groups was easily predictable based on their pre–World War I patterns of conflict and accommodation. Moreover, the affirming social groupings inherited from the monarchy were still intact although the peace treaties had effectively eliminated the mass base of non-German national groupings. There were no Lorrainers, many fewer Poles, and only a few Danes inside the new Germany. But the German Catholics and the working class maintained their integrity throughout the period as did the rural East Elbians for much of it. Thus, while voters might move frequently from party to party, there was minimal interchange among the three main groupings inherited from the Wilhelmine era—Catholic, working class, and Protestant *Bürgertum*. Even in the crucial period of realignment during the election of 1930 and the first election of 1932, the net change among these three groups was only 1.8 percent and 1.3 percent, respectively.[6]

Yet this apparent stability only hid what I believe to be very important differences within the social groupings and in their relationship to each other. The social groupings remained, but the system had changed. The Wilhelmine electoral system had an integrity whereby each part tended to reinforce the other. These same parts in Weimar were uncoordinated.

Weimar's inheritance was thus like those toys that get passed on to fire stations for the next Christmas. All or most of the parts might luckily be there, but some were repaired, changed, or so worn that they no longer fitted together effectively. And, in at least one case, a part was changed altogether in an attempt to remedy an original defect, which only succeeded in making the whole operation more problematic.

Although the Catholic and working-class social groupings remained intact until their referent parties were dissolved by force in 1933, they were not as strong as the affirming parties of the Wilhelmine era. The Catholic vote throughout the 1920s continued the steep deline that had commenced during the last Wilhelmine election; many defected to the working-class parties. Both the working-class and Catholic cohesion was weakened by the proliferation of referent parties. After 1919, class-conscious workers could also vote for another party, eventually the Communists, and believing Catholics for the Bavarian People's party as well as the Center. The loyalists who remained in the parties founded before 1914 tended to be among the less activist components of the political spectrum. The Center party held a greater attraction for women than for men; the Social Democratic party was aging. The strength of the SPD and also of its electorate lay in those young men who had joined before World War I, now aging and presenting a serious social barrier to the effective assimilation of the younger generations. The East Elbians were in an even greater dilemma; they had no unambiguous party referent. The DNVP which most of them supported until 1930 proclaimed to have ended the 100-year history of specific Prussian-bound conservatism by uniting the conservative leadership in the industrial circles of western Germany with that of the rural eastern provinces. Yet it was precisely such rhetoric which challenged the union of monarchist symbology and agrarian interests that had so effectively supported the integrity of the social grouping before 1914. Nevertheless the East Elbians followed their leaders for a considerable time and formed the core of the DNVP mass support. At its height in the first election of 1924, the DNVP was above its nationwide average in only two of the 22 districts west of the Elbe and in eight of the ten districts east of the Elbe. Yet such persistence only indicated a delayed reaction to the changes in the Weimar polity; in 1930 these same conservative voters were among the first to engage in mass defections to the National Socialists.[7]

The Protestant *Bürgertum*, including the East Elbian rurals, demonstrates the same difficulty of upholding political styles rooted in the Wilhelmine era. The Weimar *Bürgertum* was until the 1930s even more fragmented than its Wilhelmine predecessor. The war and the postwar economic conditions adversely affected a large part of the *Bürgertum*, especially the old middle class, defined as predominantly consisting of professionals, civil servants, small businessmen, and craftsmen. Most of the

Bürgertum parties were involved in unpopular political solutions to the economic dislocations caused by the inflation of 1923 and later the depression. None of the larger parties (the DDP, the DVP, the DNVP) were able to restructure their programs so as to satisfy the perceived grievances of their clienteles, some of whom defected to interest-oriented parties. The older parties also failed to reconstruct their methods of electoral campaigning and management to meet the needs of the time. Thomas Childers comments in a recent study of Weimar electoral politics that "the specifics of particular issues, no matter how vehemently debated on the Reichstag floor, assumed a secondary position in the campaign strategies of Weimar parties, each of which was determined above all else to establish its position on the traditional lines of class and/or confessional cleavage."[8]

Nor could elections be easily controlled by the local elites who for so long had represented the core of *Bürgertum* political management. The elite themselves were weakened by the process of democratization, which had allowed the entrance of formerly deviant groups such as the SPD into the administration of cities and the various states. Local elites were also undermined by the process of centralization in interest-group politics, which left them with little power to effect policy vis-à-vis the great corporations, interest groups, and nationally organized self-protection associations.

Germany was not the only country where the political power of local elites was threatened, but the German local elites in the 1920s had less immediate remedies available to them. The German Reichstag deputy had never had a successful mediator between local interest and the national government, and the electoral system installed after the war did not make such a task easier. Germany adopted the strictest form of proportional representation at all levels. There was no possible way for a deputy to be connected with a district. In the first place, the districts were too large; there were only thirty-five of them. The local elites could do little to influence candidate selection, which was the perogative of the national parties. The initial placement and the position of the candidate on the list was determined by party leadership. Voters could not affect this position in any way, either by changing their order of preference or striking a candidate off the list. Candidates were elected in rotation from the top of the list downwards, one for every 60,000 votes.

This was hardly a method of electing that was designed to support the local elites of the Protestant *Bürgertum*. In fact, the German Left believed the new system would protect voters against manipulation or misdirection by local notables, allowing the voters to follow their judgments instead of concentrating on the personality and social position of the candidate. The committee which drew up the final German electoral laws believed that it was important to assure that electors moved "from party to party rather than from person to person."[9] The worker, particularly, would thus become immunized from antidemocratic ideologies present in the elites. This view of P.R. as liberation was not unique to Germany. Eighteen European nations had adopted some form of proportional representation by 1926. Even the French had engaged in a short-term experiment, and that bastion of plurality voting, the British House of Commons, had only defeated a proportional representation measure by eighty votes in 1918. And it was rooted in the Wilhelmine inheritance since the Wilhelmine Left had believed that this system would permanently install democratic and reforming governments in Germany, an obvious fallacy when viewed in hindsight. There is little evidence that any change in the method of counting would fundamentally alter political realities anywhere. Proportional representation had not undermined the power of local elites in other nations. The contact between deputy and district in Germany had always been problematical and was seldom viewed as necessary. In this case, proportional representation only intensified the Wilhelmine inheritance but did not overturn it. All arguments are suspect which claim that the method of counting was primarily responsible for the fate of nations. There is no evidence to support the contention of German refugee scholars in the 1930s that proportional representation fostered depoliticization. It may have proliferated parties based on interest groups (the Economic party, the *Landbund*) and radical stances, that is, National Socialism. However, a plurality method of counting would have propelled the National Socialists into power by the summer of 1932.[10]

The sum of the foregoing analysis is that the Wilhelmine system remained recognizably alive until 1930, if not fully intact and certainly in desperate need of repair. Proportional representation, an unworkable political structure for local elites, the failures to generate economic and social solutions to important problems, and the slow decay of affirming loyalties all served to weaken the inheritance but could not even collectively destroy it. Yet there was no doubt also that the forces which generated predictable and habitual articulation of citizenship roles were very much undermined. The system was thus more easily toppled than it had been in 1918. Still, it required the most fundamental reordering of political and economic conditions to destroy it. Only the victory of National Socialism thus meant the end of the Wilhelmine electoral system.

The National Socialists and their precursors were also essential to the development of a new style of political violence in the new republic, a response that would eventually lead to restructuring the entire political system. Of course, violence was present in Wilhelmine society, and more of it could have been induced with the right leadership and the right situations. The power of the authoritarian state to a certain extent stimulated violence, particularly in the opinion of dissenters and political deviants. But in fact street violence in Wilhelmine Germany was very rare. This statement is supported by recent research on violence. The thinnest folders in provincial archives of the Wilhelmine period are often those labeled "internal unrest."[11]

After 1918, Germans became increasingly mobilized on the streets, often with guns in hand. It was an experience that transformed the perception of politics among those who first envisioned their potential political role while voting. Others, without that form of political experience, would become totally socialized as potential *Putschtists* or as "Red Revolutionaries." Thus these acts in the streets might often have more immediate and more direct meaning than voting, even when the consequences of voting for the first time could be translated into governmental policy.

This is not to say that street actions do not breed interest in electoral politics or that turnout might not very well increase because of the intense politicization through violence. This certainly happened in the elections immediately before and after the National Socialists came into power. But politicization through street actions and politicization through the polling booth are not always complementary activities. The first requires expensive and dangerous commitments, even if they are short-run; the second can produce only long-term results, such as a growing consciousness of the individual's political role based on repetitive but not death-defying actions.

Thus violence spread through society not only by touching all social classes; it became more geographically dispersed. In the Wilhelmine era street violence was generally confined to a few instances in specific industrial areas. In 1918–20, widespread areas of Germany were immune from any armed insurrection. By the 1930s armed and uniformed paramilitary groups had spread throughout the entire country. The differences between the Wilhelmine and the immediate pre-Hitler era can be illustrated by an anecdote found in the government files of the Prussian province of Hesse-Cassel in the decade before World War I. There the rural gendarmerie seldom even had to police, let alone take care of, political actions. Therefore, it seemed appropriate to send some of them off to the neighboring mining regions of the Ruhr in case of a major coal strike. With typical Prussian thoroughness, the police constructed lists of officers who would be transferred to the mining districts in case of an emergency. In due course, the proper officials in Cassel received a request from a gendarmerie sergeant in a remote station near Fritzlar. The post had a particularly vicious police dog who could be handled only by this one officer. And this officer had been chosen to go to the Ruhr in times of trouble. The sergeant pleaded with his superiors for the substitution of any other officer at the station rather than be faced with the problem of the dog.[12] In the early 1930s there was plenty of activity to keep the officer at home. The sergeant would have been happier; the dog would have been calmer; but the price was the destruction of political society.

The increased political violence of the early 1930s was but one indication of a generalized and deepening crisis of the capitalist system. It was this crisis that caused an explosive disintegration of former patterns of political behavior and resulted in the formation of new allegiances; it was this crisis that not only felled the Weimar Republic but the inheritance of the Wilhelmine electoral system as well. The economic collapse affected not only the marginal but also the most stable group of voters in the 1920s. The persistent rural voting patterns had endured throughout the early 1920s despite a continual postwar crisis in agriculture. This agrarian crisis had even deepened by the later 1920s, particularly for small farmers faced with heavy burdens of debt repayment and a declining agrarian market. There were signs of protest and disaffection before 1929. The depression transformed an already difficult time into an unbearable event. The traditional pro-agrarian parties (including the DNVP) were committed to deflationary policies, which made rural relief impossible. The National Socialists were untainted by such actions. Rural voters had already shown strong predilections to desert the older parties. The Nazis thus made advances and had achieved organizational successes in rural areas even before they had a formal agrarian program. By 1930 there was the beginning of a brown wave in Protestant rural voting patterns, particularly in areas of predominantly small farms with high indebtedness. These protest voters were located all over Germany; they were particularly evident in East Elbia where the traditional bonds between small and large landowners were dissolved, and the small farmers' protest movement served as the basis for the destruction of social-grouping solidarities. They were evident in Hanover, Braunschweig, and Oldenburg, in Hesse and Upper Bavaria. For the most part, these were not new voters or people who never voted; they were old loyalists transformed. The National Socialists appeared to many to answer the problems of the crisis. After 1930 they promised new programs and more government aid. Equally important, they merged economic need with symbols in ways that would hardly startle peasants reared in Wilhelmine-style politics. The National Socialists emphasized their traditional nationalist commitments, their desire to regenerate Germany. Even their strong anti-Semitism could find resonance in traditional peasant belief.[13]

National Socialism was much more than a throwback to sporadic Protestant *Bürgertum* coalitions and marginally successful anti-Semitic populists of Wilhelmine Germany. It was a generalized protest party that was able to penetrate some Catholic rural areas as well as Protestant. Most important, the party made inroads into the working class in a way no other populist movement ever had. The majority of the working class remained firmly tied to the social grouping and voted for the SPD or the Communists, but there were significant defections in all the major German cities. We know little about these defectors except that they were more likely to be in general manufacturing than in the mining and metallurgical industries, which were the strongholds of labor solidarities. Many of them may have been unemployed or never employed. Some may have been young workers never fully socialized into the politics of the working class, factory workers whose allegiances to working-class politics were nonexistent or marginal, middle-class sons and daughters of workers who had heretofore maintained their socialist allegiances. Whatever their social composition, they had turned National Socialist because the economic system had failed them. This working-class rage during a depression was not unique; it is similar to that exhibited by significant numbers of American and German workers in the 1980s. There had been an earlier instance of working-class defections to similar parties after the inflationary crisis during the first election of 1924. It should be no surprise that this phenomenon would reoccur in 1930. Some of these defectors probably were only partially mobilized and came out only in "easy issue" or crisis elections; thus, they had sat out the 1928 contest conducted in relative economic prosperity. These, in turn, were joined by many more protest voters in 1930. There is not enough knowledge available to determine the depth of these conversions in 1930 or how long they might have endured. However, it would be wrong to consider all National Socialist working-class supporters as merely marginal, exhibiting only temporary aberrations. There had always been a substantial minority of working-class members in the party. The party's most violent wing, the storm troopers, tended to be composed of young, unemployed, blue-collar workers.[14]

These rural and working-class protest voters marked a significant deviation from the Wilhelmine inheritance, but they were not the only aspect of transformation evident in voting patterns of the early 1930s. By 1932 the National Socialist successes were so widespread as to appear to approximate a reconstruction of a Protestant *Bürgertum* for which so many Wilhelmine politicians had longed. However, at least for the larger cities, this comparison is invalid. There were striking differences between the new Nazi big-city coalitions and the Wilhelmine-inspired Protestant *Bürgertum* agglomerations. The acceptance of the National Socialists as the principal anti-Marxist party in the big Protestant cities was, of course, reminiscent of the attempts to unite the Protestant *Bürgertum* in 1907 and 1912. But this so-called *Bürgertum* vote of 1930 and 1932 consisted of large numbers of workers, eliminating the absolute distinctions of class voting upon which such coalitions had been based in the Wilhelmine period. Nor could the National Socialists by program or by action be conceived as adherents and protectors of the power of the business-oriented elites in these large cities. The Nazis sustained the oppression by the rich but they did not support the peace and order essential for these elites' control; the Nazis may have been purveyors of popular anti-Semitic and nationalist ideas to which many of the elites adhered, but the party was clearly not an agent for reconstituting this elite's rule. Thus the very strong support for the National Socialists in the richest sections of these cities and the willingness of the elite-oriented press to accept the National Socialist as part of an anti-Marxist coalition is only a sign of the inability of the elites themselves to contain and control the threats to their privileged position. For this reason, they turned to the Hitler party, which was precisely the opposite of the traditional *Bürgertum* coalition, to a party that even in its most respectable dress was led by new men with antiestablishment and antiauthority positions, reminiscent more of some nascent attempts at creating populist nationalism before 1914 than of the mainstream *Bürgertum* politics before the war.[15]

It was not in the big cities but in the small towns and rural areas where National Socialism reconstituted the Protestant *Bürgertum*. By 1932 the brown tide had overwhelmed almost all other *Bürgertum* parties and was well on its way to control all the positions of local power and influence, dominating the municipal councils, local agencies of interest groups, choral and fraternal societies, and social clubs. Part of this success was due to the already weakened structures of traditional politics and the inability of local elites to maintain their positions of political influence through attachment to established voting blocs and parties. Part of this was due to the National Socialists themselves who brought a new style of politics into many small towns and rural areas, a style adumbrated by populist movements before the war. The National Socialists were extraordinarily energetic. They held frequent meetings, marches, and rallies, not only during electoral campaigns but in the intervals between them. They were untainted with responsibility for unpopular government policies. And the National Socialists had an effective leader who was even more popular than the party.

The most striking relationship between National Socialism and prewar electoral practices did not concern new or improved methods of political mobilization but consisted in the ability of the Nazis to accommodate themselves to the more traditional stances prevalent in these small towns and rural areas. The National Socialist program could appear to articulate stands that had already become familiar before 1914. National Socialist propaganda skillfully hid some of its radical implications and emphasized its apparently traditional national stands, placed itself as the protector of local economic interests and adjusted its programs to local needs, posed as the only effective shield against the Red menace, often abandoned its antireligious and antitraditional tone, and always marched under the banners of national regeneration. Local elites could easily ac-

commodate themselves to such statements and move into the fold, especially when their traditional political stances had proven ineffective. The
role of these elites in the National Socialist successes is an open question,
but there can be no doubt that the party was riddled with local elites and
interest group leaders by 1932.[16]

Yet this combination of an efficient party and a compatible program
does not explain the successes of National Socialism or articulate the
dominant theme of a Wilhelmine inheritance. The Nazi level of organization was well above that of the populist movements of the 1890s. Hitler
was clearly a more effective leader than the prewar populist politicians.
Despite its rhetorical bows to *Bürgertum* centrality, National Socialism
practiced a much more violent and intransigent brand of politics than the
prewar period would allow. National Socialism was clearly a party of
the postwar period; its ultimate success was due to the depression of the
1930s. The enormous increase in the Nazi vote was a sign of a great crisis
in the capitalist system, of a crisis that undermined many stable political
allegiances that had endured through both empire and republic. All that
we know about electoral decision making mitigates against such rapid
movement by so many except in periods of crisis. Swings of this kind are
not explained by interpretations that emphasize better organization and
ease of transition. They do not tell us why whole communities that had
produced the most stable patterns of voting in the 1920s moved un-
characteristically and almost en masse to reorient their political allegiances. And they did move. In rural areas the party often increased its
share of the vote as much as ten times in 1930. Moreover, those rural
areas where the National Socialist vote had been 40 or 50 percent of the
electorate in 1930 would reach figures of 80 or 90 percent in 1932. In the
same way, the Nazis totally dominated Protestant small-town and rural-
interest and fraternal groups by 1932, methodically dispatching the opposition as swiftly and efficiently as a good vacuum cleaner. Some of this
was due to a community effect; even voters in the solitary confines of the
balloting area sometimes operate as if in crowds, particularly when there
is no voiced opposition.

The National Socialists were ideally placed to achieve political gains
from the crisis. They had no responsibility for the depression and the
general situation of Germany; they posed global solutions that carried
soothing promise. Much of this was rooted in the fatherland rhetoric of
the Wilhelmine era, especially in the call to unity above party, against Socialism, and for an adventuresome foreign policy. The same Wilhelmine
inheritance was present in the economic programs that the National Socialists advocated. But the National Socialists had an enormous advantage over all those pre–World War I activists in the *Bürgertum* cause. In
the depression of the 1930s, there was less possibility of fulfilling the economic needs of any group; this perception tended to displace into the fu-

ture those conflicts which had heretofore characterized Protestant *Bür-gertum* interest-group politics. Thus shop clerks, small farmers, and civil servants could respond positively to the specific programs outlined by National Socialism without asking questions about priorities or how conflicts among these various groups would be resolved. The alleviation of specific economic ills had become subsumed under the large category of national regeneration, a series of vague and excessive promises, precisely the prescription for a people living in a time of collapse and often unable to cope with the fallout from this catastrophe.[17]

National Socialist voters were thus an amalgam of the fearful and threatened, driven more by their convictions about the total decline of economic and social order rather than by any specific remedy. It was this search for global solutions that united the protest voters, including the workers, with the rush of *Bürgertum* supporters who entered the National Socialist fold after 1930. Although using the rhetoric and symbols of pre-1914 nationalist populism, the National Socialists were not simply a continuation of prewar trends. The party was the only legitimate heir of a system collapse in which many Germans, including those politicized in the Wilhelmine era, had come to view their economic and political system, along with its Wilhelmine inheritances, as operating in a state of chaos. These Germans turned toward radical and untried solutions in order to reestablish their sense of security. The working-class supporters, the rural protest voters, the fearful middle class of the cities, the Protestant *Bürgertum* in distress, all responded to the politics of rage against the uncertainties of life in the depression.

National Socialism was a means for alleviating this rage and uncertainty. It represented a vote for a future which, however unclear, was better than an unendurable present. The outlines of this future may have appeared assured and predictable for some, but for many they were probably no more than vague hopes for improvement. This does not mean that an immediate return to prosperity, even if such were possible, would have destroyed the National Socialist movement entirely. National Socialism was too well entrenched as early as September 1930, if not before. Its electoral success in the 1930s was in part due to the fact that a significant number of *völkisch* protest voters had already been mobilized as early as the first election of 1924. And the successful penetration into the areas of the Protestant *Bürgertum* during the depression provided a means for consolidating support. However, there were limits to this growth. The Catholic and working-class social groupings remained relatively impenetrable to National Socialism before 1933. The Social Democrats and Communists combined did incur some losses, but the Catholic parties actually increased their share of the vote in the elections of 1930 and 1932, and many National Socialist voters could not be indefinitely sustained on the course. The strength of the party and its leadership did not preclude defections to other parties or to nonvoting. The patterns of *völkisch* protest voting suggest that many National Socialist supporters were marginal, "easy issue" voters whose loyalties were not habituated and difficult to sustain from election to election. Many of them could disappear among the nonvoters as they evidently had in the election of 1928. Thus the decline in both turnout and National Socialist vote in the autumn of 1932 might have been a sign that the voting bloc which supported the Nazis was diminishing. The Nazi promises had been substantial and needed fulfillment or large numbers of their adherents would vanish.[18]

These nonhabituated National Socialist voters were in sharp contrast to those Wilhelmines who related to seemingly permanent social ties. Wilhelmine voters overwhelmingly affirmed cleavages that were deeply embedded in everyday life. The National Socialist supporters were voting to escape everyday life for a future against the present, for at best an ersatz instead of a real past. Wilhelmines were voting for past, present, and future as embodied in continuing and durable social groupings. The Wilhelmine inheritance then was a series of stable commitments by a politicized electorate exercising its citizenship roles. It was an inheritance that far from crippled the first German democracy, and it sustained those elements that remained loyal to the democratic regime until the end. This rejected inheritance is the root of a genuine paradox: that the most positive citizenship roles were fulfilled in an authoritarian state and diminished in a democratic one. In one sense, it is a trivial dilemma. The Weimar regime endured a series of shocks that might have undermined any capitalist system and destroyed any democracy. Moreover the whole purpose of this study has been to disengage the predispositions of high politics from the interpretations of mass electoral systems. Following this assumption, there should be no reason to expect that every democratic electoral system would function better than every authoritarian one. Yet I believe that this paradox has important implications for understanding the nature of universal suffrage systems and in identifying certain problems of German history. Its very existence is unnerving, especially for those progressivist and liberal predispositions to which this author and many of his readers still adhere.

APPENDIX

Statistical Symbols and Their Meanings

Symbol	Term	Definition
r	Correlation Coefficient	Shows gross relationship between two variables. A coefficient close to 1 means that a percentile increase of 1 in the indicator (x) will yield an increase of close to 1 percentile in (y). A decrease in x by close to 1 should show a very large decrease in y. Most coefficients are considerably less than 1.
r^2	Coefficient of Determination	Shows the amount of total variation explained. An r^2 of .64 means that 64 percent of the variation in y is attributable to changes in x and vice versa.
partial	r and r^2	Shows the relationship when the effects of other variables on both x and y are removed. Thus we will know the effect of x only, controlling for z and q.
R^2	Multiple Coefficient of Determination	This represents the cumulative effect of several variables on y; i.e., finding the effect of x only, then adding the effect of z on y controlling for x, etc.
p	Significance	Describes the probability that a given relationship would be expected by chance; i.e., p should be quite low for the result to be considered statistically significant (probably not the result of chance). The symbol $p = .05$ means that the coefficient might be expected by chance only 5 times out of 100.
B	Beta or Standardized Regression Coefficient	Directly measures change caused by one variable upon another when the effects of other variables are excluded, i.e., controls for effects of other variables in a multiple regression statement. Thus the beta for y on x would show precisely what change in y is caused by x, controlling for z, q, and any other named variables.

Limits	Use of Measurement
-1 to $+1$	If percent Catholic and Center vote have a high coefficient, e.g., .8, their statistical relationship can be said to be significant. If it were $-.001$, it would be statistically insignificant. The closer toward $+1$ or -1, the more the two items vary together; the closer to 0, the less.
0 to $+1$	A relatively high percentage then has high explanatory value in terms of statistics. A very low percentage leaves a great deal more to be explained, hopefully by adding new variables.
same as r and r^2	Allows us to explain two factors controlling for others. Thus the partial r for percent Catholic and Center vote might be .6 when controlling for rurality and industrialization.
0 to $+1$	This allows for incremental increases, showing the effect. If percent Catholic yields an r^2 of .64 and the addition of industrialization is .07, then R^2 equals .71.
0 to 1	This study generally accepts as statistically significant all results that yield a level of $p = .05$ or less.
varies	Because beta is a standardized measure, a small beta weight might still be statistically significant. A beta weight of .5 for y on x means that for every change of 1 in x there will be a change of .5 in y.

NOTES

CHAPTER I

1. See particularly Rokkan, *Citizens, Elections, Parties.* The classic study of the universal suffrage systems in operation at the turn of the century is Ostrogorski, *Democracy and the Organization of Political Parties.* For Germany see Vogel, Nohlen, Schultze, *Wahlen in Deutschland,* and Faul, ed., *Wähler und Wahlen in Deutschland.* For the transition in Great Britain see Thompson, *John Stuart Mill and Representative Government;* Hanham, *Elections and Party Management,* and David C. Moore, *The Politics of Deference;* Nossiter, *Influence, Opinion and Political Idioms in Reformed England.* Particularly relevant are the cross-national data collected and interpreted by Tingsten, *Political Behavior.*

2. Quoted in HStA Wiesbaden, Regierung Wiesbaden, 405, 4324.

3. *Verhandlungen des Reichstages,* 245: 4324.

4. Rose and Massawir, "Voting and Elections: A Functional Analysis," p. 85. For the literature on abstaining, see McPhee and Ferguson, "Political Immunization," pp. 155–201; Berelson, Lazarsfeld, McPhee, *Voting;* Butler and Stokes, *Political Change in Britain,* pp. 25–29; Miller, *Electoral Dynamics in Britain since 1918.* American studies of use are Kleppner, *The Cross of Culture;* Kleppner, *The Third Electoral System, 1853–1892;* Lipset, *Political Man,* pp. 230–34; Jensen, *The Winning of the Middle West.* For the view of the uniqueness of the American situation, see Verba, Nie, Kim, *Participation and Political Equality,* pp. 308–9. On the dysfunctions of the ethno-cultural model for the twentieth century, see Lichtman, *Prejudice and Old Politics.* The most important theory of rational voting is that of Anthony Downs propounded in his *Economic Theory of Democracy,* an excerpt of which can be found reprinted in Niemi and Weisberg, *Controversies in American Voting Behavior,* pp. 33–40; Downs has been attacked so much that there is great doubt about the possibilities of making the theory work; see Ferejohn and Fiorini, "The Paradoxes of Voting," pp. 525–36; Fishburn, "Paradoxes of Voting," pp. 537–46; Kelley and Miner, "The Simple Act of Voting," pp. 572–79. It is also challenged by Sidney Verba and Norman Nie, *Participation in America,* pp. 106–7. Denis Mueller has recently been equally unable to unravel the problem in *Public Choice.*

5. Berelson, Lazarsfeld, McPhee, *Voting,* p. 312. This author relies heavily on the findings of Anglo-American electoral research, particularly on the specific reconstruction of the voter's world, in Campbell, Converse, Miller, *The American Voter;* Nie, Verba, Petrocik, *The Changing American Voter;* and Butler and Stokes, *Political Change in Britain.* For a criticism of this approach applied to recent Germany, see Meyer, "Thesen und Kritik der empirischen Wahlforschung in der Bundesrepublik Deutschland," pp. 169–94.

6. For a definition of democracy, see Dahl and Lindbloom, *Politics, Economics, Welfare,* p. 309.

7. *Vierteljahreshefte zur Statistik des Deutschen Reichs 1907*: II. The tax and tariff struggles were always presented to some group of the electorate; see also Gustav Stolper, *German Economy, 1870−1940*, p. 30. Wilhelm Altrichter argues that there was even a consensus foreign policy; see *Konstitutionalismus und Imperialismus*, pp. 90ff.

8. For Bismarck's and William's disposition to *Staatsstreich* see Zechlen, *Staatsstreichspläne Bismarck und Wilhelm II*; Michael Stürmer, "Konservatismus und Revolution in Bismarcks Politik," in Stürmer, ed., *Das kaiserliche Deutschland*, pp. 143−63. For dangers of *Staatsstreich*, see Hohenloe-Schillingfürst, *Denkwürdigkeiten der Reichskanzlerzeit*, p. 67.

9. A good overview can be found in Huber, *Deutsche Verfassungsgeschichte 4* (1968), and in Bergsträsser, *Geschichte der politischen Parteien in Deutschland*, pp. 122−93. For a brief traditional account of German politics, there is still Hartung, *Deutsche Geschichte 1871−1918*, to be used in conjunction with the new synthesis by Wehler, *Das deutsche Kaiserreich 1871−1918*; Crothers, *The German Election of 1907*; Bertram, *Die Wahlen zum deutschen Reichstag vom Jahre 1912*; Nipperdey, *Die Organisation der deutschen Parteien vor 1918*; Ritter, *Wahlgeschichtliches Arbeitsbuch*.

10. Jarausch, *The Enigmatic Chancellor*, p. 89.

11. "New orthodoxy" works include Boldt, "Deutsches Konstitutionalismus," pp. 119−42; Puhle, "Parlament, Parteien und Interessenverbände," pp. 312−39; Peter-Christian Witt, *Die Finanzpolitik des Deutschen Reiches*, pp. 32−39; Wehler, *Krisenherde des Kaiserreichs*. For a criticism of the "new orthodoxy," see Sheehan, "Review: Gerhard Ritter, *Gesellschaft, Parlament und Regierung*," pp. 565−67. For a debate on this school see Eley, "Die 'Kehrites' und das Kaiserreich," pp. 91−107; Puhle, "Zur Legende von der 'Kerschen Schule,'" pp. 109−19.

12. Stürmer, "Caesar's Laurel Crown," p. 206. See also Stürmer, "Bismarckstaat und Cäsarismus oder das Problem es nicht gegeben haben Kann," pp. 626−69; Mitchell, "Bonapartism as a Model," pp. 181−99.

13. Wehler, *Das deutsche Kaiserreich*. There are numerous criticisms, among them Nipperdey, "Wehlers 'Kaiserreich,'" pp. 529−60; Eley, "Recent Work in Modern German History," pp. 463−79; Evans, "Wilhelm II's Germany and the Historians," pp. 1−40; Hildebrand, "Geschichte oder 'Gesellschaftsgeschichte,'" pp. 328−57; Rohl, "Introduction," pp. 5−22; Zmarzlik, "Das Kaiserreich in neuer Sicht?" pp. 105−26. Wehler's reply can be found in "Kritik und kritische Antikritik," pp. 349−81 and is supported by Berghahn, "Politik und Geschichte im Wilhelmischen Deutschland," pp. 164−95. Also consult Langewiesche, "Deutsche Kaiserreich," pp. 628−42.

14. For an enunciation of this position, see particularly Gerhard A. Ritter, "Entwicklungsprobleme des deutschen Parlamentarismus," pp. 11−12. A full discussion of the problems of this approach and its critics is contained in Mock, "'Manipulation von oben' oder Selbstorganisation der Basis?" pp. 358−75.

15. Wehler, *Das deutsche Kaiserreich*, pp. 63−69 and passim. A number of other historians support Wehler; see Berghahn, *Der Tirpitz-Plan* and the essays by Wolfgang Mommsen, the most accessible of which is "Domestic Questions in German Foreign Policy," pp. 223−67.

16. Lepsius, "Parteisystem und Sozialstruktur," p. 67. See chapter 4 for a fuller discussion.

17. Veblen, *Imperial Germany and the Industrial Revolution*; Gershenkron, *Bread and Democracy in Germany*; Plessner, *Die verspätete Nation*; Wehler, *Modernisierungstheorie und Geschichte*. For similar American views see Apter, *The Politics of Modernization*, Shils, *Political Development in the New States*, and the discussion of asynchronic development in Organski, *The Stages of Political Development*.

18. Dahrendorf, *Society and Democracy in Germany*, p. 99.

19. Ibid., p. 68.

20. Eley, *Reshaping the German Right*, p. 354. See also Evans, "Wilhelm II's Germany and the Historians," pp. 11–39; Blackbourn, *Class, Religion and Local Politics*; Sheehan, *German Liberalism in the Nineteenth Century*, pp. 222–71; Rohe, "Wahlanalyse im historischen Kontext," pp. 337–57; Büsch, "Historische Wahlforschung als Zugang zur Geschichte," pp. 1–37; Conze, "Politische Willensbildung im deutschen Kaiserreich als Forschungsaufgabe historischer Wahlsoziologie," pp. 331–47; Steinbach, "Politische Partizipationsforschung," pp. 171–234. Arno Mayer believes that modernization had proceeded slowly on all levels; see *The Persistence of the Old Regime*. Criticism of modernization theory can be found in Tipps, "Modernization Theory and the Study of National Societies," pp. 199–226; Grew, "Modernization and Its Discontents," pp. 289–308.

21. Particularly striking examples of this can be found in election materials in HStA Wiesbaden, Regierung Wiesbaden, 405, 2473–75; HStA Marburg, LA Gelnhausen, 180, 3856; StA Detmold, Regierung Minden, Mi. 1, 25.

22. National Liberal leaflet, 1907, HStA Marburg, LA Gelnhausen, 180, 3856.

23. *Dortmunder Zeitung*, 25 June 1903.

24. *Arbeiter Zeitung* (Dortmund), 31 January 1907.

25. Ibid., 23 January 1907.

26. Stadtarchiv Dortmund, Do.N. 206.

27. In leaflet for June 1895 election, Bundesarchiv Koblenz, Payer Nachlass, 7.

CHAPTER 2

1. Würzburg, "Die 'Partei' der Nichtwähler," pp. 383–84; Würzburg, *Deutsches Statistisches Zentralblatt* 21: 58.

2. The data for this calculation were found in Grosse and Raith, *Beiträge zur Geschichte und Statistik der Reichstags- und Landtagswahlen in Württemberg seit 1871*, pp. 25–26, and in the poor lists for the Stadtarchiv Stuttgart, 25.

3. Carmines and Stimson, "The Two Faces of Issue Voting," pp. 78–89.

4. Mackie and Rose, *International Almanac of Electoral History*, p. 386; Tingsten, *Political Behavior*, p. 219; F. W. Craig, *British Election Results, 1885–1919*, pp. 582–83.

5. Mackie and Rose, pp. 88–92; *Historical Statistics of the United States*, pp. 1070–71; Vogel et al., *Wahlen in Deutschland*, pp. 290–97.

6. Lipset, *Political Man*, p. 229; Tingsten, *Political Behavior*; Rokkan, *Citizens, Elections, Parties*, pp. 46ff.; Burnham, *Critical Elections*. For the most far-reaching exchange between Burnham and his critics, see Burnham, "Theory and Voting Research," pp. 1002–23; Converse, "Comment," pp. 1024–27; Rusk, "Comment," pp. 1028–49 and the attack by Converse that inspired the exchange in "Change in the American Electorate," Campbell and Converse, eds., *The Human Meaning of Social Change*, pp. 263–330.

7. Burnham, "The Changing Shape of the American Political Universe," pp. 7–28.

8. The data come from Vogel et al., *Wahlen in Deutschland*. For the method see Burnham, *Critical Elections*, p. 17; Ezekial and Fox, *Methods of Correlation and Regression Analysis*, pp. 328–29.

9. Spindler, ed., *Handbuch der bayerischen Geschichte* 4: 1296–97; *Zeitschrift des Königlichen Preussischen Statistischen Bureaus*, Ergänzungsheft 30: VIII, IX; *Statistisches Jahrbuch für den Preussischen Staat*, 1915; for the national Reichstag statistics see *Monatshefte zur Statistik des Deutschen Reichs*, 1885, 1, 1887, 4: 1–43, 1890, 4: 23–69; *Vierteljahreshefte zur Statistik des Deutschen Reichs*, 1893, 4: 1–55; 1898 Ergänzungsheft 1: 1–101, 1903 Ergänzungsheft 4: 1–93, 1907 Ergänzungsheft 3: 1–131; *Statistik des Deutschen Reichs*, Neue Folge 250, 2: 1–141. Some of this material was coded directly for machine; other times the author used material from the Interuniversity Consortium. For a bibliography of voting statistics, see Diederich et al., *Wahlstatistik in Deutsch-*

land, pp. 168–69; Vogel et al., *Wahlen in Deutschland*, p. 428. See also Max von Seydel and Robert Piloty, *Bayerisches Staatsrecht* for Bavarian voting rights. For Prussia see chapter 6.

10. *Württembergische Jahrbücher für Statistik und Landeskunde*, 1907, Teil 2, 38–39; *Statistische Mitteilungen über das Grossherzogtum Baden*, Neue Folge, 6: 120–21; *Vierteljahreshefte zur Statistik des Deutschen Reichs*, 1907, 3: 82–86. For similar Hessian data, see *Beiträge zur Statistik des Grossherzogtums Hessen* 62: Heft 5, 10–11. For a discussion of voting rights in Württemberg and Baden see Walz, *Das Staatsrecht des Grossherzogtums Baden*, pp. 15–16, 70–71, 500–501; Göz, *Das Staatsrecht des Königreichs Württemberg*, pp. 26, 118, 287. For further discussion of the problems of constitutional reform in the south, see chapter 6.

11. Thränhardt, *Wahlen und politische Strukturen in Bayern 1848–1953*, pp. 96–126; White, *The Splintered Party*; Blackbourn, *Class, Religion and Local Politics in Wilhelmine Germany*.

12. *Geschäftsbericht der sozialdemokratischen Landes-Organisation, Grossherzogtum Hesse* (Offenbach, 1912), p. 27. See also Kurt, *Wähler und Wahlen in Wahlkreis Offenbach*, pp. 46–64.

13. Schwarzwaldkreis report to Interior Ministry, 6 April 1908, HStA Stuttgart, Ministry of Interior, E150, 2046.

14. *Frankfurter Zeitung*, 26 January 1907.

15. Preserved in HStA Marburg, LA Ziegenhain, 180, 4442.

16. Würzburg, "Die 'Partei'"; Merriam and Gosnel, *Non-Voting*, pp. 26, 36.

17. Rokkan, *Citizens, Elections, Parties*, pp. 191–99. A number of recent American studies have gone farther and have considered voting a particularly passive act unrelated to more intensive forms of participation: see Lester Milbrath, *Political Participation*, pp. 18ff. and Verba et al. *The Modes of Democratic Participation*, p. 64. However these studies do not replicate the reality of entrance into a political system, a fact which characterized nineteenth-century voting. A more congenial approach for the historical reality can be found in Merriam and Gosnel, *Non-Voting*, p. 26 and passim; Berelson et al., *Voting*, pp. 336–67; and in the recent emphasis upon entrance into the system characterized by Robert Salisbury's article, "Recent Research on Political Participation," pp. 323–41.

18. *Provinziell Parteitag für westliche Westfalen, 1911*, Dortmund Stadtarchiv, Do.n. 263; Kreis reports to the Minister of Interior, Stuttgart, particularly Neckarkreis 19 April 1904, 7 May 1908, Schwarzwaldkreis 8 March 1906, Jagstkreis 20 February 1908, all in HStA Stuttgart, Ministry of Interior, E150, 2046; *Tremonia* (Dortmund), 11 March 1913; Sheehan, "Liberalism and the City in Germany," pp. 126–37; Croon, *Die gesellschaftliche Auswirkungen des Gemeindewahlrechts in den Gemeinden und Kreisen des Rheinlands und Westfalen im neunzehnten Jahrhundert*, pp. 13ff.

19. Sheehan, *German Liberalism in the Nineteenth Century*, p. 231.

20. Police report 1 August 1912, Dortmund Stadtarchiv, Do.n. 263; police report 30 April 1908, ibid., Do.n. 224; police report 19 June 1909, ibid., Do.n. 180; Dortmund Landrat report, October 1890, StA Münster, Regierung Arnsberg, I, 92; Dortmund County report 14 August 1900; Police Commissioner Dortmund report 5 October 1899, ibid., Regierung Arnsberg, I, 96, Oberbürgermeister Dortmund report 28 August 1907, ibid., Regierung Arnsberg, I, 99; *Dortmunder Tageblatt*, 3 June 1903, 10–13 January 1912; *Tremonia*, 16 February 1908; Lützenkirchen, *Der sozialdemokratische Verein für den Reichstagswahlkreis Dortmund-Hörde*, pp. 87–92 and passim; Graf, *Die Entwicklung der Wahlen und politischen Parteien in Gross-Dortmund*, pp. 23–27; *Protokoll über die Verhandlungen des Parteitags der sozialdemokratischen Partei Deutschlands 1912*, pp. 77–78.

21. Hirschfeld, *Die freien Gewerkschaften in Deutschland*, pp. 16–17, 84–85, 276–

77; Emil Ritter, *Die Katholisch-soziale Bewegung im neunzehnten Jahrhundert und der Volksverein*, pp. 253 and passim; *Geschäftsbericht des preussischen Landes-Kriegerverbände 1910* in HStA Wiesbaden, Regierung Wiesbaden, 405, 2676; Report of *Christ.-patriotischer Männerverein*, p. 35 in HStA Marburg, Regierung Cassel, 165, 1242; *Jahresbericht des deutschen Flotten-Verein, 1904*.

22. See Hirschfeld, *Die freien Gewerkschaften*, pp. 1ff., Socialist *Parteitag*, pp. 70–84; *Landes-Kriegerverbände*; Fricke, *Die bürglichen Parteien in Deutschland*, 1: 28, 33, 2: 297, 811.

23. Fricke, *Die bürglichen Parteien*; Groh, *Negative Integration und revolutionärer Attentismus*, pp. 744–45; *Encyclopedia of the Social Sciences* 15: 14.

24. See note 20 and Oberbürgermeister Dortmund, 19 October 1906, StA Münster, I 15, 7801; *Organisations-Handbuch der Nationalliberalen Partei* (Berlin, 1915), pp. 159–66.

CHAPTER 3

1. MacKenzie, "Representation in Plural Societies," p. 69.

2. The information about changing polling locations in winter is in Landrat report 18 February 1907, StA Detmold, Regierung Minden, Mi. 1, 253. The general information can be found in *Handbuch der Reichstages 1912* (Berlin, 1912), pp. 93–111; *Die Reichstagswahl 1912* (Berlin, 1912), pp. 84–99.

3. The material for this statement was collected from the yearly *Kriminalstatistik des Deutschen Reichs* and is part of a cooperative study the author is currently undertaking. See also Hall, *Scandal, Sensation and Social Democracy*, pp. 41–88.

4. Huber, *Deutsche Verfassungsgeschichte* 4: 9.

5. Bertram, *Die Wahlen zum deutschen Reichstag vom Jahre 1912*, pp. 129–33; the instructions to the local election commissioners were very explicit about obeying the rules.

6. *Verhandlungen des Reichstages*, Legislaturperiode 9, Session 2, Anlageband 1: Nr. 109–10.

7. Ibid., 152: 1285.

8. Ministry of Interior to Regierungspräsident Cassel, January 1907 and accompanying documents, HStA Marburg, LA Gelnhausen, 3856. For a comprehensive study of German official and election campaigning, see O'Donnell, "National Liberalism and the Mass Politics of the German Right, 1890–1907," pp. 396–460 and passim. For a definition of political officials see John Gillis, *The Prussian Bureaucracy in Crisis*, pp. 139, 150. For the role of higher officials in nineteenth-century, and particularly Wilhelmine, Germany, see Rejewski, *Die Pflicht zur politischen Treue im preussischen Beamtenrecht*, pp. 105–54; Fenske, "Preussische Beamtenpolitik vor 1918," pp. 339–56; Röhl, "Higher Civil Servants in Germany, 1890–1900," pp. 16–18. The expectations that Württemberg officials should support the regime were very evident in the reports to the Ministry of Interior HStA Stuttgart, E150, 2046; however, the Württemberg officials were not legally bound to support the regime; see Kötz, *Staatsrecht des Königreichs Württemberg*, pp. 180–81. In contrast, for the moral pressure on Reich officials, see Labard, *Deutsches Reichstaatsrecht*, pp. 104–6.

9. For registration attempts, see GStA Berlin, Regierung Danzig, 180, 19250; Rejewski, *Die Pflicht*, pp. 134–35; for a typical list of the Bülow era see GStA Berlin, Regierung Danzig, 180, 19151; for railway problem see Minister of Interior instructions, 25 March 1910, HStA Marburg, Regierung Cassel, 165, 2141, and note. For Artillery incident see *Verhandlungen des Reichstages*, Legislaturperiode 9, Session 2, Anlageband 2: Nr. 126.

10. Röhl, "Higher Civil Servants," pp. 118–19; Rejewski, *Die Pflicht*, pp. 118–25;

Sheehan, "Leadership in the German Reichstag, 1871–1914," pp. 518–19; Molt, *Der Reichstag vor der improvisierten Revolution*, pp. 142–51; Kremer, *Der soziale Aufbau der Parteien des Deutschen Reichstages von 1871–1918*, pp. 78–79.

11. National Liberal pamphlet, August 1911, HStA Wiesbaden, Regierung Wiesbaden, 405, 2474. This story is well told in Wolf-Arno Kropat, "Die Beamte und die Politik in wilhelminischer Zeit," pp. 173–190.

12. Eugene and Pauline Anderson, *Political Institutions and Social Change in Continental Europe in the Nineteenth Century*, p. 336. See also Wehler, *Das deutsche Kaiserreich*, pp. 72–78.

13. The best works on non-German corruption are Scott, *Comparative Political Corruption*, pp. 76–157; Gwyn, *Democracy and the Costs of Politics*, pp. 50–75; Hanham, *Elections and Party Management*, pp. 262–83; Nossiter, *Influence, Opinion, and Political Idioms in Reformed England*, pp. 6–87; Jensen, *The Winning of the Middle West*, pp. 34–57; Allen and Allen, "Vote Fraud and Data Validity," pp. 153–94. There is no study of corruption in Germany.

14. Bund der Landwirte Report, 1911, HStA Wiesbaden, Regierung Wiesbaden, 405, 2474. This is also reproduced in Kropat, "Die Beamte," pp. 186–90.

15. *Verhandlungen des Reichstages*, Legislaturperiode 9, Session 2, Anlageband 1: Nr. 186.

16. *Dortmunder Tageblatt*, 11 June 1898.

17. Stadtarchiv Frankfurt, Magistratsakte R143/III; Stadtarchiv Stuttgart, Bu 25; GStA Berlin, Strasburg County, 205.

18. Frielendorf Gendarmerie report 29 May 1903, HStA Marburg, LA Ziegenhain, 180, 4442; Regierung President Wiesbaden report 25 January 1906, ibid., Oberpräsidium Kassel, 150, 633; *Die Volksstimme* (Frankfurt am Main), 20 December 1911; Keil, *Erlebnisse eines Sozialdemokraten*, 1: 174; Severing, *Mein Lebensweg*, 1: 184.

19. *Verhandlungen der Württembergischen Kammer der Abgeordneten 1901*, Beilage 2: 702.

20. *Verhandlungen des Reichstages*, Legislaturperiode 9, Session 3, Anlageband 1: Nr. 14, 102; Legislaturperiode 10, Session 1, Anlageband 2: Nr. 214; vol. 299, Nr. 373, 412; vol. 198, Nr. 30; *Arbeiter Zeitung* (Dortmund), 17 January 1907; Binder, *The Other German*, p. 17.

21. *Verhandlungen des Reichstages*, Legislaturperiode 9, Session 3, Anlageband 1: Nr. 164.

22. Grosse and Raith, *Beiträge zur Geschichte und Statistik der Reichstags- und Landtagswahlen in Württemberg seit 1871*, pp. 1*ff.; *Handbuch für hessische Zentrumswähler* (Mainz, 1911), pp. 67–99; GStA Berlin, Kreis Strasburg, 205, 209; HStA Marburg, LA Ziegenhain, 3490; *Oberhessische Zeitung* (Marburg), 7 February 1907, 23 January 1912.

23. Provincial Tax Director to Landrat, 27 October 1903, GStA Berlin, Thorn County, 207, 610; police report, 19 January 1912 and other correspondence, ibid., Schwetz County, 204, 3037; Polish Election Committee letter, 22 February 1912, ibid., Schwetz County, 204, 3073; a large number of violations in state elections are reported in Regierung Danzig, 180, 19296; *Verhandlungen des Reichstages*, Legislaturperiode 9, Session 2, Anlageband 2: Nr. 168; vol. 301, Nr. 788; vol. 299, Nr. 382; vol. 302, Nr. 1062; Bertram, *Die Wahlen*, pp. 133ff.

24. *Verhandlungen des Reichstages*, Legislaturperiode 9, Session 2, Anlageband 1: Nr. 22.

25. Gendarmerie report, 3 May 1903, GStA Berlin, Schwetz County, 204, 3073.

26. GStA Berlin, Strasburg County, 205; *Statistisches Jahrbuch für den Preussischen Staat 1914*, p. 20.

27. *Dortmunder General Anzeiger*, 13 February 1896 in StA Münster, Regierung Arnsberg, I, 96.

28. *Verhandlungen des Reichstages* vol. 299: Nr. 403.

CHAPTER 4

1. Hans Rosenberg, *Grosse Depression und Bismarckzeit*, p. 128. For a definition of interest group see Zeigler and Peak, *Interest Groups in American Society*; Truman, *Government and Processes*; Castles, *Pressure Groups and Political Culture*; Garson, *Group Theories of Politics*; Moe, *The Organization of Interests*.

2. Neumann, *Die Parteien der Weimarer Republik*, p. 25. Thomas Nipperdey, the leading scholar of Wilhelmine party structure, takes up Neumann's argument literally in *Die Organisation der deutschen Parteien vor 1918*, p. 396 and passim.

3. Heinrich Winkler, *Pluralismus oder Protektionismus*; Puhle, *Agrarische Interessenpolitik und preussischer Konservatismus im Wilhelmischen Reich* (Hanover, 1967); Puhle, "Parlament, Parteien und Interessenverbände," pp. 312−29; Ullmann, *Der Bund der Industriellen*, pp. 147ff.; Kaelble, *Industrielle Interessenpolitik in der Wilhelmischen Gesellschaft*; Kaelble, "Industrielle Interessenverbände vor 1918," pp. 180−212; Jaeger, *Unternehmer in der deutschen Politik*; Mielke, *Der Hansabund für Gewerbe Handel und Industrie*; Nipperdey, "Organisierter Kapitalismus und die Krise des Kaiserreichs," pp. 418−30; Schulz, "Über Entstehung und Formen von Interessengruppen in Deutschland seit Beginn der Industrialisierung," pp. 41−47; Wolfram Fischer, "Staatsverwaltung und Interessenverbände im Deutschen Reich 1871−1914," pp. 146−48.

4. Kleppner, *The Third Electoral System, 1853−1892*, p. 10. The interior quote is from Devine, *The Political Culture of the United States*, pp. 14−18; see also Almond and Verba, *The Civic Culture*; Almond and Powell, *Comparative Politics*, pp. 169−97; Bruce Campbell, *The American Electorate*, pp. 70−109.

5. Siegfried, *Géographie électorale de L'Ardeche sous la troisième république*, p. 61. See also Michelat and Simon, *Classe, religion et comportment politique*; Kleppner, *The Cross of Culture*; Kleppner, *The Third Electoral System*, pp. 145ff.; Jensen, *The Winning of the Middle West*, pp. 58ff.; Vandermeer, "Religion, Society and Politics," pp. 3−24; Lichtman, "Political Realignment and 'Ethnocultural' Voting in Late Nineteenth Century America," pp. 55−82 for further criticism. See also Wald, *Crosses on the Ballot*, pp. 162−201; Neal Blewitt, *The Peers, the Parties and the People*, pp. 339ff.; Joyce, *Work, Society and Politics*, pp. 240ff.; Hamer, *The Politics of Electoral Pressure*, pp. 91ff.; Miller and Raab, "The Religious Alignment at English Elections between 1918 and 1970," pp. 227−60; Miller, *Electoral Dynamics in Britain since 1918*, pp. 141ff.; Butler and Stokes, *Political Change in Britain*, pp. 157−71.

6. Taylor and Johnston, *Geography of Elections*, pp. 164−66. See also a similar study, which identifies the most partisan voters, in Rose, "Comparability in Election Studies," pp. 14−16; Liphardt, "Religious vs. Linguistic vs. Class Voting: The 'Crucial Experiment' of Comparing Belgium, Canada, South Africa and Switzerland," pp. 442−58.

7. Lepsius, "Parteisystem und Sozialstruktur: Zum Problem der Demokratisierung der deutschen Gesellschaft," p. 67. See also Wandruska, "Österreichs politische Struktur," pp. 291ff.; Thränhardt, *Wahlen und politische Strukturen in Bayern 1848−1953*, pp. 127ff.; Roth, *The Social Democrats in Imperial Germany*, pp. 159−63, 212−48. Clagett et al., "Political Leadership and the Development of Political Cleavages," pp. 654−62. For a contemporary critic, see Peter Reichel, "Politische Kultur," pp. 383−97.

8. Dawson and Prewitt, *Political Socialization*, pp. 181−83.

9. Angus Campbell et al., *The American Voter*, pp. 295−332. The following discussion on the ecological fallacy can be found in Blalock, *Causal Inferences in Nonexperimental Research*, pp. 95−116, and Goodman, "Some Alternatives to Ecological Correlation," pp. 610−25; Irwin and Lichtman, "Across the Great Divide: Inferring Individual Level Behavior from Aggregate Data," pp. 411−39; Langbein and Lichtman, *Ecological Inference*; Shade, "'New Political History': Some Statistical Questions Raised," pp. 171−96. Shade correctly states that significance tests do not have formal statistical meaning when there is no sampling; however, I believe that significance can still be used to deter-

mine those relationships which have the greatest possibilities of offering reasonable explanations. For an attack on Shade, see Lichtman and Langbein, "Ecological Regression versus Homogeneous Units," pp. 172–93. Karl Rohe correctly calls attention to the fact that nationwide aggregate data do not take into account local or regional differentiation. Thus nationwide analysis may hide community as well as individual effects and the importance of local elites. I would agree to a certain extent, yet the force of my local studies tends to support the nationwide data; see Rohe, "Konfession, Klasse und lokale Gesellschaft," pp. 110–26.

10. Hickey, "The Shaping of the German Labour Movement," pp. 218–19, 238; Klöcker, Konfession der sozialdemokratischen Wählerschaft, pp. 5ff. Croon and Utermann, Zeche und Gemeinde, pp. 22–99. For the view that enclosed communities have an effect, see Berelson et al., Voting, pp. 98ff. For the propensity of Catholics in Westphalia to maintain their isolation, see Vierhaus, "Wahlen und Wählerverhalten in Ostwestfalen und Lippe," p. 68. There is some evidence that political Catholicism benefited from a renewed religious commitment of Catholics in the last half of the nineteenth century; see Sperber, "Roman Catholic Religious Identity in Rhineland-Westphalia, 1800–70," pp. 305–18, but until the Kulturkampf, the Center drew some Protestant voters; see Claggett et al., "Political Leadership and the Development of Political Cleavages," p. 67. Both Claggett and Margaret Anderson suggest that the Center solidarities were in part the result of anti-Catholic government policy. Anderson believes that the Center would have withered away without this government policy; see Margaret Anderson, Windthorst: A Political Biography, pp. 191–98. There is some difficulty in determining the extent to which anti-Catholicism prevailed in the Protestant communities. See Antiultramontanes Handbuch, pp. 66–68, 211–14, 245 for discussion of Catholic boycotts against the dominant community; see also Buchheim, Ultramontanismus und Demokratie, pp. 354ff. Perhaps the best indication of anti-Catholic attitudes comes from the work of Max Weber. Weber's Protestant Ethic and the Spirit of Capitalism was, in large measure, a response to a contention by two Catholic scholars that Catholicism was compatible with capitalism. Weber attacked this position with some solid statistics that had been collected in Baden, and a picture-book which contended that the Alsatian Catholics had their adjustment into modern society disrupted by the French Church. See Wittich, Deutsche und französische Kultur im Elsass, pp. 18–21 and passim; Weber, Aufsätze zur Religions-Soziologie, pp. 14–25. Useful but beyond this period is the Catholic-originated Staatslexikon.

11. This technique is explicated in E. Terrence Jones, "Ecological Inference and Electoral Analysis," pp. 249–62; Kousser, "Ecological Regression and Analysis," pp. 237–62. Kousser's approach is the more useful. This author has followed the suggestions in Langbein and Lichtman, Ecological Inference, pp. 50ff.

12. Data can be found in Johannes Schauf, Das Wählverhalten der deutschen Katholiken im Kaiserreich und in der Weimarer Republik, p. 171; Statistik des Deutschen Reichs, Neue Folge, 209; 250: I, 68–79. The 47 units compared include all Regierungsbezirke of Prussia (including Sigmaringen), the 8 Regierungsbezirke of Bavaria, and all states with more than 500,000 population in 1887 (the Kingdoms of Saxony, Württemberg, the Grand Duchies of Baden, Hesse, and Mecklenburg-Schwerin, Hamburg, and Alsace-Lorraine). Excluded was about 5 percent of the population in the small states. These administrative units were chosen to nullify the effect of a party not contesting a single election. The propensity of parties to contest at one election and not at the next tends to skew the data; this is especially true when it was done as some part of a regional deal in which one party withdrew from the election in one district so that it might achieve a second party's support in another district. These regional deals would tend to be encompassed within the units chosen. Moreover there is no way of satisfactorily measuring male work force for units lower than the Regierungsbezirke although there have been several estimates by election district. The data are presented in order using multiple regression.

The assumption is that religion is an indicator of more importance than work force, and work force is more important than urbanization. It is true that inspection and various groupings of the data will yield other characteristics; see Gabler, *Die Entwicklung der Parteien auf landwirtschaftlicher Grundlage*; however, the data above and from other sources contradict this; see Wolfgang Wölk, "Sozialstruktur, Parteikorrelation und Wahlenentscheidung im Kaiserreich," pp. 524–55. The statistical presentation used in the above table is similar but not equivalent to that used by McCrary et al., "Class and Party in the Secession Crisis," pp. 448–50, and see the old standbys, Blalock, *Social Statistics*; Norman Nie et al., *Statistical Package for the Social Sciences*, pp. 180–81.

13. Calculated from Max Schwarz, *MdR*, pp. 115–508.

14. Stadtarchiv Dortmund, Do.n. 206. For a history of the Center, see Ross, *Beleaguered Tower*; Bachem, *Vorgeschichte, Geschichte und Politik der deutschen Zentrum*; Zeender, *The German Center Party 1890–1906*; Blackbourn, *Class, Religion and Local Politics in Wilhelmine Germany*; Morsey, "Die deutschen Katholiken und der Nationalstaat zwischen Kulturkampf und Ersten Weltkrieg," pp. 270–98; Epstein, *Mathias Erzberger and the Dilemma of German Democracy*; Buchheim, *Geschichte der christlichen Parteien in Deutschland*, pp. 197–238, 296–313.

15. *Tremonia* (Dortmund), 16 February 1908.

16. *Deutsches Volksblatt* (Stuttgart), 4, 15 November 1912.

17. *Der Beobachter* (Stuttgart), 14 November 1912.

18. *Wiesbadener Zeitung*, 3 June 1910 in HStA Wiesbaden, Regierung Wiesbaden, 405, 2766.

19. *Rhenische Volkszeitung*, 1911, in ibid., 405, 2473.

20. *Westpreussisches Volksblatt*, 27 May 1903 in GStA Berlin, Thorn County, A 207, 610.

21. Schulte, *Struktur und Entwicklung des Parteiensystems im Königreich Württemberg*, pp. 129, 132.

22. See chapter 2, note 9 and note 11 in this chapter. The variable conflict is computed by subtracting the percentage of the vote achieved by the leading candidate in the first election from 100.

23. Ross, *Beleaguered Tower*, p. 49. See also Nipperdey, *Organisation*, pp. 315–50.

24. *Westfälische Volkszeitung*, 21 July 1907; police report Wiedenbrück, 27 February 1907, both in StA Detmold, Regierung Minden, Mi. 1, 48.

25. *Verhandlungen des Reichstages* 245: 4303–6.

26. Blackbourn, *Class, Religion and Local Politics*, p. 18. See Epstein, *Mathias Erzberger*, pp. 35ff.

27. Zangerel, "Courting the Catholic Vote: The Center Party in Baden," pp. 228–29.

28. *Schulthess' Europaischer Geschichtskalender* 34: 61. See also Franz Josef Stegmann, "Geschichte der sozialen Ideen im deutschen Katholismus," pp. 120–24; Bachem, *Vorgeschichte*, 4: 90ff. For Bavaria see Thränhardt, *Wahlen*, pp. 96–97; Albrecht, "Von Reichsgründung bis zum Ende des Ersten Weltkrieges," pp. 313ff. See also Landrat Bochum, 1899, StA Münster, Regierung Arnsberg, I Pa. 103; *Recklinghausen Zeitung*, 28 December 1906, clipping in StA Münster, Oberpräsidium, 3907; Bertram, *Die Wahlen zum deutschen Reichstag vom Jahre 1912*, pp. 142, 163–64.

29. *Recklinghausen Zeitung*, 25 July 1895, clipping in StA Münster Oberpräsidium, 3907. See also *Münstersche Zeitung*, 11 August 1908; Minister for Agriculture to Provincial President, 23 November 1913, report of Regierungsrath Hesse, 22 December 1913, Regierungspräsident Münster, 3 September 1894, Regierungspräsident Minden, 3 September 1894, StA Münster, Oberpräsidium, 3907; Emil Ritter, *Die Katholisch-soziale Bewegung im neunzehnten Jahrhundert und der Volksverein*, pp. 253 and passim. Heitzer, *Der Volksverein für das Katholische Deutschland im Kaiserreich*, pp. 102ff.

30. *Protokoll des ersten Arbeitervereins Kongresses*, Frankfurt a.M., 26 and 27 May

1912, HStA Stuttgart, E151c, 237. See also secretary statistics in *Reichsarbeitsblatt* 5: 867; Berger, *Arbeiterbewegung und Demokratisierung*, pp. 164ff.

31. Koch, *Die Bergarbeiterbewegung im Ruhrgebiet zur Zeit Wilhelm II*, p. 96. See also *Reichsarbeitsblatt* 10: 121-27; Regierungspräsident Münster quarterly report, 13 October 1906, 21 February, 12 July 1911, 12 January 1912, StA Münster, Regierung Münster, 1052, 4832, Lager VII, 75; police report at Baukau, 2 June 1906, ibid., Regierung Arnsberg, I Pa, 98; Landrat Hörde, 12 September 1907, ibid., I Pa, 96; Polizeipräsident Bochum 3 October 1907, ibid., I Pa, 99. Crew, *Town in the Ruhr*, pp. 215ff.

32. HStA Stuttgart, Ministry of Interior, E150, 876; Grosse and Raith, *Beiträge zur Geschichte und Statistik des Reichstags- und Landtagswahlen in Württemberg seit 1871*; *Die Reichspost*, 12 November 1912; *Deutsches Volksblatt*, 24 December 1906. See Schulte, *Struktur und Entwicklung der Parteisystems*, pp. 120-24. Habitual voters were calculated thusly. Württemberg in 1912 had three separate first elections—two for candidates by district at the state and Reichstag level and one for a party list in very large districts. This third so-called proportional election was conducted without visible candidates or campaign; it was the kind of election that brought out loyalists who were mobilized by party labels and not candidates, winning or losing, conflict, or any of a host of other reasons. Only those instances among the seventy county or independent city units were used in which a given party did not field a candidate for the Reichstag first election in 1912. These results were then compared to gain or loss in turnout between Reichstag and proportional elections. Thus a high correlation would mean that particular party loyalists were willing to vote even if they had no candidate from their own party for whom to cast a ballot.

33. Von Göring, Landrat Gelnhausen to Regierungspräsident Cassel, 1 February 1907, HStA Marburg, LA Gelnhausen, 180, 3856.

34. *Hanauer Anzeiger*, 6 February 1907 in ibid. See a similar document published by the National Liberal Committee for Wiesbaden, February 1907, HStA Wiesbaden, Regierung Wiesbaden, 405, 2474.

35. *Vierteljahreshefte zur Statistik des Deutschen Reichs* 1907 Ergänzungsheft 4: 102-23; *Statistik des Deutschen Reichs* 250: III, 104-25; 240. Johannes Schauff's various 1928 essays on the decline of political Catholicism are collected in *Das Wahlverhalten der deutschen Katholiken*.

36. Wolfgang Mommsen, *Deutsche Parteiprogramme*, pp. 220-24; Huber, *Deutsche Verfassungsgeschichte*, 4: 49-63; Blackbourn, *Class, Religion and Local Politics*, pp. 29-31; Zeender, "German Catholics and the Concept of an Interconfessional Party," pp. 424-39.

37. Richard Blank, "Die sozial Zusammensetzung der sozialdemokratischen Wählershaft Deutschlands," pp. 507-50; and Michels, "Die deutsche sozialdemokratie: 1," pp. 471-556. See also Fricke, ed., *Die deutsche Arbeiterbewegung, 1869-1914*; Gerhard A. Ritter, *Die Arbeiterbewegung im Wilhelmischen Reich*; Schorske, *German Social Democracy 1905-1917*; Wachenheim, *Die deutsche Arbeiterbewegung 1844 bis 1944*; Groh, *Negative Integration und revolutionärer Attentismus*. Two interesting recent collections are Hans Mommsen, ed., *Sozialdemokratie zwischen Klassenbewegung und Volkspartei*, and Vetter, ed., *Vom Sozialistengesetz zur Mitbestimmung*.

38. For the contemporary Catholic reaction, see Klöcker, *Konfession*, pp. 72-92. Tony Judt shows how excessive secularization could bring about a high negative association with religion while at the same time being the prelude for the socialist movement; see *Socialism in Provence*, pp. 175-99.

39. *Vierteljahreshefte zur Statistik des Deutschen Reichs* 1900 Ergänzungsheft 1: 4, 235ff.; 1904 Ergänzungsheft 1: 95-115; 1911 Ergänzungsheft 4; *Statistik des Deutschen Reichs*, Neue Folge, 250: III, 105-7.

40. Blank, "Die sozial Zusammensetzung," p. 550. For data on unions see Hirschfeld, *Die freien Gewerkschaften in Deutschland.*

41. *Dortmunder Tageblatt*, 26 January 1907; "Drucklisten zur Reichstagswahl, 1903," Stadtarchiv Dortmund. The method used in this estimate is discussed in Mecksroth, "Some Problems in Cross-level Inference," pp. 45–66. The Dortmund voters were divided along the lines of occupations listed in the census; category *a* was for free professionals and higher administrators, *b* for technical, *c* for workers. In addition separate categories were set up for civil servants, salespeople, insurance brokers, etc. These eventually were formed into the white-collar grouping. All those with artisan and worker designations were counted according to census categories by their occupational groups; additional categories were added for factory workers and servants. Since these occupational categories were statistically insignificant in determining vote and turnout, they were eventually merged into the blue-collar designation.

42. In addition to note 41, see Wuerth, "The Politics and Sociology of Organized Labor in a Middle-Sized German Town: Göppingen 1900–1910," p. 367; O'Donnell, "National Liberalism and the Mass Politics of the German Right, 1890–1907," pp. 481–87.

43. Steenson, *Karl Kautsky*, p. 111. For a different approach see William Maehl, "German Social Democratic Agrarian Policy, 1890, 1895," pp. 121–55; Hesselbarth, *Revolutionäre Sozialdemokraten, Opportunisten und die Bauern am Vorabend des Imperialismus*, pp. 185–242, and for statistics, pp. 243–47; Krauss, *Die politischen Kräften und das Wahlverhalten im Landkreis Giessen während der letzten 60 Jahre*, pp. 31–45; *Beiträge zur Statistik des Grossherzogtums Hessen* 62: Heft 5, 9; *Handbuch für hessische Zentrumswähler*, pp. 90–92. The Württemberg data suggest that most of the rural vote there was due to an urban effect: *Württembergische Jahrbücher*, 1907, II: 9ff. For cases of successful rural socialism, see Judt, *Socialism in Provence.*

44. Würzburg to Prussian Ministry of Interior 1908, appended in a report to the Saxon government, Auswärtiges Amt microfilm, National Archives, ACP, Roll 180, 560–62.

45. Michels, "Die deutsche Sozialdemokratie," p. 462; Lützenkirchen, *Der sozialdemokratische Verein für Dortmund-Hörde*, pp. 122–25; Fricke, ed., *Arbeiterbewegung*, pp. 263–71; Frankfurt Electoral Union, *Tätigkeits Bericht für die Zeit von 1 Januar 1906 bis 30 Juni 1907*, p. 47.

46. Fricke, ed., *Arbeiterbewegung*, p. 273; *Volksstimme* (Frankfurt), 27 January 1902; Frankfurt Electoral Union, *Tätigkeitsbericht*, p. 10.

47. Höhn, *Die vaterlandslosen Gesellen*; Saul, *Staat, Industrie und Arbeiterbewegung*; Hall, *Scandal, Sensation and Social Democracy*, pp. 42–182; Lidtke, *The Outlawed Party*. Richard Tilly and Gerd Hohorst have argued that the SPD was a force for moderation; unfortunately their data are grouped by provinces (a considerably larger unit) and are not reasonably comparable to the units used in this study. See "Sozialer Protest in Deutschland im 19. Jahrhundert," pp. 250–57. Yet this does not mean that German workers were so fundamentally integrated or apathetic as Barrington Moore claims in *Injustice: The Social Bases of Obedience and Revolt*, pp. 119–274; on the contrary, there is every reason to believe that German workers only mirrored the general law-abidance of German society; see Charles Tilly et al., *The Rebellious Century, 1830–1930*, pp. 199–229; the uniqueness of German workers' movement is also attacked in Crew, *Town in the Ruhr*, pp. 223–24.

48. Groh, *Negative Integration*, p. 38. See also Roth, *The Social Democrats in Imperial Germany*; J. P. Nettl, "The German Social Democratic Party 1880–1914 as a Political Model," pp. 65–95.

49. Quoted in HStA Stuttgart, Ministry of Interior, E150, 20436.

50. *Schwäbische Tagwacht*, 28 February 1914 in HStA Stuttgart, Ministry of Interior, E150, 2045.

51. Milatz, "Reichstagswahlen und Mandatsverteilung 1871 bis 1918," pp. 215–16.

52. See note 9, chapter 2.

53. Quoted in HStA Wiesbaden, Regierung Wiesbaden, 20746.

54. Schulte, *Struktur*, p. 136; Hunt, *The People's Party in Württemberg and Southern Germany*, pp. 111–39; Thiel, *Die Grossblockpolitik der Nationalliberalen Partei Badens 1905 bis 1914*, pp. 38–219.

55. *Herforder Kreisblatt*, 9 October 1909 in StA Detmold, Regierung Minden, Mi. 1, 78.

56. Severing, *Mein Lebensweg*, pp. 185–87.

57. Leaflet of 1903, HStA Wiesbaden, Polizeipräsidium Frankfurt, 407, 162. See also ibid., 407, 161[2,3,4], and 162[6] for party data; Oberbürgermeister Dortmund 20 February 1900, StA Münster, Regierung Arnsberg, I, 96; Lützenkirchen, *Der sozialdemokratische Verein*, p. 18.

58. Police report Frankfurt, 18 October 1907, HStA Wiesbaden, Polizei Präsidium Frankfurt, 407, 162[9].

59. Frankfurt Electoral Union, *Tätigkeitsbericht*, p. 47; Michels, "Die deutsche Sozialdemokratie," pp. 51ff.; Lützenkirchen, *Der sozialdemokratische Verein*, pp. 125–27; Nolan, *Social Democracy and Society*, pp. 99–125; Hirschfeld, *Die freien Gewerkschaften*; *Statistik des Deutschen Reichs*, Neue Folge, p. 206.

60. HStA Wiesbaden, 407, 159; Hickey, "The Shaping of the German Labour Movement," p. 237; Lützenkirchen, *Der sozialdemokratische Verein*, pp. 32ff.; Nolan, *Social Democracy and Society*, pp. 126–66.

61. Gerhard A. Ritter and Klaus Tenfelde, "Der Durchbruch der freien Gewerkschaften Deutschlands zur Massenbewegung im letzten Viertel des 19. Jahrhunderts," pp. 62–123; Kozyk, "Die 'Metalarbeiter-Zeitung' am Vorabend der Ersten Weltkriegs," in ibid., pp. 175–97. For comparison of figures see Epstein, *Political Parties in Western Democracies*, pp. 163–64; Maurice Duverger, *Political Parties*, pp. 196ff.

62. The most recent studies about social mobility disagree as to the migration patterns among skilled and other workers, yet everyone is agreed it was momentous; see Crew, "Regional Mobilität und Arbeiterklasse," pp. 99–120; Dieter Langewische, "Wanderungsbewegungen in der Hochindustrialisierungsperiode," pp. 1–40.

63. See note 48.

64. Landrat Bochum report, 12 September 1907, StA Münster, Regierung Arnsberg, I 99. See also I 95 and I 100 for similar information. The best sources of information on working-class cultures can be found in the April 1978 issue of *Journal of Contemporary History* and the second issue of *Geschichte und Gesellschaft* 5. Individual articles the author found most helpful were those of Dove, "The Workers' Choral Movement before the First World War," pp. 269–97; Lidtke, "Lieder der deutschen Arbeiterbewegung," pp. 54–82; Klaus Tenfelde, "Bergarbeiterkultur in Deutschland: Ein Überblick," pp. 12–53.

65. See the English edition of Robert Michels's 1915 work, *Political Parties*, pp. 365ff. For Göppingen, see Wuerth, "Politics and Sociology," pp. 191–259. For similar events in Dortmund, see Lützenkirchen, *Der sozialdemokratische Verein*, pp. 37–99.

66. Fricke, ed., *Die deutsche Arbeiterbewegung*, p. 520.

67. Groh, *Negative Integration*, pp. 271–72.

68. 1911 leaflet, HStA Wiesbaden, Regierung Wiesbaden, 405, 2476.

69. Neckarkreis report, 21 March 1905, HStA Stuttgart, E150, 2046.

70. 1909 handbill in StA Ludwigsburg, Stadtdirektion Stuttgart, F201, 17.

71. StA Münster, Regierung Arnsberg, I Pa, 99.

72. HStA Marburg, Regierung Kassel, 165, 1241.

73. Dortmund Oberbürgermeister, StA Münster, 26 February 1898, Regierung Arnsberg, I, 92.

74. Hechter, *Internal Colonization*, p. 114. See also Rokkan, *Citizens, Elections, Parties*, pp. 227ff.

75. For the characteristics of the Conservative party see Sittlich, *Die politischen Parteien in Deutschland*, 1: 83ff.; Booms, *Die Deutsch-Konservative Partei*, pp. 6–31; Grebing, "Position der Konservatismus in der Bundesrepublik," p. 5. Grebing takes the position that prewar conservatism was just another form of elite politics and, therefore, undifferentiable. Hans Rosenberg's belief that the feudal aristocracy was inclined only to use the forms of universal suffrage does not contradict the view that their followers did; see Rosenberg, "Die Pseudodemokratisierung der Rittergutsbesitzerklasse," pp. 301–4; Puhle, "Radikalisierung und Wandel des deutschen Konservatismus vor dem Ersten Weltkrieg," pp. 165–86.

76. Tipton, *Regional Variations in the Economic Development of Germany During the Nineteenth Century*, p. 119. See James Hunt, "Peasants, Grain Tariffs, and Meat Quotas: Imperial German Protectionism Reexamined," p. 327; similar ideas to Hunt's can be found in Lepsius, "Parteisystem," pp. 70–71.

77. GStA Berlin, Regierung Danzig, A180, 19196. Similar responses are found throughout the German east; see also Herman Lebovics, "Agrarians versus 'Industrializers,'" pp. 31–65; Barkin, *The Controversy over German Industrialization*, pp. 131ff.

78. Booms, *Die Deutsch-Konservative Partei*, p. 37.

79. Frank, *Die Brandenburger als Reichstagswähler*, pp. 174–75. For views of this class and the politics of obedience, see Görlitz, *Die Junker*; Siegfried Korth, "Die Entstehung und Entwicklung des ostdeutschen Grossgrundsitzes," pp. 165–70; Graf zu Stolberg-Wernigerode, *Die unentschiedene Generation*, pp. 168–227; Gershenkron, *Bread and Democracy*, pp. 21–89.

80. *Hersfelder Kreisblatt*, 7 June 1898, HStA Marburg, Regierung Kassel, 165, 1241.

81. Specht and Schwabe, *Reichstagswahlen*, pp. 335–36.

82. Rosenberg, "Pseudodemokratisierung," p. 304.

83. Puhle, *Agrarische Interessenpolitik*, pp. 47ff.; Puhle, "Der Bund der Landwirte im Wilhelminischen Reich," pp. 145–62; O'Donnell, "National Liberalism," pp. 198–308; Peck, *Radicals and Reactionaries*, pp. 40ff.; Eley, *Reshaping the German Right*, pp. 29ff.

84. See Rokkan, *Citizens, Elections, Parties*, pp. 181ff.

85. For the effects of emancipation see Katz, *Out of the Ghetto*; Rürup, *Emanzipation und Antisemitismus*, pp. 81ff., partially in an English version in *Yearbook of the Leo Baeck Institute* 14: 67–91; Cecil, "Jew and Junker in Imperial Berlin," pp. 47–58; Mosse, *Germans and Jews*; Tal, *Christians and Jews in Germany*; Pulzer, *The Rise of Political Anti-Semitism in Germany and Austria*; Massing, *Rehearsal for Destruction*; Levy, *The Downfall of the Anti-Semitic Political Parties in Imperial Germany*; Volkov, *The Rise of Popular Antimodernism in Germany*, pp. 313–38; Volkov, "Antisemitism as a Cultural Code," pp. 25–46; also the discussion on Böckel in chapter 5.

86. Lamberti, *Jewish Activism in Imperial Germany*, pp. 1–54, 105ff.; Toury, *Die politische Orientierungen der Juden in Deutschland*, pp. 110ff.; Hamburger, *Juden in öffentlichen Leben Deutschlands*; Pulzer, "Die jüdische Beteiligung an der Politik," in Mosse, ed., *Juden im Wilhelminischen Deutschland*, pp. 143–240, and a shortened English version in Bronsen, *Jews and Germans from 1860 to 1933*, pp. 79–91.

87. Lamberti, "The Attempts to Formulate a Jewish Bloc," pp. 91–92; see Toury, *Die politische Orientierungen der Juden*, pp. 271–85; Pulzer, "Die jüdische Beteiligung an der Politik," pp. 185–93; Levy, *The Downfall of Anti-Semitic Political Parties in Wilhelmine Germany*, pp. 153–65; Ragins, *Jewish Responses to Anti-Semitism in Germany*; Reinharz, *Fatherland or Promised Land*. For an interesting comparison with France see Marrus, *European Jewry and the Politics of Assimilation*; Hyman, *From Dreyfus to Vichy*.

88. A good introduction to the Polish problem can be found in Wehler, *Krisenherde des*

Kaiserreichs, pp. 181–200; Hauser, "Polen und Dänen im Deutschen Reich," pp. 291–318; Silverman, *Reluctant Union: Alsace Lorraine and Imperial Germany*; Falk, "The Reichstag Election of 1912: A Statistical Study," pp. 181–207.

89. *Statistik des Deutschen Reichs*, Neue Folge, 250; Wilhelm Winkler, *Statistisches Handbuch des gesamten Deutschtums*, pp. 35–63.

90. Hagen, *Germans, Poles and Jews*; Rose, "Prussian Poland, 1850–1914," W. F. Reddaway et al., eds., *The Cambridge History of Poland*, pp. 409–31; and Adam Galos, Felix-Heinrich Gentzen, Witold Jakóbczyk, *Die Hakatistien*; and chapter 8 of this work.

91. Translation from Polish press, 1913, GStA Berlin, 209, 21.

92. Police report of meeting in Schwelatowa, 3 May 1908, GStA Berlin, Schwetz County, 204, 3073.

93. Police report, Thorn, January 1907, ibid., Strasburg County, 205, 302.

94. Hagen, *Germans, Poles and Jews*, p. 254.

95. Ibid., p. 247.

96. GStA Berlin, Regierung Danzig, 180, 19197.

97. 1907 leaflet, Strasburg, ibid., Strasburg County, 205, 301.

98. See note 91.

99. Police report, 24 January 1912, GStA Berlin, Strasburg County, 205, 302.

100. The election material comes from the data in note 89. The demographic material comes from *Statistisches Jahrbuch für den Preussischen Staat* 1913: II: 20–26.

101. Schwidetzky, *Die polnische Wahlbewegung in Oberschlesien*; Haines, *Economic-Demographic Interrelations in Developing Agriculture Regions*; Norman Pounds, *The Upper Silesian Industrial Region*, pp. 1–120; Ross, *Beleaguered Tower*, pp. 68–71.

102. Klessman, *Polnische Bergarbeiter im Ruhrgebiet*, p. 127. See also Wehler, "Die Polen in Ruhrgebiet bis 1918," Wehler, ed., *Modern deutsche Sozialgeschichte*, pp. 437–55; Falk, "The Reichstag Elections of 1912," pp. 200–207, 231ff.; Hickey, "The Shaping of the German Labour Movement," pp. 217–18; police reports, StA Münster, Regierung Arnsberg, I Pa, 95, 100a; also see Richard Murphy, "The Polish Trade Unions in the Ruhr Coal Fields," pp. 335–47 and chapter 9.

CHAPTER 5

1. Joyce, *Work, Society and Politics*, pp. 268ff.; Nossiter, *Influence, Opinion and Political Idioms*, pp. 107ff.

2. James Sheehan, *German Liberalism in the Nineteenth Century*, p. 246. See also White, *The Splintered Party*; O'Donnell, "National Liberalism and the Mass Politics of the German Right"; Sell, *Die Tragödie des deutschen Liberalismus*, pp. 254–353; Elm, *Zwischen Fortschritt und Reaktion*; Milatz, "Die linksliberalen Parteien und Gruppen in den Reichstagswahlen 1907–1912," pp. 273–92; Wegner, *Theodor Barth und die Freisinnige Vereinigung*; Wegner, "Linksliberalismus im wilhelmischen Deutschland und in der Weimarer Republik," pp. 120–27.

3. Fenske, *Wahlrecht und Parteiensystem*, pp. 118–19; Milatz, "Reichstagswahlen und Mandatsverteilung," pp. 215–16.

4. The definitions of class are very slippery in the nineteenth century; still Richard Evans criticizes James Sheehan for not using the term in Evans, "Review: James Sheehan, German Liberalism," pp. 126–31. However, Judith Matras uses "strata" in explaining social inequality, in *Social Inequality, Stratification, and Mobility*, pp. 85–134; Roland Mousnier has similarly suggested that bipolar class definitions do not apply for most of modern European history, *Social Hierarchies*; and R. S. Neale has suggested a five-class structure to overcome the difficulties of definition of middle class, *Class and Ideology in the Nineteenth Century*, pp. 15–74. For recent literature on *Mittelstand*, see Conze,

"Mittelstand," pp. 62–89; Lebovics, *Social Conservativism and the Middle Classes in Germany*, pp. 4–12; Gall, "Liberalismus und 'bürgerliche Gesellschaft,'" pp. 334–56; Wolfgang Mommsen, "Liberalismusinterpretationen," pp. 86–90; Blackbourn, "The *Mittelstand* in German Society and Politics, 1871–1914," pp. 409–33; Sedatis, *Liberalismus und Handwerk in Südwestdeutschland*, pp. 183–84. For the Norwegian comparison, see Valen and Rokkan, "Norway: Conflict Structure and Mass Politics in a European Periphery," pp. 315–70.

5. *Schwäbische Tagwacht*, 8 June 1893. See notes 41 and 42, chapter 4.

6. Wölk, "Sozialstruktur, Parteienkorrelation und Wahlenentscheidung im Kaiserreich," pp. 521–22. For further statements on liberal diversity, see Elm, *Zwischen Fortschritt und Reaktion*; Nipperdey, *Die Organisation der deutschen Parteien vor 1918*, pp. 26ff.; Nipperdey, "Die Organisation der bürgerlichen Parteien in Deutschland," pp. 114ff.; Simon, *Die württembergischen Demokraten 1890–1920*, pp. 17–44.

7. Police reports, Regierung Wiesbaden, HStA Wiesbaden, 407, 150–51, 159, 160; police reports, Stadtarchiv Dortmund, Do.n. 180, 186, 217; *Dortmunder Zeitung*, 1 June 1898.

8. Left-wing liberals include all votes labeled democratic, fortschrittlich, freisinnige, and the South German Succession and People's parties. Compare these figures with the Democratic party of the United States, which varied in paired elections between 1884/88 and 1908/12 in the following ways: .86, .59, .01, .61, .88, .85; Walter Burnham, "The United States: The Politics of Heterogeneity," p. 673.

9. *Frankfurter Zeitung*, 23 December 1911; see also a series of local government reports in Wiesbaden, 1906–9; HStA Wiesbaden, Regierung Wiesbaden, 405, 24, 75–77.

10. Police report 11, 30 April 1909, Stadtarchiv Dortmund, Do.n. 244; *Verzeichnis der städtischen Behörden und Kommissionen in Dortmund für 1901–02; Dortmunder Tageblatt*, 5 June 1903; *Dortmunder Zeitung*, 6 June 1898; Croon, *Bürgertum und Verwaltung in den Städten des Ruhrgebiets im 19 Jahrhundert*.

11. White, *The Splintered Party*, p. 197.

12. Jessop, *Traditionalism, Conservatism and British Political Culture*, p. 77.

13. Greiper, *Wie Kam's in Alzey Bingen*, p. 35. For the background to this struggle, see *Süddeutsche Nationalliberale Korrespondenz für der Wahlkreis Alzey Bingen*, n.d., HStA Wiesbaden, Regierung Wiesbaden, 405, 2761; White, *The Splintered Party*, pp. 179–88; Kriegbaum, *Die parlamentarische Tätigkeit des Freiherrn c. W. Heyl zu Hernsheim*, pp. 198ff.; *Darmstädter Zeitung*, 30 September, 6 November 1911.

14. National Liberal handbill, 15 December 1911, HStA Wiesbaden, Regierung Wiesbaden, 405, 2766; *Naussauer-Bote* (Limburg), 32 February 1903, ibid., 2766; *Die Reichspost*, 12 November 1912; *Schwäbische Merkur*, 28 April 1906; Heckart, *From Bassermann to Bebel*; Wegner, *Barth*, pp. 111–36.

15. For examples see HStA Wiesbaden, Regierung Wiesbaden, 405, 2475; O'Donnell, "National Liberalism," pp. 175–80. German Conservative data were collected and analyzed in the same manner as that of the liberals. The basic study of *Sammlungspolitik* is Ekhardt Kehr's prewar work, *Battleship Building and Party Politics in Germany*; the most recent criticism of Kehr can be found in the debate between Geoff Eley and Hans-Jürgen Puhle, see note 11, chapter 1.

16. Mielke, *Der Hansa-Bund*, p. 160. See Stegmann, *Die Erben Bismarcks*, pp. 159ff.; Ullmann, *Die Bund der Industriellen*, pp. 140ff.; Bertram, *Die Wahlen vom Jahre 1912*, pp. 102–7; Nipperdey, "Organisierter Kapitalismus," pp. 419–31.

17. White, *The Splintered Party*, pp. 156–57.

18. Leaflet 1912, HStA Wiesbaden, Reg. Wiesbaden, 405, 2476.

19. Leaflets 1893 found in Stadtarchiv Stuttgart, Magistrats-Archiv 25, 30.

20. See note 13, chapter 4.

21. Sheehan, *German Liberalism*, p. 252; Riedel, "Bürger," pp. 720–26.

22. *Reichsherold* (Marburg), 5 May 1893.

23. Report from Wiedenbrück, 5 May 1903, StA Detmold, Regierung Minden, Mi. 1, 253.

24. Found in HStA Marburg, Regierung Cassel, 165, 1241.

25. Ibid.

26. Maier, *Recasting Bourgeois Europe*, p. 30.

27. Oberbürgermeister Dortmund, 22 November 1898, StA Münster, Regierung Arnsberg, I Pa, 103. Kupisch, *Die deutschen Landeskirchen im 19. und 20. Jahrhundert*, pp. 1–92; Heussi, *Kompendium der Kirchengeschichte*, pp. 457ff.; Scholder, *Die Kirchen und das Dritte Reich*, p. 37; *Lexikon für Theologie und Kirche* 1: 271–73; Nipperdey, "Grundprobleme der deutschen Parteigeschichte im 19. Jahrhundert," p. 36; Monshausen, *Politische Wahlen im Regierungsbezirk Koblenz 1880 bis 1897*, pp. 296–97; for suggestive views on Teetotalism, see Stein Rokkan, "Toward a Generalized Concept of *Verzuiling*: A Preliminary Note," p. 570; Roberts, "Der Alkoholkonsum deutschen Arbeiter im 19. Jahrhundert," pp. 241–42.

28. StA Detmold, Regierung Minden, Mi. 1, 253. The proliferation of bourgeois organizations and its effect on the state can be seen in the organizational lists for Aalen, Württemberg, for 1909–13 in StA Ludwigsburg, F15. There is a vast and not very useful body of royalist hagiography; an exception to the rule is Fehrenbach, "Images of Kaiserdom," pp. 269–86.

29. Gerhard A. Ritter, *Historisches Lesebuch 1871–1914*, p. 207. For the means by which this transformation was achieved, see Mosse, *The Nationalization of the Masses*, pp. 47–126; Nipperdey, "Nationalidee und Nationaldenkmal in Deutschland im 19. Jahrhundert," pp. 559–85; Langsam, "Nationalism and History in the Prussian Elementary Schools," pp. 242ff.; Schellenberg, *Zum Geschichtsbild der Wilhelmischen Ära und der Weimarer Zeit*, and especially Schieder, *Der deutsche Kaiserreich von 1871 als Nationalstaat*.

30. State instruction 14 December 1906, Auswärtiges Amt microfilm ACP, Roll 396, 158. A similar document was discovered by Dieter Fricke, "Der deutsche Imperialismus und die Reichstagswahlen von 1907," pp. 549–56. The best study on the 1907 election is Crothers, *The German Election of 1907*.

31. Liberal campaign leaflet, 1907, Regierung Minden, StA Detmold, Mi. 1, 254.

32. Fricke, "Der Reichsverband gegen die Sozialdemokratie," p. 276. See also Crothers, *The German Election of 1907*, pp. 142–63; Eley, *Reshaping the German Right*, pp. 157ff.; Stegmann, *Die Erben Bismarcks*, pp. 47–50.

33. See note 31.

34. *Casseler Allgemeine Zeitung*, 23 January 1907.

35. Ibid., 4 February 1907.

36. Ministry of Interior recommended leaflet 24 November 1898, StA Minden, Regierung Minden, Mi. 1, 251.

37. Can be found in HStA Stuttgart, Ministry of Interior, E150, 246.

38. *Kreisblatt* (Frankenberg), 14 June 1898 found in HStA Marburg, LA Frankenberg, 180, 1120.

39. *Schwäbische Merkur*, 28 January 1896.

40. *Darmstädter Zeitung*, 11 January 1908, 6 December 1908.

41. Schulte, *Struktur und Entwicklung der Parteisystems*, pp. 26–32; see note 32, chapter 3 for data base.

42. Saul, "Der 'Deutsche Kriegerverband' zur innenpolitischen Funktion eines nationalen Verbandes im kaiserlichen Deutschland," pp. 95–160; Hansjoachim Henning, "Kriegervereine in den preussischen Westprovinzen," pp. 430–75; O'Donnell, "National Liberalism," pp. 358–68. See also the material collected in StA Münster, Regierung Arnsberg, I, 16, 17, 40. See the letter from priest in Lippstadt 17 January 1912, Hoover

Institute Microfilms of NSDAP Hauptarchiv, Reel 9A; the von Boldenschwingh problem is discussed in Studt to Minister of Interior, 6 May 1900, ibid., Reel 10A.

43. GStA Berlin, Regierung Danzig, 180, 13071.

44. Leaflet can be found in HStA Stuttgart, Ministry of Interior, E150, 2046.

45. Fabrikant Schulz, StA Münster, Regierung Arnsberg, I, 40; see Landrat report, Reg. Arnsberg, I, 100; *Dortmunder Zeitung*, 8 January 1908; Neckarkreis report, 21 March 1905, HStA Stuttgart, Ministry of Interior, E150, 2046.

46. The material can be found in StA Münster, Regierung Arnsberg, I, 105; see also Crew, *Town in the Ruhr*, pp. 103–58.

47. Siegen soldiers' union and left-wing political material can be found in StA Münster, Regierung Arnsberg, I, 40, 100a; also for a persistence of old settlers see ibid., Oberpräsidium Münster, 3795; Buch, *Die Stoeckerbewegung im Siegerland*, pp. 115–40; Croon and Utermann, *Zeche und Gemeinde*, pp. 22–99.

48. Of particular help in this definition is the work of Eley, *Reshaping the German Right*, pp. 196–203; see also Minogue, "Populism as a Political Movement," pp. 197–211; Gino Germani, *Authoritarianism, Fascism and National Populism*; Organski, *The Stages of Political Development*. The "nostalgic" element in American populism was certainly different from that in European populism; see Goodwyn, *Democratic Promise*, pp. 515–55; it was considerably more economic than cultural in its strongest manifestations in the Trans-Mississippi west; see Parsons, *The Populist Context*, pp. 109ff.; Wright, *The Politics of Populism*, pp. 124ff. The racist connotation of southern populism is discussed by Hackney, *Populism to Progressivism in Alabama*, pp. 32–47; C. Vann Woodward, *Origins of the New South*, pp. 254ff., and many others.

49. Farr, "Populism in the Countryside: The Peasant Leagues in Bavaria in the 1890s," pp. 136–55; Thränhardt, *Wahlen*, pp. 57–120.

50. For an example of German Socialists' bourgeois style, see the criticism found in Zeman and Scharlau, *The Merchant of Revolution*, p. 74 and passim.

51. Weber, *Gesammelte politische Schriften*, p. 319.

52. Ibid., p. 375.

53. Schauff, "Die Entwicklung zum Proportionalwahlsystem in Deutschland," p. 129.

54. For an account of Westarp's campaign, see his *Konservative Politik im letzten Jahrzehnt des Kaiserreiches*, pp. 29–31; see also Mayer to Payer, 25 May 1893, Bundesarchiv Koblenz, Payer Nachlass, 7.

55. Hessisches Statistisches Landesamt, *Historisches Gemeindeverzeichnis für Hessen* (Wiesbaden, 1968), pp. 58ff.; *Statistik des Deutschen Reichs*, Neue Folge, 209, 212.

56. Leaflet 1887, HStA Marburg, LA Frankenberg, 180, 1120; *Reichsherold*, 18 February, 4 March, 12 August 1887; 10 July, 19 December 1890; Schmal, *Entwicklungen der völkischen Bewegung*; Mack, "Otto Böckel und die anti-semitische Bauernbewegung in Hessen 1889–1914," pp. 113–47; Levy, *The Downfall of the Anti-Semitic Political Parties in Germany*, pp. 43–76 and passim; how far the movement spread to subsidiary parties can be seen in Strück, "Zur ideenpolitischen Vorbereitung des Bundeslandes Hessen," p. 295; and Knobel, *Die Hessische Rechtspartei*, pp. 126ff.

57. 1898 leaflet, HStA Marburg, Regierung Cassel, 165, 47.

58. Ibid.

59. Ibid.

60. Ibid.

61. Bader leaflet, ibid.

62. Ibid.

63. Ibid.

64. Böckel leaflet, ibid.

65. Gerlach, *Von Rechts nach Links*, pp. 171ff.

66. See reports and statistics on these elections in HStA Marburg, LA Marburg, 740; LA Frankenberg, 1122; *Oberhessische Zeitung,* 20 January 1912.

67. See note 64; the Liebermann campaigns are reported in HStA Marburg, LA Ziegenhain, 2552, 2553, 4442; Levy, *Downfall,* pp. 198−200 and passim. Blackbourn argues for the persistence of these movements, see "Peasants and Politics in Germany," pp. 63−8.

68. For a discussion of the Frankfurt *Mittelstand* movement see Polizeipräsidium Frankfurt, 30 December 1906, in HStA Wiesbaden, Regierung Wiesbaden, 405, 2475; and police report on same, especially 3 October and 3 November 1901, HStA Wiesbaden, Polizeipräsidium Frankfurt, 407, 159^2; Heuss, *Friedrich Naumann,* pp. 87−189; Düding, *Der Nationalsoziale Verein 1896−1903,* pp. 124ff.

69. Volkov, *The Rise of Popular Antimodernism in Germany;* Hans Rosenberg, *Grosse Depression und Bismarckzeit,* pp. 97−115; Heinrich Winkler, *Mittelstand, Demokratie und Nationalsozialismus,* pp. 46−54; Heinrich Winkler, "Die rückversicherte Mittelstand," pp. 163−79; Fricke, *Die bürgerliche Parteien,* pp. 200−208; Gellately, *The Politics of Economic Despair,* pp. 149ff.; Stegmann, *Die Erben Bismarcks,* pp. 239ff.; Eley, "The Wilhelmine Right: How It Changed," pp. 121−31; Sheehan, *German Liberalism,* pp. 253−54; Blackbourn, "The *Mittelstand,*" pp. 431−33; Sedatis, *Liberalismus und Handwerk,* pp. 187−93; Ullmann, *Die Bund der Industriellen,* pp. 237ff.; Schäfter, "Die Gelben Gewerkschaften," pp. 41−76.

70. Police report, 12 December 1912, Stadtarchiv Dortmund, Do.n. 266.

71. Eley, *Reshaping the German Right,* pp. 44−45. For the connection with anti-Semitism, see note 85, chapter 4; George Mosse, *The Crisis of German Ideology,* pp. 150ff.; Volkov, "Antisemitism as a Cultural Code." An interesting comparative view can be found in the study of Russian populism by Franco Venturi, *Roots of Revolution.*

CHAPTER 6

1. Lavies, *Nichtwähler als Kategorie des Wahlverhaltens,* pp. 131−34; Milbrath and Goel, *Political Participation,* pp. 106−10; Rokkan, *Citizens, Elections, Parties,* pp. 226−42. The whole problem of deviant cases relating to urbanism and turnout is just being considered in the United States; see Moore, "Urbanism and Voter Turnout: A Note on Some Unexpected Findings," pp. 71−78; Johnson, "Research Note on Correlates of Voter Behavior," pp. 107−23. Otto Büsch has discovered some evidence for weak rural turnout and increased turnout in areas of swift urbanization, but his research is unconfirmed by nationwide or statewide statistical analysis; see Büsch, "Gedanken und Thesen zur Wählerbewegung im Deutschland," pp. 148−55.

2. Much of this view can be found in Kornhauser, *The Politics of Mass Society,* pp. 69ff.; Angus Campbell et al., *The American Voter,* pp. 105−6; Almond and Verba, *The Civic Culture;* Lazarsfeld and Berelson, *The People's Choice;* Dowse and Hughes, *Political Sociology,* pp. 302−12; Tingsten, *Political Behavior;* Milbrath and Goel, *Political Participation,* pp. 43−85. This author found especially useful the work of Verba, Nie, Kim, *Participation and Political Equality,* pp. 119−124 and passim.

3. These voting lists can be found in HStA Marburg, LA Ziegenhain, 180, 2520−21.

4. Ibid.

5. Summa, *Kasseler Unterschichten im Zeitalter der Industrialisierung,* pp. 27−30, 55ff.; Karl Demeter, *Geschichte des Landes Hessen,* p. 320; Karlheinz Müller, *Preussischer Adler und Hessische Löwe,* pp. 5ff. See also Friedrich-Wilhelm Henning, "Die Einführung der Gewerbefreiheit und ihre Auswirkungen auf das Handwerk in Deutschland"; Volkov, "The Decline of German Handicrafts," pp. 165−84; Tingsten, *Political Behavior,* pp. 79−119.

6. See note 41, chapter 5.

7. Würzburg, "Die 'Partei' der Nichtwähler," pp. 383–84.

8. Hackett, "The German Women's Movement and Suffrage, 1890–1914," pp. 354–86. Very important is the work of Richard Evans, which can be found in *The Feminists*, pp. 103–13, 159–65, 199–201; Evans, "Liberalism and Society: The Feminist Movement and Social Change," pp. 186–208; Evans, *The Feminist Movement in Germany, 1894–1933*, pp. 87ff. Bäumer, "Die Geschichte der Frauenbewegung in Deutschland," 1: 148ff.; Quatert, *Reluctant Feminists in German Social Democracy*, pp. 161ff.; police report Dortmund, 14 June 1910, Stadtarchiv Dortmund, Do.n. 263; reports on SPD activity in Arnsberg 1906–8, StA Münster, Regierung Arnsberg, I Pa, 99, 100a; see also Ralf Lützenkirchen, *Der sozialdemokratische Verein für Dortmund-Hörde*, pp. 114–19; *Verhandlungen des Reichstages* 332: 21255–466; Anlage Nr. 3949; Dieter Fricke, *Die bürgerlichen Parteien* 1: 202–15; Fricke, *Arbeiterbewegung*.

9. *Bericht, XX Delegiertentag des Verbandes Süddeutscher Kath. Arbeiterverein*, 28 August 1912 in HStA Stuttgart, Ministry of Interior, E151c, 2317.

10. Can be found in Oberpräsidium Cassel, HStA Marburg, 150, 640.

11. *Archiv des deutschen Landwirtschaftsrats*, 36: 458.

12. Deutsche Landwirtschaftsrat, Protocol of Standing Committee November 1916 can be found in HStA Stuttgart, Ministry of Interior, E150, 2351.

13. Fricke, *Arbeiterbewegung*, p. 351. See also Fricke, *Parteien*, 1: 162–67; *Der Beobachter*, 26 July 1914; *Arbeiter Zeitung* (Dortmund), 20 April 1910; *Deutsche Reichspost*, 6 May 1913; Esslingen City Police, 26 July 1913, HStA Stuttgart, Ministry of Interior, E150, 2048; Lützenkirchen, *Der Sozialdemokratische Verein*, pp. 108–13. Herle, *Die deutsche Jugendbewegung*, pp. 20–66.

14. Police report Esslingen, 13 June 1907, police report Ravensburg, 25 May 1900, HStA Stuttgart, Ministry of Interior, E150, 180; E151c, 2317, 2318.

15. *Deutsches Volksblatt*, 22 June 1914.

16. *Die Volksstimme*, 2 November 1906. See also *Polizeipräsidium* report, 16 November 1911, HStA Wiesbaden, 405, 2476 and HStA Stuttgart, Ministry of Interior, E151, 2046.

17. Tipton, *Regional Variation*, pp. 3–17; Taylor and Johnston, *Geography of Elections*, pp. 152ff. Rohe persuasively argues for regional variation and local differentials of voting patterns in "Wahlanalyse im historischen Kontext," pp. 341–45, but he does not demonstrate differences in turnout patterns among regions. There is some reason to believe that these peripheries were politicized at a differential rate; see Steinbach, "Polisierung und Nationalisierung der Region im 19. Jahrhundert," pp. 342–43; Rohe, "Die verspätete Region," pp. 231–52.

18. Manziger, *Verfassungsrevision und Demokratisierung im Königreich Württemberg*, pp. 141ff.; Kleine, *Der württembergische Ministerpräsident Frh. Hermann von Mittnacht*, p. 69; Grube, *Der Stuttgarter Landtag*, pp. 542–50.

19. See table 4:4.

20. *Württembergische Jahrbücher*, 1889: Heft I, 173; 1895: Heft III, 186; 1900: Heft III, 208; 1907: Heft II, 1908; *Deutsches Volksblatt*, *Schwäbische Merkur*, both 19 November 1912. See also Schulte, *Struktur und Entwicklung des Parteisystems*, Appendix, pp. 26–30.

21. Blackbourn, *Class, Religion, and Local Politics*, pp. 236–37. See also Zeldin, *France: 1848–1945*, 1: 574–91; Priouret, *La république des députés*; Bryce, *Modern Democracies*, pp. 250–51. Ostrogorski had corroborating evidence for Great Britain in *Democracy and the Organization of Political Parties*, 1: 496–97.

22. See chapter 4 for taxes and Socialism; Hessian agrarian revolt will be discussed later; for tobacco see White, *The Splintered Party*, pp. 59ff.

23. Reports to Provincial President, 5 July, 20 August 1901 from Regierung Wiesbaden and Cassel, HStA Marburg, Oberpräsidium Cassel, 150, 510.

24. *Verhandlungen des Württembergischen Kammer der Abgeordneten*, vol. 223.

25. *Rem Zeitung* (Gmünd), 5 March 1900, in ibid.

26. 1890 leaflet, Bundesarchiv Koblenz, Payer Nachlass, 6; Blackbourn, *Class, Religion and Local Politics*, p. 118.

27. Prussian Minister to Württemberg, 8 February 1899, Auswärtiges Amt Microfilm, ACP, Roll 180, 48.

28. Gieger to Payer, 25 June 1895, Bundesarchiv Koblenz, Payer Nachlass, 7.

29. Payer leaflet 1890, ibid.

30. *Mindener Post*, 26 February 1898, StA Detmold, Regierung Minden, Mi. 1, 251.

31. Roon leaflet, in ibid.

32. *Bielefelder Zeitung*, 28 June 1898, ibid.

33. *Lübbecke Kreisblatt Extrablatt*, 20 June 1898, ibid.

34. *Vierteljahreshefte zur Statistik des Deutschen Reichs* 1899 Ergänzungshefte 3: 65–69; 1903, 4: 80–84; *Statistik des Deutschen Reichs*, Neue Folge, 250: III, 90–93; Grosse and Raith, *Beiträge zur Geschichte und Statistik der Wahlen in Württemberg*, pp. 28–31.

CHAPTER 7

1. Oldenburg-Januschau, *Erinnerungen*, p. 60.

2. Muhl, *Studien zur westpreussischen Gütergeschichte*; *Statistik des Deutschen Reichs*, Neue Folge, 112; 209; Sombart, *Die deutsche Volkswirtschaft im neunzehnten Jahrhundert*, pp. 606–26; Franke, *Das Ruhrgebiet und Ostpreussen*, p. 53; Mechow, *Die Ost- und Westpreussen in Berlin*, p. 113; *Landwirtschaftliche Jahrbücher* 19, Ergänzungsband 4: 1–38; note 77, chapter 4.

3. Puder, *Die Stadt Elbing und ihre Umgebung*. There are various publications on the Marienburg castle and its environs; see Carl Wünch, "Kurze Baugeschichte der Marienburg," pp. 21–30; note 77, chapter 4.

4. Kerstan, *Die Geschichte des Landkreises Elbing*; Zacharias, *Neues Marienburger Heimatbuch*, p. 549 and passim. See also aforementioned Reich statistics (note 2 above) in vol. 112.

5. Oldenburg-Januschau, *Erinnerungen*, p. 40.

6. Ibid., p. 117.

7. Ibid., p. 44.

8. Ibid., p. 45.

9. Ibid., p. 39.

10. Puhle, *Agrarische Interessenpolitik*, pp. 45ff.; Stegmann, *Die Erben Bismarcks*, pp. 356–60, 429; note 83, chapter 4.

11. *Danziger Neueste Nachrichten*, 6 November 1899 in GStA Berlin, Regierung Danzig, 180, 13317.

12. Specht, *Die Reichstagswahlen von 1871 bis 1903*, p. 12.

13. These can be found in GStA Berlin, Thorn County, 207, 190; ibid., Regierungsbezirk Danzig, 1890, 196.

14. *Elbinger Zeitung*, 24 May 1903, in ibid., 207, 610.

15. *Marienburger Zeitung*, 24 May 1903, in ibid.

16. Reported in GStA Berlin, Regierung Danzig, 180, 16138; see also *Nogat Zeitung*, 22 January 1907, ibid.

17. Statistics can be found in GStA Berlin, Regierung Danzig, 14664, 13290.

18. *Marienburger Zeitung*, 29 January 1907, in ibid.

19. Ritter, *Das Deutsche Kaiserreich*, p. 40.

20. *Danziger Allgemeine Zeitung*, 20 August 1910, in GStA Berlin, Regierung Danzig,

180, 13352; see also *Marienburger Zeitung*, 7 November 1910, *Danziger Zeitung*, 21 November 1910, in ibid., 180, 19250.

21. Oldenburg-Januschau, *Erinnerungen*, p. 118.

22. Ibid.

23. See chapter 1, note 15.

24. Oldenburg-Januschau, *Erinnerungen*, p. 120.

25. *Königsberger Volkszeitung*, 28 December 1906, in GStA Berlin, Regierung Danzig, 180, 16138.

26. Hoffmann, *The History of the German Resistance 1933–1945*, p. 20.

CHAPTER 8

1. See *Zeitschrift des Königlichen Preussischen Statistischen Bureaus*, 33: 189ff.

2. *Statistisches Jahrbuch für den Preussischen Staat*, 1898: 120ff.; 1903: 208ff.; 1913: 20ff.; *Statistik des Deutschen Reichs*, Neue Folge, 150: 192; *Zeitschrift des Königlichen Preussischen Statistischen Bureaus*, 42: 273ff.; Wirminghaus, "Stadt und Land unter dem Einfluss der Binnenwanderung," pp. 161ff.

3. Galos et al., *Die Hakatistien*, pp. 156–59.

4. These petitions can be found in GStA Berlin, Regierung Danzig, 180, 16138, and ibid., 209, 22.

5. 1907 leaflet, Strasburg, GStA Berlin, Strasburg County, 205, 301.

6. *Statistik des Deutschen Reichs*, Neue Folge, 212; Coelle, "Die Landwirtschaft und ihre Geschichte im Wandel der Zeiten," pp. 165–92.

7. Police reports, Strasburg 18 December 1911, 23 January 1912, Wrotzk 24 January 1912, GStA Berlin, Strasburg County, 205, 302.

8. Leaflet in Berent County 1907, ibid., Regierung Danzig, 180, 19250.

9. Calculated from data in table 3:2.

10. See Specht, *Die Reichstagswahlen*, pp. 18–19.

11. *Statistik des Deutschen Reichs*, Neue Folge, 209; Nordwein Diest-Koeber, "Gesellschaftliches Leben im 19. Jahrhundert," pp. 399–412.

12. 1907 leaflet, GStA Berlin, Strasburg County, 205, 301.

13. Police report, 18 December 1911, ibid.; see note 10.

14. Leaflet, 20 January 1912, GStA Berlin, Schwetz County, 204, 3045.

15. Police report, 24 January 1912, ibid., Strasburg County, 205, 302.

CHAPTER 9

1. Pascho, *Der Raum Dortmund*; *100 Jahre Industrie- und Handelskammer zum Dortmund*; Hellgrew, *Dortmund als Industrie- und Arbeiterstadt*; *Dortmunder Zeitung*, Jubiläumsausgabe, 1928; *Statistik des Deutschen Reichs*, Neue Folge, 209.

2. Lützenkirchen, *Der sozialdemokratische Verein für den Reichstagswahlkreis Dortmund-Hörde*, p. 77.

3. Ibid., pp. 87ff.; *Dortmunder Zeitung, Tremonia, Arbeiter Zeitung, Dortmunder Tageblatt*, all Dortmund for January 1912.

4. Police reports, 29 August 1910, 15 August 1911, 1 August 1912, Stadtarchiv Dortmund, Do.n. 263.

5. *Tremonia*, 16 February 1908.

6. *Arbeiter Zeitung*, 4 June 1898.

7. Graf, *Die Wahlen in Dortmund*, pp. 185–86.

8. *Verhandlungen des Reichstages*, Legislaturperiode 9, Session 1, Anlageband 1: Nr. 292.

9. Ibid., Legislaturperiode 9, Session 3, Anlageband 1: Nr. 134, Legislaturperiode 9, Session 3, 2450B-2452.

10. *Arbeiter Zeitung*, 7 June 1898.

11. *Dortmunder Zeitung*, 29 May 1898; *Arbeiter Zeitung*, 23 June 1898.

12. *Dortmunder Zeitung*, 11 June 1898.

13. Ibid., 13 June 1898.

14. Ibid., 30 November 1902; *Dortmunder Tageblatt*, 11, 24 June 1903; police reports, 23 January, 28 September 1902, Stadtarchiv Dortmund, Do.n. 224.

15. *Dortmunder Zeitung*, 24 June 1903.

16. Center leaflet 1903, StA Detmold, Regierung Minden, Mi. 1, 253.

17. For methods and data, see notes 4 and 27, chapter 3.

18. *Arbeiter Zeitung*, 1 January 1907.

19. Ibid., 5 January 1907.

20. Ibid., 18 January 1907.

21. Ibid., 20 January 1907.

22. Police report, 19 June 1909, Stadtarchiv Dortmund, Do.n. 180; *Provinziell Parteitag für westliche Westfalen*, Dortmund, 1909, ibid., Do.n. 260; Lützenkirchen, *Der sozialdemokratische Verein*, pp. 42–44.

23. *Arbeiter Zeitung*, 31 January 1907.

24. *Dortmunder Zeitung*, 26 January 1903, 26 January, 6 February 1907.

25. Ibid.

26. *Dortmunder Zeitung*, 4 February 1907.

27. *Mitteilungen des Nationalliberalen Vereins*, 18 February 1907, StA Detmold, Regierung Minden, Mi. 1, 98. There was no populist *Mittelstand* Catholic movement as in Bochum; Crew, *Town in the Ruhr*, pp. 129–37.

28. *Statistik des Deutschen Reichs*, Neue Folge, 250: I, 32–33. The musings about the reasons for this effect are solely the author's.

29. *Arbeiter Zeitung*, 6 February 1907.

30. *Tremonia*, 16 February 1908.

31. *Der Volksfreund*, 23 January 1912, Stadtarchiv Dortmund, Hörde County, Ho.c., 8/13.

CHAPTER 10

1. 1898 leaflet, HStA Marburg, Regierung Cassel, 165, 47.

2. The best discussion of candidate selection can be found in Nipperdey, *Die Organisation der deutschen Parteien vor 1918*, pp. 23ff.

3. Repeated time and time again in Minden-Lübbecke; see StA Detmold, Mi. 1, 25; also see Haussmann Nachlass, HStA Stuttgart, I, 47; Payer Nachlass, Bundesarchiv Koblenz, 6.

4. Vogel et al., *Wahlen in Deutschland*, pp. 98–102; Fenske, *Strukturprobleme der deutschen Parteiengeschichte*, pp. 77–79; Misch, *Das Wahlsystem zwischen Theorie und Taktik*, pp. 130–40; Johannes Schauff, "Die parteipolitische Struktur Deutschlands," pp. 139–50.

5. Vogel et al., *Wahlen in Deutschland*, pp. 290–93.

6. Ibid.; Schauff, "Die parteipolitische Struktur Deutschlands," p. 148.

7. Donald Ziegler, *Prelude to Democracy*, pp. 25–26.

8. *Verhandlungen des Reichstages* 289: 4821.

9. Misch, *Das Wahlsystem zwischen Theorie und Taktik*, p. 142. Bernstein's statements can be found in the same work, pp. 150ff.

10. See note 8.

11. Tingsten, *Political Behavior*, p. 156. Dropoff calculated from same material as in chapter 1.

12. Walter Gagel, *Die Wahlrechtsfrage in der Geschichte der deutschen liberalen Parteien*, pp. 114–47; Vogel et al., *Wahlen in Deutschland*, pp. 125–28; Jastrow, *Das Dreiklassensystem*.

13. Kleine, *Frh. von Mittnacht*, p. 81.

14. Magnus Biermer, *Die gegenwärtige politische Lage in Hessen*, p. 18.

15. Savigny, *Das parlamentarische Wahlrecht im Reich und in Preussen und seine Reform*, p. 26. See also Gagel, *Die Wahlrechtsfrage*, pp. 127–36; Gerlach, *Die Geschichte des preussischen Wahlrechts*, pp. 188–202; Kurt Dieter, *Parlaments und Wahlrechts-Reform*.

16. *Die Volksstimme*, 17 December 1902. See also SPD leaflet in HStA Marburg, Oberpräsidium Cassel, 150, 633.

17. Schorske, *German Social Democracy 1905–1917*, pp. 36ff.; *Arbeiter Zeitung* (Dortmund), 19 April 1910; and Leo Stern, ed., *Die Russische Revolutionen von 1905–07 im Spiegel der deutschen Presse*; Evans, "'Red Wednesday' in Hamburg," pp. 1–31.

18. Stern, *Die Russische Revolutionen*, 2: Part 5, 1279.

19. Can be found in HStA Marburg, LA Ziegenhain, 180, 4442.

20. Stern, *Die Russische Revolutionen*, 5: Part 6, 1772–73.

21. Ibid., 5: Part 5, 1302–3.

22. Cabinet minutes 4 March 1898 in Auswärtiges Amt microfilm, National Archives, ACP, Rolls 304, 580.

23. *Verhandlungen des Reichstages* 321: 4288.

24. Gagel, *Die Wahlrechtsfrage*, pp. 105–9, 143–58; Heckart, *From Bassermann to Bebel*, p. 160; Huber, *Deutsche Verfassungsgeschichte*, 4: 375–78, 404–9; Warren, *The Red Kingdom of Saxony*, pp. 58–90. See the various reports of the Prussian minister to Saxony in Auswärtiges Amt microfilm, National Archives, ACP, Rolls 180, 639, 649, 657–90. For Hessian reform see the reports of 14 July 1904 and 7 December 1909, Rolls 170, 206–12, 295–97; White, *The Splintered Party*, pp. 174–76.

25. *Preussische Jahrbücher* 133 (1910): 367.

26. Roth, *Social Democrats*, pp. 324–25. For the view of permanent crises, see notes 13–15, chapter 1; the more optimistic views are treated in chapter 11. For the view of a rising struggle for hegemony based on Gramsci's theories, see Eley, *Reshaping the German Right*, pp. 163ff.

CHAPTER 11

1. The most inclusive postwar attempts to make National Socialism comparable and therefore not characteristically German can be found in Ritter, *Europa und die deutsche Frage* and in *Dämonie der Macht*. A more recent attempt in that direction is Nolte, "Deutscher Scheinkonstitutionalismus." The next generations challenged this view and raised unfavorable comparisons with the U.S. as evident in Puhle, *Von der Agrarkrise zum Präfschismus*; Kocka, *White Collar Workers in America, 1890–1940*. For unfavorable comparisons with Great Britain, see Schmidt, "Parlamentarisierung oder Präventive Konterrevolution," pp. 249–78, and Eyck, *Gladstone* and *Bismarck and the German Empire*. The most recent attack on the unique nature of German history is Blackbourn and Eley, *Mythen deutscher Geschichtsschreibung*. See the criticisms of Eley's approach in Wehler,

"Deutscher Sonderweg oder allgemeine Probleme des westlichen Kapitalismus?" pp. 478–87; Moeller, "Die Suche nach der Kontinuität in der modernen deutschen Geschichte," pp. 430–38. See also Hildebrand, "Staatskunst oder Systemzwang," pp. 624–44.

2. Mann, *Betrachtungen eines Unpolitischen*, pp. 222–374; Keller, *Der unpolitische Deutsche*, pp. 44–64; Stern, *The Failure of Illiberalism*, pp. 3–25; Jarausch, "Illiberalism and Recent German History in Search of a Paradigm," pp. 268–84.

3. Eschenberg, *Die improvisierte Demokratie*, p. 6.

4. Bracher, *The German Dilemma*, p. 54. The key to this interpretation is based on Arthur Rosenberg's 1928 essay *Imperial Germany*. There is a massive literature on the topic; for a recent work emphasizing analytic approaches, see Rittenberg, "Revolution or Pseudo-Democratization," pp. 299–398.

5. Frauendienst, "Demokratisierung des deutschen Konstitutionalismus," pp. 721–46; Frauendienst, "Das deutsches Reich von 1890 bis 1914," pp. 27–93, 168–264; Grosser, *Vom monarchischen Konstitutionalismus zur parlamentarischen Demokratie*; Rauh, *Föderalismus und Parlamentarismus im Wilhelminischen Reich*, pp. 9–15; Zmarzlik, "Das Kaiserreich in neuer Sicht?" pp. 105–26; Domann, *Sozialdemokratie und Kaisertum unter Wilhelm II*; Schoenbaum, *Zabern 1913*.

6. Shively, "Party Identification and Party Choice: The Weimar Case," pp. 1220–22. See Neumann, *Die Parteien der Weimarer Republik*, p. 6; Unwin, "Germany: Continuity and Change in German Electoral Politics," pp. 127–30; Lepsius, "Parteisystem und Sozialstruktur," pp. 62–64; Milatz, *Wähler und Wahlen in der Weimarer Republik*, pp. 88–106; Thränhardt, *Wahlen und politische Strukturen in Bayern*, pp. 125ff.; Molt, "Vom kaiserlichen Reichstag zum Bundestag," pp. 118–19. For the movements within these three main groupings, see Albertin, *Liberalismus und Demokratie*, pp. 158–64; Eliasberg, *Der Ruhrkrieg von 1920*, pp. 254–56; Kühr, *Parteien und Wahlen im Stadt und Landkreis Essen*, pp. 75ff.

7. Richard Hunt, *German Social Democracy in the Weimar Republic*, pp. 105 and passim; Suzanne Miller, *Die Bürde der Macht*, pp. 445–51; Breitman, *German Socialism and Weimar Democracy*; Schauff, *Wählverhalten*; Tingsten, *Political Behavior*, pp. 50–59; Bessel, "Eastern Germany as a Structural Problem," pp. 199–218; Milatz, *Wähler und Wahlen*, pp. 102–6. For a more traditional view, see Liebe, *Die Deutschnationale Volkspartei*, pp. 16–17 and passim.

8. Childers, *The Nazi Voter*, p. 61. For the problems of the *Mittelstand*, see Larry Eugene Jones, "The Dying Middle Class," pp. 22–54; Larry Eugene Jones, "Inflation, Revaluation and the Crisis of Middle Class Politics," pp. 143–68; Heinrich Winkler, *Mittelstand, Demokratie und Nationalsozialismus*.

9. Schauff, "Die partei politische Struktur Deutschlands," p. 142.

10. Braunias, "Verhältniswahl und Persönlichkeitswahl," pp. 14–24; Ziegler, *Prelude to Democracy*, pp. 102ff.; Misch, *Das Wahlsystem zwischen Theorie und Taktik*, pp. 219–39. The exile scholarship is represented by Hermens, *Democracy or Anarchy*, p. 162; Hermens, *The Representative Republic*, pp. 326–29; Brecht, *Prelude to Silence*, pp. 131–32. An earlier attack along similar lines was Gosnel, *Why Europe Votes*, pp. 117, 236–88. Recent work tends to downplay the decisiveness of any electoral system; see Rae, *The Politics of Electoral Laws*, pp. 71–98; Fenske, *Wahlrecht und Parteiensystem*, pp. 161–66. The best defense of proportional representation can be found in Lakeman, *How Democracies Vote*.

11. The best discussion of the permeating violence is in Merkl, *The Making of a Stormtrooper*, pp. 28ff. Richard Tilly agrees that political violence had a debilitating effect; see Tilly et al., *The Rebellious Century*, pp. 199–200. For similar views, see Lipset, *Political Man*, pp. 63–65.

12. For the shaggy-dog story, see HStA Marburg, Oberpräsidium Cassel, 150, 1312.

13. Heberle, *Landbevölkerung und Nationalsozialismus*; Tilton, *Nazism, Neo-Nazism*

and the Peasantry, pp. 1–71; Passchier, "The Electoral Geography of the Nazi Landslide," pp. 283–300; Zofka, Die Ausbreitung des Nationalsozialismus auf dem Land, pp. 49–122; Noakes, The Nazi Party in Lower Saxony, pp. 118–26; Grill, "The Nazi Party's Rural Perspective before 1928," pp. 149–85; Grill, The Nazi Movement in Baden, pp. 169ff.; Childers, The Nazi Voter, pp. 29ff.

   14. Hamilton, Who Voted for Hitler?, pp. 65ff.; Childers, The Nazi Voter, pp. 98, 174ff. Mühlberger, "The Sociology of the NSDAP: The Question of Working Class Membership," pp. 494–511; Stokes, "The Social Composition of the Nazi Party in Euten, 1925–32," pp. 4–15; Kater, "Quantifizierung und NS-Geschichte," p. 462; Kater, The Nazi Party, pp. 52–55; Mason, "National Socialism and the Working Class," pp. 49–82; Conan Fischer, "The Occupational Background of the SA's Rank and File Membership during the Depression Years," pp. 131–59.

   15. The main support for this argument can be found in Hamilton, Who Voted for Hitler?, pp. 83ff. Hamilton attacks the proposition that the movement was essentially lower middle class, particularly propounded by Kocka, White Collar Workers, pp. 265ff., and most succinctly in Heinrich Winkler, "Extremismus der Mitte," pp. 175–91. The voting analyses of Childers seem to cast doubt on parts of this general middle class theory, particularly the view that the new middle classes or the craftsmen were overrepresented among voters during the crucial elections; see Childers, The Nazi Voter, pp. 92–93, 172ff. For an attack on this Mittelstand proposition, see Eley, "What Produces Fascism: Preindustrial Traditions or a Crisis of the Capitalist State," pp. 57–63. Winkler has taken some earlier criticisms into account in his new formulations, see "Mittelstandbewegung oder Volkspartei?" pp. 98–104.

   16. The classic account of the takeover is Bracher, Die Auflösung der Weimarer Republik, pp. 96ff. Also helpful are Pridham, Hitler's Rise to Power; Orlow, History of the Nazi Party; Noakes, The Nazi Party in Lower Saxony; Allen, The Nazi Seizure of Power; Kershaw, "The Führer Image and Political Integration," pp. 135–50; Zofka, Die Ausbreitung des Nationalsozialismus auf dem Land, pp. 133ff.; Fröhlich, "Die Partei auf lokaler Ebene," pp. 255–62; Broszart, "Die Struktur der NS-Massenbewegung," pp. 52–76.

   17. I am indebted for this proposition to Zofka, Die Ausbreitung, pp. 347–50.

   18. Childers, The Nazi Voter, pp. 93ff.; Kershaw, Popular Opinion and Political Dissent in the Third Reich, pp. 21–29.

BIBLIOGRAPHY

A. ARCHIVAL SOURCES

1. Germany, Aüswartiges Amt microfilms deposited in National Archives, Washington, D.C., ACP rolls, 136, 170, 180, 206–12, 295–97, 305, 639–90
2. Bundesarchiv Koblenz, Payer Nachlass
3. Geheimes Staatsarchiv Berlin-Dahlem
   Regierung Danzig
   Counties Berent, Schwetz, Strasburg, Thorn
4. Staatsarchiv Detmold
   Regierung Minden
5. Stadtarchiv Dortmund
   Dortmund and Hörde city documents
6. Stadtarchiv Frankfurt
   Magistratsakten
7. Staatsarchiv Ludwigsburg
   Oberamt Aalen
   Stadtamt Stuttgart
8. Hauptstaatsarchiv Marburg
   Oberpräsidium Cassel
   Regierung Cassel
   Landesamt Gelnhausen, Marburg, Ziegenhain, Frankenberg
9. Staatsarchiv Münster
   Oberpräsidium Münster
   Regierung Münster
   Regierung Arnsberg
10. Hauptstaatsarchiv Stuttgart
    Staatsministerium
    Innenministerium
    Conrad Haussmann Nachlass
11. Stadtarchiv Stuttgart
    Political Archives
12. Hauptstaatsarchiv Wiesbaden
    Regierung Wiesbaden
    Polizeipräsidium Frankfurt

B. PUBLISHED SOURCES

1. Germany
   Monatshefte zur Statistik des Deutschen Reichs, 1885–90
   Vierteljahreshefte zur Statistik des Deutschen Reichs, 1890–1907
   Statistik des Deutschen Reichs, Neue Folge, 150, 192, 209, 250
   Verhandlungen des Reichstages, Legislaturperiode 9–
   Reichsarbeitsblatt 5
2. United States
   Historical Statistics of the United States
3. Baden
   Statistische Mitteilungen über das Grossherzogtum Baden, Neue Folge, 6
4. Hesse
   Beiträge zur Statistik des Grossherzogtums Hessen 62
   Historisches Gemeindeverzeichnis für Hessen
5. Prussia
   Zeitschrift des Königlichen Preussischen Statistischen Bureaus, Ergänzungsheft
   30, 33, 42
   Statistisches Jahrbuch für den Preussischen Staat, 1898–1915
6. Württemberg
   Württembergische Jahrbücher für Statistik und Landeskunde, 1887–1907
   Verhandlungen des Württembergischen Kammer der Abgeordneten, 1900–

C. NEWSPAPERS

Arbeiter Zeitung (Dortmund)
Der Beobachter (Stuttgart)
Casseler Allgemeiner Zeitung
Darmstädter Zeitung
Deutsches Volksblatt (Stuttgart)
Dortmunder Tageblatt
Dortmunder Zeitung
Frankfurter Zeitung
Münsterische Zeitung
Oberhessische Zeitung (Marburg)
Reichsherold (Marburg)
Die Reichspost (Stuttgart)
Schwäbische Merkur (Stuttgart)
Schwäbische Tagwacht (Stuttgart)
Tremonia (Dortmund)
Die Volksstimme (Frankfurt)

D. BOOKS AND ARTICLES

Abel, Wilhelm, et al. *Handwerksgeschichte in neuer Sicht.* Göttingen, 1970.
Adamson, Walter. *Hegemony and Revolution.* Berkeley, 1980.
Albertin, Lothar. *Liberalismus und Demokratie am Anfang der Weimarer Republik.* Düsseldorf, 1972.
Albrecht, Dieter. "Vom Reichsgründung bis zum Ende des Ersten Weltkrieges." In *Handbuch der Bayerischen Geschichte*, edited by Max Spindler, vol. 4. Munich, 1967–75.

Allen, Howard, and Allen, Kay. "Vote Fraud and Data Validity." In *Analyzing Electoral History*, edited by Jerome Clubb, William Flanigan, and Nancy Zingale, pp. 153–94. Beverly Hills, 1981.

Allen, William S. *The Nazi Seizure of Power*. Chicago, 1965.

Almond, Gabriel; Flanagan, Scott; and Mundt, Robert, eds. *Crisis, Choice and Change*. Boston, 1973.

———, and Powell, G. Bingham, Jr. *Comparative Politics*. Boston, 1966.

———, and Verba, Sidney. *The Civic Culture*. Boston, 1966.

Altrichter, Wilhelm. *Konstitutionalismus und Imperialismus*. Frankfurt a.M., 1977.

Anderson, Eugene, and Anderson, Pauline. *Political Institutions and Social Change in Continental Europe in the Nineteenth Century*. Berkeley, 1967.

Anderson, Margaret. *Windthorst: A Political Biography*. Oxford, 1981.

Apter, David. *The Politics of Modernization*. Chicago, 1975.

Archiv des deutschen Landwirtschaftsrat.

Bachem, Karl. *Vorgeschichte, Geschichte und Politik der deutschen Zentrum*. Cologne, 1927–32.

Barkin, Kenneth. *The Controversy over German Industrialization*. Chicago, 1970.

Bartel, Horst, and Engleberg, E., eds. *Die grosspreussisch-militarische Reichsgründung 1870/71*. Berlin, 1971.

Bäumer, Gertrud. "Die Geschichte der Frauenbewegung in Deutschland." In *Handbuch der Frauenbewegung*, edited by Gertrud Bäumer and Helene Lange, pp. 1–156. Berlin, 1901.

Benedikt, Heinrich, ed. *Geschichte der Republik Österreich*. Vienna, 1954.

Berelson, Bernard R.; Lazarsfeld, Paul F.; and McPhee, William. *Voting*. Chicago, 1954.

Berger, Michael. *Arbeiterbewegung und Demokratisierung*. Freiburg, 1970.

Berghahn, Volker. *Der Tirpitz-Plan*. Düsseldorf, 1971.

———. "Politik und Geschichte in Wilhelmischen Deutschland." *Neue Politische Literatur* 24 (1979): 164–95.

Bergsträsser, Ludwig. *Geschichte der politischen Parteien in Deutschland*. Munich, 1965.

Bertram, Jürgen. *Die Wahlen zur deutschen Reichstag vom Jahre 1912*. Düsseldorf, 1964.

Bessel, Richard. "Eastern Germany as a Structural Problem in the Weimar Republic." *Social History* 3 (1978): 199–218.

Bezucha, Robert, ed. *Modern European Social History*. Lexington, Mass., 1972.

Biermer, Magnus. *Die gegenwärtige politische Lage in Hessen*. n.p., n.d.

Binder, David. *The Other German*. Washington, 1975.

Blackbourn, David. *Class, Religion and Local Politics in Wilhelmine Germany*. New Haven, 1980.

———. "The *Mittelstand* in German Society and Politics, 1871–1914." *Social History* 4 (1979): 409–33.

———. "Peasants and Politics in Germany, 1871–1914," *European History Quarterly* 14 (1984): 47–75.

———, and Eley, Geoff. *Mythen deutscher Geschichtsschreibung*. Frankfurt am Main, 1980.

Blalock, Hubert M. *Causal Inferences in Nonexperimental Research*. Chapel Hill, 1964.

———. *Social Statistics*. New York, 1960.

Blank, Richard. "Die soziale Zusammensetzung der sozialdemokratischen Wählerschaft Deutschlands." *Archiv für Sozialwissenschaft und Sozialpolitik* 20 (1905): 507–50.

Blewitt, Neal. *The Peers, the Parties and the People*. London, 1972.

Böckenförde, Ernst-Wolfgang, and Wahl, Rainer, eds. *Moderne deutsche Verfassungsgeschichte*. Cologne, 1972.

Boldt, Hans. "Deutsches Konstitutionalismus und Bismarckreich." In *Das Kaiserliche Deutschland*, edited by Michael Stürmer, pp. 119–42. Düsseldorf, 1970.

Booms, Hans. *Die Deutsch-Konservative Partei.* Düsseldorf, 1954.
Bracher, Karl Dietrich. *Die Auflösung der Weimarer Republik.* Stuttgart, 1955.
———. *The German Dilemma.* New York, 1975.
Braunias, Karl. "Verhältniswahl oder Persönlichkeitswahl im europäischen Ausland." In *Neues Wahlrecht*, edited by Johannes Schauff, pp. 85–96. Berlin, 1929.
Brecht, Arnold. *Prelude to Silence.* New York, 1944.
Breitman, Richard. *German Socialism and Weimar Democracy.* Chapel Hill, 1981.
Bronsen, David. *Jews and Germans from 1860 to 1933.* Tübingen, 1979.
Broszart, Martin. "Die Struktur des NS-Massenbewegung." *Vierteljahrshefte für Zeitgeschichte* 31 (1983): 52–76.
Brunner, Otto, et al., eds. *Geschichtliche Grundbegriffe.* Stuttgart, 1978.
Bryce, James. *Modern Democracies.* New York, 1924.
Buch, Helmut. *Die Stoeckerbewegung im Siegerland.* Siegen, 1968.
Buchheim, Karl. *Geschichte der christlichen Parteien in Deutschland.* Munich, 1953.
———. *Ultramontanismus und Demokratie.* Munich, 1963.
Burnham, Walter Dean. *Critical Elections.* New York, 1970.
———. "The Changing Shape of the American Political Universe." *American Political Science Review* 59 (1965): 7–28.
———. "Theory and Voting Research: Some Reflections on Converse's 'Change in the American Electorate.'" *American Political Science Review* 68 (1974): 1002–23.
———. "The United States: The Politics of Heterogeneity." In *Electoral Behavior: A Comparative Handbook*, edited by Richard Rose, pp. 653–726. New York, 1974.
Büsch, Otto. "Gedanken und Thesen zur Wählerbewegung in Deutschland." In *Wählerbewegung in der deutschen Geschichte*, edited by Otto Büsch, Wolfgang Wölk, and Monika Wölk, pp. 125–70. Berlin, 1977.
———. "Historische Wahlforschung als Zugang zur Geschichte." In *Wählerbewegung in der deutschen Geschichte*, edited by Otto Büsch, Wolfgang Wölk, and Monica Wölk, pp. 1–37. Berlin, 1977.
———; Wölk, Wolfgang; and Wölk, Monika, eds. *Wählerbewegung in der deutschen Geschichte.* Berlin, 1977.
Butler, David, and Stokes, Donald. *Political Change in Britain.* London, 1974.
Campbell, Angus, and Converse, Philip, eds. *The Human Meaning of Social Change.* New York, 1972.
———; Converse, Philip; and Miller, Warren. *The American Voter.* New York, 1960.
Campbell, Bruce. *The American Electorate.* New York, 1979.
Carmines, Edward, and Stimson, James. "The Two Faces of Issue Voting." *American Political Science Review* 74 (1980): 78–89.
Castles, Francis. *Pressure Groups and Political Culture.* London, 1957.
Cecil, Lamar. "Jew and Junker in Imperial Berlin." *Yearbook of the Leo Baeck Institute* 20 (1975): 47–58.
Center Party. *Handbuch für Hessische Zentrumswähler.* Mainz, 1911.
Childers, Thomas. *The Nazi Voter: The Social Foundations of Fascism in Germany, 1919–33.* Chapel Hill, 1983.
———. "The Social Basis of the National Socialist Vote." *Journal of Contemporary History* 11 (1976): 17–43.
Claggett, William; Loesch, Jeffrey; Shively, W. Phillips; and Snell, Ronald. "Political Leadership and the Development of Political Cleavages: Imperial Germany, 1871–1912." *American Journal of Political Science* 26 (1982): 644–63.
Coelle, Ernst. "Die Landwirtschaft und ihre Geschichte im Wandel der Zeiten." In *Die Stadt und der Landkreis Graudenz*, edited by Nordwein von Diest-Koeber, Gerhard Meissner, and Hans-Jürgen Schuch, pp. 165–92. Osnabrück, 1976.
Converse, Philip. "Change in the American Electorate." In *The Human Meaning of Social*

Change, edited by Angus Campbell and Philip Converse, pp. 263–330. New York, 1972.

———. "Comment." *American Political Science Review* 68 (1974): 1024–27.

Conze, Werner. "Mittelstand." In *Geschichtliche Grundbegriffe*, edited by Otto Brunner, Werner Conze, and Reinhart Koselleck, 4: 49–92. Stuttgart, 1978.

———. "Politische Willensbildung im deutschen Kaiserreich also Forschungsaufgabe historischer Wahlsoziologie." In *Vom Staat des Ancien Regime zum modernen Parteienstaat*, edited by Helmut Berding, Kurt Düwell, Lothar Gall, Wolfgang Mommsen, and Hans-Ulrich Wehler, pp. 331–47. Munich, 1978.

Craig, F. W. *British Election Results, 1885–1919*. London, 1974.

Crew, David. "Regionale Mobilität und Arbeiterklasse." *Geschichte und Gesellschaft* 1 (1974): 99–120.

———. *Town in the Ruhr*. New York, 1979.

Croon, Helmuth. *Bürgertum und Verwaltung in den Städten des Ruhrgebiets im 19 Jahrhundert*. Cologne, 1964.

———. *Die gesellschaftliche Auswirkungen des Gemeindewahlrechts in den Gemeinden und Kreisen des Rheinlands und Westfalen im neunzehnten Jahrhundert*. Cologne, 1960.

———, and Utermann, Kurt. *Zeche und Gemeinde*. Tübingen, 1958.

Crothers, George. *The German Election of 1907*. New York, 1941.

Dahl, Robert, and Lindbloom, Charles. *Politics, Economics, Welfare*. New York, 1953.

Dahrendorf, Ralf. *Society and Democracy in Germany*. New York, 1969.

Dawson, Richard, and Prewitt, Kenneth. *Political Socialization*. Boston, 1969.

Demeter, Karl. *Geschichte der Landes Hessen*. Cassel, 1959.

Devine, Donald. *The Political Culture of the United States*. Boston, 1972.

Diederich, Nils; Fuchs, Neidhard; Kullack, Irene; and Schmollinger, Horst. *Wahlstatistik in Deutschland*. Berlin, 1976.

Diest-Koeber, Nordwein von. "Gesellschaftliches Leben im 19. Jahrhundert." In *Die Staat und der Landkreis Graudenz*, edited by Nordwein von Diest-Koeber, Gerhard Meissner, Hans-Jürgen Schuch, pp. 389–422. Osnabrück, 1976.

———; Meissner, Gerhard; and Schuch, Hans-Jürgen, eds. *Die Stadt und der Landkreis Graudenz*. Osnabrück, 1976.

Dieter, Kurt. *Parlaments und Wahlrechts-Reform*. Hanover, 1906.

Domann, Peter. *Sozialdemokratie und Kaisertum unter Wilhelm II*. Wiesbaden, 1974.

Dove, Dieter. "The Workers' Choral Movement before the First World War." *Journal of Contemporary History* 13 (1978): 269–96.

Downs, Anthony. *Economic Theory of Democracy*. New York, 1957.

Dowse, Robert, and Hughes, John. *Political Sociology*. London, 1972.

Düding, Dieter. *Der Nationalsoziale Verein 1896–1903*. Munich, 1972.

Duverger, Maurice. *Political Parties*. London, 1964.

Earle, Edward, ed. *Nationalism and Internationalism*. New York, 1950.

Eley, Geoff. "Die 'Kehrites' und das Kaiserreich." *Geschichte und Gesellschaft* 4 (1978): 91–107.

———. "Recent Work in Modern German History." *The Historical Journal* 23 (1980): 463–79.

———. *Reshaping the German Right*. New Haven, 1980.

———. "The Wilhelmine Right and How It Changed." In *Society and Politics in Wilhelmine Germany*, edited by Richard Evans, pp. 112–35. London, 1978.

———. "What Produces Fascism: Preindustrial Traditions or a Crisis of the Capitalist State." *Politics and Society* 12 (1983): 53–82.

———, and Nield, Keith. "Why Does Social History Ignore Politics?" *Social History* 5 (1980): 249–72.

Eliasberg, Georg. *Der Ruhrkrieg von 1920*. Bonn, 1974.

Elm, Ludwig. *Zwischen Fortschritt und Reaktion*. Berlin, 1968.

Epstein, Klaus. *Mathias Erzberger and the Dilemma of German Democracy*. Princeton, 1959.

Epstein, Leon. *Political Parties in Western Democracies*. London, 1967.

Eschenburg, Theodor. *Die improvisierte Demokratie*. Munich, 1964.

————, et al. *The Path of Dictatorship*. Garden City, 1966.

Evans, Richard. "Liberalism and Society: The Feminist Movement and Social Change." In *Society and Politics in Wilhelmine Germany*, edited by Richard Evans, pp. 186–214. London, 1978.

————. *The Feminist Movement in Germany, 1894–1933*. London, 1976.

————. *The Feminists*. London, 1977.

————. "'Red Wednesday' in Hamburg." *Social History* 4 (1979): 1–31.

————. "Review: James Sheehan, *German Liberalism in the Nineteenth Century*." *Social History* 6 (1981): 126–31.

————. "Wilhelm II's Germany and the Historians." In *Society and Politics in Wilhelmine Germany*, edited by Richard Evans, pp. 11–39. London, 1978.

————, ed. *Society and Politics in Wilhelmine Germany*. London, 1978.

Eyck, Erich. *Bismarck and the German Empire*. London, 1950.

————. *Gladstone*. London, 1938.

Ezekial, Mordecai, and Fox, Karl. *Methods of Correlation and Regression Analysis*. New York, 1959.

Falk, Marvin. "The Reichstag Election of 1912: A Statistical Study." Ph.D. Dissertation, University of Iowa, 1976.

Farr, Ian. "Populism in the Countryside: The Peasant Leagues in Bavaria in the 1890s." In *Society and Politics in Wilhelmine Germany*, edited by Richard Evans, pp. 136–59. London, 1978.

Faul, Erwin, ed. *Wähler und Wahlen in Deutschland*. Villingen, 1960.

Fehrenbach, Elisabeth. "Images of Kaiserdom: German Attitudes to Kaiser Wilhelm II." In *Kaiser Wilhelm II*, edited by John Röhl, pp. 221–48. Cambridge, 1982.

Fenske, Hans. "Preussische Beamtenpolitik vor 1918." *Der Staat* 12 (1973): 339–56.

————. *Strukturprobleme der deutschen Parteiengeschichte*. Frankfurt a.M., 1976.

————. *Wahlrecht und Parteiensystem*. Frankfurt, 1972.

Ferejohn, John, and Morris, Fiorini. "The Paradoxes of Voting." *American Political Science Review* 68 (1974): 525–36.

Feuchtwanger, E. J., ed. *Upheaval and Continuity*. Pittsburgh, 1973.

Fischer, Conan. "The Occupational Background of the SA's Rank and File Membership during the Depression Years, 1929 to mid-1934." In *The Shaping of the Nazi State*, edited by Peter Stachura, pp. 131–59. London, 1978.

Fischer, Fritz. *Germany's Aims in the First World War*. New York, 1967.

————. *The War of Illusions*. New York, 1974.

Fischer, Wolfram. "Staatsverwaltung und Interessenverbände im Deutschen Reich 1871–1914." In *Interessenverbände in Deutschland*, edited by Heinz Josef Varain, pp. 139–61. Cologne, 1973.

Fishburn, Peter. "Paradoxes of Voting." *American Political Science Review* 68 (1974): 537–46.

Frank, Robert. *Die Brandenburger als Reichstagswähler*. Berlin, 1934.

Franke, Eberhard. *Das Ruhrgebiet und Ostpreussen*. Essen, 1936.

Frauendienst, Werner. "Demokratisierung des deutschen Konstitutionalismus in der Zeit Wilhelms II." *Zeitschrift für die gesamte Staatswissenschaft* 113 (1957): 721–46.

————. "Das deutsche Reich von 1890 bis 1914." In *Handbuch der deutschen Geschichte*, edited by Leo Just, Abschnitt 4, Teil 1. Constance, 1965.

Fricke, Dieter. *Die bürgerlichen Parteien in Deutschland*, vol. 1, 2. Leipzig, 1968–70.

———. *Die deutsche Arbeiterbewegung, 1869–1914: Ein Handbuch über ihre Organisation und Tätigkeit im Klassenkampf*. Berlin, 1976.

———. "Der deutsche Imperialismus und die Reichstagswahlen von 1907," *Zeitschrift für Geschichtswissenschaft* 9 (1961): 538–76.

———. "Der Reichsverband gegen die Sozialdemokratie." *Zeitschrift für Geschichtswissenschaft* 2 (1954): 237–80.

Fröhlich, Elke. "Die Partei lokaler Ebene." In *The "Führer State": Myth and Reality*, edited by Gerhard Hirschfeld and Lothar Kettenacker, pp. 255–69. Stuttgart, 1981.

Gabler, Helmut. *Die Entwicklung der Parteien auf landwirtschaftlicher Grundlage*. Berlin, 1934.

Gagel, Walter. *Die Wahlrechtsfrage in der Geschichte der deutschen liberalen Parteien*. Düsseldorf, 1958.

Gall, Lothar. "Bismarck und der Bonapartismus." *Historische Zeitschrift* 223 (1976): 618–37.

———. "Liberalismus und 'bürgerliche Gesellschaft.'" *Historische Zeitschrift* 222 (1976): 334–56.

Galos, Adam; Gentzen, Felix-Heinrich; and Jakóbczyk, Witold. *Die Hakatistien*. Berlin, 1966.

Garson, David. *Group Theories of Politics*. Beverly Hills, 1978.

Gellately, Robert. *The Politics of Economic Despair*. London, 1974.

Gerlach, Hellmut von. *Die Geschichte des preussischen Wahlrechts*. Berlin, 1908.

———. *Von Rechts nach Links*. Zurich, 1937.

German Naval League. *Jahresbericht*.

Grebing, Helga. "Position der Konservatismus in der Bundesrepublik." In *Konservatismus: Eines deutsche Bilanz*, by Martin Grieffenhagen, Helga Grebing, et al., pp. 4–56. Munich, 1971.

———. *Geschichte der deutschen Arbeiterbewegung*. Munich, 1970.

Greiffenhagen, Martin; Grebing, Helga; et al. *Konservatismus: Eines deutsche Bilanz*. Munich, 1971.

Greiper, Richart. *Wie Kam's in Alzey Bingen*. Worms, 1909.

Grew, Raymond. "Modernization and Its Discontents." *American Behavioral Scientist* 21 (1977): 289–308.

Grill, John Peter Horst. *The Nazi Movement in Baden*. Chapel Hill, 1983.

———. "The Nazi Party's Rural Propaganda before 1928." *Central European History* 15 (1982): 149–85.

Groh, Dieter. *Negative Integration und revolutionärer Attentismus*. Frankfurt, 1973.

Grosse, D., and Raith, G. *Beiträge zur Geschichte und Statistik der Reichstags- und Landtagswahlen in Württemberg seit 1871*. Stuttgart, 1912.

Grosser, Dieter. *Vom monarchischen Konstitutionalismus zur parlamentarischen Demokratie*. The Hague, 1970.

Grube, Karl. *Der Stuttgarter Landtag*. Stuttgart, 1959.

Gwyn, William. *Democracy and the Costs of Politics*. London, 1962.

Hackett, Amy. "The German Women's Movement and Suffrage, 1890–1914." In *Modern European Social History*, edited by Robert Bezucha, pp. 354–86. Lexington, Mass., 1972.

Hackney, Sheldon. *Populism to Progressivism in Alabama*. Princeton, 1969.

Hagen, William. *Germans, Poles and Jews*. Chicago, 1980.

Haines, Michale. *Economic-Demographic Interrelations in Developing Agriculture Regions*. New York, 1977.

Hall, Alex. *Scandal, Sensation and Social Democracy*. Cambridge, 1977.

Hamburger, Ernst. *Juden im öffentlichen Leben Deutschlands*. Tübingen, 1968.

Hamer, D. A. *The Politics of Electoral Pressure*. Hassock, Sussex, 1977.
Hamilton, Richard. *Who Voted for Hitler?* Princeton, 1982.
Hanham, H. H. *Elections and Party Management*. London, 1959.
Hartung, Fritz. *Deutsche Geschichte 1871–1918*. Stuttgart, 1952.
Hauser, Otto. "Polen und Dänen im Deutschen Reich." In *Die grosspreussische-militäristische Reichsgründung*, edited by Horst Bartel and E. Engleberg, pp. 291–318. Berlin, 1971.
Heberle, Rudolf. *Landbevölkerung und Nationalsozialismus*. Stuttgart, 1963.
Hechter, Michel. *Internal Colonization*. Berkeley, 1977.
Heckart, Beverly. *From Bassermann to Bebel*. New Haven, 1974.
Heitzer, Horstwalter. *Der Volksverein für das Katholische Deutschland im Kaiserreich*. Mainz, 1979.
Hellgrew, Henny. *Dortmund als Industrie- und Arbeiterstadt*. Dortmund, 1951.
Henning, Friedrich-Wilhelm. "Die Entführung der Gewerbefreiheit und ihre Auswirkungen auf der Handwerk in Deutschland." In *Handwerksgeschichte in neuer Sicht*, edited by Wilhelm Abel, et al., pp. 147–78. Göttingen, 1970.
Henning, Hansjoachim. "Kriegervereine in den preussischen Westprovinzen." *Rhenische Vierteljahrsblätter* 32 (1963): 430–75.
Herle, Theo. *Die deutsche Jugendbewegung*. Gotha, 1924.
Hermens, Ferdinand. *Democracy or Anarchy*. Notre Dame, 1941.
———. *The Representative Republic*. Notre Dame, 1958.
Hesselbarth, Hellmut. *Revolutionäre Sozialdemokraten, Opportunisten und die Bauern am Vorabend des Imperialismus*. Berlin, 1968.
Heuss, Theodor. *Friedrich Naumann*. Stuttgart, 1949.
Heussi, Karl. *Kompendium der Kirchengeschichte*. Tübingen, 1976.
Hickey, Stephen. "The Shaping of the German Labour Movement: Miners in the Ruhr." In *Society and Politics in Wilhelmine Germany*, edited by Richard Evans, pp. 215–40. London, 1978.
Hildebrand, Klaus. "Geschichte oder 'Gesellschaftsgeschichte.'" *Historische Zeitschrift* 223 (1976): 328–57.
———. "Staatskunst oder Systemzwang?" *Historische Zeitschrift* 228 (1979): 624–44.
Hirschfeld, Paul. *Die freien Gewerkschaften in Deutschland*. Jena, 1908.
Hoffman, Peter. *The History of the German Resistance 1933–1945*. Cambridge, Mass., 1977.
Hohenlohe-Schillingsfürst, Chlodwig. *Denkwürdigkeiten der Reichskanzlerzeit*. Munich, 1967.
Höhn, Reinhard. *Die vaterlandslosen Gesellen*. Cologne, 1964.
Huber, Ernst Rudolf. *Deutsche Verfassungsgeschichte*. Stuttgart, 1957–69.
———. *Nationalstaat und Verfassungsstaat*. Stuttgart, 1965.
Hunt, James. "Peasants, Grain Tariffs, and Meat Quotas: Imperial German Protectionism Reexamined." *Central European History* 7 (1974): 311–31.
———. *The People's Party in Württemberg and Southern Germany*. Stuttgart, 1975.
Hunt, Richard. *German Social Democracy in the Weimar Republic*. New Haven, 1964.
Hyman, Paula. *From Dreyfus to Vichy*. New York, 1979.
Industrial and Trade Chamber, Dortmund. *100 Jahre Industrie- und Handelskammer zum Dortmund*. Dortmund, 1977.
Ionescu, Ghita, and Gellner, Ernest, eds. *Populism: Its Meaning and National Characteristics*. London, 1969.
Irwin, Laura, and Lichtman, Alan J. "Across the Great Divide: Inferring Individual Level Behavior from Aggregate Data." *Political Methodology* 3 (1976): 412–39.
Jaeger, Hans. *Unternehmer in der deutschen Politik*. Bonn, 1967.

Jarausch, Konrad. *The Enigmatic Chancellor.* New Haven, 1973.
———. "From Second to Third Reich." *Central European History* 12 (1979): 69–81.
———. "Illiberalism and Beyond: German History in Search of a Paradigm." *Journal of Modern History* 55 (1983): 268–84.
———, ed. *Quantifizierung in der Geschichtswissenschaft.* Düsseldorf, 1976.
Jastrow, J. *Das Dreiklassensystem.* Berlin, 1894.
Jensen, Richard. *The Winning of the Middle West.* Chicago, 1971.
Jessop, Bob. *Traditionalism, Conservatism and British Political Culture.* London, 1974.
Johnson, Gerald. "Research Note on Correlates of Voter Behavior." *American Political Science Review* 69 (1975): 107–23.
Jones, E. Terrence. "Ecological Inference and Electoral Analysis." *Journal of Interdisciplinary History* 2 (1971): 249–62.
Jones, Larry Eugene. "'The Dying Middle': Weimar Germany and the Fragmentation of Bourgeois Politics." *Central European History* 5 (1972): 22–54.
———. "Inflation, Revaluation and the Crisis of Middle Class Politics." *Central European History* 12 (1979): 143–68.
Joyce, Patrick. *Work, Society and Politics.* New Brunswick, 1980.
Judt, Tony. *Socialism in Provence.* Cambridge, 1979.
Just, Leo, ed. *Handbuch der deutschen Geschichte,* vol. 4, Abschnitt 1a: 5–23, 94–112.
Kaelble, Hartmut. *Industrielle Interessenpolitik in der Wilhelmischen Gesellschaft.* Berlin, 1967.
———. "Industrielle Interessenverbände vor 1918." In *Zur soziologischen Theorie und Analyse des 19 Jahrhunderts,* edited by Walter Ruegg and Otto Neuloh, pp. 180–212. Göttingen, 1975.
Karl, Heinz. *Die deutsche Arbeiterklasse im Kampf um die Enteignung der Fürsten.* Berlin, 1957.
Kater, Michael. *The Nazi Party.* Cambridge, Mass., 1983.
———. "Quantifizierung und NS-Geschichte." *Geschichte und Gesellschaft* 3 (1977): 453–84.
Katz, Jakob. *Out of the Ghetto: The Social Background of Jewish Emancipation.* Cambridge, Mass., 1973.
Kehr, Ekhardt. *Battleship Building and Party Politics in Germany.* Chicago, 1975.
Keil, Wilhelm. *Erlebnisse eines Sozialdemokraten.* Stuttgart, 1947.
Keller, Ernst. *Der unpolitische Deutsche.* Berlin, 1965.
Kelley, Stanley, Jr., and Mirer, Thad. "The Simple Act of Voting." *American Political Science Review* 68 (1974): 572–91.
Kershaw, Ian. "The Führer Image and Political Integration." In *The "Führer State": Myth and Reality,* edited by Gerhard Hirschfeld and Lothar Kettenacker, pp. 133–64. Stuttgart, 1981.
———. *Popular Opinion and Political Dissent in the Third Reich.* Oxford, 1983.
Kerstan, Eugen. *Die Geschichte des Landkreises Elbing.* Elbing, 1925.
Kleine, George. *Der württembergische Ministerpräsident Frh. Hermann von Mittnacht.* Stuttgart, 1969.
Kleppner, Paul. *The Cross of Culture.* New York, 1970.
———. *The Third Electoral System, 1853–1892.* Chapel Hill, 1979.
Klessman, Christoph. *Polnische Bergarbeiter im Ruhrgebiet.* Göttingen, 1978.
Klöcker, Alfons. *Konfession der sozialdemokratischen Wählerschaft.* Mönchen-Gladbach, 1913.
Knobel, Enno. *Die Hessische Rechtspartei.* Marburg, 1975.
Koch, Max Jürgen. *Die Bergarbeiterbewegung im Ruhrgebiet zur Zeit Wilhelm II.* Düsseldorf, 1954.

Kocka, Jürgen. "Amerikanische Angestellte in Wirtschaftskrise und New Deal." *Viertel-jahrshefte für Zeitgeschichte* 20 (1975): 334–75.
———. *White Collar Workers in America, 1890–1940.* London, 1980.
Kolb, Eberhard. *Vom Kaiserreich zur Weimarer Republik.* Cologne, 1972.
Kornhauser, William. *The Politics of Mass Society.* Glencoe, 1959.
Korth, Siegfried. "Die Entstehung und Entwicklung des ostdeutschen Grossgrundsitzes." *Jahrbuch der Albertums-Universitäts zur Königsberg* 3 (1953): 165–70.
Kötz, Karl. *Staatsrecht des Königreichs Württemberg.* Tübingen, 1908.
Kousser, J. Morton. "Ecological Regression and Analysis." *Journal of Interdisciplinary History* 4 (1973): 237–62.
Kozyk, Kurt. "Die 'Metallarbeiter-Zeitung' am Vorabend der Ersten Weltkriegs." In *Vom Sozialistengesetz zur Mitbestimmung*, edited by Heinz Oskar Vetter, pp. 175–97. Cologne, 1975.
Krauss, Erwin. *Die politischen Kräften und das Wahlverhalten im Landkreis Giessen während der letzten 60 Jahre.* Giessen, 1961.
Kremer, Willy. *Der soziale Aufbau der Parteien des Deutschen Reichstages von 1871–1918.* Emsdetten, 1934.
Kriegbaum, Günter. *Die parlamentarische Tätigkeit des Freiherrn c. W. Heyl zu Harnsheim.* Meisenheim am Glan, 1962.
Kropat, Wolf-Arno. "Die Beamte und die Politik in wilhelminischer Zeit." *Nassauische Annalen* 83 (1974): 173–90.
Kühr, Herbert. *Parteien und Wahlen im Stadt und Landkreis Essen in der Zeit der Weimarer Republik.* Düsseldorf, 1973.
Kupisch, Karl. *Die deutschen Landeskirchen im 19. und 20. Jahrhundert.* Göttingen, 1966.
Kurt, Alfred. *Wähler und Wahlen in Wahlkreis Offenbach.* Offenbach, 1966.
Labard, Paul. *Deutsches Reichstaatsrecht.* Seventh edition. Tübingen, 1919.
Lacqueur, Walter, and Mosse, George, eds. *Education and Social Structure in the Twentieth Century.* New York, 1967.
Lakeman, Enid. *How Democracies Vote.* London, 1970.
Lamberti, Marjorie. "The Attempts to Formulate a Jewish Bloc." *Central European History* 13 (1980): 91–92.
———. *Jewish Activism in Imperial Germany.* New Haven, 1978.
Langbein, Laura Irwin, and Lichtman, Alan J. *Ecological Inference.* Beverly Hills, 1978.
Lange, Helene, and Gäumer, Gertrude, eds. *Handbuch der Frauenbewegung.* Berlin, 1901.
Langewiesche, Dieter. "Das Deutsche Kaiserreich—Bemerkungen zur Diskussion über Parlamentärisierung und Demokratisierung Deutschlands." *Archiv für Sozialgeschichte* 19 (1980): 628–42.
———. "Wanderungsbewegungen in der Hochindustrialisierungsperiode." *Vierteljahrshefte für Sozial und Wirtschaftsgeschichte* 64 (1971): 1–40.
Langsam, Walter. "Nationalism and History in the Prussian Elementary Schools." In *Nationalism and Internationalism*, edited by Edward Mead Earle, pp. 241–80. New York, 1950.
LaPalombara, Joseph, and Weiner, Myron, eds. *Political Parties and Political Development.* Princeton, 1968.
Lavies, Ralf-Rainer. *Nichtwähler als Kategorie des Wahlverhaltens.* Düsseldorf, 1973.
Lebovics, Herman. "Agrarians versus 'Industrializers.'" *International Review of Social History* 12 (1967): 31–65.
———. *Social Conservatism and the Middle Classes in Germany.* Princeton, 1969.
Lepsius, M. Rainer. "Parteisystem und Sozialstruktur: Zum Problem der Demokrati-

sierung der deutschen Gesellschaft." In *Die deutschen Parteien vor 1918*, edited by Gerhard A. Ritter, pp. 56–80. Cologne, 1973.

Levy, Richard. *The Downfall of the Anti-Semitic Political Parties in Imperial Germany*. New Haven, 1975.

Lichtman, Alan. "Political Realignment and 'Ethnocultural' Voting in Late Nineteenth Century America." *Journal of Social History* 16 (1983): 55–82.

———. *Prejudice and Old Politics*. Chapel Hill, 1979.

Lidtke, Vernon. "Lieder der deutschen Arbeiterbewegung, 1864–1914." *Geschichte und Gesellschaft* 5 (1979): 54–82.

———. *The Outlawed Party*. Princeton, 1966.

Liebe, Werner. *Die Deutschnationale Volkspartei*. Düsseldorf, 1956.

Liphardt, Arendt. "Religious vs. Linguistic vs. Class Voting: The 'Crucial Experiment' of Comparing Belgium, Canada, South Africa and Switzerland." *American Political Science Review* 73 (1979): 442–58.

Lipset, Seymour Martin. *Political Man*. Garden City, 1963.

Lützenkirchen, Ralf. *Der sozialdemokratische Verein für den Reichstagswahlkreis Dortmund-Hörde*. Dortmund, 1970.

McCrary, Peyton; Miller, Clark; and Baum, Dale. "Class and Party in the Secession Crisis." *Journal of Interdisciplinary History* 8 (1978): 448–50.

Mack, Rüdiger. "Otto Böckel und die anti-semitische Bauernbewegung in Hessen 1889–1914." *Wetterauer Geschichtsblätter* 16 (1967): 113–47.

MacKenzie, J. M. "Representation in Plural Societies." *Political Studies* 2 (1954): 54–69.

Mackie, Thomas, and Rose, Richard. *International Almanac of Electoral History*. London, 1974.

McPhee, William, ed. *Public Opinion and Congressional Elections*. Glencoe, 1962.

———, and Ferguson, Jack. "Political Immunization." In *Public Opinion and Congressional Elections*, edited by William McPhee, pp. 155–201. Glencoe, 1962.

Maehl, William. "German Social Democratic Agrarian Policy, 1890, 1895." *Journal of Central European Affairs* 12 (1953): 121–55.

Maier, Charles. *Recasting Bourgeois Europe*. Princeton, 1975.

Mann, Thomas. *Gesammelte Werke*, vol. 13, *Betrachtungen eines Unpolitischen*. Berlin, 1918.

Manziger, Rosemarie. *Verfassungsrevision und Demokratisierung im Königreich Württemberg*. Stuttgart, 1969.

Marrus, Michael. *European Jewry and the Politics of Assimilation*. London, 1971.

Mason, Tim. "The Coming of the Nazis." *Times Literary Supplement* 1974: 94–98.

———. "National Socialism and the Working Class, 1925–1933." *New German Critique*, no. 11 (1977): 49–92.

Massing, Paul. *Rehearsal for Destruction*. New York, 1975.

Matras, Judith. *Social Inequality, Stratification, and Mobility*. Englewood Cliffs, 1975.

Mayer, Arno. *The Persistence of the Old Regime*. New York, 1981.

Mechow, Max. *Die Ost- und Westpreussen in Berlin*. Berlin, 1975.

Mecksroth, Theodore. "Some Problems in Cross-level Inference." *American Journal of Political Science* 18 (1974): 45–66.

Merkl, Peter. *The Making of a Stormtrooper*. Princeton, 1980.

Merriam, Charles, and Gosnel, Harold. *Non-Voting*. Chicago, 1927.

Meyer, Gerd. "Thesen und Kritik der empirischen Wahlforschung in der Bundesrepublik Deutschland." *Politische Vierteljahrsschrift* 18 (1977): 169–94.

Michelat, Guy, and Simon, Michel. *Classe, religion et comportement politique*. Paris, 1977.

Michels, Robert. "Die deutsche Sozialdemokratie: 1." *Archiv für Sozialwissenschaft und Sozialpolitik* 23 (1908): 471–556.

———. *Political Parties*. Glencoe, 1949.

Mielke, Siegfried. *Der Hansabund für Gewerbe Handel und Industrie*. Göttingen, 1976.

Mierendorff, Carl. "Die Gründe gegen Verhältniswahl und das bestehende Listenver-fahren." In *Neues Wahlrecht*, edited by Johannes Schauff. Berlin, 1929.

Milatz, Alfred. "Die linksliberalen Parteien und Gruppen in den Reichstagswahlen 1907–1912." *Archiv für Sozialgeschichte* 12 (1973): 273–92.

———. "Reichstagswahlen und Mandatsverteilung 1871 bis 1918." In *Gesellschaft, Parlament und Regierung*, edited by Gerhard A. Ritter, pp. 207–24. Cologne, 1973.

———. *Wähler und Wahlen in der Weimarer Republik*. Bonn, 1965.

Milbrath, Lester. *Political Participation*. Chicago, 1965.

———, and Goel, M. L. *Political Participation*. Chicago, 1977.

Miller, Suzanne. *Die Bürde der Macht*. Düsseldorf, 1978.

Miller, William L. *Electoral Dynamics in Britain Since 1918*. New York, 1977. and 1970." *Political Studies* 25 (1975): 227–60.

Minogue, Kenneth. "Populism as a Political Movement." In *Populism: Its Meaning and National Characteristics*, edited by Ghita Ionescu and Ernest Gellner, pp. 197–211. London, 1969.

Misch, Axel. *Das Wahlsystem zwischen Theorie und Taktik*. Berlin, 1977.

Mitchell, Allan. "Bonapartism as a Model for Bismarckean Politics." *Journal of Modern History* 49 (1977): 181–209.

Mock, Wolfgang. "'Manipulation von oben' oder Selbstorganisation der Basis?" *Historische Zeitschrift* 232 (1981): 358–75.

Moe, Terry. *The Organization of Interests*. Chicago, 1980.

Moeller, Robert. "Die Suche nach Kontinuität in der modernen deutschen Geschichte." *Neue Politische Literatur* 27 (1982): 430–38.

Molt, Peter. *Der Reichstag vor der improvisierten Revolution*. Cologne, 1963.

———. "Vom kaiserlichen Reichstag zum Bundestag." In *Wahlen in Deutschland*, edited by Erwin Faul, pp. 1–134. Villingen, 1960.

Mommsen, Hans, ed. *Sozialdemokratie zwischen Klassenbewegung und Volkspartei*. Frankfurt, 1974.

Mommsen, Wolfgang. *Deutsche Parteiprogramme*. Munich, 1960.

———. "Domestic Questions in German Foreign Policy." In *Imperial Germany*, edited by James Sheehan, pp. 223–68. New York, 1976.

———. "Gegenwärtige Tendenzen in der Geschichtsschreibung der Bundesrepublik." *Geschichte und Gesellschaft* 7 (1981): 150–88.

———. "Liberalismusinterpretationen." *Geschichte und Gesellschaft* 4 (1978): 77–90.

Monshausen, Theodor. *Politische Wahlen im Regierungsbezirk Koblenz 1880 bis 1897*. Bonn, 1969.

Moore, Allen. "Urbanism and Voter Turnout." *American Journal of Political Science* 21 (1977): 71–8.

Moore, Barrington. *Injustice: The Social Bases of Obedience and Revolt*. White Plains, 1978.

Moore, David C. *The Politics of Deference*. New York, 1977.

Morsey, Rudolf. "Die deutschen Katholiken und der Nationalstaat zwischen Kulturkampf und Ersten Weltkrieg." In *Die Deutschen Parteien vor 1918*, edited by Gerhard A. Ritter, pp. 270–98. Cologne, 1973.

Moses, John. *The Politics of Illusion*. New York, 1975.

Mosse, George. *The Crisis of German Ideology*. New York, 1964.

———. *Germans and Jews*. New York, 1970.

———. *The Nationalization of the Masses*. New York, 1975.

Mosse, Werner, ed. *Juden im Wilhelminischen Deutschland*. Tübingen, 1976.

Mouffe, Chantal, ed. *Gramsci and Marxist Theory*. London, 1979.

Mousnier, Roland. *Social Hierarchies.* New York, 1973.

Mueller, Denis. *Public Choice.* Cambridge, 1979.

Muhl, Jon. *Studien zur westpreussischen Gütergeschichte.* Danzig, 1925.

Mühlberger, Dieter. "The Sociology of the NSDAP: The Question of Working Class Membership." *Journal of Contemporary History* 15 (1980): 493–512.

Müller, Karlheinz. *Preussischer Adler und Hessische Löwe.* Wiesbaden, 1966.

National Liberal Party. *Organisations-Handbuch.* Berlin, 1915.

Neale, R. S. *Class and Ideology in the Nineteenth Century.* London, 1972.

Nettl, J. P. "The German Social Democratic Party 1880–1914 as a Political Model." *Past and Present* Nr. 30, 65–95.

Neumann, Sigmund. *Die Parteien der Weimarer Republik,* reprint of 1932 edition. Stuttgart, 1965.

Nie, Norman. *Statistical Package for the Social Sciences.* New York, 1975.

———; Verba, Sidney; and Petrocik, John. *The Changing American Voter.* Cambridge, Mass., 1976.

Niemi, Richard, and Weisberg, Herbert. *Controversies in American Voting Behavior.* San Francisco, 1976.

Nipperdey, Thomas. "Grundprobleme der deutschen Parteigeschichte im 19. Jahrhundert." In *Die Deutschen Parteien vor 1918,* edited by Gerhard A. Ritter, pp. 32–55. Cologne, 1973.

———. "Nationalidee und Nationaldenkmal in Deutschland im 19. Jahrhundert." *Historische Zeitschrift* 206 (1968): 559–85.

———. "1933 und die Kontinuität der deutschen Geschichte." *Historische Zeitschrift* 227 (1978): 86–111.

———. "Die Organisation der bürgerlichen Parteien in Deutschland." In *Die Deutschen Parteien vor 1918,* edited by Gerhard A. Ritter, pp. 100–119. Cologne, 1973.

———. *Die Organisation der deutschen Parteien vor 1918.* Düsseldorf, 1961.

———. "Organisierter Kapitalismus und die Krise des Kaiserreichs." *Geschichte und Gesellschaft* 5 (1979): 418–30.

———. "Wehlers 'Kaiserreich.' Eine kritische Auseinandersetzung." *Geschichte und Gesellschaft* 1 (1975): 539–60.

Noakes, Jeremy. *The Nazi Party in Lower Saxony.* London, 1971.

Nolan, Mary. *Social Democracy and Society.* Cambridge, 1981.

Nolte, Ernst. "Deutscher Scheinkonstitutionalismus." *Historische Zeitschrift* 228 (1979): 531–50.

Nossiter, T. J. *Influence, Opinion and Political Idioms in Reformed England.* Brighton, 1975.

O'Donnell, Anthony J. "National Liberalism and the Mass Politics of the German Right, 1890–1907." Ph.D. Dissertation, Princeton University, 1973.

Oldenburg-Januschau, Elard von. *Erinnerungen.* Leipzig, 1936.

Organski, A. F. K. *The Stages of Political Development.* New York, 1965.

Orlow, Dietrich. *The History of the Nazi Party.* Pittsburgh, 1969.

Ostrogorski, M. *Democracy and the Organization of Political Parties.* New York, 1908.

Parsons, Stanley. *The Populist Context.* Westport, Conn., 1973.

Pascho, Otto. *Der Raum Dortmund.* Dortmund, 1971.

Passchier, Nico. "The Electoral Geography of the Nazi Landslide." In *Who Were the Fascists: The Social Roots of European Fascism,* edited by Stein Larsen Ugelvik, Berny Hagtvet, Jan Petter Myklevust, pp. 283–300. Bergen, 1980.

Peck, Abraham. *Radicals and Reactionaries: The Crisis of Conservatism in Wilhelmine Germany.* Washington, 1978.

Plesner, Helmuth. *Die verspätete Nation.* Stuttgart, 1959.

Poulantzas, Nicos. *Political Power and Social Classes.* London, 1978.

Pounds, Norman. *The Upper Silesian Industrial Region*. Bloomington, 1958.
Pridham, Geoffrey. *Hitler's Rise to Power*. London, 1973.
Priouret, Roger. *La république des députés*. Paris, 1959.
Puder, Erich. *Die Stadt Elbing und ihre Umgebung*. Elbing, 1907.
Pugh, Martin. *Electoral Reform in War and Peace*. London, 1978.
Puhle, Hans-Jürgen. *Agrarische Interessenpolitik und preussischer Konservatismus im Wilhelminischen Reich*. Hanover, 1967.
———. "Der Bund der Landwirte im Wilhelminischen Reich." In *Zur soziologischen Theorie und Analyse des 19. Jahrhunderts*, edited by Walter Ruegg and Otto Neuloch, pp. 145–62. Göttingen, 1975.
———. "Parlament, Parteien und Interessenverbände 1890–1914." In *Das Kaiserliche Deutschland*, edited by Michael Stürmer, pp. 312–39. Düsseldorf, 1970.
———. "Radikalisierung und Wandel des deutschen Konservatismus vor dem Ersten Weltkrieg." In *Die deutschen Parteien vor 1918*, edited by Gerhard A. Ritter, pp. 165–86. Cologne, 1973.
———. *Von der Agrarkrise zum Präfaschismus*. Wiesbaden, 1972.
———. "Zur Legende von der 'Kehrschen Schule.'" *Geschichte und Gesellschaft* 4 (1978): 100–109.
Pulzer, Peter. "Die Beteiligung an der Politik." In *Juden im Wilhelminischen Deutschland*, edited by Werner Mosse, pp. 143–240. Tübingen, 1978.
———. *The Rise of Political Anti-Semitism in Germany and Austria*. New York, 1965.
Quatert, Jean. *Reluctant Feminists in German Social Democracy*. Princeton, 1979.
Rae, Douglas. *The Politics of Electoral Laws*. New Haven, 1971.
Ragins, Sanford. *Jewish Responses to Anti-Semitism in Germany*. Cincinnati, 1980.
Rauh, Manfred. *Föderalismus und Parlamentarismus im Wilhelminischen Reich*. Düsseldorf, 1973.
Reddaway, W. F., et al. *The Cambridge History of Poland*. Cambridge, 1941.
Reichel, Peter. "Politische Kultur." *Politische Vierteljahrsschrift* 21 (1980): 383–97.
Reinharz, Jehuda. *Fatherland or Promised Land*. Ann Arbor, 1975.
Rejewski, Harro-Jürgen. *Die Pflicht zur politischen Treue im preussischen Beamtenrecht*. Berlin, 1973.
Riedel, Manfred. "Bürger." In *Geschichtliche Grundbegriffe*, edited by Otto Brunner, Werner Conze, and Reinhart Koselleck, 1: pp. 672–725. Stuttgart, 1972.
Ringer, Fritz. *The Decline of the German Mandarins*. Cambridge, Mass., 1969.
Rittenberg, Volker. "Revolution or Pseudo-Democratization: The Formation of the Weimar Republic." In *Crisis, Choice, and Change*, edited by Gabriel Almond and Scott Flanagan, pp. 299–398. Boston, 1973.
Ritter, Emil. *Die Katholisch-soziale Bewegung im neunzehnten Jahrhundert und der Volksverein*. Cologne, 1954.
Ritter, Gerhard. *Die Dämonie der Macht*. Stuttgart, 1960.
———. *Europa und die deutsche Frage*. Munich, 1948.
Ritter, Gerhard A. *Arbeiterbewegung, Parteien und Parlamentarismus*. Göttingen, 1976.
———. *Die Arbeiterbewegung im Wilhelmischen Reich*. Berlin, 1963.
———. "Entwicklungsprobleme des deutschen Parlamentarismus." In *Gesellschaft, Parlament und Regierung*, pp. 11–54. Düsseldorf, 1974.
———. *Historisches Lesebuch 1871–1914*. Frankfurt, 1967.
———. *Wahlgeschichtliches Arbeitsbuch*. Munich, 1980.
———, ed. *Die deutschen Parteien vor 1918*. Cologne, 1973.
———, ed. *Gesellschaft, Parlament und Regierung*. Düsseldorf, 1974.
———, and Tenfelde, Klaus. "Der Durchbruch der freien Gewerkschaften Deutschlands zur Massenbewegung im letzten Viertel des 19. Jahrhunderts." In *Vom*

Sozialistengesetz zur Mitbestimmung, edited by Heinz Oskar Vetter, pp. 64–123. Cologne, 1975.

Roberts, James. "Der Alkoholkonsum deutschen Arbeiter im 19. Jahrhundert." *Geschichte und Gesellschaft* 6 (1980): 220–42.

Rohe, Karl. "Konfession, Klasse und lokale Gesellschaft." In *Politische Parteien auf dem Weg zur parlamentarischen Demokratie in Deutschland*, edited by Lothar Albertin and Werner Linke, pp. 109–26. Düsseldorf, 1981.

———. "Die verspätete Region." In *Partzipation im Modernisierungsprozess*, edited by Peter Steinbach, pp. 321–49. Stuttgart, 1983.

———. "Wahlanalyse im historischen Kontext." *Historische Zeitschrift* 234 (1982): 337–57.

Röhl, John. *Germany without Bismarck*. London, 1967.

———. "Higher Civil Servants in Germany." In *Education and Social Structure in the Twentieth Century*, edited by Walter Lacqueur and George Mosse, pp. 123–38. New York, 1967.

———. "Introduction." In *Kaiser Wilhelm II: New Interpretations*, edited by John Röhl and Nicolaus Sombart, pp. 11–22. Cambridge, 1982.

Rokkan, Stein. *Citizens, Elections, Parties*. Oslo, 1970.

———. "Toward a Generalized Concept of *Verzuiling*: A Preliminary Note." *Political Studies* 25 (1977): 570.

Romeyk, Horst. *Die politischen Wahlen in Regierungsbezirk Koblenz 1898 bis 1918*. Bonn, 1969.

Rose, Richard. "Comparability in Electoral Studies." In *Electoral Behavior: A Comparative Handbook*, edited by Richard Rose, pp. 3–25. New York, 1974.

———, ed. *Electoral Behavior: A Comparative Handbook*. New York, 1974.

———, and Massawir, Harve. "Voting and Elections: A Functional Analysis." In *Empirical Democratic Theory*, edited by Charles Gnudde and Deane Neubauer, pp. 69–97. Chicago, 1969.

Rose, W. J. "Prussian Poland, 1850–1914." In *The Cambridge History of Poland*, edited by F. W. Reddaway et al., pp. 409–31. London, 1941.

Rosenberg, Arthur. *Imperial Germany*. New York, 1970.

Rosenberg, Hans. *Grosse Depression und Bismarckzeit*. Berlin, 1967.

———. "Die Pseudodemokratisierung der Rittergutsbesitzerklasse." In *Moderne deutsche Sozialgeschichte*, edited by Hans-Ulrich Wehler, pp. 287–308. Cologne, 1966.

Ross, Ronald. *Beleaguered Tower*. South Bend, 1975.

Roth, Guenther. *The Social Democrats in Imperial Germany*. Totawa, 1963.

Ruegg, Walter, and Neuloch, Otto, eds. *Zur soziologischen Theorie und Analyse des 19. Jahrhunderts*. Göttingen, 1975.

Rürup, Reinhard. *Emanzipation und Antisemitismus*. Göttingen, 1975.

———. "Problems of the German Revolution 1918–1919." *Journal of Contemporary History* 5 (1970): 109–36.

———, ed. *Arbeiter und Soldatenräte im rhenisch-westfälischen Industriegebiet*. Wuppertal, 1975.

Rusk, Jerrold. "Comment." *American Political Science Review* 68 (1974): 1028–49.

Salisbury, Robert. "Recent Research on Political Participation." *American Journal of Political Science* 19 (1975): 323–41.

Saul, Klaus. "Der 'Deutsche Kriegerverband' zur innenpolitischen Funktion eines nationalen Verbandes im kaiserlichen Deutschland." *Militärgeschichtliche Mitteilungen* 1962: 95–160.

———. *Staat, Industrie und Arbeiterbewegung*. Düsseldorf, 1974.

Savigny, Leo von. *Das parlamentarische Wahlrecht im Reich und in Preussen und seine Reform*. Berlin, 1907.

Schäfter, Hermann. "Die Gelben Gewerkschaften," *Vierteljahrsschrift für Sozial- und Wirtschaftsgeschichte* 59 (1966): 41–76.

Schauff, Karin. "Die Entwicklung zum Proportionalwahlsystem in Deutschland." In *Neues Wahlrecht*, edited by Johannes Schauff, pp. 126–38. Berlin, 1929.

Schauff, T. Johannes. "Die parteipolitische Struktur Deutschlands." In *Neues Wahlrecht*, edited by Johannes Schauff, pp. 139–50. Berlin, 1929.

————. *Das Wählverhalten der deutschen Katholiken im Kaiserreich und in der Weimarer Republik*. Mainz, 1975.

————, ed. *Neues Wahlrecht*. Berlin, 1929.

Schellenberg, Horst. *Zum Geschichtsbild der Wilhelmischen Ära und der Weimarer Zeit*. Düsseldorf, 1964.

Schieder, Theodor. *Der deutsche Kaiserreich von 1871 als Nationalstaat*. Cologne, 1961.

Schiffers, Reinhard. *Elemente direkter Demokratie im Weimarer Regierungssystem*. Düsseldorf, 1971.

Schmal, Eugen. *Entwicklungen der völkischen Bewegung*. Giessen, 1933.

Schmidt, Gustav. "Parlamentarisierung oder Präventive Konterrevolution." In *Gesellschaft, Parlament und Regierung*, edited by Gerhard A. Ritter, pp. 249–78. Düsseldorf, 1974.

Schoenbaum, David. *Zabern 1913: Consensus Politics in Imperial Germany*. London, 1982.

Scholder, Klaus. *Die Kirchen und das Dritte Reich*. Frankfurt, 1977.

Schölgen, Gregor. "Wer machte im Kaiserreich Politik?" *Neue Politische Literatur* 25 (1980): 75–97.

Schorske, Carl. *German Social Democracy 1905–1917*. Cambridge, Mass., 1955.

Schulte, Wolfgang. *Struktur und Entwicklung des Parteiensystems in Königreich Württemberg*. Stuttgart, 1970.

Schulz, Gerhard. "Über Entstehung und Formen von Interessengruppen in Deutschland seit Beginn der Industrialisierung." In *Interessenverbände in Deutschland*, edited by Heinz Josef Varain, pp. 25–54. Cologne, 1973.

Schüren, Ulrich. *Der Volksentscheid zur Fürstenenteignung*. Düsseldorf, 1978.

Schwarz, Max. *MdR*. Hanover, 1965.

Schwidetzky, Ilse. *Die polnische Wahlbewegung in Oberschlesien*. Breslau, 1934.

Scott, James C. *Comparative Political Corruption*. Englewood Cliffs, 1972.

Sedatis, Helmut. *Liberalismus und Handwerk in Südwestdeutschland*. Stuttgart, 1979.

Sell, Friedrich. *Die Tragödie des deutschen Liberalismus*. Stuttgart, 1953.

Severing, Carl. *Mein Lebensweg*. Cologne, 1950.

Seydel, Max von, and Piloty, Robert. *Bayerisches Staatsrecht*. Tübingen, 1913.

Shade, William. "'New Political History'; Some Statistical Questions Raised." *Social Science History* 5 (1981): 171–96.

Sheehan, James. *German Liberalism in the Nineteenth Century*. Chicago, 1978.

————. "Leadership in the German Reichstag, 1871–1914." *American Historical Review* 74 (1968): 518–19.

————. "Liberalism and the City in Germany." *Past and Present* Nr. 51: 126–37.

————. "Review: Gerhard Ritter, *Gesellschaft, Parlament und Regierung*." *Journal of Modern History* 48 (1976): 565–67.

————, ed. *Imperial Germany*. New York, 1976.

Shils, Edward. *Political Development in the New States*. The Hague, 1962.

Shiveley, W. Philipps. "Party Identification and Party Choice: The Weimar Case." *American Political Science Review* 66 (1972): 1203–25.

Siegfried, André. *Géographie électorale de L'Ardeche sous la troisième république*. Paris, 1948.

Silverman, Dan. *Reluctant Union: Alsace Lorraine and Imperial Germany.* University Park, Pa., 1972.

Simon, Klaus. *Die württembergischen Demokraten 1890–1920.* Stuttgart, 1969.

Sittlich, Otto. *Die politischen Parteien in Deutschland.* Leipzig, 1905.

Social Democratic Party. *Protokoll über die Verhandlungen des Parteitags.*

———. *Geschäftsbericht der sozialdemokratischen Landesorganisation, Grossherzogtum Hesse.* Offenbach, 1912.

———. *Tätigkeitsbericht für die Zeit von 1 Januar bis 30 Juni 1907, Frankfurt a.M.*

Sombart, Werner von. *Die deutsche Volkswirtschaft im neunzehnten Jahrhundert.* Berlin, 1903.

Specht, Fritz. *Die Reichstagswahlen von 1871 bis 1903.* Berlin,

Sperber, Johnathan. "Roman Catholic Religious Identity in Rhineland-Westphalia, 1800–70." *Social History* 7 (1982): 305–18.

Spindler, Max, ed. *Handbuch der bayerischen Geschichte.* Munich, 1967–75.

Stachura, Peter. "Die NSDAP und die Reichstagswahlen von 1928." *Vierteljahrshefte für Zeitgeschichte* 26 (1978): 66–99.

Steenson, Gary. *Karl Kautsky.* Pittsburgh, 1978.

Stegmann, Dirk. *Die Erben Bismarcks.* Cologne, 1970.

Stegmann, Franz Josef. "Geschichte der sozialen Ideen im deutschen Katholismus." In *Geschichte der deutschen Arbeiterbewegung,* edited by Helga Grebing, pp. 325–512. Munich, 1970.

Steinbach, Peter. "Politische Partizipationsforschung." In *Probleme der Modernisierung in Deutschland,* edited by Hartmut Kaelble, Peter Steinbach et al., pp. 171–234. Berlin, 1978.

———. "Polisierung und Nationalisierung: der Region im 19. Jahrhundert. In *Partizipation im Modernisierungsprozess,* edited by Peter Steinbach, pp. 231–52. Stuttgart, 1983.

Stern, Fritz. *The Failure of Illiberalism.* New York, 1972.

Stern, Leo, ed. *Die Russische Revolutionen von 1905–07 im Spiegel der deutschen Presse.* Berlin, 1961.

Stokes, Lawrence. "The Social Composition of the Nazi Party in Eutin, 1925–32." *International Review of Social History* 23 (1978): 2–32.

Stolberg-Wernigerode, Otto Graf zu. *Die unentschiedene Generation.* Munich, 1968.

Stolper, Gustav. *German Economy, 1870–1940.* New York, 1940.

Stoltenberg, Gerhard. *Politische Strömungen im schleswig-holsteinischen Landvolk 1918–1933.* Düsseldorf, 1962.

Strück, Wolf-Heino. "Zur ideenpolitischen Vorbereitung des Bundeslandes Hessen." *Hessisches Jahrbuch für Landesgeschichte* 20 (1970): 282–324.

Stürmer, Michael. *Bismarck und die preussisch-deutsche Politik.* Munich, 1970.

———. "Bismarckstaat und Cäserismus." *Der Staat* 12 (1973): 457–98.

———. "Caesar's Laurel Crown—The Case for a Comparative Concept." *Journal of Modern History* 49 (1977): 203–6.

———. "Cäsarismus oder das Problem es nicht gegeben haben Kann." *Historische Zeitschrift* 229 (1979): 626–29.

———. *Koalition und Opposition in der Weimarer Republik 1924–1928.* Düsseldorf, 1967.

———, ed. *Das kaiserliche Deutschland.* Düsseldorf, 1970.

Summa, Rudolf. *Kasseler Unterschichten im Zeitalter der Industrialisierung.* Darmstadt, 1978.

Tal, Uriel. *Christians and Jews in Germany.* Ithaca, 1975.

Taylor, P. J., and Johnston, R. J. *Geography of Elections.* New York, 1979.

Tenfelde, Klaus. "Bergarbeiterkultur in Deutschland: Ein Überblick." *Geschichte und Gesellschaft* 5 (1979): 12–53.
Thiel, Jürgen. *Die Grossblockpolitik der Nationalliberalen Partei Badens 1905 bis 1914.* Stuttgart, 1976.
Thompson, Dennis. *John Stuart Mill and Representative Government.* Princeton, 1976.
Thränhardt, Dietrich. *Wahlen und politische Strukturen in Bayern 1848–1953.* Düsseldorf, 1973.
Tilly, Charles; Tilly, Louise; and Tilly, Richard. *The Rebellious Century, 1830–1930.* Cambridge, Mass., 1975.
Tilly, Richard, and Hohorst, Gerd. "Sozialer Protest in Deutschland im 19. Jahrhunderts." In *Quantifizierung in der Geschichtswissenschaft,* edited by Konrad Jarausch, pp. 232–78. Düsseldorf, 1976.
Tilton, Timothy. *Nazism, Neo-Nazism and the Peasantry.* Bloomington, 1975.
Tingsten, Herbert. *Political Behavior.* New York, 1937.
Tipps, Dean. "Modernization Theory and the Study of National Societies." *Comparative Studies in Society and History* 18 (1976): 199–226.
Tipton, Frank, Jr. *Regional Variations in the Economic Development of Germany During the Nineteenth Century.* Middletown, Conn., 1976.
Toury, Jakob. *Die politische Orientierungen der Juden in Deutschland.* Tübingen, 1966.
Truman, David. *Government and Processes.* New York, 1954.
Ullmann, Hans P. *Der Bund der Industriellen.* Göttingen, 1976.
Unwin, Derek. "Germany: Continuity and Change in Electoral Politics." In *Electoral Behavior: A Comparative Handbook,* edited by Richard Rose, pp. 109–70. New York, 1974.
Valen, Henry, and Rokkan, Stein. "Norway: Conflict Structure and Mass Politics in a European Periphery." In *Electoral Behavior: A Comparative Handbook,* edited by Richard Rose, pp. 315–70. New York, 1974.
Vandermeer, Philip. "Religion, Society and Politics." *Social Science History* 5 (1981): 3–24.
Varain, Heinz Josef, ed. *Interessenverbände in Deutschland.* Cologne, 1973.
Veblen, Thorstein. *Imperial Germany and the Industrial Revolution.* London, 1915.
Venturi, Franco. *Roots of Revolution.* New York, 1960.
Verba, Sidney, and Nie, Norman. *Participation in America.* New York, 1972.
———; Nie, Norman; and Kim, Jae-on. *The Modes of Democratic Participation.* Beverly Hills, 1971.
———; Nie, Norman; and Kim, Jae-on. *Participation and Political Equality.* Cambridge, 1978.
Vetter, Heinz Oskar, ed. *Vom Sozialistengesetz zur Mitbestimmung.* Cologne, 1975.
Vierhaus, Rudolf. "Wählen und Wählerverhalten in Ostwestfalen und Lippe." *Westfälische Forschungen* 21 (1959): 59–70.
Vogel, Reinhard; Nohlen, Dieter; and Schultze, Rainer-Olaf. *Wahlen in Deutschland.* Berlin, 1971.
Volkov, Shulamit. "Antisemitism as a Cultural Code." *Yearbook of the Leo Baeck Institute* 23 (1978): 25–46.
———. "The Decline of German Handicrafts." *Vierteljahrsschrift für Sozial- und Wirtschaftsgeschichte* 61 (1967): 165–84.
———. *The Rise of Popular Antimodernism in Germany.* Princeton, 1978.
Wachenheim, Hedwig. *Die deutsche Arbeiterbewegung 1844 bis 1944.* Cologne, 1967.
Wald, Kenneth. *Crosses on the Ballot.* Princeton, 1983.
Walz, Ernst. *Das Staatsrecht des Grossherzogtums Baden.* Tübingen, 1909.
Wandruska, Adam. "Österreichs politische Struktur." In *Geschichte der Republik Österreich,* edited by Heinrich Benedikt, pp. 289–485. Vienna, 1954.

Warren, Donald. *The Red Kingdom of Saxony*. The Hague, 1964.

Weber, Max. *Aufsätze zur Religions-Soziologie*. Tübingen, 1963.

———. *Gesammelte politische Schriften*. Tübingen, 1958.

Wegner, Konstanze. "Linksliberalismus im wilhelmischen Deutschland und in der Weimarer Republik." *Geschichte und Gesellschaft* 4 (1978): 120–27.

———. *Theodor Barth und die Freisinnige Vereinigung*. Tübingen, 1968.

Wehler, Hans-Ulrich. *Das deutsche Kaiserreich 1871–1918*. Göttingen, 1973.

———. "'Deutscher Sonderweg' oder allgemeine Probleme des westlichen Kapitalismus." *Merkur* 35 (1981): 480–87.

———. *Krisenherde des Kaiserreichs*. Göttingen, 1970.

———. "Kritik und kritische Antikritik." *Historische Zeitschrift* 225 (1977): 349–84.

———. "Moderne Politikgeschichte oder 'Grosse Politik der Kabinette.'" *Geschichte und Gesellschaft* 1 (1975): 344–69.

———. *Modernisierungstheorie und Geschichte*. Göttingen, 1975.

———. "Die Polen im Ruhrgebiet bis 1918." In *Moderne deutsche Sozialgeschichte*, edited by Hans-Ulrich Wehler, pp. 437–55. Cologne, 1968.

———, ed. *Moderne deutsche Sozialgeschichte*. Cologne, 1968.

Westarp, Kuno. *Konservative Politik im letzten Jahrzehnt des Kaiserreiches*. Berlin, 1935.

White, Dan. *The Splintered Party*. Cambridge, Mass., 1976.

Winkler, Heinrich. "Extremismus der Mitte," *Vierteljahrshefte für Zeitgeschichte* 20 (1972): 175–91.

———. *Mittelstand, Demokratie und Nationalsozialismus*. Cologne, 1972.

———. "Mittelstandsbewegung oder Volkspartei? Zur sozialen Basis der NSDAP." In *Faschismus als soziale Bewegung*, edited by Wolfgang Schieder, pp. 97–118. Hamburg, 1976.

———. *Pluralismus oder Protektionismus*. Wiesbaden, 1972.

———. "Die rückverischerte Mittelstand." In *Zur soziologischen Theorie und Analyse des 19. Jahrhunderts*, edited by Walter Ruegg and Otto Neuloch, pp. 163–79. Göttingen, 1975.

Winkler, Wilhelm. *Statistisches Handbuch des gesamten Deutschtums*. Berlin, 1927.

Wirminghaus, Alfred. "Stadt und Land unter dem Einfluss der Binnenwanderung." *Jahrbuch für Nationalökonomie und Statistik*, 3 Folge, 9: 161ff.

Witt, Peter-Christian. *Die Finanzpolitik des Deutschen Reiches von 1903 bis 1913*. Lübeck, 1970.

Wittich, Werner. *Deutsche und französische Kultur in Elsass*. Strasburg, 1900.

Wölk, Wolfgang. "Sozialstruktur, Parteienkorrelation und Wahlenentscheidung im Kaiserreich." In *Wählerbewegung in der deutschen Geschichte*, edited by Otto Büsch, Wolfgang Wölk, and Monika Wölk, pp. 505–48. Berlin, 1977.

Woodward, C. Vann. *Origins of the New South*. Baton Rouge, 1951.

Wright, James. *The Politics of Populism*. New Haven, 1974.

Wuerth, Dieter. "The Politics and Sociology of Organized Labor in a Middle-Sized German Town: Göppingen 1900–1910." Ph.D. Dissertation, University of Wisconsin, 1974.

Wünch, Carl. "Kurze Baugeschichte der Marienburg." *Westpreussen Jahrbuch* 25 (1975): 21–30.

Würzburg, Eugen. "Die 'Partei' der Nichtwähler." *Jahrbücher für Nationalökonomie und Statistik* 3 Folge, 33: 383–84.

Zacharias, Rainer. *Neues Marienburger Heimatbuch*. Herford, 1967.

Zangerel, Carl. "Courting the Catholic Vote: The Center Party in Baden." *Central European History* 10 (1976): 228–29.

Zechlen, Edgmont. *Staatsstreichspläne Bismarck und Wilhelm II*. Stuttgart, 1929.

Zeender, John. "German Catholics and the Concept of an Interconfessional Party." *Journal of Central European Affairs* 23 (1964): 424–39.

———. *The German Center Party 1890–1906.* Philadelphia, 1976.

Zeigler, L. Harmon, and Peak, G. Wayne. *Interest Groups in American Society.* Englewood Cliffs, N.J., 1972.

Zeldin, Theodore. *France: 1848–1945.* Oxford, 1973.

Zeman, Z. A. B., and Scharlau, W. B. *The Merchant of Revolution.* Oxford, 1965.

Ziegler, Donald. *Prelude to Democracy.* Lincoln, Neb., 1958.

Zmarzlik, Hans-Günter. "Das Kaiserreich in neuer Sicht?" *Historische Zeitschrift* 222 (1976): 105–26.

Zofka, Zdenek. *Die Ausbreitung des Nationalsozialismus auf dem Land.* Munich, 1979.

INDEX